1974

EX LIBRIS

E. BERGQUIST

The CIA
and the Cult
of Intelligence

The CIA
and the Cult
of Intelligence

Victor Marchetti
and John D. Marks

INTRODUCTION BY MELVIN L. WULF

Alfred A. Knopf   New York   1974

THIS IS A BORZOI BOOK
PUBLISHED BY ALFRED A. KNOPF, INC.

Library of Congress Number: 74-4995
ISBN: 0-394-48239
Manufactured in the United States of America
First Edition

AND YE SHALL KNOW THE TRUTH,

AND THE TRUTH SHALL MAKE YOU FREE.

John, VIII: 32

(inscribed on the marble wall
of the main lobby at CIA headquarters,
Langley, Virginia)

Contents

Publisher's Note

By federal court order, the authors were required to submit the manuscript of this book to the CIA for review prior to publication. Under the terms of the court ruling, the CIA ordered the deletion of 339 passages of varying length. Later, following demands to the CIA by legal counsel for the authors—and the commencement of litigation by the publisher and the authors against the CIA challenging the censorship involved—all but 168 of these deletions were reinstated.

An additional 140 passages, plus parts of two others, were cleared for publication by a federal judge, but because of continuing appeals they are not available for inclusion. For a full account of these events, see the Introduction by Melvin L. Wulf, Legal Director of the American Civil Liberties Union, which begins on page xix.

As it presently exists, therefore, the manuscript of *The CIA and the Cult of Intelligence* demonstrates with remarkable clarity the actual workings of the CIA's "classification" system. In this edition, passages the CIA originally ordered excised—and then reluctantly permitted to be reinstated—are printed in **boldface type.** Firm deletions, including the 140-plus passages cleared but still tied up in litigation, are indicated by blank spaces preceded and followed by parentheses: **(DELETED).** The spaces correspond to the actual length of the cuts.

Authors' Prefaces

I

My introduction to the intelligence business came during the early years of the Cold War, while serving with the U.S. Army in Germany. There, in 1952, I was sent to the European Command's "special" school at Oberammergau to study Russian and the rudiments of intelligence methods and techniques. Afterward I was assigned to duty on the East German border. The information we collected on the enemy's plans and activities was of little significance, but the duty was good, sometimes even exciting. We believed that we were keeping the world free for democracy, that we were in the first line of defense against the spread of communism.

After leaving the military service, I returned to college at Penn State, where I majored in Soviet studies and history. Shortly before graduation, I was secretly recruited by the CIA, which I officially joined in September 1955; the struggle between democracy and communism seemed more important than ever, the CIA was in the forefront of that vital international battle. I wanted to contribute.

Except for one year with the Clandestine Services, spent largely in training, most of my career with the CIA was devoted to analytical work. As a Soviet military specialist, I did research, then current intelligence, and finally national estimates—at the time, the highest form of intelligence production. I was at one point the CIA's—and probably the U.S. government's—leading expert on Soviet military aid to the countries of the Third World. I was involved in uncovering Moscow's furtive efforts that culminated in the Cuban missile crisis of 1962 and, later, in unraveling the enigma of the "Soviet ABM problem."

From 1966 to 1969 I served as a staff officer in the Office of the

Director of the CIA, where I held such positions as special assistant to the Chief of Planning, Programming, and Budgeting, special assistant to the Executive Director, and executive assistant to the Deputy Director. It was during these years that I came to see how the highly compartmentalized organization performed as a whole, and what its full role in the U.S. intelligence community was. The view from the Office of the Director was both enlightening and discouraging. The CIA did not, as advertised to the public and the Congress, function primarily as a central clearinghouse and producer of national intelligence for the government. Its basic mission was that of clandestine operations, particularly covert action—the secret intervention in the internal affairs of other nations. Nor was the Director of CIA a dominant—or much interested—figure in the direction and management of the intelligence community which he supposedly headed. Rather, his chief concern, like that of most of his predecessors and the agency's current Director, was in overseeing the CIA's clandestine activities.

Disenchanted and disagreeing with many of the agency's policies and practices, and, for that matter, with those of the intelligence community and the U.S. government, I resigned from the CIA in late 1969. But having been thoroughly indoctrinated with the theology of "national security" for so many years, I was unable at first to speak out publicly. And, I must admit, I was still imbued with the mystique of the agency and the intelligence business in general, even retaining a certain affection for both. I therefore sought to put forth my thoughts—perhaps more accurately, my feelings—in fictional form. I wrote a novel, *The Rope-Dancer*, in which I tried to describe for the reader what life was actually like in a secret agency such as the CIA, and what the differences were between myth and reality in this overly romanticized profession.

The publication of the novel accomplished two things. It brought me in touch with numerous people outside the inbred, insulated world of intelligence who were concerned over the constantly increasing size and role of intelligence in our government. And this, in turn, convinced me to work toward bringing about an open review and, I hoped, some reform in the U.S. intelligence system. Realizing that the CIA and the intelligence community are in-

capable of reforming themselves, and that Presidents, who see the system as a private asset, have no desire to change it in any basic way, I hoped to win support for a comprehensive review in Congress. I soon learned, however, that those members of Congress who possessed the power to institute reforms had no interest in doing so. The others either lacked the wherewithal to accomplish any significant changes or were apathetic. I therefore decided to write a book—this book—expressing my views on the CIA and explaining the reasons why I believe the time has come for the U.S. intelligence community to be reviewed and reformed.

The CIA and the government have fought long and hard—and not always ethically—first to discourage the writing of this book and then to prevent its publication. They have managed, through legal technicalities and by raising the specter of "national security" violations, to achieve an unprecedented abridgment of my constitutional right to free speech. They have secured an unwarranted and outrageous *permanent* injunction against me, requiring that anything I write or say, "*factual, fictional or otherwise*," on the subject of intelligence must first be censored by the CIA. Under risk of criminal contempt of court, I can speak only at my own peril and must allow the CIA thirty days to review, and excise, my writings— prior to submitting them to a publisher for consideration.

It has been said that among the dangers faced by a democratic society in fighting totalitarian systems, such as fascism and communism, is that the democratic government runs the risk of imitating its enemies' methods and, thereby, destroying the very democracy that it is seeking to defend. I cannot help wondering if my government is more concerned with defending our democratic system or more intent upon imitating the methods of totalitarian regimes in order to maintain its already inordinate power over the American people.

VICTOR MARCHETTI

Oakton, Virginia
February 1974

II

Unlike Victor Marchetti, I did not join the government to do intelligence work. Rather, fresh out of college in 1966, I entered the Foreign Service. My first assignment was to have been London, but with my draft board pressing for my services, the State Department advised me that the best way to stay out of uniform was to go to Vietnam as a civilian advisor in the so-called pacification program. I reluctantly agreed and spent the next eighteen months there, returning to Washington just after the Tet offensive in February 1968. From personal observation, I knew that American policy in Vietnam was ineffective, but I had been one of those who thought that if only better tactics were used the United States could "win." Once back in this country, I soon came to see that American involvement in Indochina was not only ineffective but totally wrong.

The State Department had assigned me to the Bureau of Intelligence and Research, first as an analyst of French and Belgian affairs and then as staff assistant to State's intelligence director. Since this bureau carries on State's liaison with the rest of the intelligence community, I was for the first time introduced to the whole worldwide network of American spying—not so much as a participant but as a shuffler of top-secret papers and a note-taker at top-level intelligence meetings. Here I found the same kind of waste and inefficiency I had come to know in Vietnam and, even worse, the same sort of reasoning that had led the country into Vietnam in the first place. In the high councils of the intelligence community, there was no sense that intervention in the internal affairs of other countries was not the inherent right of the United States. "Don't be an idealist; you have to live in the 'real' world," said the professionals. I found it increasingly difficult to agree.

For me, the last straw was the American invasion of Cambodia

in April 1970. I felt personally concerned because only two months earlier, on temporary assignment to a White House study group, I had helped write a relatively pessimistic report about the situation in Vietnam. It seemed now that our honest conclusions about the tenuous position of the Thieu government had been used in some small way to justify the overt expansion of the war into a new country.

I wish now that I had walked out of the State Department the day the troops went into Cambodia. Within a few months, however, I found a new job as executive assistant to Senator Clifford Case of New Jersey. Knowing of the Senator's opposition to the war, I looked at my new work as a chance to try to change what I knew was wrong in the way the United States conducts its foreign policy.

During my three years with Senator Case, when we were concentrating our efforts on legislation to end the war, to limit the intelligence community, and to curb presidential abuses of executive agreements, I came to know Victor Marchetti. With our common experience and interest in intelligence, we talked frequently about how things could be improved. In the fall of 1972, obviously disturbed by the legal action the government had taken against the book he intended to write but which he had not yet started, he felt he needed someone to assist him in his work. Best of all would be a coauthor with the background to make a substantive contribution as well as to help in the actual writing. This book is the result of our joint effort.

I entered the project in the hope that what we have to say will have some effect in influencing the public and the Congress to institute meaningful control over American intelligence and to end the type of intervention abroad which, in addition to being counterproductive, is inconsistent with the ideals by which our country is supposed to govern itself. Whether such a hope was misguided remains to be seen.

JOHN D. MARKS

Washington, D.C.
February 1974

Acknowledgments

Work on *The CIA and the Cult of Intelligence* began in early 1972 and from the beginning the effort was plagued with problems, largely generated by an angry CIA and a misguided U.S. government. Throughout the ordeal, our friend and agent, David Obst, was a constant source of encouragement and help. Similarly, the good people at the American Civil Liberties Union—Aryeh Neier, Sandy Rosen, John Shattuck, Mimi Schneider, and others, but especially Mel Wulf—provided more than free counsel and an effective legal defense of our constitutional rights. They have been friends of the best sort. We owe a special debt of gratitude to our editor, Dan Okrent, and to Tony Schulte of Knopf, who never lost faith and always offered inspiration. To the president of Random House, Robert Bernstein, who had the courage to go forward with the book in the face of intimidating odds, we are deeply indebted. And, lastly, to Jim Boyd of the Fund for Investigative Journalism and all the others who helped in various ways but must in the circumstances remain anonymous, we say thank you.

V.M. and J.D.M.

Introduction

by Melvin L. Wulf
Legal Director
American Civil Liberties Union

On April 18, 1972, Victor Marchetti became the first American writer to be served with an official censorship order issued by a court of the United States. The order prohibited him from "disclosing in any manner (1) any information relating to intelligence activities, (2) any information concerning intelligence sources and methods, or (3) any intelligence information."

To secure the order, government lawyers had appeared in the chambers of Judge Albert V. Bryan, Jr., of the United States District Court for the Eastern District of Virginia, in Alexandria, on the morning of April 18, without having notified Marchetti. The government's papers recited that Marchetti had worked at the CIA from 1955 to 1969, that he had signed several "secrecy agreements" in which he had agreed not to reveal any information learned during his employment, that after he left the CIA he had revealed forbidden information, that he was planning to write a non-fiction book about the agency, and that publication of the book would "result in grave and irreparable injury to the interests of the United States."

Among the papers presented to the judge was an affidavit (classified "Secret") from Thomas H. Karamessines, Deputy Director of the Central Intelligence Agency, the head of the CIA's covert-activities branch. The affidavit said that a magazine article and an outline of a proposed book, both written by Marchetti, had been turned over to the CIA and that they contained information about the CIA's secret activities. The affidavit related several of the items and described how their disclosure would, in the CIA's opinion, be harmful to the United States. On the basis of that affidavit and others, including one by CIA Director Richard Helms, Judge Bryan signed a temporary restraining order forbidding Mar-

chetti to disclose any information about the CIA and requiring him to submit any "manuscript, article or essay, or other writing, factual or otherwise," to the CIA before "releasing it to any person or corporation." It was that order which United States marshals served upon Marchetti. The next month was consumed by a hectic and unsuccessful effort to have the order set aside.

Marchetti asked the ACLU for assistance the day after receiving the order, and was in New York the following day to meet his lawyers and prepare his defense. At the first court appearance, on Friday, April 21, we unsuccessfully urged Judge Bryan to dissolve the temporary restraining order. He also refused to order the government to allow Marchetti's lawyers to read the "secret" affidavit, because none of us had security clearance. The following Monday we were in Baltimore to arrange an appeal to the United States Court of Appeals to argue there that the temporary restraining order should be dissolved. The court agreed to hear argument two days later. During the Baltimore meeting the government lawyers announced that they had conferred security clearance upon me and that I would be able to read the secret affidavit but could not have a copy of it. They said they would clear the other defense lawyers during the next few days. We were also told that any witnesses we intended to present at trial, to be held that Friday, would also require security clearance before we could discuss the secret affidavit with them. That was a hell of a way to prepare for trial; we couldn't even talk to prospective witnesses unless they were approved by the government.

We argued the appeal before the Court of Appeals on Wednesday, but that too was unsuccessful, and the temporary restraining order remained in effect. Our only satisfaction was an order by the court prohibiting both the CIA and the Department of Justice from trying to influence our witnesses in any way.

On Friday we appeared before Judge Bryan and reluctantly asked for a two-week postponement because it had been impossible for us to secure witnesses who could testify that day. The need for security clearance had made it impossible for us to discuss the case with those witnesses who had at least tentatively agreed to testify for the defense. But, more depressing, we had had great

difficulty finding people willing to testify at all. We had called a few dozen prospects, largely former members of the Kennedy and Johnson administrations who had reputations as liberals and even, in some cases, reputations as civil-libertarians. I'm still waiting for half of them to return my calls. Of the other half, most were simply frightened at the idea of being identified with the case, and some, including a few who had themselves revealed classified information in their published memoirs, agreed with the government that Marchetti's pen should be immobilized. In the end, our list of witnesses was short but notable: Professor Abram Chayes of Harvard Law School, and former Legal Advisor to the Department of State in the Kennedy administration; Professor Richard Falk, Milbank Professor of International Law at Princeton; Morton Halperin, former Deputy Assistant Secretary of Defense and staff member of the National Security Council under Kissinger; and Professor Paul Blackstock, an intelligence expert from the University of South Carolina.

The next two weeks were consumed by the frustrating hunt for witnesses and by other pre-trial requirements, including examination of Karamessines and the CIA's Security Director, who were to be the government's chief witnesses.

The trial started and ended on May 15. Essentially, it consisted of Karamessines repeating the contents of his secret affidavit. As interesting as it would be to describe the day in detail, I am forbidden to, for the public was excluded and the testimony of the government witnesses is classified. The result, however, is public. It was a clean sweep for the CIA, and Judge Bryan issued a permanent injunction against Marchetti.

The results on appeal were not much better. The validity of the injunction was broadly affirmed. The only limitation imposed by the Court of Appeals was that only *classified* information could be deleted from the book by the CIA. The litigation finally came to an end in December 1972 when the Supreme Court refused to hear the case. It was a great defeat for Marchetti, for his lawyers— and for the First Amendment.

American law has always recognized that injunctions against publication—"prior restraints," in legal jargon—threaten the root

and branch of democratic society. Until 1971, when the *New York Times* was enjoined from printing the Pentagon Papers, the federal government had never attempted to impose a prior restraint on publication, and the handful of such efforts by the states were uniformly denounced by the Supreme Court. As we learned from the Pentagon Papers Case, however, the Nixon administration was not going to be deterred by a mere two hundred years of history from becoming the first administration to try to suppress publication of a newspaper. They ultimately failed in their specific goal of suppressing publication of a newspaper—but, for fifteen days, a newspaper actually was restrained from publishing, the first such restraint in American history.

The *Times'* resumption of publication of the Pentagon Papers immediately after the Supreme Court decision would seem to mean that the case ended victoriously. Although it was a victory, it was not a sound victory, for only Justices Black and Douglas said that injunctions against publication were constitutionally forbidden under *any* circumstances. The other members of the court made it perfectly clear that they could imagine circumstances where such injunctions would be enforced, notwithstanding the First Amendment's guarantee of a free press. Nixon-administration lawyers could read the opinions as well as ACLU lawyers, and they too saw that the decision in the Pentagon Papers Case was not a knockout punch. So only ten months after being beaten off by the *New York Times,* they were back in court trying the same thing again with Victor Marchetti.

Nine opinions were written in the Pentagon Papers Case. Out of all those opinions one standard emerges under which a majority of the Justices would have allowed information to be suppressed prior to publication: proof by the government that disclosure would "surely result in direct, immediate and irreparable injury to the Nation or its people." We were comfortable with that standard because we were confident that nothing Marchetti had disclosed or would disclose in the future would have that effect. But we were not permitted to put the government to its proof through the testimony of our four witnesses because Judge Bryan agreed with the government that Marchetti's case was different from the

Pentagon Papers Case. "We are not enjoining the press in this case," the government lawyers said. "We are merely enforcing a contract between Marchetti and the CIA. This is not a First Amendment case, it's just a contract action." The contract to which they were referring was, of course, Marchetti's secrecy agreement.

All employees of the CIA are required to sign an agreement in which they promise not to reveal any information learned during their employment which relates to "intelligence sources or methods" without first securing authorization from the agency. The standard form of the agreement includes threats of prosecution and promises to deliver the most awful consequences upon the slightest violation. The only trouble with the threats is that until now they have been unenforceable. Apart from disclosure of information classified by the Atomic Energy Commission, it is not a crime to disclose classified information unless it is done under circumstances which involve what is commonly understood as espionage—spying for a foreign nation. The government tried, in the prosecution of Daniel Ellsberg, to stretch the espionage statutes to punish his disclosure of the Pentagon Papers, even though he had had no intent to injure the United States, as required by the statute. Though that prosecution was aborted under the most dramatic circumstances, including a surreptitious attempt by President Nixon to influence the trial judge, it is unlikely that the appeals courts would have upheld such an expansive application of the espionage laws—assuming that the jury would even have brought in a guilty verdict.

In any case, being doubtful about how far the threat of prosecution under a dubious statute would deter Marchetti from publicly criticizing the CIA and inevitably disclosing some of its practices, the CIA fell upon the contract theory as a device for trying to suppress his book before it was put into print. The theory struck a harmonious note with the federal judges who heard the case, and proved more successful than the government probably ever dared to hope and certainly more than we had ever expected. But it cheapens the First Amendment to say that an agreement by an employee of the United States not to reveal some

government activity is the same as an agreement to deliver a hundred bales of cotton. It ignores the compelling democratic principle that the public has a right to be well informed about its government's actions.

Of course, some will be heard to say, "But these are secrets," and indeed much of the information you will read in this book has been considered to be secret. But "secrets" have been revealed before—there were literally thousands of them in the Pentagon Papers. Every high government official who writes his memoirs after leaving office reveals "secrets" he learned while in government service, and most had signed secrecy agreements too. "Secrets" are regularly leaked to the press by government officers, sometimes to serve official policy, sometimes only to serve a man's own ambitions. In fact, disclosure of so-called secrets—even CIA secrets—has a long and honorable history in our country, and the practice has proved to be valuable because it provides the public with important information that it must have in order to pass judgment on its elected officials.

Furthermore, disclosure of "secret" information is rarely harmful because the decision inside government to classify information is notoriously frivolous. Experts have estimated that up to 99 percent of the millions of documents currently classified ought not be classified at all. But not only is disclosure of "secret" information generally harmless, it is a tonic that improves our nation's health. Government officers cried that disclosure of the Pentagon Papers would put the nation's security in immediate jeopardy. When they were finally published in their entirety, the only damage was to the reputation of officials in the Kennedy and Johnson administrations who were shown to have deceived the nation about the war in Vietnam.

When you read this book, you will notice that, unlike any other book previously published in the United States, this one contains blanks. That is the remarkable effect of the government's success. You will also notice that the book has two authors, Victor Marchetti and John Marks. That is another remarkable effect of the government's success. After being enjoined, defeated in his attempts to win relief in the appellate courts, virtually ignored by

the press, shunned by his former colleagues at the CIA, unable even to discuss the progress of his work with his editor at Knopf (because the very purpose of the injunction was to forbid the publisher to see the manuscript before the CIA had had the opportunity to censor it), there was serious question whether Marchetti would be able to write the book at all. His discouragement was profound and his bitterness sharp. If he had not written the book, the government's success would have been complete, for that was its real objective. Luckily, Marchetti and Marks came together, and with a shared perspective on the evils of clandestine activities, they were able to do together what the government hoped would not be done at all.

When the manuscript was completed at the end of August 1973, it was delivered to the CIA. Thirty days later, the time allowed by the injunction, we received a letter from the CIA which designated 339 portions of the book that were to be deleted. Some of the deletions were single words, some were several lines, some were portions of organizational charts, and many were whole pages. In all, 15 to 20 percent of the manuscript was ordered deleted. I won't soon forget that September evening when Marchetti, Marks, and I sat in the ACLU office for several hours literally cutting out the deleted parts of the manuscript so that we could deliver the remains to Knopf. It was the Devil's work we did that day.

We filed suit in October, together with Knopf, challenging the CIA's censorship. By the time we went to trial on February 28, the agency had reduced the number of deletions from 339 to 168. Withdrawal of half their original objections should not be taken as a sign of the CIA's generosity. On the contrary, it was the result of our insistent demands over a period of four months, and the agency's recognition that we would go to the mat over the very last censored word. The authors gave up nothing, and rejected several invitations to re-write parts of the book so that it would be satisfactory to the CIA.

There were three issues to be decided at the trial: did the censored portions of the book consist of classified information? Was that information learned by the authors during their government employment? And was any of it in the public domain?

After a two-and-a-half day trial, including testimony by the five highest-ranking officials of the CIA, Judge Bryan decided the case on March 29. It was a major victory for the authors and the publisher. Bryan held that the agency had failed, with a few exceptions, to prove that the deleted information was classified.

The decision was probably more surprising to the CIA. Accustomed as they have become to having their way, it is unlikely to have occurred to them that a mere judge of the United States would contradict their declarations about classified information, for it was the government's theory throughout the case that material was classified if high-ranking officials *said* it was classified. Our view, presented through the expert testimony of Morton Halperin, was that concrete proof of classification was required. In the absence of documents declaring specific information to be classified, or testimony by the employee who had in fact classified specific information, Judge Bryan flatly rejected mere assertions by ranking CIA officers that such information was classified.

Of the 168 disputed items, he found only 27 which he could say were classified. On the other hand, he found that only seven of the 168 had been learned by Marchetti and Marks outside their government employment, and that none of the information was in the public domain.

The decision is obviously important. It allows virtually the entire book to be published (though the present edition still lacks the deleted sections cleared by Judge Bryan, since he postponed enforcement of his decision to allow the government its right to appeal); it desanctifies the CIA; and it discards the magical authority that has always accompanied government incantation of "national security." Hopefully, the higher courts will agree.

There will necessarily be differences of opinion on the subject of the disclosure of secret information. The reader of this book can decide whether the release of the information it contains serves the public's interest or injures the nation's security. For myself, I have no doubts. Both individual citizens and the nation as a whole will be far better off for the book's having been published. The only injury inflicted in the course of the struggle to publish the book is the damage sustained by the First Amendment.

PART I

ONE

The Cult
of Intelligence

But this secrecy . . . has become
a god in this country, and those
people who have secrets travel
in a kind of fraternity . . . and
they will not speak to anyone else.

—SENATOR J. WILLIAM FULBRIGHT
Chairman, Senate Foreign
Relations Committee
November 1971

THERE exists in our nation today a powerful and dangerous secret cult—the cult of intelligence.

Its holy men are the clandestine professionals of the Central Intelligence Agency. Its patrons and protectors are the highest officials of the federal government. Its membership, extending far beyond governmental circles, reaches into the power centers of industry, commerce, finance, and labor. Its friends are many in the areas of important public influence—the academic world and the communications media. The cult of intelligence is a secret fraternity of the American political aristocracy.

The purpose of the cult is to further the foreign policies of the U.S. government by covert and usually illegal means, while at the same time containing the spread of its avowed enemy, communism. Traditionally, the cult's hope has been to foster a world order in which America would reign supreme, the unchallenged international leader. Today, however, that dream stands tarnished by time and frequent failures. Thus, the cult's objectives are now less grandiose, but no less disturbing. It seeks largely to advance America's self-appointed role as the dominant arbiter of social, economic, and political change in the awakening regions of Asia, Africa, and Latin America. And its worldwide war against communism has to some extent been reduced to a covert struggle to maintain a self-serving stability in the Third World, using whatever clandestine methods are available. For the cult of intelligence, fostering "stability" may in one country mean reluctant and passive acquiescence to evolutionary change; in another country, the active maintenance of the *status quo*; in yet another, a determined effort to reverse popular trends toward independence and democracy. The cult attempts that which it believes it can accomplish and which—in the event of failure or exposure—the U.S. government can plausibly deny.

The CIA is both the center and the primary instrument of the cult of intelligence. It engages in espionage and counterespionage, in propaganda and disinformation (the deliberate circulation of false information) in psychological warfare and paramilitary activities. It penetrates and manipulates private institutions, and creates its own organizations (called "proprietaries") when necessary. It recruits agents and mercenaries; it bribes and blackmails foreign officials to carry out its most unsavory tasks. It does whatever is required to achieve its goals, without any consideration of the ethics involved or the moral consequences of its actions. As the secret-action arm of American foreign policy, the CIA's most potent weapon is its covert intervention in the internal affairs of countries the U.S. government wishes to control or influence.

Romanticized by myths, the operations of the CIA are also beclouded by false images and shielded by official deceptions. Its practices are hidden behind arcane and antiquated legalisms which prevent the public and even Congress from knowing what the mysterious agency is doing—or why. This the cult of intelligence justifies with dramatic assertions that the CIA's purpose is to preserve the "national security," that its actions are in response to the needs of the nation's defense. No one—in an age in which secrecy is the definitional operative of security—need know more than that.

The cult is intent upon conducting the foreign affairs of the U.S. government without the awareness or participation of the people. It recognizes no role for a questioning legislature or an investigative press. Its adherents believe that only they have the right and the obligation to decide what is necessary to satisfy the national needs. Although it pursues outmoded international policies and unattainable ends, the cult of intelligence demands that it not be held accountable for its actions by the people it professes to serve. It is a privileged, as well as secret, charge. In their minds, those who belong to the cult of intelligence have been ordained, and their service is immune from public scrutiny.

The "clandestine mentality" is a mind-set that thrives on secrecy and deception. It encourages professional amorality—the belief

that righteous goals can be achieved through the use of unprincipled and normally unacceptable means. Thus, the cult's leaders must tenaciously guard their official actions from public view. To do otherwise would restrict their ability to act independently; it would permit the American people to pass judgment on not only the utility of their policies, but the ethics of those policies as well. With the cooperation of an acquiescent, ill-informed Congress, and the encouragement and assistance of a series of Presidents, the cult has built a wall of laws and executive orders around the CIA and itself, a wall that has blocked effective public scrutiny.

When necessary, the members of the cult of intelligence, including our Presidents (who are always aware of, generally approve of, and often actually initiate the CIA's major undertakings), have lied to protect the CIA and to hide their own responsibility for its operations. The Eisenhower administration lied to the American people about the CIA's involvement in the Guatemalan *coup d'état* in 1954, about the agency's support of the unsuccessful rebellion in Indonesia in 1958, and about Francis Gary Powers' 1960 U-2 mission. The Kennedy administration lied about the CIA's role in the abortive invasion of Cuba in 1961, admitting its involvement only after the operation had failed disastrously. The Johnson administration lied about the extent of most U.S. government commitments in Vietnam and Laos, and all of the CIA's. And the Nixon administration publicly lied about the agency's attempt to fix the Chilean election in 1970. For adherents to the cult of intelligence, hypocrisy and deception, like secrecy, have become standard techniques for preventing public awareness of the CIA's clandestine operations, and governmental accountability for them. And these men who ask that they be regarded as honorable men, true patriots, will, when caught in their own webs of deceit, even assert that the government has an inherent right to lie to its people.

The justification for the "right to lie" is that secrecy in covert operations is necessary to prevent U.S. policies and actions from coming to the attention of the "enemy"—or, in the parlance of the clandestine trade, the "opposition." If the opposition is oblivious to the CIA's operations, the argument runs, then it cannot

respond and the CIA activities stand a good chance of succeeding. Nonetheless, in many instances the opposition knows exactly what covert operations are being targeted against it, and it takes counter-action when possible. The U-2 overflights and, later, those of the photographic satellites were, and are, as well known to the Soviets and the Chinese as Soviet overhead reconnaissance of the United States is to the CIA; there is no way, when engaging in operations of this magnitude, to keep them secret from the opposition. It, too, employs a professional intelligence service. In fact, from 1952 to 1964, at the height of the Cold War, the Soviet KGB electronically intercepted even the most secret messages routed through the code room of the U.S. embassy in Moscow. This breach in secrecy, how-ever, apparently caused little damage to U.S. national security, nor did the Soviet government collapse because the CIA had for years secretly intercepted the private conversations of the top Russian leaders as they talked over their limousine radio-telephones. Both sides knew more than enough to cancel out the effect of any leaks. The fact is that in this country, secrecy and deception in intelligence operations are as much to keep the Congress and the public from learning what their government is doing as to shield these activities from the opposition. The intelligence establishment operates as it does to maintain freedom of action and avoid accountability.

A good part of the CIA's power position is dependent upon its careful mythologizing and glorification of the exploits of the clan-destine profession. Sometimes this even entails fostering a sort of perverse public admiration for the covert practices of the opposi-tion intelligence services—to frighten the public and thereby justify the actions of the CIA. Whatever the method, the selling of the intelligence business is designed to have us admire it as some sort of mysterious, often magical, profession capable of accomplishing terribly difficult, if not miraculous, deeds. Like most myths, the intrigues and successes of the CIA over the years have been more imaginary than real. What is real, unfortunately, is the willingness of both the public and adherents of the cult to believe the fictions that permeate the intelligence business.

The original mission of the CIA was to coordinate the intelligence-collection programs of the various governmental departments and agencies, and to produce the reports and studies required by the national leadership in conducting the affairs of U.S. foreign policy. This was President Truman's view when he requested that Congress establish the secret intelligence agency by passing the National Security Act of 1947. But General William "Wild Bill" Donovan, Allen Dulles, and other veterans of the wartime Office of Strategic Services—a virtually unregulated body, both romantic and daring, tailor-made to the fondest dreams of the covert operator—thought differently. They saw the emergency agency as the clandestine instrument by which Washington could achieve foreign-policy goals not attainable through diplomacy. They believed that the mantle of world leadership had been passed by the British to the Americans, and that their own secret service must take up where the British left off. Thus, they lobbied Congress for the power to conduct covert operations.

That Truman attempted to create an overt intelligence organization, one which would emphasize the gathering and analysis of information rather than secret operations, was commendable. That he thought he could control the advocates of covert action was, in retrospect, a gross miscalculation. Congress, in an atmosphere of Cold War tension, allowed itself to be persuaded by the intelligence professionals. With the passage of the National Security Act of 1947 it allowed the new agency special exemptions from the normal congressional reviewing process, and these exemptions were expanded two years later by the Central Intelligence Agency Act of 1949. Of the greatest and most far-reaching consequence was the provision in the 1947 law that permitted the CIA to "perform such other functions and duties related to intelligence . . . as the National Security Council may from time to time direct." From those few innocuous words the CIA has been able, over the years, to develop a secret charter based on NSC directives and presidential executive orders, a charter almost completely at variance with the apparent intent of the law that established the agency. This vague phrase has provided the CIA with freedom to engage in covert action, the

right to intervene secretly in the internal affairs of other nations. It has done so usually with the express approval of the White House, but almost always without the consent of Congress, and virtually never with the knowledge of the American public.

Knowing nothing has meant that the public does not even realize how frequently the CIA has failed. In the field of classical espionage, the CIA's Clandestine Services have been singularly unsuccessful in their attempts to penetrate or spy on the major targets. The Penkovsky case in the early 1960s, the only espionage operation against the Soviets that the agency can point to with pride, was a fortuitous windfall which British Intelligence made possible for the CIA. The loudly heralded Berlin tunnel operation of the mid-1950s—actually a huge telephone wiretap—produced literally tons of trivia and gossip, but provided little in the way of high-grade secret information that could be used by the agency's intelligence analysts. The operation's true value was the embarrassment it caused the KGB and the favorable publicity it generated for the CIA. Against China, there have been no agent-related espionage successes whatever.

Fortunately for the United States, however, the CIA's technical experts, working with their counterparts in the Pentagon and in the private sector, have been able over the years to develop a wide array of electronic methods for collecting much useful information on the U.S.S.R. and China. From these collection systems, supplemented by material accumulated through diplomatic channels and open sources (newspapers, magazines, and so on), the analysts in the CIA and elsewhere in the intelligence community have been able to keep abreast of developments within the communist powers.

The CIA's Clandestine Services have fared better in the area of counterespionage than in classical espionage. But here, too, the gains have been largely fortuitous. Most of the successes were not scored by spies, but secured through the good offices of defectors who, in return for safety, provided whatever information they possessed. And one must subtract from even these limited achieve-

ments the misinformation passed on by "deceptions"—double agents sent out or "surfaced" by the opposition to defect to, and confuse, the CIA.

In its favorite field of operational endeavor, covert action, the agency has enjoyed its greatest degree of success, but its blunders and failures have caused much embarrassment to the United States. Clearly, the CIA played a key role in keeping Western Europe free of communism in the early Cold War period, although it sadly erred in its attempts to roll back the Iron and Bamboo curtains in the late 1940s and in the 1950s. And it did perform successfully, if questionably, in the effort to contain the spread of communism elsewhere in the world. Some of its "victories," however, have since come back to haunt the U.S. government. One cannot help but wonder now if it might not have been wiser for the CIA not to have intervened in Guatemala or Cuba or Chile, not to have played its clandestine role in Iran or elsewhere in the Middle East, not to have become so deeply involved in the affairs of Southeast Asia, particularly Indochina. But the agency did, and our nation will have to live with the consequences of those actions.

When its clandestine activities are criticized, the CIA's leadership often points with disingenuous pride to the work of the intelligence analysts. But here, too, the agency's record is spotty. Its many errors in estimating Soviet and Chinese strategic military capabilities and intentions have been a constant source of aggravation to government officials. Often, however, it has accurately judged the dangers and consequences of U.S. involvement in the Third World, especially Southeast Asia and Latin America. Ironically, the clandestine operatives who control the agency rely little on the views of the analysts within their own organization, and the White House staff functionaries tend to be equally heedless of the analysts' warnings. And since the CIA's secret intelligence is largely retained within the executive branch, there is of course no opportunity for Congress or others to use these warnings to question the policies of the administration and the covert practices of the CIA.

Occasionally, clandestine operations backfire spectacularly in public—the U-2 shootdown and the Bay of Pigs invasion, for example—and, further, investigations by journalists and uncowed

members of Congress have in these instances given the public some idea of what the CIA actually does. Most recently, investigation of the Watergate scandal has revealed some of the CIA's covert activities within the United States, providing a frightening view of the methods which the agency has employed for years overseas. The assistance given the White House "plumbers" by the CIA and the attempts to involve the agency in the cover-up have pointed up the dangers posed to American democracy by an inadequately controlled secret intelligence organization. As the opportunities for covert action abroad dwindle and are thwarted, those with careers based in clandestine methods are increasingly tempted to turn their talents inward against the citizens of the very nation they profess to serve. Nurtured in the adversary setting of the Cold War, shielded by secrecy, and spurred on by patriotism that views dissent as a threat to the national security, the clandestine operatives of the CIA have the capability, the resources, the experience—and the inclination—to ply their skills increasingly on the domestic scene.

There can be no doubt that the gathering of intelligence is a necessary function of modern government. It makes a significant contribution to national security, and it is vital to the conduct of foreign affairs. Without an effective program to collect information and to analyze the capabilities and possible intentions of other major powers, the United States could neither have confidently negotiated nor could now abide by the S.A.L.T. agreements or achieve any measure of true *détente* with its international rivals. The proven benefits of intelligence are not in question. Rather, it is the illegal and unethical clandestine operations carried out under the guise of intelligence and the dubious purposes to which they are often put by our government that are questionable—both on moral grounds and in terms of practical benefit to the nation.

The issue at hand is a simple one of purpose. Should the CIA function in the way it was originally intended to—as a coordinating agency responsible for gathering, evaluating, and preparing foreign intelligence of use to governmental policy-makers—or should it be permitted to function as it has done over the years—as an opera-

tional arm, a secret instrument of the Presidency and a handful of powerful men, wholly independent of public accountability, whose chief purpose is interference in the domestic affairs of other nations (and perhaps our own) by means of penetration agents, propaganda, covert paramilitary interventions, and an array of other dirty tricks?

The aim of this book is to provide the American people with the inside information which they need—and to which they without question have the right—to understand the significance of this issue and the importance of dealing with it.

TWO

The Clandestine Theory

For some time I have been
disturbed by the way CIA
has been diverted from its
original assignment. It
has become an operational
arm and at times a policy-
making arm of the Government.

—PRESIDENT HARRY S TRUMAN
December 1963

(**DELETED**
) Henry Kissinger made that
statement not in public, but at a secret White House meeting on
June 27, 1970. The country he was referring to was **Chile.**

In his capacity as Assistant to the President for National Security
Affairs, Kissinger was chairman of a meeting of the so-called 40
Committee, an interdepartmental panel responsible for overseeing
the CIA's high-risk covert-action operations. The 40 Committee's
members are the Director of Central Intelligence, the Under Secretary of State for Political Affairs, the Deputy Secretary of Defense,
and the Chairman of the Joint Chiefs of Staff. (At the time of the
Chilean meeting, Attorney General John Mitchell was also a member.) It is this small group of bureaucrats and politicians—in close
consultation with the President and the governmental departments
the men represent—that directs America's secret foreign policy.

On that Saturday in June 1970, the main topic before the 40
Committee was: (
                              DELETED

) **The Chilean election was scheduled for
the following September, and Allende, a declared Marxist, was one
of the principal candidates. Although Allende had pledged to maintain the democratic system if he was elected, the U.S. ambassador
to Chile (**

                              DELETED

)

Most of the American companies with large investments in Chile
were also fearful of a possible Allende triumph, and at least two
of those companies, the International Telephone and Telegraph

Corporation (ITT) and Anaconda Copper, were spending substantial sums of money to prevent his election.

**Ambassador Korry's superiors at the State Department in
Washington** (

DELETED

)

**Richard Helms, then director of the CIA, represented a some-
what divided** (

DELETED

) press—perhaps with help
from the Soviet KGB—or by American reporters, and that such
disclosures would only help Allende.

Helms' position at the 40 Committee meeting was influenced by
memories of the Chilean presidential election of 1964. At that
time he had been chief of the Clandestine Services and had been
actively involved in planning the CIA's secret efforts to defeat
Allende, who was then running against Eduardo Frei.** Frei had

* The official name for this part of the CIA is the Directorate of Operations (until early 1973 the Directorate of Plans), but it is more appropriately
referred to within the agency as the Clandestine Services. Some members of
Congress and certain journalists call it the "Department of Dirty Tricks," a
title never used by CIA personnel.

**Nine years later Laurence Stern of the *Washington Post* finally exposed
the CIA's massive clandestine effort in the 1964 Chilean election. He quoted
a strategically placed U.S. intelligence official as saying, "U.S. government

won the Presidency, but now, six years later, he was constitutionally forbidden to succeed himself, and Allende's candidacy therefore seemed stronger than before.

Anti-American feeling had grown in Chile since 1964, and one reason was widespread resentment of U.S. interference in Chile's internal affairs. The Chilean leftist press had been full of charges of CIA involvement in the 1964 elections, and these reports had not been without effect on the electorate. Additionally, in 1965 the exposure of the Pentagon's ill-advised Project Camelot had further damaged the reputation of the U.S. government. Ironically, Chile was not one of the principal target countries of the Camelot project, a multimillion-dollar social-science research study of possible counterinsurgency techniques in Latin America. But the existence of Camelot had first been made public in Chile, and newspapers there—of all political stripes—condemned the study as "intervention" and "imperialism." One paper said, in prose typical of the general reaction, that Project Camelot was "intended to investigate the military and political situation prevailing in Chile and to determine the possibility of an anti-democratic coup." Politicians of both President Frei's Christian Democratic Party and Allende's leftist coalition protested publicly. The final result was to cause Washington to cancel first Camelot's limited activities in Chile, and then the project as a whole. While the CIA had not been a sponsor of Camelot, the project added to the fears among Chileans of covert American intelligence activities.

In 1968 the CIA's own Board of National Estimates, after carefully studying the socio-political problems of Latin America, had produced a National Intelligence Estimate on that region for the U.S. government's planners and policy-makers. **The central conclusion had been that forces for change in the developing Latin nations were so powerful as to be beyond outside manipulation.** This estimate had been endorsed by the United States

---

intervention in Chile was blatant and almost obscene." Stern reported that both the State Department and the Agency for International Development cooperated with the CIA in funneling up to $20 million into the country, and that one conduit for the funds was an ostensibly private organization called the International Development Foundation.

Intelligence Board, whose members include the heads of the government's various intelligence agencies, and had then been sent to the White House and to those departments that were represented on the 40 Committee.

The 1968 estimate had in effect urged against the kind of intervention that the 40 Committee was in 1970 considering with regard to Chile. But as is so often the case within the government, the most careful advance analysis based on all the intelligence available was either ignored or simply rejected when the time came to make a decision on a specific issue. (

DELETED

)

Henry Kissinger, the single most powerful man at the 40 Committee meeting on Chile, (

DELETED

DELETED

)
**During the next two months, before Allende was officially en-
dorsed as President by the Chilean congress, (**

DELETED

)
Some months afterward President Nixon disingenuously ex-
plained at a White House press conference: "As far as what hap-
pened in Chile is concerned, we can only say that for the United
States to have intervened in a free election and to have turned it
around, I think, would have had repercussions all around Latin
America that would have been far worse than what happened in
Chile."

The following year, in the fall of 1972, CIA Director Helms,
while giving a rare public lecture at Johns Hopkins University, was
asked by a student if the CIA had mucked about in the 1970
Chilean election. His response: "Why should you care? Your side
won."

Helms was understandably perturbed. Columnist Jack Anderson
had only recently reported "the ITT story," which among other
things revealed that the CIA had indeed been involved in an effort
to undo Allende's victory—even after he had won the popular
vote. Much to the agency's chagrin, Anderson had shown that
during September and October 1970, William Broe, chief of the
Western Hemisphere Division of the CIA's Clandestine Services,
had met several times with high officials of ITT to discuss ways
to prevent Allende from taking office. (The ITT board member
who later admitted to a Senate investigative committee that he had
played the key role in bringing together CIA and ITT officials
was John McCone, director of the CIA during the Kennedy administration and, in 1970, a CIA consultant.) Broe had proposed

to ITT and a few other American corporations with substantial financial interests in Chile a four-part plan of economic sabotage which was calculated to weaken the local economy to the point where the Chilean military authorities would move to take over the government and thus frustrate the Marxist's rise to power. ITT and the other firms later claimed they had found the CIA's scheme "not workable." But almost three years to the day after Allende's election, at a time when severe inflation, truckers' strikes, food shortages, and international credit problems were plaguing Chile, he was overthrown and killed in a bloody *coup d'état* carried out by the combined action of the Chilean armed services and national police. His Marxist government was replaced by a military junta. What role American businesses or the CIA may have played in the coup is not publicly known, and may never be. ITT and the other giant corporations with investments in Chile have all denied any involvement in the military revolt. So has the U.S. government, although CIA Director William Colby admitted in secret testimony before the House Foreign Affairs Committee (revealed by Tad Szulc in the October 21, 1973, *Washington Post*) that the agency "had some intelligence coverage about the various moves being made," that it had "penetrated" all of Chile's major political parties, and that it had secretly furnished "some assistance" to certain Chilean groups. Colby, himself the former director of the bloody Phoenix counterintelligence program in Vietnam, also told the Congressmen that the executions carried out by the junta after the coup had done "some good" because they reduced the chances that civil war would break out in Chile—an excellent example of the sophistry with which the CIA defends its strategy of promoting "stability" in the Third World.

Even if the CIA did not intervene directly in the final *putsch,* the U.S. government as a whole did take a series of actions designed to undercut the Allende regime. Henry Kissinger set the tone of the official U.S. position at a background press conference in September 1970, when he said that Allende's Marxist regime would contaminate Argentina, Bolivia, and Peru—a stretch of the geopolitical imagination reminiscent of the Southeast Asian domino theory. Another measure of the White House attitude—and an

indication of the methods it was willing to use—was the burglarizing of the Chilean embassy in Washington in May 1972 by some of the same men who the next month staged the break-in at the Watergate. And the U.S. admittedly worked to undercut the Allende government by cutting off most economic assistance, discouraging private lines of credit, and blocking loans by international organizations. State Department officials testifying before Congress after the coup explained it was the Nixon administration's wish that the Allende regime collapse economically, thereby discrediting socialism.

Henry Kissinger has dismissed speculation among journalists and members of Congress that the CIA helped along this economic collapse and then engineered Allende's downfall; privately he has said that the secret agency wasn't competent to manage an operation as difficult as the Chilean coup. Kissinger had already been supervising the CIA's most secret operations for more than four years when he made this disparaging remark. Whether he was telling the truth about the CIA's non-involvement in Chile or was simply indulging in a bit of official lying (called "plausible denial"), he along with the President would have made the crucial decisions on the Chilean situation. For the CIA is not an independent agency in the broad sense of the term, nor is it a governmental agency out of control. Despite occasional dreams of grandeur on the part of some of its clandestine operators, the CIA does not on its own choose to overthrow distasteful governments or determine which dictatorial regimes to support. Just as the State Department might seek, at the President's request, to discourage international aid institutions from offering loans to "unfriendly" governments, so does the CIA act primarily when called upon by the Executive. The agency's methods and assets are a resource that come with the office of the Presidency.

Thus, harnessing the agency's clandestine operators is not the full, or even basic, solution to the CIA problem. The key to the solution is controlling and requiring accountability of those in the White House and elsewhere in the government who direct or approve, then hide behind, the CIA and its covert operations. This elusiveness, more than anything else, is the problem posed by the CIA.

Intelligence Versus Covert Action

The primary and proper purpose of any national intelligence organization is to produce "finished intelligence" for the government's policy-makers. Such intelligence, as opposed to the raw information acquired through espionage and other clandestine means, is data collected from all sources—secret, official, and open—which has been carefully collated and analyzed by substantive experts specifically to meet the needs of the national leadership. The process is difficult, time-consuming, and by no means without error. But it is the only prudent alternative to naked reliance on the unreliable reporting of spies. Most intelligence agencies, however, are nothing more than secret services, more fascinated by the clandestine operations—of which espionage is but one aspect—than they are concerned with the production of "finished intelligence." The CIA, unfortunately, is no exception to this rule. Tactics that require the employment of well-placed agents, the use of money, the mustering of mercenary armies, and a variety of other covert methods designed to influence directly the policies (or determine the life-spans) of foreign governments—such are the tactics that have come to dominate the CIA. This aspect of the modern intelligence business —intervention in the affairs of other countries—is known at the agency as covert action.

The United States began engaging in covert-action operations in a major way during World War II. Taking lessons from the more experienced British secret services, the Office of Strategic Services (OSS) learned to use covert action as an offensive weapon against Germany and Japan. When the war ended, President Truman disbanded the OSS on the grounds that such wartime tactics as paramilitary operations, psychological warfare, and political manipulation were not acceptable when the country was at peace. At the same time, however, Truman recognized the need for a permanent organization to coordinate and analyze all the intelligence available to the various governmental departments. He believed that if there had been such an agency within the U.S. government in 1941, it

would have been "difficult, if not impossible" for the Japanese to attack Pearl Harbor successfully.

It was, therefore, with "coordination of information" in mind that Truman proposed the creation of the CIA in 1947. Leading the opposition to Truman's "limited" view of intelligence, Allen Dulles stated, in a memorandum prepared for the Senate Armed Services Committee, that "Intelligence work in time of peace will require other techniques, other personnel, and will have rather different objectives. . . . We must deal with the problem of conflicting ideologies as democracy faces communism, not only in the relations between Soviet Russia and the countries of the west but in the internal political conflicts with the countries of Europe, Asia, and South America." It was Dulles—to become CIA director six years later—who contributed to the eventual law the clause enabling the agency to carry out "such other functions and duties related to intelligence as the National Security Council may from time to time direct." It was to be the fulcrum of the CIA's power.

Although fifteen years later Truman would claim that he had not intended the CIA to become the covert-action arm of the U.S. government, it was he who, in 1948, authorized the first postwar covert-action programs, although he did not at first assign the responsibility to the CIA. Instead he created a largely separate organization called the Office of Policy Coordination (OPC), and named a former OSS man, Frank G. Wisner, Jr., to be its chief. Truman did not go to Congress for authority to form OPC. He did it with a stroke of the presidential pen, by issuing a secret National Security Council Intelligence directive, NSC 10/2. (The CIA provided OPC with cover and support, but Wisner reported directly to the secretaries of State and Defense.) Two years later, when General Walter Bedell Smith became CIA director, he moved to consolidate all major elements of national intelligence under his direct control. As part of this effort, he sought to bring Wisner's operations into the CIA. Truman eventually concurred, and on January 4, 1951, OPC and the Office of Special Operations (a similar semi-independent organization established in 1948 for covert intelligence collection) were merged into the CIA, forming

the Directorate of Plans or, as it became known in the agency, the Clandestine Services. Allen Dulles was appointed first chief of the Clandestine Services; Frank Wisner was his deputy.

With its newly formed Clandestine Services and its involvement in the Korean war, the agency expanded rapidly. **From less than 5,000 employees in 1950, the CIA grew to about 15,000 by 1955** —and recruited thousands more as contract employees and foreign agents. During these years the agency spent well over a billion dollars to strengthen non-communist governments in Western Europe, to subsidize political parties around the world, to found Radio Free Europe and Radio Liberty for propaganda broadcasts to Eastern Europe, to make guerrilla raids into mainland China, to create the Asia Foundation, to overthrow leftist governments in Guatemala and Iran, and to carry out a host of other covert-action programs.

While the agency considered most of its programs to have been successful, there were more than a few failures. Two notable examples were attempts in the late 1940s to establish guerrilla movements in Albania and in the Ukraine, in keeping with the then current national obsession of "rolling back the Iron Curtain." Almost none of the agents, funds, and equipment infiltrated by the agency into those two countries was ever seen or heard from again.

In the early 1950s another blunder occurred when the CIA tried to set up a vast underground apparatus in Poland for espionage and, ultimately, revolutionary purposes. The operation was supported by millions of dollars in agency gold shipped into Poland in installments. Agents inside Poland, using radio broadcasts and secret writing techniques, maintained regular contact with their CIA case officers in West Germany. In fact, the agents continually asked that additional agents and gold be sent to aid the movement. Occasionally an agent would even slip out of Poland to report on the operation's progress—and ask for still more agents and gold. It took the agency several years to learn that the Polish secret service had almost from the first day co-opted the whole network, and that no real CIA underground operation existed in Poland. The Polish service kept the operation going

only to lure anti-communist Polish émigrés back home—and into prison. And in the process the Poles were able to bilk the CIA of millions of dollars in gold.

One reason, perhaps the most important, that the agency tended from its very beginnings to concentrate largely on covert-action operations was the fact that in the area of traditional espionage (the collection of intelligence through spies) the CIA was able to accomplish little against the principal enemy, the Soviet Union. With its closed society, the U.S.S.R. proved virtually impenetrable. The few American intelligence officers entering the country were severely limited in their movements and closely followed. The Soviet Union's all-pervasive internal security system made the recruitment of agents and the running of clandestine operations next to impossible. Similar difficulties were experienced by the CIA in Eastern Europe, but to a lesser degree. The agency's operators could recruit agents somewhat more easily there, but strict security measures and efficient secret-police establishments still greatly limited successes.

Nevertheless, there were occasional espionage coups, such as the time CIA operators found an Eastern European communist official able to provide them with a copy of Khrushchev's 1956 de-Stalinization speech, which the agency then arranged to have published in the *New York Times*. Or, from time to time, a highly knowledgeable defector would bolt to the West and give the agency valuable information. Such defectors, of course, usually crossed over of their own volition, and not because of any ingenious methods used by CIA. A former chief of the agency's Clandestine Services, Richard Bissell, admitted years later in a secret discussion with selected members of the Council on Foreign Relations: "In practice however espionage has been disappointing. . . . The general conclusion is that against the Soviet bloc or other sophisticated societies, espionage is not a primary source of intelligence, although it has had occasional brilliant successes."*

It had been Bissell and his boss Allen Dulles who by the mid-

* This and all subsequent quotes from the Bissell speech come from the official minutes of the meeting. The minutes do not quote Bissell directly but, rather, paraphrase his remarks.

1950s had come to realize that if secret agents could not do the job, new ways would have to be found to collect intelligence on the U.S.S.R. and the other communist countries. Increasingly, the CIA turned to machines to perform its espionage mission. By the end of the decade, the agency had developed the U-2 spy plane. This high-altitude aircraft, loaded with cameras and electronic listening devices, brought back a wealth of information about Soviet defenses and weapons. Even more important was communications intelligence (COMINT), electronic transmissions monitored at a cost of billions of dollars by the Defense Department's National Security Agency (NSA).

Both Bissell and Dulles, however, believed that the successful use of human assets was at the heart of the intelligence craft. Thus, it was clear to them that if the Clandestine Services were to survive in the age of modern technical espionage, the agency's operators would have to expand their covert-action operations—particularly in the internal affairs of countries where the agency could operate clandestinely.

In the immediate postwar years, CIA covert-action programs had been concentrated in Europe, as communist expansion into Western Europe seemed a real threat. The Red Army had already occupied Eastern Europe, and the war-ravaged countries of the West, then trying to rebuild shattered economies, were particularly vulnerable. Consequently, the CIA subsidized political parties, individual leaders, labor unions, and other groups, especially in West Germany, France, and Italy. It also supported Eastern European émigré groups in the West as part of a program to organize resistance in the communist countries. "There were so many CIA projects at the height of the Cold War," wrote columnist Tom Braden in January 1973, "that it was almost impossible for a man to keep them in balance." Braden spoke from the vantage point of having himself been the CIA division chief in charge of many of these programs. By the end of the 1950s, however, pro-American governments had become firmly established in Western Europe, and the U.S. government, in effect, had given up the idea of "rolling back the Iron Curtain."

Thus, the emphasis within the Clandestine Services shifted to-

ward the Third World. This change reflected to a certain extent the CIA's bureaucratic need as a secret agency to find areas where it could be successful. More important, the shift came as a result of a hardened determination that the United States should protect the rest of the world from communism. A cornerstone of that policy was secret intervention in the internal affairs of countries particularly susceptible to socialist movements, either democratic or revolutionary. Years later, in a letter to *Washington Post* correspondent Chalmers Roberts, Allen Dulles summed up the prevailing attitude of the times. Referring to the CIA's coups in Iran and Guatemala, he wrote: "Where there begins to be evidence that a country is slipping and Communist takeover is threatened . . . we can't wait for an engraved invitation to come and give aid."

The agency's orientation toward covert action was quite obvious to young officers taking operational training during the mid-1950s at **"The Farm," the CIA's West Point, located near Williamsburg, Virginia, and operated under the cover of a military base called Camp Peary.** Most of the methods and techniques taught there at that time applied to covert action rather than traditional espionage, and to a great extent training was oriented toward such paramilitary activities as infiltration/exfiltration, demolitions, and nighttime parachute jumps. Agency officers, at the end of their formal clandestine education, found that most of the job openings were on the Covert Action Staff and in the Special Operations Division (the CIA's paramilitary component). Assignments to Europe became less coveted, and even veterans with European experience were transferring to posts in the emerging nations, especially in the Far East.

The countries making up the Third World offered far more tempting targets for covert action than those in Europe. These nations, underdeveloped and often corrupt, seemed made to order for the clandestine operators of the CIA, Richard Bissell told the Council on Foreign Relations: "Simply because [their] governments are much less highly organized there is less security consciousness; and there is apt to be more actual or potential diffusion of power among parties, localities, organizations, and individuals outside the central government." And in the frequent power struggles within

such goverments, all factions are grateful for outside assistance. Relatively small sums of money, whether delivered directly to local forces or deposited (for their leaders) in Swiss bank accounts, can have an almost magical effect in changing volatile political loyalties. In such an atmosphere, the CIA's Clandestine Services have over the years enjoyed considerable success.

Swashbucklers and Secret Wars

During the 1950s most of the CIA's covert-action operations were not nearly so sophisticated or subtle as those Bissell would advocate in 1968. Nor were they aimed exclusively at the rapidly increasing and "less highly organized" governments of the Third World. Covert operations against the communist countries of Europe and Asia continued, but the emphasis was on clandestine propaganda, infiltration and manipulation of youth, labor, and cultural organizations, and the like. The more heavy-handed activities—paramilitary operations, coups, and countercoups—were now reserved for the operationally ripe nations of Asia, Africa, and Latin America.

Perhaps the prototype for CIA covert operations during the 1950s was the work of Air Force Colonel Edward Lansdale. His exploits under agency auspices, first in the Philippines and then in Vietnam, became so well known that he served as the model for characters in two best-selling novels, *The Ugly American* by William J. Lederer and Eugene Burdick, and *The Quiet American* by Graham Greene. In the former, he was a heroic figure; in the latter, a bumbling fool.

Lansdale was sent to the Philippines in the early 1950s as advisor to Philippine Defense Minister (later President) Ramón Magsaysay in the struggle against the Huks, the local communist guerrillas. Following Lansdale's counsel, Magsaysay prompted social development and land reform to win support of the peasantry away from the Huks. But Lansdale, backed up by millions of dollars in secret U.S. government funds, took the precaution of launching other, less conventional schemes. One such venture was the establishment of the Filipino Civil Affairs Office, which was made responsible for psychological warfare.

After a 1972 interview with Lansdale, now living in quiet retirement, journalist Stanley Karnow reported:

One [Lansdale-initiated] psywar operation played on the
superstitious dread in the Philippine countryside of the *asuang*,
a mythical vampire. A psywar squad entered an area, and
planted rumors that an asuang lived on where the Communists were based. Two nights later, after giving the rumors
time to circulate among Huk sympathizers, the psywar squad
laid an ambush for the rebels. When a Huk patrol passed, the
ambushers snatched the last man, punctured his neck vampire-
fashion with two holes, hung his body until the blood drained
out, and put the corpse back on the trail. As superstitious as
any other Filipinos, the insurgents fled from the region.

With Magsaysay's election to the Philippine Presidency in 1953,
Lansdale returned to Washington. In the eyes of the U.S. government, his mission had been an unquestioned success: the threat of
a communist takeover in the Philippines had been eliminated.

A year later, after Vietnam had been provisionally split in
two by the Geneva Accords, Lansdale was assigned to South
Vietnam to bolster the regime of Ngo Dinh Diem. He quickly became involved in organizing sabotage and guerrilla operations
against North Vietnam, but his most effective work was done in the
South. There he initiated various psychological-warfare programs
and helped Diem in eliminating his political rivals. His activities,
extensively described in the Pentagon Papers, extended to pacification programs, military training, even political consultation:
Lansdale helped design the ballots when Diem formally ran for
President of South Vietnam in 1955. He used red, the Asian good-
luck color, for Diem and green—signifying a cuckold—for Diem's
opponent. Diem won with an embarrassingly high 98 percent of
the vote, and Lansdale was widely credited within American
government circles for having carried out another successful operation. He left Vietnam soon afterward.

Meanwhile, other agency operators, perhaps less celebrated than
Lansdale, were carrying out covert-action programs in other
countries. Kermit Roosevelt, of the Oyster Bay Roosevelts, master-

minded the 1953 *putsch* that overthrew Iran's Premier Mohammed Mossadegh. The Guatemala coup of 1954 was directed by the CIA. Less successful was the attempt to overthrow Indonesian President Sukarno in the late 1950s. **Contrary to denials by President Eisenhower and Secretary of State Dulles, the CIA gave direct assistance to rebel groups located on the island of Sumatra. Agency B-26s even carried out bombing missions in support of the insurgents. On May 18, 1958, the Indonesians shot down one of these B-26s and captured the pilot, an American named Allen Pope. Although U.S. government officials claimed that Pope was a "soldier of fortune," he was in fact an employee of a CIA-owned proprietary company, Civil Air Transport.** Within a few months after being released from prison four years later, Pope was again flying for the CIA—this time with **Southern Air Transport, an agency proprietary** airline based in Miami.

As the Eisenhower years came to an end, there still was a national consensus that the CIA was justified in taking almost any action in that "back alley" struggle against communism—this despite Eisenhower's clumsy effort to lie his way out of the U-2 shootdown, which lying led to the cancellation of the 1960 summit conference. Most Americans placed the CIA on the same above-politics level as the FBI, and it was no accident that President-elect Kennedy chose to announce on the same day that both J. Edgar Hoover and Allen Dulles would be staying on in his administration.

It took the national shock resulting from the abortive Bay of Pigs invasion in 1961 to bring about serious debate over CIA operations—among high government officials and the public as a whole. Not only had the CIA failed to overthrow the Castro regime, it had blundered publicly, and the U.S. government had again been caught lying. For the first time, widespread popular criticism was directed at the agency. And President Kennedy, who had approved the risky operation, came to realize that the CIA could be a definite liability—to both his foreign policy and his personal political fortunes—as well as a secret and private asset of the Presidency. Determined that there would be no repetition of the Bay of Pigs, Kennedy moved quickly to tighten White House control of the agency. He reportedly vowed "to splinter the CIA in

a thousand pieces and scatter it to the winds." But the President's anger was evidently more the result of the agency's failure to overthrow Castro than a reaction to its methods or techniques. While neither agency funding nor operations were cut back in the aftermath, the Bay of Pigs marked the end of what was probably the CIA's Golden Age. Never again would the secret agency have so totally free a hand in its role as the clandestine defender of American democracy. Kennedy never carried through on his threat to destroy the CIA, but he did purge three of the agency's top officials, and thus made clear the lines of accountability. If Allen Dulles had seemed in Kennedy's eyes only a few months earlier to be in the same unassailable category as J. Edgar Hoover, the Bay of Pigs had made him expendable. In the fall of 1961 John McCone, a defense contractor who had formerly headed the Atomic Energy Commission, replaced Dulles as CIA Director; within months Major General Marshall "Pat" Carter took over from Major General Charles Cabell as Deputy Director, and Richard Helms became chief of the Clandestine Services in place of Richard Bissell.

Kennedy also ordered General Maxwell Taylor, then special military advisor to the President and soon to be Chairman of the Joint Chiefs of Staff, to make a thorough study of U.S. intelligence. Taylor was joined by Attorney General Robert Kennedy, Dulles, and Naval Chief Admiral Arleigh Burke. The Taylor committee's report was to a large extent a critique of the tactics used in—not the goals of—the Bay of Pigs operation. It did not call for any fundamental restructuring of the CIA, although many outside critics were urging that the agency's intelligence-collection and analysis functions be completely separated from its covert-action arm. The committee's principal recommendation was that the CIA should not undertake future operations where weapons larger than hand guns would be used.

Taylor's report was accepted, at least in principle, by the Kennedy administration, but its primary recommendation was disregarded almost immediately. CIA never shut down its two anti-Castro operations bases located in southern Florida, and agency-sponsored raids against Cuba by exile groups continued

into the mid-1960s, albeit on a far smaller scale than the Bay of Pigs. The agency also became deeply involved in the chaotic struggle which **broke out in the Congo in the early 1960s. Clandestine Service operators regularly bought and sold Congolese politicians, and the agency supplied money and arms to the supporters of Cyril Adoula and Joseph Mobutu. By 1964, the CIA had imported its own mercenaries into the Congo, and the agency's B-26 bombers, flown by Cuban exile pilots—many of whom were Bay of Pigs veterans—were carrying out regular missions against insurgent groups.**

During these same years American involvement in Vietnam expanded rapidly, and the CIA, along with the rest of the U.S. government, greatly increased the number of its personnel and programs in that country. Among other activities, the agency organized guerrilla and small-boat attacks on North Vietnam, armed and controlled tens of thousands of Vietnamese soldiers in irregular units, and set up a giant intelligence and interrogation system which reached into every South Vietnamese village.

In neighboring Laos, the CIA actually led the rest of the U.S. government—at the White House's order—into a massive American commitment. Although the agency had been carrying out large-scale programs of political manipulation and other covert action up to 1962, that year's Geneva agreement prohibiting the presence of foreign troops in Laos paradoxically opened up the country to the CIA. For almost from the moment the agreement was signed, the Kennedy administration decided not to pull back but to expand American programs in Laos. This was justified partly because the North Vietnamese were also violating the Geneva Accords; partly because Kennedy, still smarting from his Cuban setback, did not want to lose another confrontation with the communists; and partly because of the strategic importance placed on Laos in the then-fashionable "domino theory." Since the United States did not want to admit that it was not living up to the Geneva agreement, the CIA—whose members were not technically "foreign troops"—got the job of conducting a "secret" war. The Laotian operation became one of the largest and most expensive in the agency's history: more than 35,000 opium-growing Meo and

other Lao mountain tribesmen were recruited into the CIA's private army, L'Armée Clandestine; CIA-hired pilots flew bombing and supply missions in the agency's own planes; and, finally, when L'Armée Clandestine became less effective after long years of war, the agency recruited and financed over 17,000 Thai mercenaries for its war of attrition against the communists.

By the late 1960s, however, many CIA career officers were expressing opposition to the agency's Laotian and Vietnamese programs—not because they objected to the Indochina wars (few did), but because the programs consisted for the most part of huge, unwieldy, semi-overt paramilitary operations lacking the sophistication and secrecy that most of the agency's operators preferred. Furthermore, the wars had dragged on too long, and many officers viewed them as unwinnable messes. The agency, therefore, found itself in the awkward position of being unable to attract sufficient volunteers to man the field assignments in Vietnam. Consequently, it was forced to draft personnel from other areas of its clandestine activity for service in Southeast Asia.

Covert-Action Theory

It was in such an atmosphere of restiveness and doubt, on a January evening in 1968, that a small group of former intelligence professionals and several other members of the cult of intelligence met to discuss the role of the CIA in U.S. foreign policy, not at CIA headquarters in Langley, Virginia, but at the Harold Pratt House on Park Avenue—the home of the Council on Foreign Relations. The discussion leader was investment banker C. Douglas Dillon, previously Under Secretary of State and Secretary of the Treasury; the main speaker was Richard Bissell, the former chief of the agency's Clandestine Services, still a consultant to the CIA, and now a high-ranking executive with the United Aircraft Corporation. Like most other former agency officials, Bissell was reluctant to make his views on intelligence known to the public, and the meeting was private.

In 1971, however, as part of an anti-war protest, radical students occupied the building in Cambridge, Massachusetts, that

houses Harvard University's Center for International Affairs. Once inside, the protesters proceeded to barricade the entrances and ransack the files of faculty members who worked there. Discovered among the papers belonging to Center associate William Harris were the confidential minutes of the January 8, 1968, meeting at the Pratt House. Harris admitted privately a year later that the document in his files had been partially edited to eliminate particularly sensitive material. Even so, the purloined version was still the most complete description of the CIA's covert-action strategy and tactics ever made available to the outside world. Aside from a few newspaper articles which appeared in 1971, however, when it was reprinted by the African Research Group, the Bissell paper attracted almost no interest from the American news media.

Among the CIA's senior Clandestine Services officers, Richard Bissell was one of a very few who had not spent World War II in the OSS; in all other respects, he was the ideal agency professional. A product of Groton and Yale, he had impeccable Eastern Establishment credentials. Such a background was not absolutely essential to success in CIA, but it certainly helped, especially during the Allen Dulles years. And Bissell also had the advantage of scholarly training, having earned a doctorate in economics and then having taught the subject at Yale and MIT. He joined the CIA in 1954 and immediately showed a great talent for clandestine work. By 1958 Dulles had named Bissell head of the Clandestine Services.

At the beginning of the Kennedy administration, Bissell was mentioned in White House circles as the logical candidate to succeed Dulles, who was then near seventy. Brilliant and urbane, Bissell seemed to fit perfectly, in David Halberstam's phrase, the "best and the brightest" image of the New Frontier. But Bissell's popularity with the Kennedy administration was short-lived, for it was Bissell's Clandestine Services which planned and carried out the Bay of Pigs invasion of Cuba in April 1961. Bissell's operatives had not only failed, they were not even successful in inventing and maintaining a good cover story, or "plausible denial,"

which every covert operation is supposed to have and which might have allowed the Kennedy administration to escape the blame. Fidel Castro had told the truth to the world about American intervention in Cuba while the U.S. Secretary of State and other administration officials had been publicly caught in outright lies when their agency-supplied cover stories fell apart. So Kennedy fired the CIA officials who had got him into the Bay of Pigs, which he himself had approved; Bissell was forced out along with Dulles and Deputy Director Charles Cabell.

Bissell's replacement, Richard Helms, despite having been second in command in the Clandestine Services, had managed to stay remarkably untouched by the Bay of Pigs operation. Years later a very senior CIA official would still speak in amazement of the fact that not a single piece of paper existed in the agency which linked Helms to either the planning or the actual execution of the Bay of Pigs. This senior official was not at all critical of Helms, who had been very much involved in the overall supervision of the operation. The official simply was impressed by Helms' bureaucratic skill and good judgment in keeping his signature off the documents concerning the invasion, even in the planning stage.

Helms took over from Bissell as Clandestine Services chief on February 17, 1962, and Bissell was awarded a secret intelligence medal honoring him for his years of service to the agency. But Bissell remained in close touch with clandestine programs as a consultant; the CIA did not want to lose the services of the man who had guided the agency into some of its most advanced techniques. He had been among the first during the 1950s to understand the hopelessness of spying against the Soviets and the Chinese with classic espionage methods, and hence had pushed the use of modern technology as an intelligence tool. He had been instrumental in the development of the U-2 plane, which had been among CIA's greatest successes until the Powers incident. Bissell had also promoted, with the technical help of Kelly Johnson and the so-called Skunk Works development facilities of Lockheed Aircraft Corp., the A-11, later known as SR-71, a spy plane that

could fly nearly three times the speed of sound at altitudes even higher than the U-2.

Moreover, Bissell had been a driving force behind the development of space satellites for intelligence purposes—at times to the embarrassment of the Air Force. He had quickly grasped the espionage potential of placing high-resolution cameras in orbit around the globe to photograph secret installations in the Soviet Union and China. And due in great part to the technical advances made by scientists and engineers working under Bissell, the CIA largely dominated the U.S. government's satellite reconnaissance programs in the late 1950s and well into the 1960s. Even today, when the Air Force has taken over most of the operational aspects of the satellite programs, the CIA is responsible for many of the research and development breakthroughs. At the same time that Bissell was sparking many of the innovations in overhead reconnaissance, he was guiding the Clandestine Services into increased emphasis on covert-action programs in the Third World. It was Bissell who developed and put into practice much of the theory and technique which became standard operating procedure in the CIA's many interventions abroad.

Bissell spoke mainly about covert action that January night in 1968 at the Council on Foreign Relations in New York, and the minutes provide a virtual textbook outline of covert operations. Among his listeners were former CIA officials Allen Dulles and Robert Amory, Jr., former State Department intelligence chief Thomas Hughes, former Kennedy aide Theodore Sorensen, columnist Joseph Kraft, and fourteen others.* All those present were men who had spent most of their lives either in or on the fringes of the government. They could be trusted to remain discreet about what they heard.

Speaking freely to a friendly audience, the former Clandestine Services chief said:

* A complete listing of the participants, as well as the available minutes of the meeting, are contained in the Appendix, "The Bissell Philosophy."

Covert action [is] attempting to influence the internal affairs of other nations—sometimes called "intervention"—by covert means.

. . . the technique is essentially that of "penetration," including "penetrations" of the sort which horrify classicists of covert operations, with a disregard for the "standards" and "agent recruitment rules." Many of the "penetrations" don't take the form of "hiring" but of establishing a close or friendly relationship (which may or may not be furthered by the provision of money from time to time).

Bissell was explaining that the CIA needs to have its own agents on the inside—i.e., "penetrations"—if it wants to finance a political party, guide the editorial policy of a newspaper, or carry off a military coup. CIA clandestine operators assigned overseas are called case officers, and they recruit and supervise the "penetrations." Their tours of duty are normally two to three years, and most serve with false titles in American embassies. Some live under what is called "deep cover" in foreign countries posing as businessmen, students, newsmen, missionaries, or other seemingly innocent American visitors.

The problem of Agency operations overseas [Bissell continued] is frequently a problem for the State Department. It tends to be true that local allies find themselves dealing always with an American and an *official* American—since the cover is almost invariably as a U.S. government employee. There are powerful reasons for this practice, and it will always be desirable to have some CIA personnel housed in the Embassy compound, if only for local "command post" and communications requirements.

Nonetheless, it is possible and desirable, although difficult and time-consuming, to build overseas an apparatus of unofficial cover. This would require the use or creation of private organizations, many of the personnel of which would be non-U.S. nationals, with freer entry into the local society and less implication for the official U.S. posture.

Whatever cover the case officer has, his role is to find agents willing to work with or for the CIA. His aim is to penetrate the host government, to learn its inner workings, to manipulate it for the agency's purposes.

But for the larger and more sensitive interventions [Bissell went on], the allies must have their own motivation. On the whole the Agency has been remarkably successful in finding individuals and instrumentalities with which and through which it could work in this fashion. Implied in the requirement for a pre-existing motivation is the corollary that an attempt to induce the local ally to follow a course he does not believe in will at least reduce his effectiveness and may destroy the whole operation.

Covert action is thus an exercise in seeking out "allies" willing to cooperate with the CIA, preferably individuals who believe in the same goals as the agency; at the very least, people who can be manipulated into belief in these goals. CIA case officers must be adept at convincing people that working for the agency is in their interest, and a good case officer normally will use whatever techniques are required to recruit a prospect: appeals to patriotism and anti-communism can be reinforced with flattery, or sweetened with money and power. Cruder methods involving blackmail and coercion may also be used, but are clearly less desirable.

For covert action to be most effective, the recruitment and penetration should be made long before an actual operation is scheduled. When the U.S. government secretly decides to provoke a coup in a particular country, it is then too late for CIA case officers to be looking for local allies. Instead, if the case officers have been performing their jobs well, they will have already built up a network of agents in that country's government, military forces, press, labor unions, and other important groups; thus there is, in effect, a standing force in scores of countries ready to serve the CIA when the need arises. In the interim, many of these agents also serve the agency by turning over intelligence obtained through their official positions. This intelligence can often be of tactical value to the

CIA in determining local political power structures and calculating where covert action would be most effective. Again, Bissell:

> [There is a] need for continuing efforts to develop covert-action capabilities even where there is no immediate need to employ them. The central task is that of identifying potential indigenous allies—both individuals and organizations—making contact with them, and establishing the fact of a community of interest.

This process is called, in intelligence parlance, "building assets" or developing the operational apparatus. It is a standard function of all CIA clandestine stations and bases overseas. And when a case officer is transferred to a new assignment after several years in a post, he passes on his network of agents and contacts to his replacement, who will stay in touch with them as well as search out new "assets" himself.

Depending on the size and importance of a particular country, from one to scores of CIA case officers may operate there; together, their collective "assets" may number in the hundreds. The planners of any operation will try to orchestrate the use of the available assets so as to have the maximum possible effect. Bissell:

> Covert intervention is probably most effective in situations where a comprehensive effort is undertaken with a number of separate operations designed to support and complement one another and to have a cumulatively significant effect.

In fact, once the CIA's case officers have built up their assets, whether or not the United States will intervene at all will be based in large part on a judgment of the potential effectiveness, importance, and trustworthiness of the CIA's agents or, in Bissell's word, "allies." Yet only case officers on the scene and, to a lesser extent, their immediate superiors in the United States are in a position to make this judgment, since only the CIA knows the identity of its agents. This information is not shared with outsiders or even widely known inside the agency, where agents are listed

by code names even in top-secret documents. Thus, while the political decision to intervene must be made in the White House, it is the CIA itself (through its Clandestine Services) which supplies the President and his advisors with much of the crucial information upon which their decision to intervene is based.

Even if the CIA's reputation for honesty and accurate assessment were unassailable (which it is not), there would still be a built-in conflict of interest in the system: the CIA draws up the intervention plans; the CIA is the only agency with the specific knowledge to evaluate the merits and the feasibility of those plans; and the CIA is the action arm which carries out the plans once they are approved. When the CIA has its assets in place, the inclination within the agency is to recommend their use; the form of intervention recommended will reflect the type of assets which have been earlier recruited. Further, simply because the assets are available, the top officials of the U.S. government may well rely too heavily on the CIA in a real or imagined crisis situation. To these officials, including the President, covert intervention may seem to be an easier solution to a particular problem than to allow events to follow their natural course or to seek a tortuous diplomatic settlement. The temptation to interfere in another country's internal affairs can be almost irresistible, when the means are at hand.

It is one of the contradictions of the intelligence profession, as practiced by the CIA, that the views of its substantive experts—its analysts—do not carry much weight with the clandestine operators engaging in covert action. The operators usually decide which operations to undertake without consulting the analysts. Even when pertinent intelligence studies and estimates are readily available, they are as often as not ignored, unless they tend to support the particular covert-action cause espoused by the operators. Since the days of the OSS, clandestine operators—especially in the field—have distrusted the detached viewpoint of analysts not directly involved in covert action. To ensure against contact with the analysts (and to reduce interference by high-level staff members, even those in the Office of the Director) the operators usually resort to tight operational security—the "need-to-know" principle

—and to bureaucratic deceptions when developing or seeking approval of a covert-action operation. Thus, it is quite possible in the CIA for the intelligence analysts to say one thing, and for the covert-action officers to get the authorization to do another. Although the analysts saw little chance for a successful rebellion against President Sukarno in 1958, the Clandestine Services supported the abortive *coup d'état*. Despite the analysts' view that Castro's government had the support of the Cuban people, the agency's operators attempted—and failed—at the Bay of Pigs to overthrow him. In spite of large doubts on the part of the analysts for years as to the efficacy of Radio Free Europe and Radio Liberty, the CIA continued to fund these propaganda efforts until 1971, when forced by Congress to withdraw its support. Although the analysts clearly indicated that the wars in Laos and Vietnam were not winnable, the operational leadership of the CIA never ceased to devise and launch new programs in support of the local regimes and in the hope of somehow bringing about victory over the enemy. **The analysts had warned against involvement in Latin American politics, but covert action was attempted anyway to manipulate the 1964 and 1970 Chilean presidential elections.**

In theory, the dichotomy that exists between the analytical and clandestine components of the CIA is resolved at the top of the agency. It is at the Director's level that the CIA's analytical input is supposed to be balanced against the goals and risks of the covert-action operation. But it does not always, or even often, work that way. Directors like Allen Dulles and Richard Helms, both long-time clandestine operators, tended to allow their affinity for secret operations to influence their judgment. Even a remote chance of success was enough to win their approval of a covert-action proposal. The views of the analysts, if requested at all, and if they survived the bureaucratic subterfuge of the clandestine operators, were usually dismissed by the agency's leadership on the grounds that they were too vague or indecisive for the purposes of operational planning.

Still, regardless of the preference of the Director of Central Intelligence, it is the President or his National Security Advisor who provides the ultimate direction and grants the final approval for

any significant covert-action program undertaken by the CIA. Often in proposing such a program the agency's operators are responding solely to a presidential directive or to orders of the National Security Council. And always when a CIA covert-action proposal is submitted for approval, the plans are reviewed by the 40 Committee, the special interdepartmental group chaired by the President's National Security Advisor. Thus, the desire of the President or his advisor to move secretly to influence the internal events of another country is frequently the stimulus that either sparks the CIA into action or permits its operators to launch a dubious operation. Only then does the apparatus get into motion; only then do the analysts become meaningless. But "only then" means "almost always."

Tactics

In his talk at the Council on Foreign Relations, Bissell listed eight types of covert action, eight different ways that the CIA intervenes in the domestic affairs of other nations:

> (1) political advice and counsel; (2) subsidies to an individual; (3) financial support and "technical assistance" to political parties; (4) support of private organizations, including labor unions, business firms, cooperatives, etc.; (5) covert propaganda; (6) "private" training of individuals and exchange of persons; (7) economic operations; and (8) paramilitary [or] political action operations designed to overthrow or to support a regime (like the Bay of Pigs and the program in Laos). These operations can be classified in various ways: by the degree and type of secrecy required by their legality, and, perhaps, by their benign or hostile character.

Bissell's fifth and eighth categories—covert propaganda and paramilitary operations—are so large, so important, that they will be discussed at length in later chapters; they are, as well, somewhat self-defining. But the other six categories need some explanation at this point.

The first three categories—political advice and counsel, subsidies to an individual, and financial support and technical assistance to political parties—are usually so closely related that they are nearly impossible to separate. (

DELETED

) The reporters who covered that affair on April 10, 1971, apparently failed to notice anything unusual about the guests. Seated in the State Dining Room at long white tables forming a large E was the usual assortment of foreign dignitaries, high U.S. government officials, and corporate executives who have become fixtures at such occasions during the Nixon years. The guest list supplied by the White House press office gave the titles and positions for almost all the diners.(

DELETED

) years later, he was elected mayor of West Berlin. Throughout this period, (

DELETED

) He was a hard-working politician in Allied-occupied Berlin, and his goal of making the Social Democratic party a viable alternative to communism (

DELETED

) And that evening after dinner, singer Pearl Bailey entertained the White House crowd in the East Room. The *Washington Post* reported the next day that she had "rocked" the White House. (

DELETED

DELETED

)
In certain countries where the CIA has been particularly active, the agency's chief of station (COS) maintains closer ties with the head of state than does the U.S. ambassador. Usually, the ambassador is kept informed of the business transacted between the COS (who is officially subordinate to the ambassador) and the head of state (to whom the ambassador is officially accredited as the personal representative of the President of the United States). But Bissell mentioned cases in which the CIA's relationship with the local head of state was so special that the American ambassador was not informed of any of the details, because either the Secretary of State or the head of the host government preferred that the ambassador be kept ignorant of the relationships. (

DELETED

DELETED

)

Still another example of a country where the CIA enjoys a special relationship is Nationalist China. In Taiwan, however, the CIA's link is not with President Chiang Kai-shek, but with his son and heir apparent, Premier Chiang Ching-kuo. One former CIA chief of station, Ray Cline, until late 1973 the State Department's Director of Intelligence and Research, became something of a legend within the Clandestine Services because of his frequent all-night drinking bouts with the younger Chiang. (

DELETED

)

In South Vietnam, Ambassador Ellsworth Bunker insisted on personally conducting all important meetings with President Thieu;

sometimes Bunker was accompanied by the CIA chief when there was agency business to be discussed. But there has been another CIA officer in Saigon who has known Thieu for many years and who has retained access to the Vietnamese President. According to a former assistant to Ambassador Bunker, this CIA officer has served as conduit between Thieu and the American government when a formal meeting is not desired or when Thieu wishes to float an idea. (

DELETED

DELETED

) Each man has been thought by the agency to represent a strong anti-communist force that would maintain stability in a potentially volatile country.

Generally speaking, the CIA's ties with foreign political leaders who receive advice and money from the agency are extremely delicate. The CIA is interested in moving the leader and, through him, his party and country into policies to the advantage of the United States. In most countries of the Third World, the United States policy is usually to maintain the *status quo,* so most subsidies are designed to strengthen the political base of those in power. The foreign leader who receives money from the CIA is typically furthering both his own career and, presumably, what he believes are the legitimate aims of his country. But even that presumption is shaky; any politician's ability to rationalize his actions probably increases once he has made the decision to accept such funds.

Extensive CIA involvement with private institutions at home and overseas (Bissell's fourth category of covert-action tactics) is one of the few aspects of the agency's covert-action effort to have received a good deal of public attention. The 1967 exposé by *Ramparts* magazine of the CIA's clandestine connections with the National Student Association was quickly followed by a flurry of articles in the press concerning agency subsidies to scores of other organizations. Some of these institutions, particularly those used as conduits for covert funds, were under direct CIA control. Others simply were financed by the agency and steered toward policies that

it favored through the manipulation of only a few of the organization's key personnel. Sam Brown, a former head of the National
Student Association's National Supervisory Policy Board and later
a leader in the 1968 McCarthy campaign and in the anti-war movement, told David Wise and Thomas B. Ross that in the case of the
NSA, the CIA would select one or two association officers as its
contacts. These officers were told that they should be aware of
certain secrets and were asked to sign an oath pledging silence.
"Then," Brown said,

> they were told, "You are employed by the CIA." At that
> point they were trapped, having signed a statement not to
> divulge anything. . . . This is the part of the thing that I found
> to be most disgusting and horrible. People were duped into this
> relationship with the CIA, a relationship from which there
> was no out.

Not all the student leaders recruited over the years by the CIA,
however, were displeased with the arrangement. Some later joined
the agency formally as clandestine operatives, and one rose to become executive assistant to Director Richard Helms. It was this same
man who sometimes posed as an official of the Agency for International Development to entrap unsuspecting NSA officers, revealing
his "cover" only after extracting pledges of secrecy and even NSA
commitments to cooperate with specific CIA programs.

Tom Braden, who headed the CIA's International Organizations
Division from 1950 to 1954 when that component of the Clandestine Services was responsible for subsidizing private organizations,
described his own experiences in a 1967 *Saturday Evening Post*
article entitled "I'm Glad the CIA Is 'Immoral' ":

> It was my idea to give the $15,000 to Irving Brown [of the
> American Federation of Labor]. He needed it to pay off his
> strong-arm squads in Mediterranean ports, so that American
> supplies could be unloaded against the opposition of Com-
> munist dock workers. . . . At [Victor Reuther's] request, I
> went to Detroit one morning and gave Walter [Reuther]

$50,000 in $50 bills. Victor spent the money, mostly in West Germany, to bolster labor unions there. . . .

I remember the enormous joy I got when the Boston Symphony Orchestra won more acclaim for the U.S. in Paris than John Foster Dulles or Dwight D. Eisenhower could have bought with a hundred speeches. And then there was *Encounter*, the magazine published in England and dedicated to the proposition that cultural achievement and political freedom were interdependent. Money for both the orchestra's tour and the magazine's publication came from the CIA, and few outside of the CIA knew about it. We had placed one agent in a Europe-based organization of intellectuals called the Congress for Cultural Freedom. Another agent became an editor of *Encounter*. The agents could not only propose anti-Communist programs to the official leaders of the organizations but they could also suggest ways and means to solve the inevitable budgetary problems. Why not see if the needed money could be obtained from "American foundations"? As the agents knew, the CIA-financed foundations were quite generous when it came to the national interest.

The CIA's culture-loving, optimistic, freewheeling operators, however, made serious tactical errors in funding these "private" institutions. Over the years, the agency became involved with so many groups that direct supervision and accounting were not always possible. Moreover, the agency violated a fundamental rule of intelligence in not carefully separating the operations of each organization from all the others. Thus, when the first disclosures of CIA involvement were published early in 1967, enterprising journalists found that the financing arrangements and the conduit foundations were so intertwined and overused that still other groups which had been receiving CIA funds could be tracked down. Bissell acknowledged this sloppiness of technique when he said, " . . . it is very clear that we should have had greater compartmenting of operations."

In the aftermath of the disclosures, President Johnson appointed a special committee consisting of Under Secretary of State Nicholas

Katzenbach as chairman, CIA Director Richard Helms, and HEW Secretary John Gardner to study the CIA's relationship with private organizations. On March 29, 1967, the committee unanimously recommended—and the President accepted as the national policy —that: "No federal agency shall provide any covert financial assistance or support, direct or indirect, to any of the nation's educational or private voluntary organizations." The report said that exceptions to this policy might be granted in case of "overriding national security interests," but that no organizations then being subsidized fitted this category. The Katzenbach committee noted that it expected the CIA largely, if not entirely, to terminate its ties with private organizations by the end of 1967.

Yet, a year later Richard Bissell told the Council on Foreign Relations:

> If the Agency is to be effective, it will have to make use of private institutions on an expanding scale, though those relations which have "blown" cannot be resurrected. We need to operate under deeper cover, with increased attention to the use of "cut-outs" [i.e., intermediaries]. CIA's interface with the rest of the world needs to be better protected. If various groups hadn't been aware of the source of their funding, the damage subsequent to disclosure might have been far less than occurred. The CIA interface with various private groups, including business and student groups, must be remedied.

Bissell's comments seemed to be in direct contradiction to the official U.S. government policy established by the President. But Bissell, no longer a CIA officer, wasn't challenging presidential authority, and his audience understood that, just as it understood what, indeed, the Katzenbach committee had recommended. Bissell was merely reflecting the general view within the CIA and the cult of intelligence that President Johnson had been pressured by liberals and the press into taking some action to reduce the agency's involvement with private groups; that by naming Katzenbach (then considered by the CIA to be a "friend") as chairman of the com-

mittee and by making CIA Director Helms the second of its three members, the President was stacking the deck in the CIA's favor; that the agency certainly could be criticized for its lack of professional skill in so sloppily funding the private groups; *but* that, essentially, the President did not wish to change appreciably the CIA's covert-action programs.

Once the Katzenbach report appeared, the CIA arranged secret exceptions to the much-heralded new policy. Two CIA broadcasting stations, Radio Free Europe and Radio Liberty, which together received more than $30 million annually in CIA funds, were immediately placed outside the restrictions of the presidential order. And the CIA delayed withdrawing its support for other organizations whose agency ties had been exposed until new forms of financing them could be developed. Thus, as **late as 1970 the CIA was still subsidizing a major international youth organization through a penetration who was one of the organization's officers.** In some cases, "severance payments" were made that could keep an organization afloat for years.

Although the CIA had been widely funding foreign labor unions for more than fifteen years and some of the agency's labor activities were revealed in Tom Braden's *Saturday Evening Post* article, the Katzenbach committee did not specify unions as the type of organizations the CIA was barred from financing. At the 1968 Council on Foreign Relations meeting at which Bissell spoke, Meyer Bernstein, the Steelworkers Union's Director of International Labor Affairs, commented:

the turn of events has been unexpected. First, there hasn't been any real problem with international labor programs. Indeed, there has been an increase in demand for U.S. labor programs and the strain on our capacity has been embarrassing. Formerly, these foreign labor unions knew we were short of funds, but now they all assume we have secret CIA money, and they ask for more help.

Worse yet, Vic Reuther, who had been alleging that others were receiving CIA money, and whose brother's receipt of

$50,000 from CIA in old bills was subsequently disclosed by Tom Braden, still goes on with his charges that the AFL-CIO has taken CIA money. Here again, no one seems to listen. "The net result has been as close to zero as possible. We've come to accept CIA, like sin." So, for example, British Guiana's [Guyana] labor unions were supported through CIA conduits, but now they ask for more assistance than before. So, our expectations to the contrary, there has been almost no damage.

In Vietnam, enthusiastic officials of the U.S. embassy in Saigon were fond of saying during the late 1960s that Tran Ngoc Buu was the Samuel Gompers of the Vietnamese labor movement. They did not say—and most probably did not know—(

DELETED

)

Bissell also identified " 'private' training of individuals and ex-change of persons" as a form of covert action:

Often activities have been initiated through CIA channels be-cause they could be started more quickly and informally but do not inherently need to be secret. An example might be certain exchange-of-persons programs designed to identify potential political leaders and give them some exposure to the United States. It should be noted, however, that many such innocent programs are more effective if carried out by private auspices than if supported officially by the United States Government. They do not need to be covert but if legitimate private entities such as the foundations do not initiate them, there may be no way to get them done except by covert support to "front" organizations.

He was referring to the so-called people-to-people exchange programs, most of which are funded openly by the State De-partment, the Agency for International Development, the U.S.

Information Agency, and various private organizations and foundations. But the CIA has also been involved to a lesser extent, and has brought foreigners to the United States with funds secretly supplied to conduit organizations. **On occasion, the agency will sponsor the training of foreign officials at the facilities of another government agency. A favorite site is AID's International Police Academy in Washington. The academy is operated by AID's Public Safety (police) Division, which regularly supplies cover to CIA operators all over the world. And the CIA takes advantage of exchange programs to recruit** agents. While a systematic approach is not followed, the agency considers foreigners visiting the United States to be legitimate targets for recruitment.

The CIA has undertaken comparatively few economic covert-action programs (Bissell's seventh category) over the years, preferring the more direct approach of paramilitary operations or propaganda. And those economic programs attempted by the agency have not been notably successful. During the mid-1960s Japanese investors were used in an effort to build up the South Vietnamese economy, because American companies tended to shy away from making substantial investments in Vietnam. The U.S. government hoped that the Japanese would fill the void at least partially, and eventually lighten U.S. aid requirements. Thus, CIA representatives promised certain Japanese businessmen that the agency would supply the investment capital if the Japanese would front for the operation and supply the technical expertise for large commercial farms. After long and detailed negotiations, the deal faltered and then failed.

A few years earlier the CIA had tried to disrupt Cuba's sugar trade as part of its program to undercut Fidel Castro's regime. At one point the Clandestine Services operatives proposed that the CIA purchase large amounts of sugar and then dump it in a certain foreign country so as to destroy the market for Cuban sugar. This plan also fell through, but a more serious attack on Cuban sugar occurred in August 1962 when a British freighter under lease to the Soviets docked in Puerto Rico for repairs. The freighter,

carrying Cuban sugar destined for the Soviet Union, was placed in a bonded warehouse while the ship was in dry dock. CIA agents broke into the warehouse and contaminated the sugar with a non-poisonous but unpalatable substance.

As pointed out earlier, one of the advantages a secret agency like the CIA provides to a President is the unique pretext of being able to disclaim responsibility for its actions. Thus, a President can direct or approve high-risk clandestine operations such as a manned overflight of the Soviet Union on the eve of a summit conference, a Bay of Pigs invasion, penetration and manipulation of private youth, labor, or cultural organizations, paramilitary adventures in Southeast Asia, or intervention in the domestic politics of Chile without openly accepting the consequences of these decisions. If the clandestine operations are successful—good. If they fail or backfire, then usually all the President and his staff need do to avoid culpability is to blame the CIA.

In no instance has a President of the United States ever made a serious attempt to review or revamp the covert practices of the CIA. Minor alterations in operational methods and techniques have been carried out, but no basic changes in policy or practice have ever been demanded by the White House. And this is not surprising: Presidents *like* the CIA. It does their dirty work—work that might not otherwise be "do-able." When the agency fails or blunders, all the President need do is to deny, scold, or threaten.

For the CIA's part, being the focus of presidential blame is an occupational hazard, but one hardly worth worrying about. It is merely an aspect of the cover behind which the agency operates. Like the other aspects of cover, it is part of a deception. The CIA fully realizes that it is too important to the government and the American political aristocracy for any President to do more than tinker with it. The CIA shrugs off its blunders and proceeds to devise new operations, secure in the knowledge that the White House usually cannot resist its offerings, particularly covert action—covert action that dominates, that determines, that defines the shape and purpose of the CIA. America's leaders have not yet reached the

point where they are willing to forsake intervention in the internal affairs of other countries and let events naturally run their course. There still is a widely held belief in this country that America has the right and the responsibility to become involved in the internal political processes of foreign nations, and while faith in this belief and that of doctrinaire anti-communism may have been somewhat shaken in the last decade (

DELETED

)

THREE

The CIA and the Intelligence Community

It is the task of the Director
of Central Intelligence,
utilizing his influence in the
various interdepartmental
mechanisms, to create out of
these diverse components a
truly national estimate, useful to
the national interest and not
just to a particular bureaucratic
preference. This is not
an easy task.

—HARRY HOWE RANSOM
The Intelligence Establishment

THE CIA is big, very big. Officially, it has authorized manpower of **16,500**, and an authorized budget of **$750** million—and even those figures are jealously guarded, generally made available only to Congress. Yet, regardless of its official size and cost, the agency is far larger and more affluent than these figures indicate.

The CIA itself does not even know how many people work for it. The **16,500** figure does not reflect the tens of thousands who serve under contract (mercenaries, agents, consultants, etc.) or who work for the agency's proprietary companies.* Past efforts to total up the number of foreign agents have never resulted in precise figures because of the inordinate secrecy and compartmentalization practiced by the Clandestine Services. Sloppy record-keeping—often deliberate on the part of the operators "for security purposes"—is also a factor. There are one-time agents hired for specific missions, contract agents who serve for extended periods of time, and career agents who spend their entire working lives secretly employed by the CIA. In some instances, contract agents are retained long after their usefulness has passed, but usually are known only to the case officers with whom they deal. One of the Watergate burglars, Eugenio Martinez, was in this category. When he was caught inside the Watergate on that day in June 1972, he still was receiving a $100-a-month stipend from the agency for work apparently unrelated to his covert assignment for the Committee to Re-Elect the President. The CIA claims to have since dropped him from the payroll.

A good chunk of the agency's annual operational funds, called

---

* Nor does the figure include the guard force which protects the CIA's buildings and installations, the maintenance and char force, or the people who run the agency's cafeterias. The General Services Administration employs most of these personnel.

"project money," is wasted in this fashion. Payments to no-longer-productive agents are justified on several grounds: the need to maintain secrecy about their operations even though these occurred years ago; the vague hope that such agents will again prove to be useful (operators are always reluctant to give up an asset, even a useless one), and the claim that the agency has a commitment to its old allies—a phenomenon known in the CIA as "emotional attachment." It is the last justification that carries the most weight within the agency. Thus, hundreds—perhaps thousands—of former Cuban, East European, and other minor clandestine agents are still on the CIA payroll, at an annual cost to the taxpayers of hundreds of thousands, if not millions, of dollars a year.

All mercenaries and many field-operations officers used in CIA paramilitary activities are also contractees and, therefore, are not reflected in the agency's authorized manpower level. The records kept on these soldiers of fortune are at best only gross approximations. In Laos and Vietnam, for example, the Clandestine Services had a fairly clear idea of how many local tribesmen were in its pay, but the operators were never quite certain of the total number of mercenaries they were financing through the agency's numerous support programs, some of which were fronted for by the Department of Defense, the Agency for International Development, and, of course, the CIA proprietary, Air America.

Private individuals under contract to—or in confidential contact with—the agency for a wide variety of tasks other than soldiering or spying are also left out of the personnel totals, and complete records of their employment are not kept in any single place.* In 1967, however, when the CIA's role on American campuses was under close scrutiny because of the embarrassing National Student Association revelations, Helms asked his staff to find out just how many university personnel were under secret contract to the CIA. After a few days of investigation, senior CIA officers reported back that they could not find the answer. Helms immediately ordered a full study of the situation, and after more than a month

* Attempts to computerize the complete CIA employment list were frustrated and eventually scuttled by Director Helms, who viewed the effort as a potential breach of operational security.

of searching records all over the agency, a report was handed in to Helms listing hundreds of professors and administrators on over a hundred campuses. But the staff officers who compiled the report knew that their work was incomplete. Within weeks, another campus connection was exposed in the press. The contact was not on the list that had been compiled for the director.

Just as difficult as adding up the number of agency contractees is the task of figuring out how many people work for its proprietaries. CIA headquarters, for instance, has never been able to compute exactly the number of planes flown by the airlines it owns, and personnel figures for the proprietaries are similarly imprecise. An **agency** holding company, the Pacific Corporation, including Air America and Air Asia, alone accounts for almost 20,000 people, more than the entire workforce of the parent **CIA.** For years this vast activity was dominated and controlled by one contract agent, George Doole, who later was elevated to the rank of a career officer. Even then his operation was supervised, part time, by only a single senior officer who lamented that he did not know "what the hell was going on."

Well aware that the agency is two or three times as large as it appears to be, the CIA's leadership has consistently sought to downplay its size. During the directorship of Richard Helms, when the agency had a career-personnel ceiling of **18,000,** CIA administrative officers were careful to hold the employee totals to 200 or 300 people below the authorized complement. Even at the height of the Vietnam war, while most national-security agencies were increasing their number of employees, the CIA handled its increased needs through secret contracts, thus giving a deceptive impression of personnel leanness. Other bureaucratic gambits were used in a similar way to keep the agency below the **18,000** ceiling. Senior officers were often rehired on contract immediately after they retired and started to draw government pensions. Overseas, agency wives were often put on contract to perform secretarial duties.

Just as the personnel figure is deceptive, so does the budget figure not account for a great part of the CIA's campaign chest. The agency's proprietaries are often money-making enterprises, and

Size and Cost of the CIA
(Approximate)

	Personnel	$ Millions
Office of the Director	400	10
Clandestine Services	6,000	440
(Directorate of Operations)		
Espionage/Counterespionage	(4,200)	(180)
Covert Action	(1,800)	(260)
Directorate of Management and Services	5,300	110
Communications	(2,000)	(70)
Other Support	(3,300)	(40)
Directorate of Intelligence	3,500	70
Analysis	(1,200)	(50)
Information Processing	(2,300)	(20)
Directorate of Science and Technology	1,300	120
Technical Collection	(1,000)	(50)
Research and Development	(300)	(70)
	16,500*	750**

* Nearly 5,000 CIA personnel serve overseas, the majority (60–70 percent) being members of the Clandestine Services. Of the remainder, most are communications officers and other operational support personnel.
** Does not include the Director's Special Contingency Fund.

thus provide "free" services to the parent organization. The prime examples of this phenomenon are the airlines (Air America, Air Asia, and others) organized under the CIA holding company, the Pacific Corporation, which have grown bigger than the CIA itself by conducting as much private business as possible and continually reinvesting the profits. These companies generate revenues in the tens of millions of dollars each year, but the figures are imprecise because detailed accounting of their activities is not normally required by agency bookkeepers. For all practical purposes, the proprietaries conduct their own financial affairs with a minimum of oversight from CIA headquarters. Only when a pro-

prietary is in need of funds for, say, expansion of its fleet of planes does it request agency money. Otherwise, it is free to use its profits in any way it sees fit. In this atmosphere, the proprietaries tend to take on lives of their own, and several have grown too big and too independent to be either controlled from or dissolved by headquarters.

Similarly, the CIA's annual budget does not show the Pentagon's annual contribution to the agency, amounting to hundreds of millions of dollars, to fund certain major technical espionage programs and some particularly expensive clandestine activities. For example, the CIA's Science and Technology Directorate has an annual budget of only a little more than **$100 million, but it actually spends well over $500 million a year. The difference is funded largely by the Air Force, which underwrites the national overhead-reconnaissance effort for the entire U.S. intelligence** community. Moreover, the Clandestine Services waged a "secret" war in Laos for more than a decade at an annual cost to the government of approximately $500 million. Yet, the CIA itself financed less than 10 percent of this amount each year. The bulk of the expense was paid for by other federal agencies, mostly the Defense Department but also the Agency for International Development.

Fully aware of these additional sources of revenue, the CIA's chief of planning and programming reverently observed a few years ago that the director does not operate a mere *multimillion*-dollar agency but actually runs a *multibillion*-dollar conglomerate—with virtually no outside oversight.

In terms of financial assets, the CIA is not only more affluent than its official annual budget reflects, it is one of the few federal agencies that have no shortage of funds. In fact, the CIA has more money to spend than it needs. Since its creation in 1947, the agency has ended almost every fiscal year with a surplus—which it takes great pains to hide from possible discovery by the Office of Management and Budget (OMB) or by the congressional oversight subcommittees. The risk of discovery is not high, however, since both the OMB and the subcommittees are usually friendly and indulgent when dealing with the CIA. Yet, each year the agency's bookkeepers, at the direction of the organization's top

leadership, transfer the excess funds to the accounts of the CIA's major components with the understanding that the money will be kept available if requested by the director's office. This practice of squirreling away these extra dollars would seem particularly unnecessary because the agency always has some **$50 to $100 million** on call for unanticipated costs in a special account called the Director's Contingency Fund.

The Director's Contingency Fund was authorized by a piece of legislation which is unique in the American system. Under the Central Intelligence Agency Act of 1949, the Director of Central Intelligence (DCI) was granted the privilege of expending funds "without regard to the provisions of law and regulations relating to the expenditure of Government funds; and for objects of confidential, extraordinary, or emergency nature, such expenditures to be accounted for solely on the certificate of the Director. . . ." In the past, the Fund (

DELETED

) **But there have been times when the fund has been used for the highly questionable purpose of paying expenses incurred by other agencies of the government.**

In 1967 Secretary of Defense Robert McNamara promised Norwegian officials that the U.S. government would provide them with some new air-defense equipment costing several million dollars. McNamara subsequently learned the equipment was not available in the Pentagon's inventories and would have to be specially purchased for delivery to Norway. He was also informed that, because of the high cost of the Vietnam war (for which the Defense Department was then seeking a supplemental appropriation from Congress), funds to procure the air-defense equipment were not immediately at hand. Further complications arose from the fact that the Secretary was then engaged in a disagreement with some members of Congress over the issue of foreign military aid. It was therefore decided not to openly request the funds for the small but potentially sticky commitment to the Norwegians. **Instead, the Pentagon asked the CIA (with White House approval)**

to supply the money needed for the purchase of air-defense equipment. The funds were secretly transferred to the Defense (

DELETED

) That same year President Johnson traveled to Punta del Este, a posh resort in Uruguay, for a meeting of the Organization of American States. He entertained the attending foreign leaders in a lavish manner which he apparently thought befitted the President of the United States, and he freely dispensed expensive gifts and souvenirs. In the process, LBJ greatly exceeded the representational allowance that the State Department had set aside for the conference. When the department found itself in the embarrassing position of being unable to cover the President's bills because of its tight budget (due in part to the economies LBJ had been demanding of the federal bureaucracy to help pay for the war in Vietnam), it was reluctant to seek additional funds from Congress. Representative John Rooney of Brooklyn, who almost singlehandedly controlled State's appropriations, had for years been a strong critic of representational funds (called the "booze allowance") for America's diplomats. Rather than face Rooney's wrath, State turned to the CIA, and the Director's Contingency Fund was used to pay for the President's fling at Punta del Este.

For some reason—perhaps because of the general view in the CIA that its operations are above the law—the agency has tended to play fiscal games that other government departments would not dare engage in. One example concerns the agency's use of its employee retirement fund, certain agent and contract-personnel escrow accounts, and the CIA credit union's capital, to play the stock market. With the approval of the top CIA leadership, a small group of senior agency officers has for years secretly supervised the management of these funds and invested them in stocks, hoping to turn a greater profit than normally would be earned through the Treasury Department's traditional low-interest but

safe bank deposits and bond issues. Originally, the investment group, consisting of CIA economists, accountants, and lawyers, dealt with an established Boston brokerage house, which made the final investment decisions. But several years ago the Boston brokers proved too conservative to suit the agency investors, some of whom were making fatter profits with their personal portfolios. The CIA group decided it could do much better by picking its own stocks, so the brokerage house was reduced to doing only the actual stock trading (still with a handsome commission, of course). Within a matter of months the agency investors were earning bigger profits than ever before. Presumably, the gains were plowed back into the retirement, escrow, and credit-union funds.*

In 1968, Senator Richard Russell of Georgia, then the chairman of the Senate joint subcommittee for overseeing the CIA's activities, privately informed Director Helms that because of increasing skepticism among certain Senators about the agency operations, it probably would be a good idea for the CIA to arrange to have its financial procedures reviewed by an independent authority. Thus, in Russell's view, potential Senate critics who might be considering making an issue of the agency's special fiscal privileges would be undercut in advance. Senator Russell suggested the names of a few private individuals who might be willing to undertake such a task on behalf of the CIA. After conferring with his senior officers, Helms chose to ask Wilfred McNeil, at that time the president of Grace Shipping Lines (

DELETED

) to serve as the confidential reviewer of the

---

* The investment practices of the CIA group in companies with overseas holdings open up some interesting questions about "insider" information. Would the CIA group have sold Anaconda Copper short in 1970 when the agency realized that its covert efforts to prevent Salvador Allende from assuming the Presidency of Chile had failed? Or in 1973, when Director James Schlesinger decided to allow William Broe, the former chief of the Clandestine Services' Western Hemisphere Division, to testify before the Senate Foreign Relations Committee and describe ITT's role in trying to provoke CIA action against Allende, might the investment group not have been tempted to dump its ITT stock (if it had any)?

agency's budgetary practices. McNeil, a former admiral and once comptroller for the Defense Department, was thought by Helms to be ideally suited, politically and otherwise, for the assignment.

McNeil accepted the task and soon came to CIA headquarters for a full briefing on the agency's most sensitive financial procedures—including an account of the methods used for purchasing and laundering currency on the international black market. He was told of the CIA's new planning, programming, and budgeting system, modeled after the innovations Robert McNamara had introduced at the Defense Department. Agency experts explained to McNeil how funds for new operations were authorized within the agency. He learned that the agency maintained a sliding-scale system for the approval of new projects or the periodic renewal of ongoing ones; that espionage operations costing up to $10,000 could be okayed by operators in the field; and that progressively more expensive operations necessitated branch, division, and Clandestine Services chief approval until, finally, operations costing over $100,000 were authorized personally by the Director. McNeil also was briefed on the agency's internal auditing system to prevent field operatives from misusing secret funds.

McNeil's reaction to his long and detailed briefing was to express surprise at the scope of the CIA's financial system and to praise the accounting practices used. When asked where and when he would like to begin his work in depth, he politely demurred and departed—never to return. A month or so later a CIA officer working in the Director's office learned that McNeil had had certain misgivings about the project and had sought the advice of former agency Director William Raborn, who had his own doubts about the reliability of the CIA's top career officers. Raborn had apparently discouraged McNeil from becoming involved in such a review. But as far as the CIA was concerned, Senator Russell's request for an independent audit had been carried out, since the agency's fiscal practices had been looked over by a qualified outsider and found to be in no need of improvement. The whole matter was then dropped.

Organization

The CIA is neatly organized into five distinct parts, a relatively small office of the Director and four functional directorates, the largest of which is the Directorate of Operations (known inside the agency as the Clandestine Services). The executive suite houses the CIA's only two political appointees, the Director of Central Intelligence (DCI) and the Deputy Director (DDCI), and their immediate staffs. Included organizationally, but not physically, in the Office of the Director are two components that assist the DCI in his role as head of the U.S. intelligence community. One is a small group of senior analysts, drawn from the CIA and the other agencies of the community, which prepares the "blue books," or National Intelligence Estimates, on such subjects as Soviet strategic defense capabilities, Chinese long-range missile developments, and the political outlook for Chile.* The other is the Intelligence Resources Advisory Committee, a group created in 1971, which provides staff assistance to the Director in his efforts to manage and streamline the $6-billion intelligence community.

The Intelligence Resources Advisory Committee, long a dream of those officers who believe the U.S. intelligence community to be too big and inefficient, has thus far proven to be something of a nightmare. Instead of eliminating wasteful and redundant activities within U.S. intelligence, it has been turned into a vehicle for the military intelligence agencies to justify and expand their already overly ambitious collection programs. Likewise, the recent revamping of the Board of National Estimates, under present Director William Colby, has been characterized by some experienced hands as "a sellout" to Pentagon power, caused in part by the political pressures of Henry Kissinger's National Security

---

* These senior analysts are called National Intelligence Officers (and sometimes "the Wise Men" by their colleagues within the community). The group has replaced the Board of National Estimates, which was a larger and more formalized body of senior officers who oversaw the preparation of national estimates.

Organization of the CIA

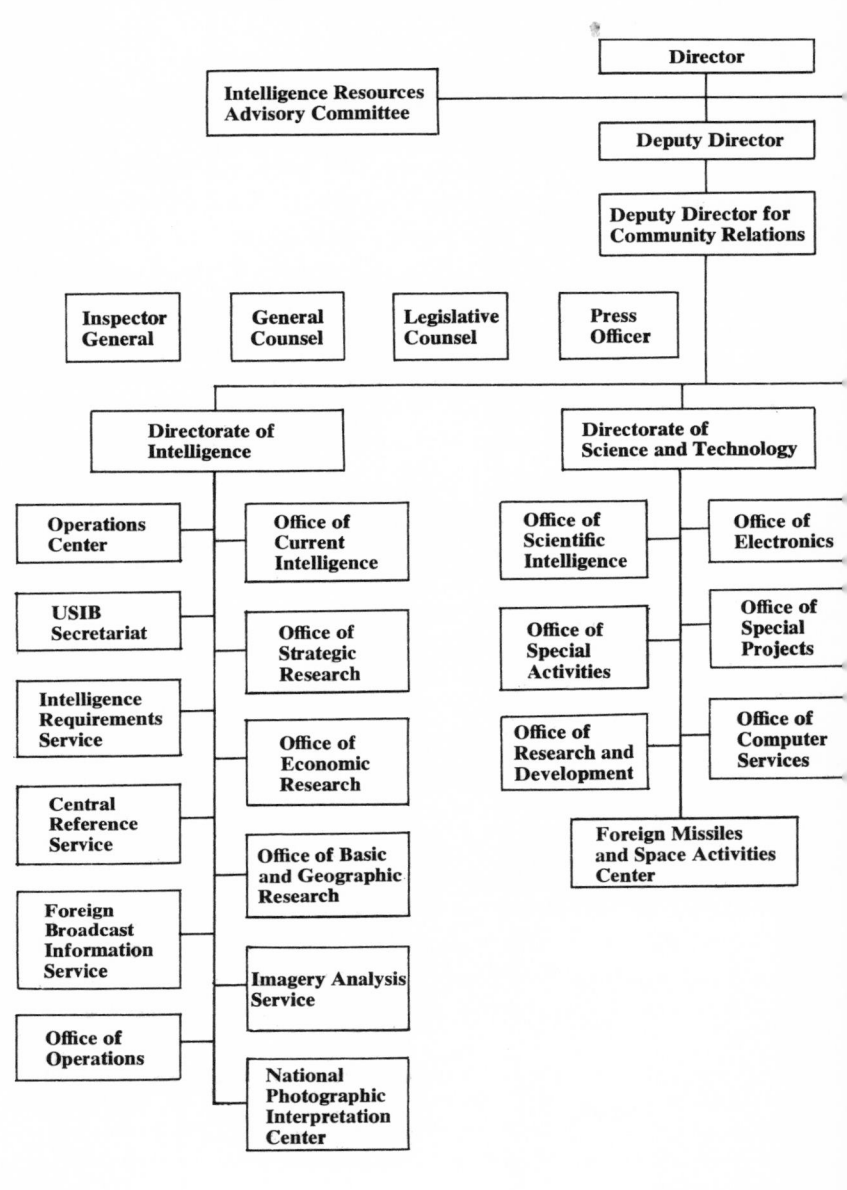

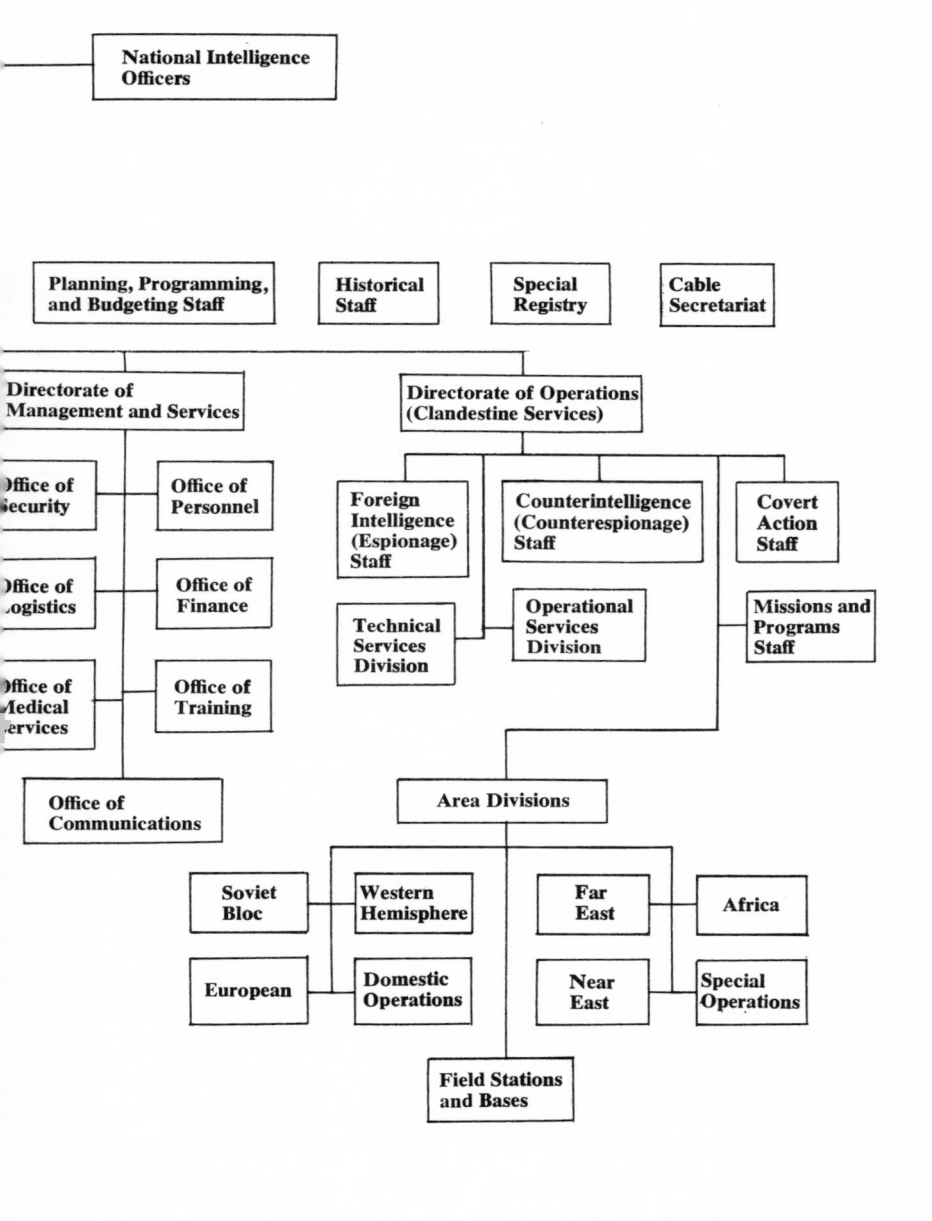

Council staff. Under Colby, the board has been greatly reduced in both prestige and independence, and has been brought under the stifling influence of military men whose first allegiance is to their parent services rather than to the production of objective, balanced intelligence assessments for the policy-makers.

The other components of the Office of the Director include those traditionally found in governmental bureaucracies: press officers, congressional liaison, legal counsel, and so on. Only two merit special note: the Cable Secretariat and the Historical Staff. The former was established in 1950 at the insistence of the Director, General Walter Bedell Smith. When Smith, an experienced military staff officer, learned that agency communications, especially those between headquarters and the covert field stations and bases, were controlled by the Clandestine Services, he immediately demanded a change in the system. "The operators are not going to decide what secret information I will see or not see," he is reported to have said. Thus, the Cable Secretariat, or message center, was put under the Director's immediate authority. Since then, however, the operators have found other ways, when it is thought necessary, of keeping their most sensitive communications from going outside the Clandestine Services.

The Historical Staff represents one of the CIA's more clever attempts to maintain the secrecy on which the organization thrives. Several years ago the agency began to invite retiring officers to spend an additional year or two with the agency—on contract, at regular pay—writing their official memoirs. The product of their effort is, of course, highly classified and tightly restricted. In the agency's eyes, this is far better than having former officers openly publish what really happened during their careers with the CIA.

The largest of the agency's four directorates is the Directorate of Operations, or the Clandestine Services, which has about **6,000** professionals and clericals. The ratio between professionals, mostly operations officers, and clericals, largely secretaries, is roughly two to one. Approximately 45 percent of the Clandestine Services personnel is stationed overseas, the vast majority using official cover

—i.e., posing as representatives of the State or Defense Department. About two out of three of the people in the Clandestine Services are engaged in general intelligence activities—liaison, espionage, and counterespionage—the remainder concentrating on various forms of covert action. Yet despite the smaller number of personnel working on covert action, these interventions in the internal affairs of other countries cost about half again as much as spying and counterspying **($260 million v. $180 million annually).** The greater expense for covert action is explained by the high costs of paying for paramilitary operations and subsidizing political parties, labor unions, and other international groups.

The Clandestine Services is broken down into fifteen separate components, but its actual operating patterns do not follow the neat lines of an organizational chart. Exceptions are the rule. Certain clandestine activities which would seem to an outsider to be logically the responsibility of one component are often carried out by another—because of political sensitivity, because of an assumed need for even greater secrecy than usual, because of bureaucratic compartmentalization, or simply because things have always been done that way.

The bulk of the Clandestine Services' personnel, about **4,800** people, work in the so-called area divisions, both at headquarters and overseas. These divisions correspond roughly to the State Department's geographic bureaus—a logical breakdown, since most CIA operators in foreign countries work under State cover. The largest area division is the Far East (with about **1,500** people), followed in order of descending size by Europe (Western Europe only), Western Hemisphere (Latin America plus Canada), Near East, Soviet Bloc (Eastern Europe), and Africa (with only **300** staff). The chain of command goes from the head of the Clandestine Services to the chiefs of the area divisions, then overseas to the chiefs of stations (COS) and their chiefs of bases (COB).

The CIA's stations and bases around the world serve as the principal headquarters of covert activity in the country in which each is located. The station is usually housed in the U.S. embassy in the capital city, while bases are in other major cities or some-

times on American or foreign military bases. For example, in West Germany, the CIA's largest site for operations, the station is located in Bonn; the chief of station is on the staff of the American ambassador. There are subordinate bases in (**DELETED**

) and a few other cities, along with several bases under American military cover scattered throughout the German countryside.

The Domestic Operations Division of Clandestine Services is, in essence, an area division, but it conducts its mysterious clandestine activities in the United States, not overseas. Its chief—like the other area-division chiefs, the civilian equivalent of a two- or three-star general—works out of an office in downtown Washington, within two blocks of the White House. Under the Washington station are bases located in other major American cities.

Also in the Clandestine Services are three staffs, Foreign Intelligence (espionage), Counterintelligence (counterespionage), and Covert Action, which oversee operational policy in their respective specialties and provide assistance to the area divisions and the field elements. For instance, in an operation to plant a slanted news story in a Chilean newspaper, propaganda experts on the Covert Action Staff might devise an article in cooperation with the Chilean desk of the Western Hemisphere Division. A **CIA proprietary,** like (**DELETED**   ) might be used to write and transmit the story to Chile so it would not be directly attributable to the agency, and then a clandestine operator working out of the American embassy in Santiago might work through one of his penetration agents in the local press to ensure that the article is reprinted. While most CIA operations abroad are carried out through the area divisions, the operational staffs, particularly the Covert Action Staff, also conduct independent activities.

The Special Operations Division is something of a hybrid between the area divisions and the operational staffs. Its main function is to provide the assets for paramilitary operations, largely the contracted manpower (mercenaries or military men on loan), the matériel, and the expertise to get the job done. Its operations, however, are organizationally under the station chief in the country where they are located.

The remaining three components of the Clandestine Services provide technical assistance to the operational components. These three are: the Missions and Programs Staff, which does much of the bureaucratic planning and budgeting for the Clandestine Services and which writes up the justification for covert operations submitted for approval to the 40 Committee; the Operational Services Division, which among other things sets up cover arrangements for clandestine officers; and the Technical Services Division, which produces in its own laboratories the gimmicks of the spy trade—the disguises, miniature cameras, tape recorders, secret writing kits, and the like.

The Directorate of Management and Services (formerly the Directorate of Support) is the CIA's administrative and house-keeping part. However, most of its budget and personnel is devoted to assisting the Clandestine Services in carrying out covert operations. (This directorate is sometimes referred to within the agency as the Clandestine Services' "slave" directorate.) Various forms of support are also provided to the Directorate of Intelligence and the Directorate of Science and Technology, but the needs of these two components for anything beyond routine administrative tasks are generally minimal. Covert operations, however, require a large support effort, and the M&S Directorate, in addition to providing normal administrative assistance, contributes in such areas as communications, logistics, and training.

The M&S Directorate's Office of Finance, for example, maintains field units in Hong Kong, Beirut, Buenos Aires, and Geneva with easy access to the international money markets. The Office of Finance tries to keep a ready inventory of the world's currencies on hand for future clandestine operations. Many of the purchases are made in illegal black markets where certain currencies are available at bargain rates. In some instances, most notably in the case of the South Vietnamese piaster, black-market purchases of a single currency amount to millions of dollars a year.

The Office of Security provides physical protection for clandestine installations at home and abroad and conducts polygraph (lie detector) tests for all CIA employees and contract personnel

and most foreign agents. The Office of Medical Services heals the sicknesses and illnesses (both mental and physical) of CIA personnel by providing "cleared" psychiatrists and physicians to treat agency officers; analyzes prospective and already recruited agents; and prepares "psychological profiles" of foreign leaders (and once, in 1971, at the request of the Watergate "plumbers," did a "profile" of Daniel Ellsberg). The Office of Logistics operates the agency's weapons and other warehouses in the United States and overseas, supplies normal office equipment and household furniture, as well as the more esoteric clandestine matériel to foreign stations and bases, and performs other housekeeping chores. The Office of Communications, employing over 40 percent of the Directorate of Management and Services's more than **5,000** career employees, maintains facilities for secret communications between CIA headquarters and the hundreds of stations and bases overseas. It also provides the same services, on a reimbursable basis, for the State Department and most of its embassies and consulates. The Office of Training operates the agency's training facilities at many locations around the United States, and a few overseas. (The Office of Communications, however, runs (

DELETED

) The Office of Personnel handles the recruitment and record-keeping for the CIA's career personnel.

Support functions are often vital for successful conduct of covert operations, and a good support officer, like a good supply sergeant in an army, is indispensable to a CIA station or base. Once a station chief has found the right support officer, one who can provide everything from housekeeping to operational support, the two will often form a professional alliance and stay together as they move from post to post during their careers. In some instances the senior support officer may even serve as the *de facto* second-in-command because of his close relationship with the chief.

Together, the Clandestine Services and the Directorate for Management and Services constitute an agency within an agency. These two components, like the largest and most dangerous part of an iceberg, float along virtually unseen. Their missions, methods, and personnel are quite different from those of the CIA's other two

directorates, which account for only less than a third of the agency's budget and manpower. Yet the CIA—and particularly former Director Richard Helms—has tried to convince the American public that the analysts and technicians of the Directorates for Intelligence and Science and Technology, the clean white tip of the CIA iceberg, are the agency's key personnel.

The Directorate of Intelligence, with **some 3,500 employees**, engages in two basic activities: first, the production of finished intelligence reports from the analysis of information (both classified and unclassified); and second, the performance of certain services of common concern for the benefit of the whole intelligence community. Included in the latter category are the agency's various reference services (e.g., a huge computerized biographical library of foreign personalities, another on foreign factories, and so on); the Foreign Broadcasting Information Service (a worldwide radio and television monitoring system); and the National Photographic Interpretation Center (an organization, run in close cooperation with the Pentagon, which analyzes photographs taken from satellites and spy planes). About two thirds of the Intelligence Directorate's **$70 million** annual budget is devoted to carrying out these services of common concern for the government's entire national-security bureaucracy. Thus, the State and Defense departments are spared the expense of maintaining duplicate facilities, receiving from the CIA finished intelligence in areas of interest to them. For example, when there is a shift in the Soviet leadership, or a new Chinese diplomat is posted to Washington, the Intelligence Directorate routinely sends biographical information (usually classified "secret") on the personalities involved to the other government agencies. Similarly, the various State Department bureaus (along with selected American academicians and newspapers) regularly receive the agency's unclassified transcripts of foreign radio and television broadcasts.

Most of the rest of the Intelligence Directorate's assets are focused on political, economic, and strategic military research. The agency's specialists produce both current intelligence—reports and explanations on a daily basis of the world's breaking events—

and long-range analysis of trends, potential crisis areas, and other matters of interest to the government's policy-makers. Turning out current intelligence reports is akin to publishing a newspaper, and, in fact, the Intelligence Directorate puts out daily and weekly publications which, except for their high security classifications, are similar to work done by the American press. These regular intelligence reports, along with special ones on topics like corruption in South Vietnam or the prospects for the Soviet wheat crop, are sent to hundreds of "consumers" in the federal government. The primary consumer, however, is the President, and he receives every morning a special publication called the President's Daily Brief. In the Johnson administration these reports frequently contained, in addition to the normal intelligence fare, rather scandalous descriptions of the private lives of certain world leaders, always avidly read by the President.* The agency found, however, that in the Nixon administration such items were not appreciated, and the tone of the daily report was changed. Even so, President Nixon and Henry Kissinger soon lost interest in reading the publication; the task was relegated to lower-ranking officials on the National Security Council staff.

The fourth and newest of the CIA's directorates. Science and Technology, also employs the smallest number of personnel, about **1,300** people. It carries out functions such as basic research and development, the operation of spy satellites, and intelligence analysis in highly technical fields. In addition to these activities, it also handles the bulk of the agency's electronic data-processing (computer) work. While the S&T Directorate keeps abreast of and does research work in a wide variety of scientific fields, its most important successes have come in developing technical espionage systems. The precursor of this directorate was instrumental in the development of the U-2 and **SR-71** spy planes. The S&T ex-

---

* President Johnson's taste in intelligence was far from conventional. A former high State Department official tells of attending a meeting at the White House and then staying on for a talk with the President afterward. LBJ proceeded to play for him a tape recording (one of those presumably made by the FBI) of Martin Luther King in a rather compromising situation.

perts have also made several brilliant breakthroughs in the intelligence-satellite field. In the late 1950s, when Clandestine Services chief Richard Bissell encouraged the technicians in their development of America's first photo-reconnaissance satellite, they produced a model which was still in use as late as 1971. And agency technicians have continued to make remarkable advances in the "state of the art." Today spy satellites, capable of producing photographs from space with less than (**DELETED**) resolution, lead all other collection means as a source of intelligence. The S&T Directorate has also been a leader in developing other technical espionage techniques, such as over-the-horizon radars, "stationary" satellites, and various other electronic information-gathering devices.

The normal procedure has been for the S&T Directorate, using both CIA and Pentagon funds, to work on a collection system through the research-and-development stage. Then, once the system is perfected, it is turned over to the Defense Department. In the case of a few particularly esoteric systems, the CIA has kept operational control, but the agency's S&T budget of about **$120 million** per year is simply not large enough to support many independent technical collection systems.

CIA technicians, for example, worked with Lockheed Aircraft at a secret site in Nevada to develop the A-11, probably the most potent airborne collection system ever to fly. In February 1964, before the plane became operational, President Johnson revealed its existence to the news media, describing it as a long-range Air Force interceptor. Five months later, at another news conference, the President disclosed that there was a second version of the aircraft, which he described as "an advanced strategic reconnaissance plane for military use, capable of worldwide reconnaissance." Three years after that, when the A-11, now the SR-71, was flying regularly, the program was turned over to the Air Force. (

DELETED

DELETED

)

Any reasonable reviewer of the CIA, after surveying the deployment of agency funds and personnel and weighing these against the intelligence gains produced by the various directorates, would probably come to the same conclusion as did Richard Helms' temporary replacement as Director, James Schlesinger. On April 5, 1973, Schlesinger admitted to the Senate Armed Forces Committee that "We have a problem . . . we just have too many people. It turns out to be too many people in the operational areas. These are the people who in the past served overseas. . . . Increasing emphasis is being placed on science and technology, and on intelligence judgments."

Schlesinger's words—and the fact that he was not a "house man" from the Clandestine Services—were auguries of hope to those many critics of the CIA who believe that it is overly preoccupied with the covert side of intelligence. But Schlesinger lasted only four months at the agency before he was named Secretary of Defense, and the changes he effected were generally confined to a 6-percent staff cut and an early-retirement program for certain superannuated employees. Schlesinger has been succeeded by William Colby—a man who had a highly successful career as a clandestine operator specializing in "dirty tricks," and who can only be expected to maintain the Dulles-Helms policy of concentration on covert action.

At present the agency uses about two thirds of its funds and its manpower for covert operations and their support—proportions that have been held relatively constant for more than ten years. Thus, out of the agency's career workforce of roughly 16,500 people and yearly budget of about $750 million, 11,000 personnel and roughly $550 million are earmarked for the Clandestine Services and those activities of the Directorate of Management and

Services (formerly the Directorate of Support), such as communications, logistics, and training, which contribute to covert activities. Only about 20 percent of the CIA's career employees (spending less than 10 percent of the budget) work on intelligence analysis and information processing. There is little reason, at present, to expect that things will change.

The Intelligence Community

Taken as a whole, U.S. intelligence is no longer made up of a small glamorous fraternity of adventurous bluebloods—men motivated by a sense of *noblesse oblige* who carry out daring undercover missions. That is the romantic myth without which there would be few spy novels, but it is not the substance of the modern intelligence profession. Today the vast majority of those in the spy business are faceless, desk-bound bureaucrats, far removed from the world of the secret agent. To be sure, the CIA still strives to keep alive such techniques as classical espionage and covert action, but its efforts have been dwarfed by the huge technical collection programs of other government intelligence organizations—chiefly military agencies.

In all, there are ten different components of the federal government which concern themselves with the collection and/or analysis of foreign intelligence. These ten agencies, complete with their hundreds of subordinate commands, offices, and staffs, are commonly referred to as the "intelligence community." Operating silently in the shadows of the federal government, carefully obscured from public view and virtually immune to congressional oversight, the intelligence community every year spends over $6 billion and has a full-time workforce of more than 150,000 people. The bulk of this money and manpower is devoted to the collection of information through technical means and the processing and analysis of that information. The intelligence community amasses data on all the world's countries, but the primary targets are the communist nations, especially the Soviet Union and China, and the most sought-after information concerns their military capabilities and intentions.

Size and Cost of
U.S. Intelligence Community
(Approximate)

ORGANIZATION	PERSONNEL	ANNUAL BUDGET
Central Intelligence Agency	16,500	$750,000,000
National Security Agency*	24,000	$1,200,000,000
Defense Intelligence Agency*	5,000	$200,000,000
Army Intelligence*	35,000	$700,000,000
Naval Intelligence*	15,000	$600,000,000
Air Force Intelligence* (Including the National Reconnaissance Office	56,000	$2,700,000,000
State Department (Bureau of Intelligence and Research)	350	$8,000,000
Federal Bureau of Investigation (Internal Security Division)	800	$40,000,000
Atomic Energy Commission (Division of Intelligence)	300	$20,000,000
Treasury Department	300	$10,000,000
TOTAL	153,250	$6,228,000,000

* Department of Defense agency

As can be seen, the intelligence community's best-known member, the CIA, accounts for less than 15 percent of its total funds and personnel. Despite the agency's comparatively small size, however, the head of the CIA is not only the number-one man in his own agency but, as a result of the National Security Act of 1947, is also the Director of Central Intelligence (DCI)—the titular chief of the entire intelligence community. However, the community which the DCI supposedly oversees is made up of fiercely independent bureaucratic entities with little desire for outside supervision. All the members except the CIA are parts of much larger governmental departments, and they look to their parent

agencies for guidance, not to the DCI. While all participants share the same profession and general aim of protecting the national security, the intelligence community has developed into an interlocking, overlapping maze of organizations, each with its own goals. In the words of Admiral Rufus Taylor, former head of Naval Intelligence and former Deputy Director of the CIA, it most closely resembles a "tribal federation."

The Director of Central Intelligence heads up several inter-agency groups which were created to aid him in the management and operation of the intelligence community. The DCI's two principal tools for managing intelligence are the Intelligence Resources Advisory Committee (IRAC) and the United States Intelligence Board (USIB). The IRAC's members include representatives from the State Department, Defense, the Office of Management and Budget, and the CIA itself. (Since the agency's Director chairs the group in his role as DCI, or head of the intelligence community, the CIA is also given a seat.) IRAC was formed in November 1971, and it is supposed to prepare a consolidated budget for the whole community and generally assure that intelligence resources are used as efficiently as possible. However, it has not been in existence long enough for its performance to be judged, especially since three different DCIs have already headed it.

The USIB's main tasks are the issuance of National Intelligence Estimates and the setting of collection requirements and priorities. Under it are fifteen permanent inter-agency committees and a variety of *ad hoc* groups for special problems. Working through these committees and groups, the USIB, among other things, lists the targets for American intelligence and the priority attached to each one,* coordinates within the intelligence community the

---

* Although in a crisis situation, like the implementation of the Arab-Israeli cease-fire in 1970, Henry Kissinger or occasionally the President himself may set the standards. In the 1970 case (

DELETED

)

The U.S. Intelligence Community

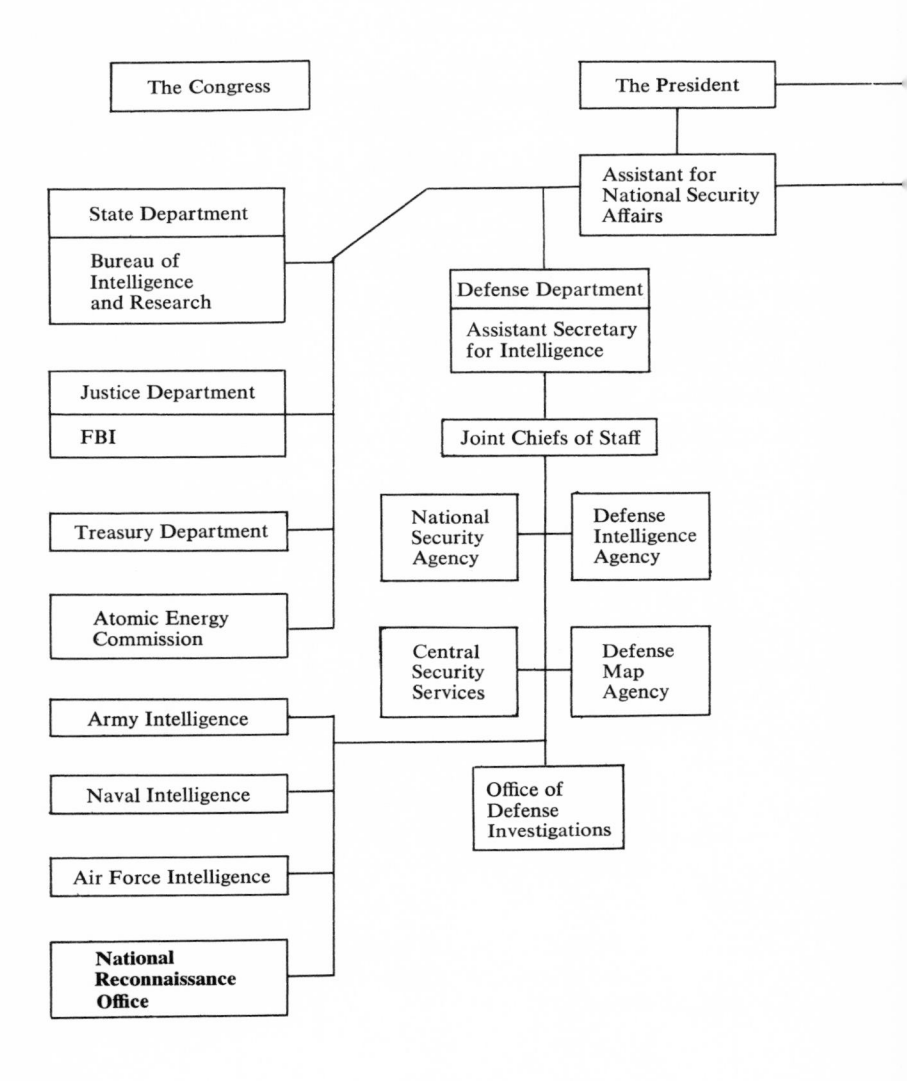

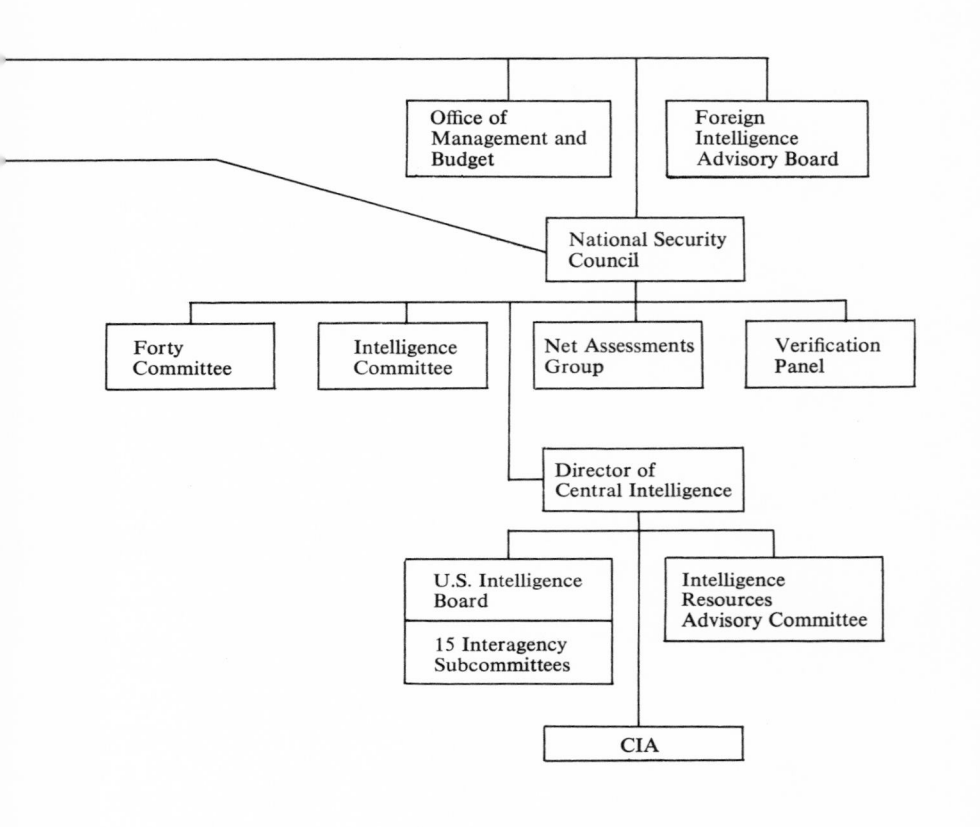

Office of Management and Budget

Foreign Intelligence Advisory Board

National Security Council

Forty Committee

Intelligence Committee

Net Assessments Group

Verification Panel

Director of Central Intelligence

U.S. Intelligence Board

15 Interagency Subcommittees

Intelligence Resources Advisory Committee

CIA

estimates of future events and enemy strengths, controls the classification and security systems for most of the U.S. government, directs research in the various fields of technical intelligence, and decides what classified information will be passed on to foreign friends and allies.*

The USIB meets every Thursday morning in a conference room on the seventh floor of CIA headquarters. At a typical meeting there are three or four subjects on the agenda, itself a classified document which the USIB secretariat circulates to each member a few days before the meeting. The first item of business is always the approval of the minutes of the last session; in the interest of security, the minutes are purposely made incomplete. Then the USIB turns to the Watch Report, which has been prepared earlier in the week by an inter-agency USIB committee responsible for keeping an eye out for any indication that armed conflict, particularly one which might threaten the United States or any of its allies, may break out anywhere in the world. A typical Watch Report might, in effect, say something like: War between the United States and the Soviet Union does not seem imminent this week, but the Soviets are going ahead with the development of their latest missile and have moved two new divisions into position along the Chinese border; North Vietnamese infiltration along the Ho Chi Minh trail (as monitored by sensors and radio intercepts) indicates that the level of violence will probably rise in the northern half of South Vietnam; and satellite photos of the Suez Canal (**DELETED**) point to a higher level of tension between Israel and Egypt.

Once the USIB gives its routine assent, the Watch Report is

---

* Intelligence reports are routinely provided to certain foreign countries, especially the English-speaking ones, on the basis of so-called intelligence agreements entered into by the DCI and his foreign equivalents. Although these agreements commit the United States government to a specified course of action enforceable under international law, they are never submitted as treaties to the U.S. Senate. In fact, they are negotiated and put into force in complete secrecy, and no member of the Senate Foreign Relations Committee has ever seen one, even for informational purposes.

forwarded to the nation's top policy-makers, who normally do not even glance at it, since they know that everything in it of any consequence has already been distributed to them in other intelligence reports. If some apocalyptic sign that war might break out were ever picked up by any agency of the community, the President and his top aides would be notified immediately, and the USIB would not be consulted; but as long as nothing of particular note is occurring, every Thursday morning the USIB spends an average of about thirty seconds discussing the Watch Report (which actually takes several man-weeks to prepare) before it is forwarded to the White House.

Next on the USIB agenda is the consideration and, almost always, the approval of the one or two National Intelligence Estimates which have been completed that week. These estimates of enemy capabilities and future events are drafted in advance by the CIA's National Intelligence Officers and then coordinated at the staff level with the various USIB-member agencies. By the time the estimates come before the USIB itself, all differences have normally been compromised in the inter-agency coordination meetings, or, failing in that accommodation, a dissenting member has already prepared a footnote stating his agency's disagreement with the conclusions or text of the NIE.

Once the USIB has approved the estimates before it (now certified as the best judgments of the intelligence community on the particular subject), the board turns to any special items which all the members have the prerogative of placing on the agenda. One Thursday in 1969 the chief of Naval Intelligence asked the USIB to reconsider a proposal, which had earlier been turned down at the USIB subcommittee level, to furnish the **Brazilian navy** with relatively advanced American cryptological equipment. Because of the sensitivity of U.S. codes and encrypting devices, exports—even to friendly countries—need the USIB's approval; the board turned down this particular request. At another meeting in 1970 the special discussion was on whether or not a very sophisticated satellite should be targeted against the (**DELETED**) part of the (**DELETED**) instead of (**DELETED**). The Air Force's

request to (**DELETED**) its satellite came to the USIB under its responsibility for setting intelligence-collection priorities; citing the great cost of the satellite and the possibility that the (**DE-LETED**) might lead to a malfunction, the USIB said no to the (**DELETED**). In another 1970 meeting the USIB considered a Pentagon proposal to lower the U.S. government's research goals for the detection of underground nuclear explosions. Again the USIB said no.*

On occasion, when extremely sensitive matters are to be discussed, the USIB goes into executive session—the practical effect of which is that all staff members leave the room and no minutes at all are kept. The USIB operated in this atmosphere of total privacy for a 1969 discussion of the Green Beret murder case and again in 1970 for a briefing of the Fitzhugh panel's recommendations on the reorganization of Pentagon intelligence (see p. 100).

Under DCI Helms, most USIB meetings were finished within forty-five minutes. Since almost all of the substantive work had been taken care of in preparatory sessions at the staff level, the USIB rarely did anything more than ratify already determined decisions, and thus the board, the highest-level substantive committee of the U.S. intelligence community, had very little work to do on its own.

The USIB and its fifteen committees deal exclusively with what is called national intelligence—intelligence needed, in theory, by the country's policy-makers. But there is a second kind of intel-

* The Pentagon claimed that there was not enough money available in its budget to attain the level of detection on the Richter scale set forth in the USIB guidelines, and that relaxing the standard reflected this financial reality. The State Department argued that a changed goal might open the intelligence community up to criticism on grounds that it had not done everything possible to achieve a comprehensive nuclear test ban—which would ultimately be dependent on both sides, being confident that cheating by the other party could be detected. DCI Helms sided with State. But the civilian victory was a hollow one, since there was no way the DCI could ensure that the Pentagon would indeed spend more money on seismic research in order to be able to meet the level of detection fixed by the USIB.

ligence—"departmental"—which is, again in theory, solely for the use of a particular agency or military service. The Army, Navy, and Air Force collect great amounts of departmental intelligence to support their tactical missions. For example, an American commander in Germany may desire data on the enemy forces that would oppose his troops if hostilities broke out, but the day-to-day movements of Soviet troops along the East German border are of little interest to high officials back in Washington (unless, of course, the Soviets are massing for an invasion, in which case the information would be upgraded to national intelligence). The dividing line between national and departmental intelligence, however, is often quite faint, and the military have frequently branded as departmental a number of wasteful collection programs that they know would not be approved on the national level.

Although the CIA has had since its creation exclusive responsibility for carrying out overseas espionage operations for the collection of national intelligence, the various military intelligence agencies and the intelligence units of American forces stationed abroad have retained the right to seek out tactical information for their own departmental requirements. During the Korean and Vietnamese wars, field commanders understandably needed data of enemy troop movements, and one way of obtaining it was through the hiring of foreign agents. But even in peacetime, with U.S. forces permanently stationed in countries like England, Germany, Italy, Morocco, Turkey, Panama, Japan, and Australia, the military intelligence services have consistently sought to acquire information through their own secret agents—the justification, of course, always being the need for departmental or tactical intelligence. To avoid duplication and proliferation of agents, all of these espionage missions are supposed to be coordinated with the CIA. But the military often fail to do this because they know the CIA would not give its approval, or because an arrangement has been previously worked out to the effect that as long as the military stay out of CIA's areas of interest, they can operate on their own. Every military unit has an intelligence section, and few commanders wish to see their personnel remain idle. Therefore, if for

no other reasons than to keep their soldiers occupied, American military intelligence units overseas are usually involved in the espionage game.

For example, a military intelligence unit assigned to Bangkok, Thailand, as late as 1971 was trying to entrap Soviet KGB officers, recruit local spies, and even was attempting to run its own agents into China through Hong Kong. Little or none of this activity was being cleared with the CIA. Similarly, in (

DELETED

) at virtually every level.

The tribalism that plagues the intelligence community is at its worst in the military intelligence agencies, and most of the personnel working for these organizations feel their first loyalty is to their parent service. The men who run military intelligence are almost all career officers who look to the Army, Navy, and Air Force for promotion and other advancement. They serve only a tour or two in intelligence before they return to conventional military life. Very few are willing to do anything in their intelligence assignments which will damage their careers, and they know all too well that analysis on their part which contradicts the views or the policies of the leadership of their parent service will not be well received. Thus, their intelligence judgments tend to be clouded by the prejudices and budgetary needs of the military service whose uniform they wear.

The Army, the Navy, and the Air Force traditionally maintained their own independent intelligence agencies—ostensibly to support their tactical responsibilities and to maintain an enemy "order of battle." Each service collected its own information and quite often was less than forthcoming to the others. The result was a large amount of duplication and an extremely parochial approach in each service's analysis of enemy capabilities.

This self-serving approach of the military services toward intelligence led to the formation in 1961 of the Defense Intelligence Agency, which was supposed to coordinate and consolidate the views and, to some extent, the functions of the three service agencies. It was planned that the DIA would replace the Army, Navy,

and Air Force at the USIB meetings, but Allen Dulles and successive DCIs have balked at leaving total responsibility for representing the Pentagon to the DIA, which has subsequently developed its own brand of parochialism as the intelligence arm of the Joint Chiefs of Staff. Thus, while only the DIA is an official USIB member, the heads of the three service agencies remain at the table for the weekly sessions, push their pet theories, and demand that footnotes be included in intelligence estimates that run contrary to their views of their service.

Aside from operating the overt system of military attachés working out of American embassies overseas, the DIA does little information collection on its own. It is largely dependent on the service intelligence agencies for its raw data, and its **5,000** employees process and analyze this material and turn it into finished intelligence reports which are circulated within the Pentagon and to the rest of the intelligence community. The DIA also prepares daily and weekly intelligence digests that are similar in form and content to the CIA publications, and makes up its own estimates of enemy capabilities. This latter function did not take on much significance in the DIA until November 1970, when the agency was reorganized and Major General Daniel Graham was given a mandate by DIA chief Lieutenant General Donald Bennett to improve the agency's estimating capability. Graham had served two earlier tours of duty in CIA's Office of National Estimates, and he quickly established the DIA office as a serious rival to the agency's estimative function.*

Although the DIA was originally intended to take over many of their functions, the service intelligence agencies have continued to grow and flourish since its founding. Indeed, each of the three is larger than the DIA, and Air Force intelligence is the biggest spy organization in the whole intelligence community, with

---

* As a colonel in the late 1960s, Graham nearly resigned from the Army to accept an offer of permanent employment with the CIA. In early 1973 DCI James Schlesinger brought him back to the agency, still in uniform, to work on military estimates. Graham was widely known in the corridors of the CIA as the funny little military officer who hung a drawing of a bayonet over his desk with a caption describing it as "The weapon of the future."

56,000 employees and an annual budget of about **$2.7 billion.** Most of this latter figure goes to pay for the extremely costly reconnaissance satellites and the rockets necessary to put them in orbit. A separate part of Air Force intelligence, the **National Reconnaissance Office, operates these satellite programs for the entire community, and the NRO's budget alone is more than $1.5 billion** a year. **The NRO** works in such intense secrecy that its very existence is classified. Its director for many years was a mysterious Air Force colonel (and later brigadier general) named Ralph Steakley, who retired in the early 1970s to take employment with Westinghouse, a defense contractor which sells considerable equipment to **the NRO.**

The Office of Naval Intelligence, with about 15,000 employees and a $600 million annual budget, is perhaps the fastest-growing member of the intelligence community. At the same time submarine-missile (Polaris and Poseidon) programs have in recent years received larger and larger budgets (**DELETED**) have similarly captured the imagination of the military planners. Naval Intelligence operates (**DELETED**) crammed with the most modern sensors, radars, cameras, and other listening devices which (

DELETED

)

The Navy formerly sent surface ships, like the *Liberty* and the *Pueblo,* on similar missions, but since the attack on the former and the capture of the latter, these missions have largely been discontinued.

Army Intelligence is the least mechanized of the three service agencies. Its mission is largely to acquire tactical intelligence in support of its field forces. Yet, due to the great size of the Army and the proliferation of G2-type units, the Army still manages to spend about **$700 million** annually and employ **35,000** people in intelligence.

The remaining large component of military intelligence is the National Security Agency. The NSA, the most secretive member of the intelligence community, breaks foreign codes and ciphers

and develops secure communications for the U.S. government—
at a cost to the taxpayer of about $1.2 billion every year. Founded
in 1952 by a classified presidential order, the NSA employs about
24,000 people. Its headquarters is at Fort Meade, Maryland, and
its hundreds of listening posts around the world eavesdrop on the
communications of most of the world's countries—enemy and
friend alike. Most of the NSA's intercept stations are operated by
special cryptological units from the armed forces, which are subordinate to the head of the NSA.

Under the Fitzhugh recommendations, which were put into effect
in 1972, the Assistant Secretary of Defense for Intelligence has
overall responsibility for military intelligence. Independent of the
Joint Chiefs of Staff and the military services, he is supposed to
coordinate and generally supervise the activities of the DIA, the
service intelligence agencies, the NSA, the Defense Mapping
Agency, and the Defense Investigative Service. These latter two
organizations were formed in early 1972 (also as a result of the
Fitzhugh recommendations) out of the three separate mapping
and investigative agencies which had previously existed in the
Army, Navy, and Air Force. The mappers, aided by satellite photography, chart nearly every inch of the earth's surface. The investigators perform counterintelligence work and look into the
backgrounds of Defense Department personnel. In the late 1960s,
however, the three units which would later become the Defense
Investigative Service devoted much of their time and effort to reporting on domestic dissident and anti-war groups. The Secretary
of Defense ordered that this military surveillance of civilians be
stopped in early 1971, but there are indications that it is still
going on.

The State Department's Bureau of Intelligence and Research
has the smallest budget in the intelligence community—only $8
million—and it is the only member with no collection capability
of its own. It is completely dependent on State Department diplomatic cables and the sources of other community members for the
data which its 350 employees turn into finished intelligence reports.
INR represents State on all the USIB and other inter-agency panels

dealing with intelligence. It coordinates within State the departmental position for 40 Committee meetings, and does the Under Secretary's staff work for these meetings. The Director of INR until the end of 1973, Ray S. Cline, spent twenty-two years with the CIA before he joined the State Department in 1969. He had risen to be the agency's Deputy Director for Intelligence before losing out in an internal CIA struggle in 1966, when he was sent off to head agency operations in West Germany. Although the German station was (and is) the CIA's largest in the world, Cline was far from the center of power in Washington. However, his absence apparently did not diminish either his bureaucratic skills or his capabilities as an intelligence analyst, and he bolstered INR's position within the community, although the bureau, without any resources of its own, still remains a comparatively minor participant.*

The FBI, the Atomic Energy Commission, and the Treasury Department—the lesser members of the USIB—are all active participants in the intelligence community although the primary functions of these organizations are unrelated to the collection of foreign intelligence. Nevertheless, the FBI's internal-security duties include protecting the country against foreign espionage attempts, a responsibility considered to be associated with that of the intelligence community. The Atomic Energy Commission has an intelligence division which concerns itself with information about nuclear developments in foreign countries and maintains technical listening posts around the world (sometimes manned by CIA personnel) to monitor foreign atomic blasts. The Treasury Department's connection with the intelligence community is based primarily in its campaign to halt drugs entering the United States.

Contrary to the National Security Act of 1947, the CIA today does not in fact perform the function of "coordinating the intelligence activities of the several governmental departments and agencies."

---

* INR's position within the intelligence community has been upgraded recently because of Henry Kissinger's assumption of the role of Secretary of State and by his appointment of long-time NSC aide and former CIA officer William Hyland to the post of director.

For a time during the early 1950s the DCI did manage some degree of control over the other agencies, but in the years that followed came the technological explosion in intelligence and with it the tremendous expansion of the community. The spying trade was transformed—everywhere but at the CIA—from a fairly small, agent-oriented profession to a machine-dominated information-gathering enterprise of almost boundless proportions. Technical collection, once a relatively minor activity in which gentlemen *did* read other gentlemen's mail, blossomed into a wide range of activities including COMINT (communications intelligence), SIGINT (signal intelligence), PHOTINT (photographic intelligence), ELINT (electronic intelligence), and RADINT (radar intelligence). Data was obtained by highly sophisticated equipment on planes, ships, submarines, orbiting and stationary space satellites, radio and electronic intercept stations, and radars—some the size of three football fields strung together. The sensors, or devices, used for collection consisted of high-resolution and wide-angle cameras, infrared cameras, receivers for intercepting microwave transmissions and telemetry signals, side-looking and over-the-horizon radars, and other even more exotic contrivances.

The proliferation of technical collection has also had a significant influence on the personnel makeup of the intelligence community. The mountains of information received gave rise to a variety of highly specialized data processors: cryptanalysts, traffic analysts, photographic interpreters, and telemetry, radar, and signal analysts, who convert the incomprehensible bleeps and squawks intercepted by their machines into forms usable by the substantive intelligence analysts. And it has created a new class of technocrats and managers who conceive, develop, and supervise the operation of systems so secret that only a few thousand (sometimes only a couple of hundred) people have high enough security clearances to see the finished intelligence product.

The information collected by the technical systems constitutes the most valuable data available to U.S. intelligence. Without it, there would be no continuing reliable way for government to determine with confidence the status of foreign—especially Soviet and Chinese—strategic military capabilities. Without it, also,

there would have been no agreement with the Soviet Union in 1972 for the limitations of strategic armaments, since that pact was absolutely dependent on each side being confident that it could monitor new military developments—even possible cheating—on the other side through its own satellites and other surveillance equipment.

The first advanced overhead-reconnaissance systems—the U-2 spy planes and the early satellites in the late 1950s and early 1960s—provided valuable information about the Soviet Union, but their successes only whetted the appetites of U.S. military planners, who had so long been starved for good intelligence on America's main adversary. Once they got a taste of the fruits of technical collection, they demanded more specific and more frequent reporting on the status of the Soviet armed forces. And the technicians, with nearly unlimited funds at their disposal, obliged them, partly because the technicians themselves had a natural desire to expand the state of their art.

A complementary circle of military intelligence requirements and technical collection methods evolved. Collection responded to requirements and, in turn, generated still further demands for information, which resulted in the development of yet bigger and better collection systems. If some particular type of data could somehow be collected, invariably one or another part of the Pentagon would certify that it was needed, and a new technical system for gathering it would be developed. The prevailing ethic became collection for collection's sake.

In the infant years of the technological explosion, Allen Dulles paid scant attention to technical collection's potential as an intelligence tool. He was far more interested in clandestine operations and the overthrowing of foreign governments. After the Bay of Pigs debacle in 1961 cut short Dulles' career as DCI, his successor, John McCone, soon grasped the importance of the new information-gathering systems. He tried to reassert the CIA's leadership position in this area, and as part of his effort he created the Directorate for Science and Technology and recruited a brilliant young scientist, Albert "Bud" Wheelon, to head the component. But try as he might, the tenacious, hard-driving McCone could not cope

with the Pentagon juggernaut, then under the direction of Robert McNamara, who energetically supported the military services in their efforts to gain maximum control of all technical collection. McCone was forced to conclude that the battle with the Defense Department was lost and the trend toward Pentagon domination was irreversible. This was one of the reasons that McCone resigned in 1965 (another being, in McCone's view, President Johnson's lack of appreciation for strategic intelligence such as the National Intelligence Estimates).

McCone was followed by Admiral William Raborn, whose ineffective tour as DCI was mercifully ended after only fourteen months, to the relief of all members of the intelligence community.

Richard Helms took over the CIA in the spring of 1966. Like Dulles, he was much more interested in the cloak-and-dagger field, where he had spent his entire career, than in the machines that had revolutionized the intelligence trade. Although he was Director of Central Intelligence, not just the head of CIA, Helms rarely challenged the Pentagon on matters regarding technical collection—or, for that matter, intelligence analysis—until, belatedly, his last years as DCI. As a result, during his directorship the CIA was completely overshadowed by the other agencies in all intelligence activities other than covert operations, and even here the military made deep inroads.

Richard Helms clearly understood the bureaucratic facts of life. He knew all too well that he did not have Cabinet status and thus was not the equal of the Secretary of Defense, the man ultimately responsible for the military intelligence budget. Helms simply did not have the power to tell the Pentagon that the overall needs of U.S. intelligence (which were, of course, his responsibility as DCI) demanded that the military cut back on a particular spying program and spend the money elsewhere. Since managing the intelligence community did not interest him very much anyway, only on a few occasions did he make the effort to exercise some measure of influence over the other agencies outside the CIA.

In 1967 Helms was urged by his staff to authorize an official review of intelligence collection by community members, with special emphasis on the many technical collection systems. How-

ever, Helms was reluctant to venture very far into this highly complex, military-controlled field, and decided only to authorize a study of the CIA's "in-house" needs. He named an experienced senior agency officer, Hugh Cunningham, to head the small group picked to make the study. Cunningham, a former Rhodes scholar, had previously served in top positions with the Clandestine Services and on the Board of National Estimates. With his broad experience, he seemed to agency insiders to be an ideal choice to carry out the review. After several months of intense investigation, he and his small group concluded—this was the first sentence of their report —"The United States intelligence community collects too much information." They found that there was a large amount of duplication in the collection effort, with two or more agencies often spending great amounts of money to amass essentially the same data, and that much of the information collected was useless for anything other than low-level intelligence analysis. The study noted that the glut of raw data was clogging the intelligence system and making it difficult for the analysts to separate out what was really important and to produce thoughtful material for the policy-makers. The study also observed that the overabundance of collection resulted in an excess of finished intelligence reports, many of which were of little use in the formulation of national policy; there simply were too many reports on too many subjects for the high-level policy-makers to cope with.

The Cunningham study caused such consternation in the CIA that Helms refused to disseminate it to the other intelligence agencies. Several of his deputies complained bitterly about the study's critical view of their own directorates and the way it seemed to diminish the importance of their work. Since the study was even harsher in dealing with the military's intelligence programs, Helms was further unwilling to risk the Pentagon's wrath by circulating it within the intelligence community. He decided to keep the controversial report within the CIA.

Always the master bureaucrat, Helms resorted to the time-honored technique of forming another special study group to review the work of the first group. He organized a new committee, the Senior Executive Group, to consider in general terms the

CIA's managerial problems. The SEG's first job was to look over the Cunningham study, but its members were hardly fitted to the task. They were the chiefs of the agency's four directorates, each of which had been heavily criticized in the original study; the Executive Director (the CIA's number-three man), a plodding, unimaginative former support officer; and—as chairman—the Deputy DCI, Admiral Rufus Taylor, a career naval officer. After several prolonged meetings, the SEG decided, not surprisingly, that the study on collection was of only marginal value and therefore not to be acted on in any significant way. A short time later Cunningham was transferred to the Office of Training, one of the CIA's administrative Siberias. The SEG never met again.

Although Richard Helms showed little talent for management —and even less interest in it—during his years as DCI he did make some efforts to restrict the expansion of the intelligence community. One such try was successful. It occurred in the late 1960s when Helms refused to give his approval for further development work on the Air Force's extremely expensive manned orbiting laboratory (MOL), which was then being promoted as being, among other things, an intelligence-collection system. Without Helms' endorsement, the Air Force was unable to convince the White House of the need for the project, and it was subsequently dropped by the Johnson administration. (Some Air Force officials viewed Helms' lack of support as retaliation for the Air Force's "capture" in 1967 of the **SR-71** reconnaissance plane, which the CIA had originally developed and would have preferred to keep under its control, but this criticism was probably unfair. Helms simply seemed to be going along with the strong pressure in the Johnson administration to cut costs because of the Vietnam war, and saw the MOL as a particularly vulnerable—and technically dubious—program in a period of tight budgets.)

Helms was always a realist about power within the government, and he recognized that, except in a rare case like that of the MOL, he simply did not have the clout to prevent the introduction of most new technical collection systems. He also understood that the full force of the Pentagon was behind these projects—as redundant or superfluous as they often were—and that if he concentrated his

efforts on trying to eliminate or even reduce unproductive and outdated systems, he was making enemies who could undercut his own pet clandestine projects overseas. But even the few efforts he did bring against these obviously wasteful systems failed (save that against the MOL), demonstrating vividly that the true power over budgets in the intelligence community lies with the Pentagon, not the Director of Central Intelligence.

In 1967, for example, Helms asked Frederick Eaton, a prominent and conservative New York lawyer, to conduct a review of the National Security Agency. For some time the NSA's cost-effectiveness as a contributor to the national intelligence effort had been highly suspect within the community, especially in view of the code-breaking agency's constantly growing budget, which had then risen over the billion-dollar mark. Eaton was provided with a staff composed of officials from several intelligence offices, including the CIA, the State Department, and the Pentagon, and this staff accumulated substantial evidence that much of the NSA's intelligence collection was of little or marginal use to the various intelligence consumers in the community. But Eaton, after extensive consultation with Pentagon officials, surprised his own staff by recommending no reductions and concluding that all of the NSA's programs were worthwhile. The staff of intelligence professionals rebelled, and Eaton had to write the conclusions of the review himself.

The lesson of the Eaton study was clear within the intelligence community. The NSA was widely recognized as the community member most in need of reform, and the professionals who had studied the matter recommended substantial change in its programs. Yet Helms' effort to improve the supersecret agency's performance through the Eaton study accomplished nothing, and if the Director of Central Intelligence could not, as the professionals said, "get a handle on" the NSA, then it was highly unlikely that he could ever influence the expanding programs of the other Pentagon intelligence agencies.

In 1968 Helms created another select inter-agency group at the insistence of his staff: the National Intelligence Resources Board (the forerunner of the Intelligence Resources Advisory Commit-

tee). Intended to bring about economies in the community by cutting certain marginal programs, the NIRB had more bureaucratic power than any of its predecessors because it was chaired by the Deputy Director of the CIA and had as members the directors of the Defense Intelligence Agency and the State Department's Bureau of Intelligence and Research. It immediately decided to take a new look at the NSA's programs, and it singled out a particular communications-intercept program, costing millions of dollars a year, as particularly wasteful. The NIRB had found that nearly all intelligence analysts within the community who had access to the results of the NSA program believed the data to be of little or no use. These findings were related to Paul Nitze, then Deputy Secretary of Defense, with the recommendation that the program be phased out. (The final decision on continuing the NSA program, of course, had to be made in the Pentagon, since the NSA is a military intelligence agency.) Nitze did nothing with the recommendation for several months. Then, as he was leaving office in January 1969, he sent a letter to Helms thanking the DCI for his advice but informing him that approval had been given by Pentagon decision-makers to continue the dubious project. And despite the NIRB's overwhelming arguments against the project, Nitze did not even bother to list any reasons why the Pentagon chose not to concur with the decision of the Director of Central Intelligence.

In the wake of such defeats, Helms gave up on making attempts at managing the intelligence community. At one point, months later, he observed to his staff that while he, as DCI, was theoretically responsible for 100 percent of the nation's intelligence activities, he in fact controlled less than 15 percent of the community's assets—and most of the other 85 percent belonged to the Secretary of Defense and the Joint Chiefs of Staff. Under such circumstances, Helms concluded, it was unrealistic for any DCI to think that he could have a significant influence on U.S. intelligence-resource decisions or the shaping of the intelligence community.

But when the Nixon administration took over in 1969, some very powerful people, including Defense Secretary Melvin Laird and the President himself, became concerned about the seemingly

uncontrolled expansion of the Pentagon's intelligence programs. Laird said in his 1970 Defense budget statement:

> Intelligence is both critical and costly. Yet we have found intelligence activities, with management overlapping or nonexistent. Deficiencies have provoked criticism that became known even outside the intelligence community. These criticisms can be summarized in five principal points:
>
> 1. Our intelligence product was being evaluated poorly.*
> 2. Various intelligence-gathering activities overlapped and there was no mechanism to eliminate the overlap.
> 3. There was no coordinated long-range program for resource management and programming.
> 4. Significant gaps in intelligence-gathering went unnoticed.
> 5. The intelligence community failed to maintain frank and unrestricted channels of internal communication.

That same year President Nixon appointed a "blue-ribbon" panel chaired by Gilbert W. Fitzhugh, chairman of the board of the Metropolitan Life Insurance Company, to conduct a review of the Defense Department's entire operations and organization. Fitzhugh declared at a July 1970 press conference that his investigation showed that the Pentagon was "an impossible organization to administer in its present form, just an amorphous lump." Then turning to military spying, he stated, "I believe that the Pentagon suffers from too much intelligence. They can't use what they get because there is too much collected. It would almost be better that they didn't have it because it's difficult to find out what's important." The Fitzhugh panel recommended a series of economies in Pentagon espionage and also urged that a new post of Assistant

---

* Some intelligence was not being evaluated at all, and, as a result, a new concept, "the linear drawer foot," entered the English language. Translated from Pentagonese, this refers to the amount of paper needed to fill a file drawer one foot in length. A 1969 House Armed Services Committee report noted that the Southeast Asia office of the DIA alone had 517 linear drawer feet of unanalyzed raw intelligence locked in its vaults.

Secretary of Defense for Intelligence be created. Under this proposal, the various military intelligence agencies, which previously had been scattered all over the Defense Department's organizational chart, were to be put under the authority of the new Assistant Secretary, who in turn would report to Secretary Laird.

By 1971, before the Fitzhugh recommendations were put into effect, the House Committee on Appropriations had become aware that military intelligence was in need of a shake-up. The committee released a little-noticed but blistering report which stated that "the intelligence operations of the Deparment of Defense have grown beyond the actual needs of the Department and are now receiving an inordinate share of the fiscal resources of the Department." The congressional report continued, "Redundancy is the watch word of many intelligence operations. . . . Coordination is less effective than it should be. Far more material is collected than is essential. Material is collected which cannot be evaluated . . . and is therefore wasted. New intelligence means have become available . . . without offsetting reductions in old procedures." With these faults so obvious even to the highly conservative and military-oriented congressional committee, strong reform measures would have seemed to be in order. But little was done by the Congress to bring the intelligence community under control. The fear on Capitol Hill of violating the sacred mystique of "national security" prevented any effective corrective action.

Finally, in November 1971, after a secret review of the intelligence community carried out by the Office of Management and Budget's James Schlesinger, who would a year later be named Director of the CIA, the Nixon administration announced "a number of management steps to improve the efficiency and effectiveness" of U.S. intelligence. The President reportedly had been grumbling for some time about the poor information furnished him by the intelligence community. Most recently he had been disturbed by the community's blunder in assuring that American prisoners were being held at the Son Tay camp in North Vietnam, which during a dramatic rescue mission by U.S. commandos in 1970 was found to be empty. Nixon was also angered by the failure of intelligence to warn about the ferocity of the North

Vietnamese response to the South Vietnamese invasion of Laos in early 1971. (In both these instances the faulty intelligence seems to have come from the Pentagon,* although there are good reasons to believe that in the Son Tay case the President's political desire to make a show of support for the prisoners outweighed the strong possibility that no prisoners would be found there.) The President, as the nation's primary consumer of intelligence, felt that he had a right to expect better information.

Whether a President takes great personal interest in intelligence, as Lyndon Johnson did, or, as in Nixon's case, delegates most of the responsibility to an aide (Henry Kissinger), the intelligence field remains very much a private presidential preserve. Congress has almost completely abdicated any control it might exercise. Thus, when President Nixon chose to revamp the intelligence structure in 1971, he did not even bother to consult in advance those few Congressmen who supposedly oversee the intelligence community.

The ostensible objective of the 1971 reorganization was to improve management of the intelligence community by giving the DCI "an enhanced leadership role . . . in planning, reviewing, coordinating, and evaluating all intelligence programs and activities, and in the production of national intelligence." Under the Nixon plan, the DCI's powers over the rest of the community for the first time included the right to review the budgets of the other members—an unprecedented step in the tribal federation of intelligence and one absolutely necessary to the exercise of any meaningful degree of control.

But with this very same plan to enhance the DCI's "leadership role," the President was also placing control over all U.S. intelligence squarely in the National Security Council staff, still headed today by Henry Kissinger, even after he also has become Secretary of State. Kissinger was put in charge of a new NSC Intelligence Committee which included as members the DCI, the Attorney General,

---

* Reporter Tad Szulc, formerly of the *New York Times*, recalls that after the Son Tay raid a CIA official approached him to emphasize that the agency had played no part in the operation and that the faulty information had originated with military intelligence.

the Under Secretary of State, the Deputy Secretary of Defense, and the Chairman of the Joint Chiefs of Staff. This Intelligence Committee was to "give direction and guidance on national intelligence needs and provide for a continuing evaluation of intelligence products from the viewpoint of the intelligence user." At the same time the President established another new body, called the Net Assessment Group, under Kissinger's control, to analyze U.S. military capabilities in comparison with those of the Soviets and Chinese as estimated by intelligence studies. Already chairman of the 40 Committee, which passes on all high-risk CIA covert operations, and the Verification Panel, which is responsible for monitoring the intelligence related to the S.A.L.T. negotiations and agreements, Kissinger, with his control now asserted over virtually all the NSC's key committees, had clearly emerged as the most powerful man in U.S. intelligence—as well as in American foreign policy.

Yet with Kissinger almost totally occupied with other matters, the President clearly intended under his November 1971 reorganization that CIA Director Helms take over and improve the actual management of the intelligence community—under Kissinger's general supervision, to be sure. Partly because of the nearly impervious tribalism of the community and partly because of Helms' pronounced lack of interest in management and technical matters, the shake-up had little effect on the well-entrenched ways of the community. Much to the amazement of his staff, Helms did virtually nothing to carry out the wishes of the President as contained in the restructuring order.

Shortly after the 1972 election, Helms was fired by the President as Director of Central Intelligence. According to his own testimony before the Senate Foreign Relations Committee, he wanted to stay on the job, but that was not the wish of the White House. The President's dissatisfaction with Helms' management of the intelligence community was certainly a factor in his ouster, as perhaps were Helms' social connections with liberal Congressmen and journalists (some of whom were on the White House "enemies" list).

From his earlier work at the Office of Management and Budget

and the Rand Corporation, James Schlesinger appeared knowl-edgeable about the problems facing the community and moved quickly, once he arrived at the CIA to replace Helms, to set up the bureaucratic structures necessary to exercise control over the other intelligence agencies. He created a new Deputy Director for Community Relations and strengthened the Intelligence Resources Advisory Committee, but his four-month tenure was too short to bring about any large-scale reform. And nothing in the record of his successor, William Colby—a clandestine operator for thirty years—indicates that he has either the management skills or the inclination to bring the spiraling growth of the intelligence com-munity under control.

Clearly, the CIA is not the hub, nor is its Director the head, of the vast U.S. intelligence community. The sometimes glamorous, incorrigibly clandestine agency is merely a part of a much larger interdepartmental federation dominated by the Pentagon. And although the Director of Central Intelligence is nominally desig-nated by each President in turn as the government's chief intelli-gence advisor, he is in fact overshadowed in the realities of Wash-ington's politics by both the Secretary of Defense and the Presi-dent's own Assistant for National Security Affairs, as well as by several lesser figures, such as the Chairman of the Joint Chiefs of Staff. Nevertheless, agency directors and the CIA itself have man-aged to survive, and at times even flourish, in the secret bureau-cratic jungle because of their one highly specialized contribution to the national intelligence effort. The CIA's primary task is not to coordinate the efforts of U.S. intelligence or even to produce finished national intelligence for the policy-makers. Its job is, for better or worse, to conduct the government's covert foreign policy.

PART II

FOUR

Special Operations

You have to make up your mind
that you are going to have an
intelligence agency and protect
it as such, and shut your eyes
some and take what
is coming.

—SENATOR JOHN STENNIS
Chairman, Joint Senate Committee
for CIA Oversight
November 23, 1971

COVERT action—intervention in the internal affairs of other nations—is the most controversial of the CIA's clandestine functions. It is the invariable means to the most variable ends. It is basic to the clandestine mentality. And the crudest, most direct form of covert action is called "special operations."

These activities, mostly of a paramilitary or warlike nature, have little of the sophistication and subtlety of political action (penetration and manipulation) or propaganda and disinformation. Although planned by the CIA's professionals, these operations are to a large extent carried out by agency contract employees and mercenaries—both American and foreign. Within the CIA's Clandestine Services, "special ops" have always been viewed with mixed emotions. Most of the professionals, especially in recent years, have looked down on such activities, even while at times recommending their use. It is widely recognized within the agency, however, that less direct forms of covert action have their limitations, especially when timely, conclusive action is thought necessary to put down a troublesome rebel movement or to overthrow an unfriendly government. In these cases, the CIA usually calls on its own "armed forces," the Special Operations Division (SOD), to do the job.

By definition, special ops are violent and brutal; most clandestine operators prefer more refined techniques. The CIA professional is a flimflam artist, involved in the creative challenge of plotting and orchestrating a clandestine campaign without resorting to violence. In such non-paramilitary covert action, the operator tends to keep his hands unbloodied, and his crimes are of the white-collar variety—conspiracy, bribery, corruption. His failure or exposure is normally punished only with expulsion from the country where he is operating. He is, in the end, merely engaging

in a "gentleman's" game. The paramilitary operator, on the contrary, is a gangster who deals in force, in terror, in violence. Failure can mean death—if not to the operator himself, then to the agents he has recruited. The SOD man wages war, albeit on a small and secret level, but none of the rules of warfare apply. His is a breed apart; in the CIA, special ops types are sometimes referred to as the "animals" of the agency.

In the CIA's early years, and especially during the Korean war, many paramilitary (PM) specialists, mostly former military men, were hired as career officers. But the CIA soon learned that their military skills were not easily transferable to other types of clandestine work and that most of the PM experts were next to useless in the bureaucratic and diplomatic settings in which the agency usually functions. At times, when special operations were at a low ebb, the agency had difficulty in finding jobs that the PM specialists could handle. Hence, during the late 1950s PM manpower was gradually reduced to a cadre of a couple of hundred operators capable of doing the planning and the training for paramilitary operations. When more men were needed, the agency would hire them on short-term contracts. These contract forces tended to be a mélange of ex-military men, adventurers, and outright mercenaries; others came to the CIA on direct loan from the armed services. The U.S. Army's Special Forces and the counterguerrilla units of the Navy (SEALs) and Air Force (SOFs) provided many of the recruits, since veterans of these branches already possessed the most up-to-date paramilitary skills. Sometimes these military men "resigned" from the service in order to accommodate the CIA's cover requirements for their activities, but they did so with the understanding that eventually they would return to military service—their time with the CIA counting toward promotion and retirement. (This process is known in the intelligence trade as "sheep-dipping.") But the agency was always careful to keep direct control over the planning, logistics, and communications of its special or paramilitary operations. The contractees merely did the dirty work.

The CIA set up training facilities in the United States and overseas to prepare both its own career operators and the temporary

personnel on contract for paramilitary work. **Camp Peary—"The Farm"—in southeastern Virginia provided the basic courses. More advanced techniques, such as demolitions and heavy weapons, were taught at a secret CIA base in North Carolina. Instruction in parachuting and air operations was provided at both these facilities and at the headquarters of Intermountain Aviation near Tucson, Arizona.** A secret installation in the Canal Zone was the site for jungle-warfare and survival training. Here the agency's trainees would play paramilitary war games, pitted against the élite of the U.S. Army's Special Forces.

Large-scale paramilitary operations also necessitated special training bases for the mercenaries. For the 1954 Guatemalan invasion, the CIA built installations in Nicaragua and Honduras. For the 1961 attack at the Bay of Pigs, sites were established again in Nicaragua and this time also in Guatemala, which had become available to the CIA as a result of its success there seven years earlier (**DELETED**   ) constructed large support facilities in Northeast India and gave (**DELETED**) the guerrillas at a deserted army base in the mountains. And for its many Southeast Asia adventures, the Special Operations Division had "a home away from home" **under Navy cover on the Pacific island of Saipan.**

Saipan, however, was not a U.S. possession, but rather a Trust Territory of the United Nations under U.S. care, and consequently there was some concern within the agency that the establishment and operation of a secret military base there would raise sticky problems in the U.N. But being masters of the art of cover and deception, the CIA contingent on Saipan merely "sanitized" the base whenever U.N. representatives visited the island on inspection tours. According to a native of the island, trainees and instructors alike disappeared; the barbed wire and "no admittance to unauthorized personnel" signs were taken down. In a day or so, the camp was made to appear just like any other jumble of military quonset huts, which the inspectors ignored. As soon as they were gone, however, all was returned to normal, and the CIA's special ops training was begun anew.

One former officer of the CIA's Clandestine Services, who was

trained in special ops, wrote this account of his experiences for *Ramparts* magazine:

The stated purpose of paramilitary school was to train and equip us to become instructors for village peasants who wanted to defend themselves against guerrillas. I could believe in that.

Some of the training was conventional: But then we moved up to the CIA's demolition training headquarters. It was here that Cubans had been, and still were [in the mid-1960s] being trained in conventional and underwater demolitions. And it was here that we received training in tactics which hardly conformed to the Geneva Convention.

The array of outlawed weaponry with which we were familiarized included bullets that explode on impact, silencer-equipped machineguns, homemade explosives and self-made napalm for stickier and hotter Molotov cocktails. We were taught demolition techniques, practicing on late model cars, railroad trucks, and gas storage tanks. And we were shown a quick method of saturating a confined area with flour or fertilizer, causing an explosion like in a dustbin or granary.

And there was a diabolical invention that might be called a mini-cannon. It was constructed of a concave piece of steel fitted into the top of a #10 can filled with a plastic explosive. When the device was detonated, the tremendous heat of friction of the steel turning inside out made the steel piece a white-hot projectile. There were a number of uses for the mini-cannon, one of which was demonstrated to us using an old army school bus. It was fastened to the gasoline tank in such a fashion that the incendiary projectile would rupture the tank and fling flaming gasoline the length of the bus interior, incinerating anyone inside. It was my lot to show the rest of the class how easily it could be done. It worked, my God, how it worked. I stood there watching the flames consume the bus. It was, I guess, the moment of truth. What did a busload of burning people have to do with freedom? What right did I have, in the name of democracy and the CIA, to

decide that random victims should die? The intellectual game was over. I had to leave.

The heavy reliance on paramilitary methods in the CIA's special operations is a direct outgrowth of the clandestine guerrilla programs undertaken by the Office of Strategic Services during World War II. The OSS, like its British counterpart, Special Operations Executive, made extensive use of indigenous underground resistance movements to sabotage the activities of German and Japanese armed forces in the occupied countries and to foment national unrest in these areas. In running such operations, the OSS officers performed as advisors and acted as channels for communications and support from the Allied powers. Basic to the success of the OSS operations was the fact that the countries in which it conducted its covert activities were under the military control of foreign armies despised by native resistance forces. Even so, the resistance movements in most occupied countries enjoyed limited success until the regular Allied forces had won sufficient victories to force the Axis powers into an essentially defensive strategy of protecting their homelands.

During the early postwar years, as we have noted, the CIA's initial reaction to the Cold War was to employ the wartime tactics of the OSS in new efforts to organize and promote paramilitary resistance movements in such areas as Albania, the Ukraine, and other parts of Eastern Europe. Almost all of these operations were complete failures. (Similar setbacks occurred in agency paramilitary operations against China and North Korea.) The controlling military forces in Eastern Europe, although supported by the Soviet Union, were for the most part of native origin—often directed by the same political elements that had cooperated with the OSS and other Allied intelligence services in the prior struggle against the Nazi occupiers. Despite a large amount of disenchantment with the communist regimes on the part of the indigenous populations, which the CIA grossly misinterpreted as revolutionary fervor, the war-weary populations were not willing to join, in significant numbers, resistance groups with little chance of success. And under the prevailing political circumstances of the times,

there was little likelihood of eventual overt military support from the U.S. armed forces. Thus, the Eastern European governments, with their rigid internal-security systems, were easily able to thwart CIA paramilitary efforts against them.

In those areas of the world not under communist domination, however, the CIA's clandestine paramilitary operations fared somewhat better, at least during the early 1950s. But unlike the OSS, which had supported partisan groups fighting against fascist-dominated governments, the CIA more often than not found itself in the position of supporting the counterinsurgency efforts of established regimes threatened from the left by local guerrilla movements. Blinded by its fear and distrust of communism, the CIA had gradually drifted into a posture whereby its paramilitary operations were in support of the *status quo*. The agency, in pursuit of "stability" and "orderly change," increasingly associated itself with protecting vested interests. In the view of much of the world, it had become a symbol of repression rather than freedom. While the CIA's paramilitary activities were at times successful, many of the victories won took on a Pyrrhic quality. They always seemed to work against legitimate social and political change— for which the U.S. government would in later years be held accountable by the peoples of these countries.

During the first years of its existence and particularly after the outbreak of the Korean war in 1950, the CIA recruited and trained large numbers of officers for special operations. Many were, of course, intended for service in Korea, but the American commander there, General Douglas MacArthur, was not particularly fond of clandestine paramilitary operations, and he did his best to keep the CIA's special-ops experts out of his theater. The agency did nevertheless manage to launch a large number of secret operations, resulting in the loss of numerous Korean agents and few, if any, meaningful gains.

With its newly expanded staff, the CIA's Special Operations Division was able to turn its attention to other countries in Asia. Attempts were made to develop resistance movements in China, but these efforts accomplished virtually nothing more than the

capture of agency officers John Downey and Richard Fecteau—and death for the Nationalist Chinese agents they were helping to infiltrate. Mainland China, like Eastern Europe, was not fertile territory for agency operations.

There were some successes elsewhere. The Huk insurgency in the Philippines was put down with CIA help. Agency-supported Nationalist Chinese troops in Burma (when not engaging in their principal pastime of trafficking in opium) were induced to conduct occasional raids into the hinterland of Communist China. In South Vietnam the CIA played a large part in consolidating the power of the Diem regime—and this was considered by the agency to be a major accomplishment.

Such gains in Southeast Asia were offset by some rather notable failures, most particularly the **agency's inability to overthrow President Sukarno of Indonesia in 1958. While this CIA-supported revolt was going on,** the U.S. government categorically denied providing any support to the anti-Sukarno forces. In March 1958, Secretary of State John Foster Dulles told a congressional committee that "we are not intervening in the internal affairs of this country." Six weeks later President Eisenhower stated that while "soldiers of fortune" probably were involved in the affair, "our policy is one of careful neutrality and proper deportment all the way through so as not to be taking sides where it is not of our business." These statements were of course false. The Indonesian government put little credence in the denials and denounced the United States for its intervention. The *New York Times,* however, chose to believe the official American version and indignantly scolded the Indonesians for circulating false reports saying that the U.S. government was giving aid to the rebels. The *Times* commented that the Secretary of State and "the President himself" had denied American involvement, and that "the United States is not ready . . . to step in to help overthrow a constituted government." The pattern of lying to cover up failure was established; it would find further manifestation during the U-2 affair, and again at the Bay of Pigs.

In 1959 the CIA found another opportunity to engage in special ops when the Tibetans revolted against the Chinese com-

munists who eight years before had imposed their rule on the mountain kingdom. Sparked by Peking's move to replace the Dalai Lama, Tibet's traditional religious and temporal ruler, with the Panchen Lama, an important religious leader controlled by the Chinese, there was a short-lived uprising. After its failure, the Dalai Lama with several thousand followers and troops escaped to India, where he and his loyalists were granted sanctuary. Then, (

DELETED

) **taken on a tour of friendly Asian and European capitals as living, though somewhat incongruous proof—since he was himself an autocrat—of Communist China's totalitarianism.** Later, he was brought to the United States for a visit, during which he appeared at the United Nations to plead his case and to denounce the Peking government. (

DELETED

) **special ops officers began secretly training and reequipping the Dalai Lama's troops—fearsome Khamba horsemen—in preparation for eventual clandestine forays into Tibet. Some of the Tibetans were quietly brought to the United States for special paramilitary training at Camp Hale, Colorado.**

Although the CIA officers led their Tibetan trainees to believe that they were being readied for the reconquering of their homeland, even within the agency few saw any real chance that this could happen. Some of the covert operators who worked directly with the Tibetans, however, eventually came to believe their own persuasive propaganda. Years later, they would flush with anger and frustration describing how they and their Tibetans had been undone by the bureaucrats back in Washington.* Several of them would turn for solace to the Tibetan prayers which they had learned during their years with the Dalai Lama.

---

* This phenomenon of "emotional attachment" is not rare in the clandestine business, but it is particularly prevalent in special operations. The officers who engage in special ops often have a deep psychological need to belong and believe. This, coupled with the dangers and hardships they willingly endure, tends to drive them to support extreme causes and seek unattainable goals.

From the beginning of the Tibetan operation, it was clear that its only value would be one of harassment. Spot raids against Chinese facilities in the backward mountain country were an annoyance to Peking and a reminder of its vulnerability. But the dream of reoccupying the land and reestablishing the Dalai Lama as its political ruler was an impossible one.

The guerrilla raids of the Dalai Lama's forces into Tibet, planned by CIA operators and on occasion led by agency contract mercenaries, were supported and covered by "private" planes of the Civil Air Transport complex, a CIA proprietary which was also instrumental in secretly supplying weapons (DELETED
) part, the raids accomplished little beyond giving the Tibetan troops some temporary satisfaction and fanning their hopes that someday they would lead a true invasion of their homeland. Communication lines were cut, some sabotage was carried out, and from time to time an ambush of a small Chinese Communist force was undertaken.

One such ambush resulted in an intelligence windfall. The Tibetans had waylaid a small military convoy on a lonely mountain road and were preparing to put the torch to the Chinese vehicles when it was discovered that one of them contained several mailbags. A quick examination disclosed that in addition to the routine mix of general correspondence, the mail included official governmental and military documents being delivered from China proper. The mailbags were salvaged and returned to India by the Tibetan guerrillas, where they were turned over to the CIA operatives working on the operation. The contents of the mailbags were later analyzed in detail by the agency's China experts in Langley, Virginia. Data and insights as to the status of the Chinese occupation of Tibet were found in abundance: While difficulties were being encountered in imposing communist rule on the feudal system of the mountain nation, it was clear that the Chinese were in full control of the situation and were determined to have their way. Even more interesting to the agency's China watchers, however, was authentic background information revealing that Mao Tse-tung's "Great Leap Forward" had failed in several crucial respects to achieve its goal of raising China from the depths of

underdevelopment. **As incredible as it may seem in retrospect, some of the CIA's economic analysts (and many other officials in Washington) were in the early 1960s still inclined to accept much of Peking's propaganda as to the success of Mao's economic experiment. The acquisition of the Tibetan documents was a significant contribution to the resolution of this particular debate within the U.S. intelligence community.**

Without any other noteworthy gains, the Tibetan operation sputtered hopelessly on. A few years later, at the end of 1964, the Chinese removed the Panchen Lama from power, setting off another minor revolt. But the Dalai Lama's **CIA-trained** troops, now more than five years in exile in India, were unable to come to the rescue of their countrymen. With the CIA's Bay of Pigs defeat still fresh in American minds, there was little interest in Washington in supporting the dreams of the Khamba horsemen. Gradually the Tibetan operation atrophied. By the late 1960s the CIA's clandestine operatives were interested only in seeking a graceful way to terminate their association with the Dalai Lama and his aging, now useless troops.

The Tibetan operation was soon overshadowed and succeeded by CIA involvement in the Congo. The chaotic strife which gripped that country almost from the moment it became independent of Belgian rule provided the CIA, along with intelligence services of many other countries, fertile ground for special operations. The U.S. government's intent was to promote a stable pro-Western regime that would protect foreign investments, and the CIA was given much of the responsibility for carrying out this policy. **At first the agency's covert activities were confined to political manipulation and cash payments to selected politicians, but as the Congolese political scene became more and more unraveled, the agency sent its paramilitary experts and mercenaries to support the new government. By 1964, CIA B-26 aircraft flown by Cuban pilots under contract with the CIA were carrying out regular bombing missions against rebel areas.** Later, in 1966, the *New York Times* would describe the CIA planes as "an instant air force." While the agency was not completely happy with this

publicity, many operators were pleased with the newspaper's recognition of the CIA's skill in putting the operation together on comparatively short notice.

Relying in large part on the considerable assistance furnished by the CIA and other U.S. government agencies, the central Congolese government under President Mobutu was finally able to impose some degree of stability throughout the country. (

DELETED

)

During the years when the Tibetan and Congolese programs were in full operation, the CIA and its Special Operations Division were already becoming increasingly preoccupied with Southeast Asia. In Laos, agency operators were organizing a private army (L'Armée Clandestine) of more than 30,000 men and building an impressive string of bases throughout the country. **A few of these bases were used as jumping-off points to send guerrilla raiding parties into North Vietnam and China.**

The secret war in Laos was viewed within the CIA with much more favor than the huge military struggle that eventually developed in Vietnam. The fighting was not highly visible to the American public or the world. In fact, the Laotian war was years along before the U.S. Congress even became aware it was going on. In Laos the CIA was in complete control, but at no time were more than forty or fifty operations officers required to direct the paramilitary effort. The dirty and dangerous work—the ground fighting —was handled by hundreds of agency contract personnel and more than 30,000 Lao tribesmen under the leadership of General Vang Pao—whom the CIA from time to time secretly decorated with "intelligence" medals. The CIA's Laotian forces were augmented by thousands of Thai "volunteers" paid by the agency. Air support, an extremely dangerous business in Laos, was supplied by Air America—a **CIA-owned airline**—and on occasion by the Thai Air Force. Thus, while the CIA's special-ops officers masterminded the war and called all the shots, largely from the Laotian capital of Vientiane or from secure bases upcountry, most were not required to run the physical risks of war. The Laotian operation was,

as special operations go, a near-perfect situation for the career officer.

Meanwhile, in Vietnam the CIA supported and financed a force of roughly 45,000 Civilian Irregular Defense Guards (CIDGs), local guerrilla troops who fought under the operational direction of the U.S. Army's Special Forces. SOD operators and agency contractees ran the Counter Terror teams which employed similar methods to oppose the Vietcong's terror tactics of kidnapping, torture, and murder. **The agency also organized guerrilla raids against North Vietnam, with special emphasis on intrusions by sea-borne commando groups coming "over the beach" on specially designed, heavily armed high-speed PT-type boats. At least one such CIA raiding party was operating in that part of the Tonkin Gulf in 1964 where two U.S. destroyers allegedly came under attack by North Vietnamese ships.** These CIA raids may well have specifically provoked the North Vietnamese action against the destroyers, which in turn led to the passage of the Tonkin Gulf resolution by the U.S. Congress in 1964, thus setting the stage for large-scale American military involvement in Indochina.

The CIA's special operations in Southeast Asia were massive in scale and an important part of the overall U.S. war effort. Many of these operations are described in detail in official U.S. government documents published in *The Pentagon Papers*. Nevertheless, a few operations not mentioned therein deserve particular note.

One involved the Nungs, a national minority of Chinese hill people who fought on the French side in the first Vietnam war and then came south in large numbers after 1954. The Nungs were known to be extremely fierce fighters, and they became a favorite source of manpower for CIA operations in South Vietnam. In fact, casual observers could nearly always spot secret CIA installations in the Vietnamese provinces by the Nung guards out front, dressed invariably in jungle camouflage uniforms.

In addition, Nung mercenaries were often sent by the CIA on forays along the Ho Chi Minh trail. Their function was to observe North Vietnamese and Vietcong supply movements and on occasion to make attacks against convoys, or to carry out sabotage on storage depots. **Since most of the Nungs were illiterate and had great**

difficulty in sending back quick, accurate reports of what they saw, the CIA technicians developed a special kind of radio transmitter for their use. Each transmitter had a set of buttons corresponding to pictures of a tank, a truck, an artillery piece, or some other military-related object. When the Nung trail watcher saw a Vietcong convoy, he would push the appropriate button as many times as he counted such objects go by him. Each push sent a specially coded impulse back to a base camp which could in this way keep a running account of supply movements on the trail. In some instances the signals would be recorded by observation planes that would relay the information to attack aircraft for immediate bombing raids on the trail.

The Nung units made special demands on their CIA case officers, and consequently they cost the agency about 100 times as much per soldier as the Meos fighting in CIA's L'Armée Clandestine in Laos, who could be put into the field for less than ten cents per man per day. The higher cost for the Nungs' services was caused by their unwillingness to go into remote regions under agency command unless they were regularly supplied with beer and prostitutes—thus, the agency had no choice but to provide flying bar and brothel services. Even though one of the **CIA's own airlines**, Air America, handled this unusual cargo, the cost of the air support was still high. The CIA's case officers would have preferred to give the Nungs whiskey, which, while more expensive to buy, was considerably lighter and hence cheaper to fly in, but the Nungs would fight only for beer. The prostitutes also presented a special problem because the agency did not want to compromise the secrecy of the operations by supplying women from local areas who might be able to talk to the Nungs. Thus, Air America brought in only prostitutes from distant parts of Southeast Asia who had no language in common with the Nungs.

With their characteristic enthusiasm for gimmicks and gadgetry, the CIA came up with two technical discoveries in the mid-1960s that were used in Vietnam with limited success but great delight. (

DELETED

DELETED

) In actual practice, however, whatever damage was caused by the chemical was quickly repaired by the Vietcong and North Vietnamese.

The agency's other discovery was a weapons-detection system. It worked by spraying a special chemical on the hands of a suspected Vietcong and then, after a few minutes, shining an ultraviolet light on his hands. If the chemical glowed in a certain manner, that meant that the suspect had held a metal object—in theory, a weapon—during the preceding twenty-four hours. The system's main drawback was that it was just as sensitive to steel farm implements as to guns and it could implicate a person who had been merely working with a hammer. The CIA considered the system such a success, however, that it passed it on through a domestic training program to the police forces of several American cities.
(

DELETED

)

Latin America in 1954 was the scene of one of the CIA's greatest paramilitary triumphs—the successful invasion of Guatemala by an agency-organized rebel force. And it was in Latin America that the CIA seven years later suffered its most notable failure—the

abortive invasion of Cuba at the Bay of Pigs. But the agency was slow to accept defeat in the Cuban operation. The only reason for the failure, the CIA's operators believed, was that President Kennedy had lost his nerve at the last minute, refusing more air support for the invasion and withholding or reducing other possible assistance by U.S. forces. Consequently, the agency continued its relationships with its "penetrations" of Cuban exile groups—in a way reminiscent of its lingering ties with Eastern European émigré organizations from the early Cold War period. And the CIA kept many of the Bay of Pigs veterans under contract, paying them regular salaries for more than a decade afterward.

(

DELETED

)

Time after time, the Cuban government would parade CIA-sponsored rebels before television cameras to display them and their equipment to the Cuban public and the world. Often the captives made full confessions of the agency's role in their activities.

Nevertheless, the CIA kept looking for new and better ways to attack the Castro government. **Under contract to the agency, the Electric Boat Division of General Dynamics at Groton, Connecticut developed a highly maneuverable high-speed boat designed for use by guerrilla raiders. The boat was supposed to be faster than any ship in the Cuban navy, and thereby able to move arms and men into Cuba at will. There were numerous delays in putting the boat into production, however, and no deliveries were made up to 1967. By that time, the U.S. was too deeply involved in Southeast Asia to think seriously about a new invasion of Cuba. The CIA, therefore, quietly dropped the boat project and turned the developmental model over the U.S. Navy.**

Also during the mid-1960s, (
DELETED

DELETED

)

By 1968, almost everyone in the Clandestine Services had finally accepted the fact that special operations against Cuba had outlived their usefulness. To be sure, there were still some diehard veterans around who would continue to propose new schemes, but even "Frank Bender"—the heavy-accented, cigar-smoking German refugee who had helped manage the Bay of Pigs fiasco—could no longer bring himself to believe in them. The death knell for CIA Cuban operations was sounded that year, seven years after the Bay of Pigs, when the agency closed down its two largest bases in Florida. One of these, located on an old naval air station at Opa-locka, had served as an all-purpose base for CIA-sponsored raids on Cuba. (

DELETED

)

While the CIA was largely concerned with Cuba in its Latin American operations during much of the 1960s, the rest of the continent was by no means neglected. For the most part, the agency's aim was not to overthrow particular Latin American governments but rather to protect them from local insurgent movements. The CIA generally avoided getting involved in any large way, instead using relatively small amounts of covert money, arms, and advisors to fight leftist groups. While this switch in tactics reflected the counterinsurgency theories popular in the Kennedy and Johnson administrations, it also came as a result of the diversion of a substantial part of the nation's military resources—covert and otherwise—to Southeast Asia.

The CIA assumed the role of coordinator of all U.S. government counterinsurgency activities in Latin America, and other agencies —particularly AID, with its police-training programs, and the

Defense Department, with its military-assistance and civic-action programs—provided the CIA with cover and additional resources. Much of the agency's manpower for Latin American special operations was furnished by the U.S. Army's Special Forces; small detachments of Green Berets were regularly placed under CIA control. These soldiers usually came from the Third Battalion of the Seventh Special Forces, located at Fort Gulick in the Canal Zone. The agency had its own paramilitary base in the Canal Zone, and even when the Special Forces carried on missions outside the CIA's direct command, agency operators kept in close touch with what was going on. Since 1962 more than 600 Special Forces "mobile training teams" have been dispatched to the rest of Latin America from Fort Gulick, either under direct CIA control or under Pentagon auspices. **Green Berets participated, for example, in what was the CIA's single large-scale Latin American intervention of the post–Bay of Pigs era. This occurred in the mid-1960s, when the agency secretly came to the aid of the Peruvian government, then plagued by guerrilla troubles in its remote eastern regions. Unable to cope adequately with the insurgent movement, Lima had turned to the U.S. government for aid, which was immediately and covertly forthcoming.**

The agency financed the construction of what one experienced observer described as "a miniature Fort Bragg" in the troubled Peruvian jungle region, complete with mess halls, classrooms, barracks, administrative buildings, parachute jump towers, amphibious landing facilities, and all the other accoutrements of paramilitary operations. Helicopters were furnished under cover of official military aid programs, and the CIA flew in arms and other combat equipment. Training was provided by the agency's Special Operations Division personnel and by Green Beret instructors on loan from the Army.

As the training progressed and the proficiency of the counter-guerrilla troops increased, the Peruvian government grew uneasy. Earlier, the national military commanders had been reluctant to provide personnel for the counterinsurgency force, and thus the CIA had been required to recruit its fighting manpower from among the available local populace. By paying higher wages than

the army (and offering fringe benefits, better training, and "esprit de corps") the agency soon developed a relatively efficient fighting force. In short order, the local guerrillas were largely wiped out.

A few months later, when Peru was celebrating its chief national holiday, the authorities refused to allow the CIA-trained troops into the capital for the annual military parade. Instead, they had to settle for marching through streets of a dusty provincial town, in a satellite observance of the great day. Realizing that many a Latin American regime had been toppled by a crack regiment, Peru's leaders were unwilling to let the CIA force even come to Lima, and the government soon moved to dismantle the unit.

As large and successful as the CIA's Peruvian operation might have been, it was outweighed in importance among agency leaders by a smaller intervention in Bolivia that occurred in 1967; for the CIA was out for bigger game in Bolivia than just local insurgents. The target was Che Guevara.

The Tracking of Che

When he vanished from the Cuban scene in the spring of 1965, there were reports that Ernesto "Che" Guevara, the Argentinian physician and comrade-in-arms of Fidel Castro, had challenged the Cuban leader's authority and, as a result, had been executed or imprisoned. There were other reports that Guevara had gone mad, beyond all hope of recovery, and was under confinement in a villa somewhere in the Cuban provinces. And there were still other reports that Che had formed a small cadre of dedicated disciples and had gone off to make a new revolution. At first no one in the CIA knew what to believe. But eventually a few clues to Guevara's whereabouts began to dribble in from the agency's field stations and bases. They were fragmentary, frustratingly flimsy, and, surprisingly, they pointed to Africa—to the Democratic Republic of the Congo, now called Zaire. Yet another insurrection was going on in the former Belgian colony, and information from the CIA's operatives in the field indicated that foreign revolutionaries were participating in it. Some of their tactics suggested the unique style of Che Guevara.

Before the intelligence could be verified, however, the rebellion in the eastern inland territories suddenly evaporated. By the fall of 1965, Lake Tanganyika was again calm. But the **CIA** mercenaries (some of them veterans of the Bay of Pigs operation), who had been assisting the Congo government in repressing the revolt, were convinced, as were their agency superiors in Africa, that Che had indeed been in the area.

Later it was learned by the CIA that Guevara and a group of more than 100 Cuban revolutionaries had infiltrated into the Congo from neighboring Tanzania in the spring of 1965. They intended to set Africa aflame with rebellion, but their revolutionary zeal was not matched by that of the native guerrillas or the local populace. In disgust, six months later Che secretly returned to Cuba to lay plans for his next adventure. At the time, however, the CIA knew only that he had once again disappeared. Again conflicting reports as to his whereabouts and status, health and otherwise, began to drift into the agency. By early 1967, almost a year and a half later, the information available to the agency pointed to the heart of South America, to Bolivia.

While many of the officers in the CIA's Clandestine Services firmly believed that Guevara was behind the insurgent movement in the southern mountains of Bolivia, a few of the agency's top officials hesitated to accept the fact. Despite the air of doubt, **some agency special operations personnel were sent** to the land-locked South American country to assist local forces in dealing with the rebel movement. Ironically, at this point not even Bolivian President René Barrientos thought that Guevara was involved in the guerrilla movement.

A couple of months later, in April, two events occurred that dramatically underscored the belief of the CIA's clandestine operators, both in Bolivia and at headquarters, that Che was leading the rebels. Early in the month a Bolivian army unit overran the base camp of the guerrillas at Ñancahuazú, capturing documents, diaries, and photographs which the fleeing insurgents had left behind. Included in the materials seized at the guerrilla base camp were photographs of a partially bald, gray-haired man with glasses who, upon close examination of certain features, bore a

striking resemblance to Che Guevara. In addition, a couple of smudged fingerprints on some of the documents seemed to match Guevara's. The documents, furthermore, clearly established that a number of the guerrillas operating in Bolivia were Cubans, probably some of the same men who were thought to have been with Guevara in the Congo.

Ten days later Regis Debray, the leftist French journalist, who had disappeared months earlier upon arriving in Bolivia to do a geopolitical study, was captured near Muyupampa, along with two other foreigners suspected of having been in contact with the rebels. According to his statements months later, the journalist Debray was saved from summary execution by the CIA men accompanying the Bolivian forces who captured him. Afterward he was confronted with secret evidence by these same CIA operatives, disclosing that the agency knew a great deal more about his activities abroad and in Bolivia than he had thought possible. Denying, at first, any knowledge of Guevara's connection with the rebel movement, Debray soon wilted and began to talk in an attempt to save himself from trial and execution.

Even with the rapidly mounting evidence, Director Richard Helms still could not accept that the legendary Cuban revolutionary had indeed reappeared to lead another rebellion. He scoffed at the claims of his clandestine operatives that they had acquired proof of Guevara's presence in Bolivia; Helms guessed Che was probably dead. Thomas Karamessines, then chief of the CIA's Clandestine Services, who had presented the case to the Director, would not, however, back down from the contention that his operatives were now hot on Guevara's trail, and Helms' attitude seemed to spur the clandestine operators to greater efforts. **More agency "advisors," including Cuban veterans of the Bay of Pigs adventure,** were soon dispatched to Bolivia to assist in the tracking down of Guevara. A team of experts from the Army's Special Forces was sent to La Paz from the Canal Zone to train Bolivian "rangers" in the art of counterinsurgency operations.

The Clandestine Services were obsessed with Guevara, and even somewhat fearful of him. He was in part a constant and irritating reminder of their failure in the Cuban operation. Unable to vent

their frustrations and anger against those U.S. officials who had undercut that desperate effort, and incapable of gaining direct retribution by destroying Fidel himself or his Soviet and Chinese allies, the CIA's Clandestine Services were left to brood over their failure—until Guevara exposed himself. In so doing he presented himself to the CIA as an inviting target; his capture or death would provide some measure of revenge for past failures.

During the summer of 1967, while the **agency's special ops experts** were assisting the Bolivian army in hunting down Guevara, information as to his entry into Bolivia became available. It was learned that in November 1966 he had come to La Paz from Havana, via Prague, Frankfurt, and São Paulo, traveling on a false Uruguayan passport and disguised as a balding, gray-haired merchant with horn-rimmed spectacles—a far cry from the familiar poster picture. He had been preceded by fifteen Cubans who would assist him in his Bolivian venture. There was no longer any doubt in anyone's mind that Che Guevara was in the country and in charge of the guerrilla movement in the southern mountains. Both President Barrientos and Helms now accepted the fact. The Bolivian government offered a reward ($4,200) for Guevara—dead or alive. It was only a matter of time until Che would be run to ground.

In the months that followed, the guerrillas suffered defeat after defeat at the hands of the American-trained, CIA-advised Bolivian rangers. One battle, on the last day of August, resulted in the death of the mysterious Tania, the lone female in Guevara's rebel band. Although she had posed as a Cuban intelligence agent, a link between the guerrillas and Havana, it was ultimately learned by the CIA that the East German woman was actually a double agent. Her primary employer was the Soviet KGB, which, like the CIA, wanted to keep tabs on Guevara's Cuban-sponsored revolutionary activities in Latin America. Less than six weeks later, on October 8, Guevara himself was wounded and captured near the small mountain village of La Higuera.

As they had done for Debray earlier, the CIA advisors with the Bolivian army tried to bring Guevara back alive to La Paz for in-depth interrogations. The Bolivian commander, however, was under

orders to execute Guevara. All that was to be brought back were the head and hands—incontestable proof that Che had failed in his mission and was dead.

While the CIA advisors stalled the Bolivian colonel, the agency's station chief in La Paz tried to convince President Barrientos of the long-range advantages of bringing Guevara out of the mountains as a prisoner of the government. Barrientos was adamant. He argued that the Debray affair had caused enough difficulties, and that the arrival of Che Guevara, alive, in the capital might spark disturbances among the students and leftists which his government would not be able to control. In desperation, the station that night appealed to Langley headquarters for assistance, but to no avail.

Going on the assumption that neither the station nor headquarters would be successful in getting Barrientos to change his position, the senior CIA operative at La Higuera, (**DELETED**) attempted to question Che. The revolutionary, however, would not cooperate. He was willing to discuss political philosophies and revolutionary movements in general, but he refused to permit himself to be interrogated about the details of his operation in Bolivia or any of his previous guerrilla activities elsewhere. The CIA would have to settle for the contents of his personal diary, which he had been carrying at the time of his capture.

Final word came from the capital early the next morning. The prisoner was to be executed on the spot and his body, strapped to the landing gear of a helicopter, was to be flown to Vallegrande for inspection at a local laundry house by a small group of reporters and government officials. Afterward the corpse was to be buried in an unmarked grave outside of town. On hearing the order, (**DELETED**) the CIA operative, hurried back to the schoolhouse where Guevara was being held, to make one last attempt at interrogating Che. There was not much time left; the execution was to be carried out in the next hour or two.

Guevara's last moments were recorded in a rare, touching message to headquarters from the CIA operator. The Cuban veteran, and agency contract officer, noted that Guevara was at first still confident of somehow surviving his ordeal, but when he finally realized that he was about to die, his pipe fell from his mouth. Che,

however, quickly recovered his composure and asked for some tobacco. His painfully wounded leg no longer seemed to bother him. He accepted his fate with a sigh of resignation, requesting no last favors. (**DELETED**) clearly felt admiration for the revolutionary and compassion for the man he had helped to capture and thereby condemn. Minutes later Che Guevara was dead.

The following summer Che's diary suddenly surfaced and soon found its way into the hands of his comrades in Havana and certain American admirers (*Ramparts* magazine), who immediately verified its authenticity and published it, much to the chagrin of the CIA and the Bolivian government, which had been releasing only those portions which buttressed their case against Guevara and his rebels. In the midst of the confusion, charges, and countercharges, Antonio Arguedas, Bolivian Minister of the Interior, disappeared in July among rumors that he had been the one who had released the document. Arguedas, as Minister of the Interior, was in charge of the Bolivian intelligence service, with which the agency had many close connections. And Arguedas himself was an agent of the CIA.

It was quickly learned that Arguedas had escaped to Chile, where he intended to ask for political asylum. Instead, authorities there turned him over to the CIA station, and the agency man who had been his original case officer was dispatched from headquarters in Washington to cool him off. But despite the CIA's counsel, Arguedas spoke out publicly against the agency and its activities in Bolivia. He denounced the Barrientos regime as a tool of American imperialism, criticized the government's handling of the Guevara affair, and then disappeared again, precipitating a major political crisis in Bolivia.

At various times during the next several months of 1968, Arguedas popped up in London, New York, and Peru. Alternately cajoled and threatened at each stop by CIA operatives who wanted him to shut up, the former minister nevertheless admitted he had been the one who had released Che's diary because, he said, he agreed with the revolutionary's motives of attempting to bring about popular social, political, and economic change in Bolivia

and elsewhere in Latin America. And ultimately, much to the horror of the CIA and the Barrientos government, Arguedas announced that he had been an agent of the CIA since 1965 and claimed that certain other Bolivian officials were also in the pay of the secret agency. He described the circumstances under which he had been recruited, charging that the CIA had threatened to reveal his radical student past and ruin his political career if he did not agree to participate in its operations.

Eventually the CIA was able to strike a bargain with Arguedas, and he voluntarily returned to Bolivia—apparently to stand trial. He told a *New York Times* reporter on the flight from Lima to La Paz that should anything untoward happen to him, a tape recording detailing his accusations against the CIA and the Barrientos government would be delivered to certain parties in the United States and Cuba. The tape, he said, was being held for him by Lieutenant Mario Terán. Terán, inexplicably, was previously identified as Che Guevara's executioner.

Arguedas, during his interview, hinted at the magnitude of his potential revelations by disclosing the names of several CIA officers with whom he had worked in the past: **Hugo Murray, chief of station; John S. Hilton, former COS; Colonel Ed Fox; Larry Sternfield; and Nick Lendiris. He also identified some of the agency's contract officers who had assisted in the tracking down of Guevara: Jolio Gabriel Garcia (Cuban), and Eddie and Mario Gonzales (Bolivians). Arguedas credited the Gonzales brothers** with having saved Debray's life. He now claimed, however, that Barrientos and even the U.S. ambassador were unaware of the full scope of the CIA's penetration of the Bolivian government, undoubtedly a concession to the powers that arranged his safe return to La Paz.

The final chapter in the episode was acted out the following summer, almost two years after Che Guevara's death. President René Barrientos was killed in a helicopter crash while returning from a visit to the provinces. Six weeks later Antonio Arguedas, the self-admitted agent of the CIA who had yet to stand trial for treason and releasing Che Guevara's diary, was shot to death on

a street in La Paz. A month later Herberto Rojas, the guide for the Bolivian rangers and their CIA advisors during the final track-down of Guevara, and one of the few people who possibly knew where the body of rebel leader was buried, was assassinated in Santa Cruz.

The incriminating tapes Arguedas claimed to have given to Mario Teran for safekeeping have never surfaced.

FIVE

Proprietary Organizations

As far as depots of "untraceable arms," airlines and other installations are concerned, one wonders how the CIA could accomplish the tasks required of it in Southeast Asia without such facilities.

—LYMAN KIRKPATRICK
Former CIA Executive Director
U.S. News and World Report
October 11, 1971

LATE one windy spring afternoon in 1971 a small group of men gathered unobtrusively in a plush suite at Washington's Mayflower Hotel. The host for the meeting was Professor Harry Howe Ransom of Vanderbilt University, author of *The Intelligence Establishment*, a respected academic study of the U.S. intelligence system. He was then doing research for another book on the subject and had invited the others for drinks and dinner, hoping to gather some new material from his guests, who included ex-CIA officials, congressional aides, and David Wise, co-author of *The Invisible Government* and *The Espionage Establishment*, two of the best books on the CIA and clandestine intelligence operations ever published. Someone brought up the CIA's use of front companies.

"Oh, you mean the Delaware corporations," said Robert Amory, Jr., a former Deputy Director of the CIA. "Well, if the agency wants to do something in Angola, it needs the Delaware corporations."

By "Delaware corporations" Amory was referring to what are more commonly known in the agency as "proprietary corporations" or, simply, "proprietaries." These are ostensibly private institutions and businesses which are in fact financed and controlled by the CIA. From behind their commercial and sometimes non-profit covers, the agency is able to carry out a multitude of clandestine activities—usually covert-action operations. Many of the firms are legally incorporated in Delaware because of that state's lenient regulation of corporations, but the CIA has not hesitated to use other states when it found them more convenient.

The CIA's best-known proprietaries were Radio Free Europe and Radio Liberty, both established in the early 1950s. The cor-

porate structures of these two stations served as something of a prototype for other agency proprietaries. Each functioned under the cover provided by a board of directors made up of prominent Americans, who in the case of RFE incorporated as the National Committee for a Free Europe and in the case of RL as the American Committee for Liberation. But CIA officers in the key management positions at the stations made all the important decisions regarding the programming and operations of the stations.

In 1960 when the agency was preparing for the Bay of Pigs invasion and other paramilitary attacks against Castro's Cuba, it set up a radio station on desolate Swan Island in the Caribbean to broadcast propaganda to the Cuban people. Radio Swan, as it was called, was operated by a New York company with a Miami address, the Gibraltar Steamship Corporation. Again the CIA had found a group of distinguished people—as usual, corporate leaders with government ties—to front for its clandestine activities. Gibraltar's president was Thomas D. Cabot, who had once been president of the United Fruit Company and who had held a high position in the State Department during the Truman administration. Another "stockholder" was Sumner Smith, also of Boston, who claimed (as did the Honduran government) that his family owned Swan Island and who was president of the Abington Textile and Machinery Works.

During the Bay of Pigs operation the following year, Radio Swan ceased its normal fare of propaganda broadcasts and issued military commands to the invading forces and to anti-Castro guerrillas inside Cuba. What little cover Radio Swan might have had as a "private" corporation was thus swept away. Ultimately, Radio Swan changed its name to Radio Americas (although still broadcasting from Swan Island), and the Gibraltar Steamship Corporation became the Vanguard Service Corporation (but with the same Miami address and telephone number as Gibraltar). The corporation, however, remained a CIA proprietary until its dissolution in the late 1960s.

At least one other agency proprietary, the Double-Chek Corporation, figured in the CIA's operations against Cuba. Double-Chek was founded in Miami (which abounds with agency

proprietaries) in 1959, and, according to the records of the Florida state government, "brokerage is the general nature of the business engaged in." In truth, Double-Chek was used by the agency to provide air support to Cuban exile groups, and it was Double-Chek that recruited the four American pilots who were killed during the Bay of Pigs invasion. Afterward the CIA, through Double-Chek, paid pensions to the dead fliers' widows and warned them to maintain silence about their husbands' former activities.

When the CIA intervened in 1964, Cuban exile pilots—some of whom were veterans of the Bay of Pigs—flew B-26 bombers against the rebels. These **pilots were hired by a company called Caramar (Caribbean Marine Aero Corporation), another CIA proprietary.**

Often the weapons and other military equipment for an operation such as that in the Congo are provided by a "private" arms dealer. The largest such dealer in the United States is the International Armament Corporation, or Interarmco, which has its main office and some warehouses on the waterfront in Alexandria, Virginia. Advertising that it specializes in arms for law-enforcement agencies, the corporation has outlets in Manchester in England, Monte Carlo, Singapore, Pretoria, South Africa, and in several Latin American cities. Interarmco was founded in 1953 by Samuel Cummings, a CIA officer during the Korean war. The circumstances surrounding Interarmco's earlier years are murky, but CIA funds and support undoubtedly were available to it at the beginning. Although Interarmco is now a truly private corporation, it still maintains close ties with the agency. And while the CIA will on occasion buy arms for specific operations, it generally prefers to stockpile military matériel in advance. For this reason, it maintains several storage facilities in the United States and abroad for untraceable or "sterile" weapons, which are always available for immediate use. Interarmco and similar dealers are the CIA's second most important source, after the Pentagon, of military matériel for paramilitary activities.

The Air Proprietaries

Direct CIA ownership of Radio Free Europe, Radio Liberty, and the Bay of Pigs proprietaries, and direct involvement in Inter-armco are largely past history now. Nevertheless, the agency is still very much involved in the proprietary business, especially to support its paramilitary operations. CIA mercenaries or CIA-supported foreign troops need air support to fight their "secret" wars, and it was for just this purpose that the agency built a huge network of clandestine airlines which are far and away the largest and the most dangerous of all the CIA proprietaries.

Incredible as it may seem, the CIA is currently the owner of one of the biggest—if not *the* biggest—fleets of "commercial" airplanes in the world. **Agency proprietaries include Air America, Air Asia, Civil Air Transport, Intermountain Aviation, Southern Air Transport, (DELETED)** and several other air charter companies around the world.

Civil Air Transport (CAT), **the original link in the CIA air empire,** was started in China in 1946, one year before the agency itself was established by Congress. CAT was an offshoot of General Claire Chennault's Flying Tigers, and during its early days it flew missions of every kind in support of Chiang Kai-shek's unsuccessful effort to retain control of the Chinese mainland. When Chiang was finally driven out of China in 1949, CAT went with him to Taiwan and continued its clandestine air operations. In 1950 CAT was reorganized as a Delaware corporation under a **CIA proprietary** holding company called the Pacific Corporation.

In a top-secret memorandum to General Maxwell Taylor on "unconventional-warfare resources in Southeast Asia" in 1961, published in *The Pentagon Papers*, Brigadier General Edward Lansdale described CAT's functions as follows:

CAT is a commercial air line engaged in scheduled and non-scheduled air operations throughout the Far East, with headquarters and large maintenance facilities located in Taiwan. CAT, a CIA proprietary, provides air logistical support under commercial cover to most CIA and other U.S. Govern-

ment agencies' requirements. CAT supports covert and clandestine air operations by providing trained and experienced
personnel, procurement of supplies and equipment through
overt commercial channels, and the maintenance of a fairly
large inventory of transport and other type aircraft under both
Chinat [Chinese Nationalist] and U.S. registry.

CAT has demonstrated its capability on numerous occasions to meet all types of contingency or long-term covert air
requirements in support of U.S. objectives. During the past
ten years, it has had some notable achievements, including
support of the Chinese Nationalist withdrawal from the mainland, air drop support to the French at Dien Bien Phu, complete logistical and tactical air support for the Indonesian
operation, air lifts of refugees from North Vietnam, more
than 200 overflights of Mainland China and Tibet, and extensive air support in Laos during the current crisis. . . .

The air drops at Dien Bien Phu occurred in 1954 when the U.S.
government decided not to come directly to the assistance of the
beleaguered French force but did approve covert military support.
1954 was also the year of the airlift of refugees from North Vietnam to the South. These were non-secret missions, but the CIA
could not resist loading the otherwise empty planes that flew to
North Vietnam with a cargo of secret agents and military equipment to be used in a clandestine network then being organized in
North Vietnam. Like other guerrilla operations against communist
countries, whether in Europe or Asia, this CIA venture was a
failure.

**By "the Indonesian operation," Lansdale was referring to the
covert air and other military support the CIA provided to the
rebels of the Sukarno government in 1958.*** The "more than 200

* Allen Pope, the pilot who was shot down and captured during this
operation by the Indonesian government, was a CAT pilot. Six months after
his release in 1962 he went to work for another CIA proprietary, Southern
Air Transport. The attorney for Southern at that time was a man named
Alex E. Carlson, who had only a year before been the lawyer for Double-
Chek Corporation when that CIA proprietary had furnished the pilots for
the Bay of Pigs.

overflights of Mainland China and Tibet" that Lansdale mentioned occurred mainly during the 1950s (but continued well into the 1960s), when the CIA supported, on its own and in cooperation with the Chiang Kai-shek government, guerrilla operations against China. CAT was the air-supply arm for these operations, and it was in a CAT plane that Richard Fecteau and John Downey were shot down by the communist Chinese in 1954.

By the end of the 1950s, CAT had split into three separate airlines, all controlled by a **CIA proprietary** holding company, the Pacific Corporation. One firm, Air America, took over most of CAT's Southeast Asia business; another, Air Asia, operated a giant maintenance facility on Taiwan. The portion still called CAT continued to fly open and covert charter missions out of Taiwan and to operate Nationalist China's scheduled domestic and international airline. CAT was best known for the extravagant service on its "Mandarin Jet," which linked Taipei to neighboring Asian capitals.

In 1964, about the time of the mysterious crash of a CAT plane,* the **CIA** decided that running Taiwan's air passenger service contributed little to the **agency's covert mission in Asia, and that the non-charter portion of CAT should be turned over to the Chinese Nationalists.** But the Nationalists' own China Air Lines had neither the equipment nor the experience at that time to take over CAT's routes, and the Nationalist government was not pre-

---

* CAT's former public-relations director, Arnold Dibble, wrote in the *Saturday Review* of May 11, 1968: "A highly suspicious crash of a C-46 claimed the lives of fifty-seven persons, including that of perhaps the richest man in Asia, Dato Loke Wan Tho—the Malaysian movie magnate—and several of his starlets from his Cathay studios. The full story of this crash has yet to be unraveled; what is known has not been told because it has been kept under official and perhaps officious wraps. There has never been, for instance, an official airing of the part played by two apparently demented military men aboard who had stolen two radar identification manuals (about the size of a mail-order catalog) in the Pescadores Islands, hollowed them out with a razor blade so each would hold a .45 caliber pistol. The manuals and one pistol were found, but fire and perhaps inadequate investigation marred the evidence. It was never definitely determined if the weapons had been fired."

pared to allow the CIA to abandon Taiwan's principal air links with the outside world. The CIA could not simply discontinue service, because such action would have offended the Chiang government and made uncertain the continued presence of the agency's other proprietaries and intelligence facilities on Taiwan.

The negotiations over CAT's passenger routes dragged on through the next four years. The CIA was so eager to reach a settlement that it sent a special emissary to Taiwan on temporary duty, but his short-term negotiating assignment eventually turned into a permanent position. Finally, in 1968 another CAT passenger plane—this time a Boeing 727—crashed near the Taipei airport. This second accident caused twenty-one deaths and provided that rarest of occurrences on Taiwan, a spontaneous public demonstration—against U.S. involvement in the airline. Bowing to public pressure, the Nationalist government then accepted a settlement with the agency: China Air Lines took over CAT's international flights; CAT, despite the agency's reluctance, continued to fly domestic routes on Taiwan; and the CIA sweetened the pot with a large cash payment to the Nationalists.

Air America, a spin-off of CAT, was set up in the late 1950s to accommodate the **agency's** rapidly growing number of operations in Southeast Asia. As U.S. involvement deepened in that part of the world, other government agencies—the State Department, the Agency for International Development (AID), and the United States Information Agency (USIA)—also turned to Air America to transport their people and supplies. By 1971, AID alone had paid Air America more than $83 million for charter services. In fact, Air America was able to generate so much business in Southeast Asia that eventually other American airlines took note of the profits to be made.

One private company, Continental Airlines, made a successful move in the mid-1960s to take some of the market away from Air America. Pierre Salinger, who became an officer of Continental after his years as President Kennedy's press secretary, led Continental's fight to gain its share of the lucrative Southeast Asian business. The Continental position was that it was a questionable, if not illegal, practice for a government-owned business (even a

CIA proprietary under cover) to compete with truly private companies in seeking government contracts. The CIA officers who had to deal with Continental were very uncomfortable. They knew that Salinger had learned during his White House days of the agency's activities in Southeast Asia and, specifically, of Air America's tie to the CIA. They feared that implicit in Continental's approach for a share of the Southeast Asian market was the threat that if the agency refused to cooperate, Continental would make its case publicly—using information supplied by Salinger. Rather than face the possibility of unwanted publicity, the CIA permitted Continental to move into Laos, where since the late 1960s it has flown charter flights worth millions of dollars annually. And Continental's best customer is the CIA itself.

But even with Continental flying in Laos, the agency was able to keep most of the flights for its own Air America. This **CIA** airline has done everything from parachuting Meo tribesmen behind North Vietnamese lines in Laos to dropping rice to refugees in the Vietnamese highlands. Air America has trained pilots for the Thai national police, transported political prisoners for the South Vietnamese government, carried paymasters and payrolls for CIA mercenaries, and, even before the Tonkin Gulf Resolution, furnished pilots for secret bombing raids on North Vietnamese supply lines in Laos. It has also been accused of participating in Southeast Asia's heroin trade. Air America's operations regularly cross national boundaries in Southeast Asia, and its flights are almost never inspected by customs authorities. It has its own separate passenger and freight terminals at airports in South Vietnam, Laos, and Thailand. At Udorn, in Thailand, Air America maintains a large base which is hidden within an even larger U.S. Air Force facility (which is ostensibly under Thai government control). The Udorn base is used to support virtually all of the "secret" war in Laos, and it also houses a "secret" maintenance facility for the planes of the Thai, Cambodian, and Laotian air forces.

Before the cease-fire in Vietnam, Air America was flying 125 planes of its own, with roughly 40 more on lease, and it had about 5,000 employees, roughly 10 percent of whom were pilots. It was one of America's largest airlines, ranking just behind National in

total number of planes. Now that the U.S. military forces have withdrawn from the Vietnamese theater, the role of maintaining a significant American influence has reverted largely to the CIA—and Air America, under the circumstances, is finding its services even more in demand than previously. Even the International Supervisory and Control Commission, despite the membership of communist Poland and Hungary, has signed a contract with the **CIA proprietary** to support its supervision of the Vietnam cease-fire. In 1973, Air America had contracts with the Defense Department worth $41.4 million.

A wholly owned subsidiary of Air America, Air Asia, operates on Taiwan the largest air repair and maintenance facility in the Pacific region. Established in 1955, Air Asia employs about 8,000 people. It not only services the **CIA's** own planes, it also repairs private and military aircraft. The U.S. Air Force makes heavy use of Air Asia and consequently has not had to build a major maintenance facility of its own in East Asia, as would have been necessary if the **CIA proprietary** had not been available. Like Air America, Air Asia is a self-sustaining, profit-making enterprise.

Until the CIA decided to sell it off in mid-1973, Southern Air Transport, another agency proprietary, operated out of offices in Miami and Taiwan. Unlike CAT, Air America, and Air Asia, it was not officially connected with the Pacific Corporation holding company, but Pacific did guarantee $6.6 million loaned to it by private banks, and Air America loaned it an additional $6.7 million funneled through yet another CIA proprietary called Actus Technology. Southern's role in the Far East was largely limited to flying profitable routes for the Defense Department. Other U.S. government agencies have also chartered Southern on occasion. In the first half of 1972 it received a $2 million AID contract to fly relief supplies to the new state of Bangladesh.

But within the CIA, Southern Air Transport was primarily important as the agency's air arm for potential Latin American interventions. This was the justification when the CIA took control of it in 1960, and it provided the agency with a readily available "air force" to support counterinsurgency efforts or to help bring down an unfriendly government. While Southern awaited its call

to be the Air America of future Latin American guerrilla wars, it "lived its cover" and cut down CIA's costs by hiring out its planes on charter. (

DELETED

) When the CIA brought Tibetan tribesmen to the United States in the late 1950s to prepare them for guerrilla forays into China, the agency's Intermountain Aviation assisted in the training program.

Then, in the early 1960s CIA air operations grew by leaps and bounds with the expansion of the wars in Southeast Asia and the constant fighting in the Congo.

(

DELETED

) But a reporter visiting Tucson in 1966 still wrote, "Anyone driving by could see more than a hundred B-26s with their armor plate, bomb bays, and gun ports." Not long after this disclosure appeared in the press, (**DELETED**) were made available to (**DELETED**) to build hangars for the parked aircraft. Prying reporters and the curious public soon saw less.

In 1965, Intermountain Aviation served as a conduit in the sale of

B-26 bombers to Portugal for use in that country's colonial wars in Africa. The sale directly violated the official United States policy against arms exports to Portugal for use in Angola, Mozambique, or Portuguese Guinea. The U.S. government, at its highest level, had decided to sell twenty B-26s to Portugal, and the CIA proprietary was following official orders. Theoretically, the embargo on weapons exports for use in Portugal's colonies remained intact—but not in fact. The U.S. government was, thus, doing covertly what it had forbidden itself to do openly.

Through the spring and summer of 1965, seven B-26s were flown from Arizona to Lisbon by an English pilot hired by an ostensibly private firm called Aero Associates. By September the operation's cover had worn so thin that Soviet and Hungarian representatives at the United Nations specifically attacked the transaction. The American U.N. delegation conceded that seven B-26s had been delivered to Portugal, but Ambassador Arthur Goldberg stated that "the only involvement of officials of the United States has been in prosecuting a malefactor against the laws of the country." This was a simple mistruth. Ambassador Goldberg, however, may have not known what the facts were. Adlai Stevenson before him had not been fully briefed on the Bay of Pigs invasion and wound up unknowingly making false statements at the U.N.

The same techniques were used to distort the prosecution of the "malefactor." Ramsey Clark, at the time Deputy Attorney General, got in contact with Richard Helms, when the latter was the CIA's Deputy Director, and the agency's General Counsel, Lawrence Houston, to discuss the Portuguese airplane matter. Agency officials assured Clark that the CIA had not been involved. Recalling the case, Clark says, "We couldn't have gone to trial if they [the CIA] had been involved. I don't see how you can just prosecute the little guys acting in the employ of a government agency."

Still, the United States had been exposed as violating its own official policy, and, for political reasons, those knowledgeable about the facts refused to intervene to aid "the little guys." Thus, one agency of the government, the Justice Department, unwittingly

found itself in the curious position of prosecuting persons who had been working under the direct orders of another government agency, the CIA. Five indictments were finally secured, but one of the accused fled the country, and charges against two of the others were dropped. But in the fall of 1966 the English pilot, John Richard Hawke, and Henri Marie François de Marin de Montmarin, a Frenchman who had been a middleman in the deal, were brought to trial in a Buffalo, New York, federal court.

Hawke admitted in court, "Yes, I flew B-26 bombers to Portugal for use in their African colonies, and the operation was arranged through the State Department and the CIA." However, CIA General Counsel Houston flatly denied under oath that the agency had been involved in the transaction. Houston did reveal that the agency "knew about" the bomber shipment on May 25, 1965, five days before it began, and that this information had been passed on to the State Department and eleven other government agencies. He also said that on July 7 the CIA was "informed" that four of the B-26s had actually been delivered to Portugal; again the CIA gave notice to State and other agencies. He did not explain why, if the U.S. government had so much intelligence on the flights, nothing was done to stop them, although their flight plans had been filed with the Federal Aviation Administration and Hawke, on one mission, even inadvertently buzzed the White House.

The jury found Hawke and Montmarin innocent. Members of the panel later let it be known that they had not been convinced that the two accused had deliberately violated the law. (

DELETED

DELETED)

Former Director Helms, however, refused to fly (**DELETED**) because he believed that its commercial cover was too transparent. He preferred instead to travel on legitimate commercial airlines. Less reluctant was Vice President Hubert Humphrey, who often used (**DELETED**) Gulfstream during his 1968 presidential campaign. (

DELETED

)

Perhaps the CIA's most out-of-the-way proprietary was located in Katmandu, Nepal. It was established to provide air support for agency-financed and -directed tribesmen who were operating in Chinese-controlled Tibet. CAT originally flew these missions, as indicated by General Lansdale's reference to CAT's "more than 200 overflights of Mainland China and Tibet." But flying planes from Taiwan to the CIA's operational base in northeastern India proved too cumbersome; thus the **Nepalese proprietary was set up. As the Tibetan operations were cut back and eventually halted during the 1960s, this airline was reduced in size to a few planes, helicopters, and a supply of spare parts. Still, up to the late 1960s, it flew charters for the Nepalese government and private organizations in the area.**

The CIA's Planning, Progamming, and Budgeting Staff back in Langley believed that the airline's usefulness as an agency asset had passed, and the decision was made to sell it off. But, for the CIA to sell a proprietary is a very difficult process. The agency feels that it must maintain the secrecy of its covert involvement, no matter how moot or insignificant the secrecy, and it does not want to be identified in any way, either before or after the actual trans-

action. Moreover, there is a real fear within the Clandestine Services that a profit will be made, and then by law, the CIA would be obliged to return the gain to the U.S. Treasury. The clandestine operatives do not want to be troubled by the bureaucratic red tape this would entail. It simply goes against the grain of the clandestine mentality to have to explain and justify such a transaction to anyone—let alone to the bookkeepers at the Treasury.

Unloading Southern Air Transport in 1973 proved to be something of a fiasco for the agency. Following past practice, the CIA tried to sell it quietly to a former employee—presumably at an attractive price—but the effort failed when three legitimate airlines protested to the Civil Aeronautics Board. They complained that Southern had been built up with government money, that it had consequently received lucrative charter routes, and that it represented unfair competition. When word of this prospective sale got into the newspapers, the CIA backtracked and voluntarily dropped Southern's CAB certification—greatly reducing the airline's value but guaranteeing that the agency could sell it off in complete secrecy.

And with the Nepalese airline, CIA found a buyer who had previously worked for other agency air proprietaries. Since he was a former "company man," secrecy was preserved. He was allowed to purchase the airlines for a small down payment. Following highly unorthodox business procedure, the airline itself served as collateral for the balance due. A CIA auditor at headquarters privately described the sale as a "giveaway," but this was the way the Clandestine Services wanted the affair handled. The new owner remained in Miami although all his airlines' operations were in Nepal. Within a comparatively short period of time, he liquidated all the airline's assets. He wound up with a considerable profit, but the agency made back only a fraction of its original costs. The Clandestine Services was pleased with the sale, in any case, because it had been able to divest itself of a useless asset in a way both to guarantee maximum security and to assure the future loyalty and availability of the buyer. (
DELETED

DELETED

)

While the ethics of transactions of this sort are questionable, conflict of interest laws presumably do not apply to the CIA; the Central Intelligence Agency Act of 1949 conveniently states that "The sums made available to the Agency may be expended without regard to the provisions of law and regulations relating to the expenditure of Government funds." In any case, the use of proprietary companies opens up to the participants an opportunity to make substantial profits while "living their cover."

The fact remains that CIA proprietaries are worth hundreds of millions of dollars, and no one outside the agency is able to audit their books. And, as will be seen later in this chapter, CIA headquarters sometimes has only the vaguest notion about what certain proprietaries are doing or what their assets are. Undoubtedly, there are wide opportunities for abuse, and many of the people involved in fields such as the arms trade, paramilitary soldiering, and covert air operations are not known for high ethical standards. While only a few agency career employees would take money for personal gain, there is little to prevent officers of the proprietaries from doing so, if they are so inclined.

As can be seen, the CIA's proprietary corporations serve largely in support of special, or paramilitary, operations. Some, of course, were established for propaganda and disinformation purposes and, like most other covert assets, proprietaries can also be used on

occasion to further the espionage and counterespionage efforts of the Clandestine Services. In the main, however, there has been a definite trend in the agency for more than a decade to develop the air proprietaries as the tactical arm for the CIA's secret military interventions in the Third World. The fleets of these CIA airlines have been continually expanded and modernized, as have been their base facilities. In the opinion of most CIA professionals, the agency's capabilities to conduct special operations would be virtually nonexistent without the logistical and other support provided by the air proprietaries.

The performance of the Pacific Corporation and its subsidiaries, Air America and Air Asia, in assisting the CIA's many special ops adventures over the years in the Far East and Southeast Asia has deeply impressed the agency's leadership. The exploits of the contract air officers in that strife-ridden corner of the world have become almost legendary within the CIA. Furthermore, the advantages of having a self-sustaining, self-run complex which requires no CIA funds and little agency manpower are indeed much appreciated by the Clandestine Services.

Without the air proprietaries, there could have been no secret raids into Communist China. There could have been no Tibetan or Indonesian or Burmese operations. And, most important of all, there could have been no "secret" war in Laos. Even many of the CIA's covert activities in Vietnam could not have been planned, much less implemented, without the assurance that **CIA airlines** were available to support such operations. Thus, it is small wonder that the agency, when it moved to intervene in the Congo (and anticipating numerous other insurgencies on the continent), hastily tried to develop the same kind of air support there that traditionally was available to special operations in Asia. And one can easily understand why the planners of the Bay of Pigs operation now regret not having made similar arrangements for their own air needs instead of relying on the U.S. armed forces.

The Fabulous George Doole

Although the boards of directors of the air proprietaries are studded with the names of eminently respectable business leaders and financiers, several of the companies' operations were actually long in the hands of one rather singular man, George Doole, Jr. Until his retirement in 1971, Doole's official titles were president of the Pacific Corporation and chief executive officer of Air America and Air Asia; it was under his leadership that the CIA air proprietaries blossomed.

Doole was known to his colleagues in the agency as a superb businessman. He had a talent for expanding his airlines and for making them, functionally if not formally, into profit-making concerns. In fact, his proprietaries proved something of an embarrassment to the agency because of their profitability. While revenues never quite covered all the costs to the CIA of the original capital investment, the huge contracts with U.S. government agencies resulting from the war in Indochina made the Pacific Corporation's holdings (CAT, Air America, and Air Asia) largely self-sufficient during the 1960s. Consequently, the CIA was largely spared having to pay in any new money for specific projects.

Some of the agency's top officials, such as the former Executive Director-Comptroller and the chief of Planning, Programming, and Budgeting, felt uncomfortable with the booming business Doole managed, but they did nothing to change it. **The Executive Director once privately explained the inaction: "There are things here better left undisturbed. The point is that George Doole and CAT provide the agency with a great number of services, and the agency doesn't have to pay for them."** Among the other services he provided was his ability as a straight-faced liar: asked by the *New York Times* in 1970 whether his airlines had any connection with the CIA, Doole said: "If 'someone out there' is behind all this, we don't know about it." **At that time Doole had been working for the CIA for seventeen years, and for most of those years had held a CIA "supergrade" position.**

Doole's empire was formally placed under the CIA's Directorate

of Support on the agency's organization chart, although many of
its operations were supervised by the Clandestine Services. But so
little was known inside CIA headquarters about the air proprietaries which employed almost as many people as the agency
itself (18,000) that in 1965 a CIA officer with extensive Clandestine Service experience was assigned to make a study of their
operations for the agency's top officials.

This officer spent the better part of a year trying to assemble the
relevant data, and he became increasingly frustrated as he proceeded. He found that the various proprietaries were constantly
trading, leasing, and selling aircraft to each other;* that the tail
numbers of many of the planes were regularly changed; and that
the mixture of profit-making and covert flight made accounting
almost impossible. He finally put up a huge map of the world in a
secure agency conference room and used flags and pins to try to
designate what proprietaries were operating with what equipment
in what countries. This officer later compared his experience to
trying to assemble a military order of battle, and his estimate was
that his map was at best 90 percent accurate at any given time.
Finally, Helms, then Deputy Director, was invited in to see the
map and be briefed on the complexity of the airlines. A witness
described Helms as being "aghast."

That same year the Executive Committee for Air (Ex Comm
Air) was formed in order to keep abreast of the various air proprietaries. Lawrence Houston, the agency's General Counsel, was
appointed chairman, and representatives were appointed from the
Clandestine Services, the Support Directorate, and the agency's
executive suite. But the proceedings were considered so secret that
Ex Comm Air's executive secretary was told not to keep minutes
or even notes.

In 1968, Ex Comm Air met to deal with a request from George
Doole for several million dollars to "modernize" Southern Air
Transport. Doole's justification for the money was that every major
airline in the world was using jets, and that Southern needed to

---

* The CAT jet that crashed on Taiwan in 1968 was on lease from
Southern Air Transport.

follow suit if it were to continue to "live its cover." Additionally, Doole said that Southern should have equipment as effective as possible in the event the agency had to call on it for future contingencies in Latin America.

Previous to Doole's request, the agency's Board of National Estimates had prepared a long-range assessment of events in Latin America. This estimate had been approved by the Director and sent to the President as the official analysis of the intelligence community. The conclusions were generally that political, economic, and social conditions in Latin America had so deteriorated that a long period of instability was at hand; that existing American policy was feeding this instability; and that there was little the United States could do, outside of providing straight economic and humanitarian assistance, to improve the situation. The estimate strongly implied that continued open U.S. intervention in the internal affairs of Latin American nations would only make matters worse and further damage the American image in that region.*

At the meeting on Southern Air Transport's modernization request, Doole was asked if he thought expanding Southern's capabilities for future interventions in Latin America conformed with the conclusions of the estimate. Doole remained silent, but a Clandestine Services officer working in paramilitary affairs replied that the estimate might well have been a correct appraisal of the Latin American situation and that the White House might accept it as fact, but that non-intervention would not necessarily become official American policy. The Clandestine Services man pointed out that over the years there had been other developments in Latin America—in countries such as Guatemala and the Dominican Republic—where the agency had been called on by the White House to take action against existing political trends; that the CIA's Director had a responsibility to prepare estimates for the White

---

* This estimate came much closer to recommending future American policy than almost any other paper previously prepared by the Board of National Estimates. The board member in charge of its preparation was a former division chief and chief of station in the Clandestine Services. He and his colleagues apparently hoped that the estimate would have a direct bearing on future agency covert operations in Latin America.

House as accurately as possible; but that the Director (and the Clandestine Services and Doole) also had a responsibility to be ready for the worst possible contingencies.

In working to strengthen Southern Air Transport and his other proprietaries, Doole and the Clandestine Services were following one of the basic maxims of covert action: Build assets now for future contingencies. It proved to be persuasive strategy, as the Director personally approved Doole's request and **Southern** received its several million dollars for jets.*

The meeting ended inconclusively. Afterward the CIA officer who had been questioning Doole and the Clandestine Services man was told that he had picked the wrong time to make a stand.

So if the U.S. government decides to intervene covertly in the internal affairs of a Latin American country—or elsewhere, for that matter—Doole's planes will be available to support the operation. These CIA airlines stand ready to drop their legitimate charter business quietly and assume the role they were established for: the transport of arms and mercenaries for the agency's "special operations." The guns will come from the CIA's own stockpiles and from the warehouses of Interarmco and other international arms dealers. The mercenaries will be furnished by the agency's Special Operations Division, and, like the air proprietaries, their connection with the agency will be "plausibly deniable" to the American public and the rest of the world.

Doole and his colleagues in the Clandestine Services have worked hard over the years to build up the airlines and the other assets for paramilitary action. Their successors will fight hard to retain this capability—both because they want to preserve their own secret empire and because they believe in the rightness of CIA clandestine intervention in other countries' internal affairs. They know all too well that if the CIA never intervened, there would be little justification for their existence.

---

* When the CIA tried to sell off Southern in 1973, only three propeller-driven planes were listed in its inventory. It is not known what happened to the jets, but it is a safe bet that somehow they have been transferred to a better-hidden CIA proprietary.

SIX

Propaganda and Disinformation

In psychological warfare . . .
the intelligence agencies of the
democratic countries suffer
from the grave disadvantage that
in attempting to damage the
adversary they must also
deceive their own public.

—VICTOR ZORZA
Washington Post
November 15, 1965

By the mid 1960s most of the professionals in the CIA's Clandestine Services thought that the day of the balloon as an effective delivery vehicle in propaganda operations had long since passed. Years before, in the early rough-and-tumble era of the Cold War, agency operators in West Germany had often used balloons to carry anti-communist literature into the denied areas behind the Iron Curtain. These operations, although lacking in plausible deniability, normally a prerequisite in covert propaganda efforts, had scored high—judging from the numerous angry protests issued by the Soviet Union and its East European satellites.

Since then the propaganda game had evolved into a subtle contest of wits, and the agency's Covert Action Staff had developed far more sophisticated methods for spreading ideological messages. Thus, **there was a sense of "déjà vu" among the covert-action staffers when officers of the Far East Division suggested in 1967 that a new balloon operation be undertaken. The target this time was to be mainland China.**

The People's Republic was at that time in the midst of the cultural revolution. Youthful Red Guards were rampaging throughout the country, shattering customs and laws alike; confusion, near chaos, engulfed the nation. But the CIA's China watchers in Hong Kong and elsewhere on the periphery of the mainland had detected that a reaction was setting in, especially in southern China around Canton and Foochow in the provinces of Kwangtung and Fukien. They believed that a kind of backlash to the excesses of the Red Guards was building, for increasingly groups within the military and among the workers were beginning to resist the Red Guards and to call for a return to traditional law and order.

To the agency's operators, these were conditions worth exploiting. No one really believed that communism could be eliminated

from the mainland, but the short-term political objectives which might be achieved through covert propaganda were too tempting to pass up. China was an avowed enemy of the United States, and the CIA felt that each bit of additional domestic turmoil that could be stirred up made the world's most populous country—already experimenting with long-range ballistic missiles—that much less of a threat to American national security. Furthermore, if Peking could be kept preoccupied with internal problems, then the likelihood of Chinese military intervention in the Vietnamese war, in a manner similar to that so effectively employed years earlier in Korea, could be diminished. Perhaps, too, China could be forced to reduce its material support to North Vietnam and to cut back on its export of revolution to other areas of the developing world.

The operation was accordingly approved by the 303 Committee (now the 40 Committee) and the agency took its balloons out of storage, shipping them to a secret base on Taiwan. There they were loaded with a variety of carefully prepared propaganda materials —leaflets, pamphlets, newspapers—and, when the winds were right, launched to float over the mainland provinces due west of the island. The literature dropped by the balloons had been designed by the agency's propagandists to appear as similar as possible in substance and style to the few publications then being furtively distributed on a small scale by conservative groups inside China. Names of no genuine anti-revolutionary organizations were used; fictitious associations, some identified with the army, others with agricultural communes or urban industrial unions, were invented.

The main thrust of all the propaganda was essentially the same, criticizing the activities (both real and imaginary) of the Red Guards and, by implication, those leaders who inspired or permitted such excesses. It was hoped that the propaganda and its attendant disinformation would create further reactions to the cultural revolution, on one hand adding to the growing domestic confusion and on the other disrupting the internal balance of power among the leadership in Peking. The CIA calculated that when the Chinese realized they were being propagandized, the U.S. government could confidently disclaim any responsibility. The assumed culprit would most likely be Chiang Kai-shek's Taiwan regime, the

agency's witting and cooperative host for the operation.

Almost immediately after it began, the balloon project was a success. The CIA's China watchers soon saw evidence of increased resistance to the Red Guards in the southern provinces. Peking, apparently believing the reaction to the cultural revolution to be greater than it actually was, displayed strong concern over developments in the south. And within weeks, refugees and travelers from the mainland began arriving in Hong Kong with copies of the leaflets and pamphlets that the agency's propagandists had manufactured—a clear indication of the credence being given the false literature by the Chinese masses. It was not long, therefore, before the Clandestine Services were searching for other ways to expand their propaganda effort against the new target.

A decision was therefore made to install on Taiwan a pair of clandestine radio transmitters which would broadcast propaganda —and disinformation—of the same nature as that disseminated by the balloon drops. If the Chinese people accepted the radio broadcasts as genuine, the CIA reasoned, then they might be convinced that the countermovement to the cultural revolution was gaining strength and perhaps think that the time had come to resist the Red Guards and their supporters still more openly.

(

DELETED

DELETED

)

Against a closed-society target, simply providing information and news that the government wishes to keep from its people can have a significant effect. If, in addition, some clever disinformation can be inserted, then so much the better. The listeners, realizing that much of what they are hearing is true, tend to believe that *all* they are told is accurate.

One source of news used by agency propagandists was the CIA's own Foreign Broadcast Information Service (FBIS), which daily monitors open radio broadcasting around the world from more than a dozen listening posts located in such varied places as Hong Kong, Panama, Nigeria, Cyprus, even San Francisco. **The product of the FBIS was also utilized to determine whether the broadcasts of the clandestine transmitters were reaching their target in China and creating the anticipated effect.**

There was a third (and deleterious) way, however, in which the monitoring service played a role in the operation, and the Clandestine Services were slow to correct it. Unlike most of the intelligence collected by the agency, the programs monitored by the FBIS are widely disseminated within the U.S. government and to certain subscribers among the press corps and the academic community. These daily reports, verbatim transcripts translated into English, are packaged and color-coded according to major geographical area— Far East (yellow), Middle East/Africa (blue), Latin America (pink), and so on. But even though the FBIS editors are members of the CIA's Intelligence Directorate, the operators in the Clandestine Services are reluctant to reveal their propaganda operations to them. As a result, for its Far East daily report the FBIS frequently monitored and distributed the texts of programs actually originating from the agency's secret stations on Taiwan

along with the transcripts of broadcasts from real counter-revolutionary organizations on the mainland.

CIA operators seemed untroubled by this development and the accompanying fact that the agency's own China analysts back at headquarters in Washington (along with their colleagues in the State and Defense departments) were being somewhat misled. Nor did they appear to mind that unwitting scholars and newsmen were publishing articles based to some extent on the phony information being reported by the FBIS. Eventually the CIA analysts at home were informed of the existence of the clandestine radios, but no steps were taken to rectify the false data passed on to the other U.S. government agencies or to the press and academia; operational security precluded such revelations. Besides, Communist China was an enemy, and the writings of recognized journalists and professors publicizing its state of near chaos and potential rebellion helped to discredit Peking in the eyes of the world—which was, after all, in keeping with the CIA's interpretation of American foreign policy at the time. **The CIA's secret radios thus proved to be highly successful, even after the Chinese government discovered their origin and announced to its people that the broadcasts were** false.

Meanwhile, the agency's operatives turned to outright disinformation in their effort to exploit China's internal difficulties. For example, (

DELETED

) began to show results. The Red Guards turned their fury on the Ministry of Foreign Affairs, demanding

that Chinese diplomats, too, be cleansed of Western ways and re-dedicated to Mao's principles of communism.

(

DELETED

)

To be sure, propaganda and disinformation are not new phe-nomena. Nations and factions within nations have long employed such techniques to enhance their own images while at the same time attempting to discredit their enemies and rivals. Yet the great advances in communications during the twentieth century have vastly changed the potential of propagandistic effort, making possible rapid, widespread distribution of propaganda material. Nazi Germany refined and made enormous use of the "big lie." The Soviet Union and other communist countries have used many of the methods invented by the Germans and have added new twists of their own. Although the United States did not actively enter the field until World War II, when the OSS and the Office of War Information (OWI) started their psychological-warfare pro-

grams, its propaganda effort has grown—under the eyes of the Covert Action Staff of the CIA's Clandestine Services—to be thoroughly expert.

Working on the CA Staff are sociologists, psychologists, historians, and media specialists—all skilled at selecting "reachable" targets, such as the youth or intellectuals of a particular country, and at getting a message through to them. In planning and carrying out its activities, the branch often works closely with other agency officers in the area divisions. The idea for an operation may be initiated by a field component—say, a station in Africa or Latin America—that sees a special need or a target of opportunity within its area of responsibility; it may originate at headquarters in Langley, either in the propaganda branch or in one of the area divisions; or it may come from the White House, the State Department, the Pentagon, or any member of the U.S. intelligence community in the form of a requirement for the CIA to take action. If it is considered to be a program of major political significance or entailing an inherent high-risk factor—that is, if its exposure would cause substantial embarrassment for the U.S. government—a project proposal developed in the Clandestine Services is submitted to the Director's office for review. Subsequently, the plan will be sent to the 40 Committee for final approval. Thenceforth, control of any propaganda operation and responsibility for its coordination within the Clandestine Services and the government may rest with either the Covert Action Staff or an area division. Certain long-standing operations, such as Radio Free Europe and Radio Liberty, were traditionally under the control of the CA Staff. But responsibility for the newer and smaller operations usually is determined on an *ad hoc* basis, with the CA Staff serving in either an advisory or controlling capacity, depending on the circumstances of the particular undertaking.

A propaganda operation might not be anything more sinister than broadcasting straight news reports or rock music to the countries of Eastern Europe. Others are far more devious. (

DELETED

DELETED

)

The CIA also makes considerable use of forged documents.* During the mid-1960s, for instance, the agency learned that a certain West African country was about to recognize the People's Republic of China and that the local government intended to force the withdrawal of the diplomatic representatives of Nationalist China. This was considered to be contrary to American foreign-policy aims, so the CIA went into action. (

DELETED

)

The Pentagon Papers have revealed some other examples of CIA propaganda and disinformation activities. One top-secret document written in 1954 by Colonel Edward Lansdale, then an agency operator, describes an effort involving North Vietnamese astrologers hired to write predictions about the coming disasters which would befall certain Vietminh leaders and their undertakings, and the success and unity which awaited the South.

Lansdale also mentioned that personnel under his control

---

* Watergate burglar E. Howard Hunt was questioned in 1973 about his forgery of a State Department cable directly linking the Kennedy administration to the assassination of South Vietnamese President Ngo Dinh Diem. "After all," Hunt told the federal prosecutor, "I had been given some training in my past CIA career to do just this sort of thing . . . floating forged newspaper accounts, telegrams, that sort of thing."

had engineered a black psywar strike in Hanoi: leaflets signed by the Vietminh instructing Tonkinese on how to behave for the Vietminh takeover of the Hanoi region in early October, including items about property, money reform, and a three-day holiday of workers upon takeover. The day following the distribution of these leaflets, refugee registration tripled. Two days later Vietminh took to the radio to denounce the leaflets; the leaflets were so authentic in appearance that even most of the rank and file Vietminh were sure that the radio denunciations were a French trick.

Lansdale's black propaganda also had an effect on the American press. One of his bogus leaflets came to the attention of syndicated columnist Joseph Alsop, who was then touring South Vietnam. The leaflet, indicating that many South Vietnamese were to be sent to China to work on the railroads, seemed to have been written by the communists. Alsop naïvely accepted the leaflet at face value and, according to Lansdale, this "led to his sensational, gloomy articles later. . . . Alsop was never told this story." Nor, of course, was the false impression left with Alsop's readers ever corrected.

CIA propaganda activities also entail the publication of books and periodicals. Over the years, the agency has provided direct subsidies to a number of magazines and publishing houses, ranging from Eastern European émigré organs to such reputable firms as Frederick A. Praeger, of New York—which admitted in 1967 that it had published "fifteen or sixteen books" at the CIA's request.

(

DELETED

DELETED   )

Many other anti-communist publishing concerns in Germany, Italy, and France were also supported and encouraged by the agency during the post–World War II years. (

DELETED   ) According to a former high-ranking agency official, (

DELETED   ) **and the Parisian newspaper, "Le Combat."** This same ex-official also recalls with an ironic smile that for several years the agency subsidized the New York communist paper, *The Daily Worker*. In fairness to the *Worker*'s staff, it must be noted that they were unaware of the CIA's assistance, which came in the form of several thousand secretly purchased prepaid subscriptions. The CIA apparently hoped to demonstrate by this means to the American public that the threat of communism in this country was indeed real.

Although the CIA inherited from the OSS responsibility for covert propaganda operations, the agency has no specific authority in the open law to engage in such operations—other than the vague charge to carry out "such other functions and duties related to intelligence affecting the national security as the National Security Council may from time to time direct." Yet since its founding in 1947 the CIA has spent over one billion dollars for propaganda activities (mainly foreign but also domestic) to further what it perceived to be the national interests of the United States.

Sometimes this means simply telling the truth to an audience (called "white" propaganda); other times a mixture of truths, half-truths, and slight distortions is used to slant the views of the audience ("gray" propaganda); and, on occasion, outright lies ("black" propaganda) are used, although usually accompanied for credibility's sake by some truths and half-truths.

"Black" propaganda on the one hand and "disinformation" on the other are virtually indistinguishable. Both refer to the spreading of false information in order to influence people's opinions or actions. Disinformation actually is a special type of "black" propaganda which hinges on absolute secrecy and which is usually supported by false documents; originally, it was something of a

Soviet specialty, and the Russian word for it, *dezinformatsiya*, is virtually a direct analogue of our own. Within the KGB there is even a Department of Disinformation.

On June 2, 1961 (less than two months after the CIA's humiliating failure at the Bay of Pigs), Richard Helms, then Deputy Director of the Clandestine Services, briefed the Senate Internal Security Subcommittee on communist forgeries. Helms discussed thirty-two fraudulent documents "packaged to look like communications to or from American officials." Twenty-two were meant to demonstrate imperialist American plans and ambitions; seventeen of these asserted U.S. interference in the affairs of several free-world countries. Of the seventeen, eleven charged U.S. intervention in private business of Asian nations. One was a fake secret agreement between the Secretary of State and Japanese Premier Kishi permitting use of Japanese troops anywhere in Asia. Another alleged that American policy in Southeast Asia called for U.S. control of the armed forces of all S.E.A.T.O. nations. Two forgeries offered proof that the Americans were plotting the overthrow of Indonesia's Sukarno; the remaining two were merely meant to demonstrate that the U.S. government, despite official disclaimers, was secretly supplying the anti-Sukarno rebels with military aid.

These last examples concerning Indonesia are especially interesting. A cursory examination of the documents, as submitted by Helms, indicates that they were indeed rather crude forgeries, **but their message was accurate. Not only did the CIA in 1958 support efforts to overthrow the Sukarno government,** but Helms himself, as second-ranking official in Clandestine Services, knew it well. And he knew that the **"official disclaimers" to which he referred were deceptions and outright lies issued by U.S. government spokesmen.** Helms' testimony was released to the public with the approval of the CIA, which was, in effect, targeting a propaganda operation against the American people. Not only did he lie about the communists' lying (which is not to say that they are not indeed culpable), but Helms in the process quite ably managed to avoid discussion of the pervasive lying the CIA commits in the name of the United States.

The Radios

Until 1971, the CIA's largest propaganda operations by far were Radio Free Europe (RFE) and Radio Liberty (RL). RFE broadcast to Poland, Hungary, Czechoslovakia, Romania, and Bulgaria, while RL was aimed at the Soviet Union. These ostensibly private stations had been started by the agency in the early 1950s at the height of the Cold War. They operated under the cover provided by their New York–based boards of directors, which were made up principally of distinguished statesmen, retired military leaders, and corporate executives. With studios in Munich and transmitters in West Germany, Spain, Portugal, and Taiwan, the two stations broadcast thousands of hours of programs a year into the communist countries. Their combined annual budgets ranged from $30 to $35 million, and the CIA financed over 95 percent of the costs.*

In their early years, both RFE and RL quite stridently promoted the "rolling back" of the Iron Curtain. (Radio Liberty was originally named Radio Liberation.) The tone of their broadcasts softened considerably in the aftermath of the 1957 Hungarian revolt, when RFE was subjected to severe criticism for its role in seeming to incite continued, but inevitably futile, resistance by implying that American assistance would be forthcoming. During and after the Hungarian events, it became quite clear that the United States would not actively participate in freeing the captive nations, and the emphasis at both RFE and RL was changed to promote liberalization within the communist system through peaceful change. The CIA continued, however, to finance both stations, to provide them with key personnel, and to control program content.

The ostensible mission of RFE and RL was to provide accurate

---

* A particularly deceptive aspect of the RFE operation was, and is, the annual fund-raising drive carried out in the United States. Under the auspices of the Advertising Council, RFE solicits funds with the clear implication that if money is not donated by the American public the station will no longer be able to function and the "truth" will not get through to Eastern Europe. Although between $12 and $20 million in free advertising time was made available in 1969, for example, less than $100,000 was raised from a not terribly alarmed public.

information to the people of Eastern Europe. In this aim they were largely successful, and their programs reached millions of listeners. While RFE and RL broadcasts contained a certain amount of distortion, they were, especially in the early years, considerably more accurate than the Eastern European media. But to many in the CIA the primary value of the radios was to sow discontent in Eastern Europe and, in the process, to weaken the communist governments. Hard-liners in the agency pointed to the social agitation in Poland which brought Wladyslaw Gomulka to power in 1956, the Hungarian uprising in 1957, and the fall of Czech Stalinist Antonin Novotny in 1967 as events which RFE helped to bring about. Others in the CIA did not specifically connect RFE or RL to such dramatic occurrences, but instead stressed the role of the two stations in the more gradual de-Stalinization and liberalization of Eastern Europe.

Like most propaganda operations, RFE's and RL's principal effect has been to contribute to existing trends in their target areas and sometimes to accentuate those trends. Even when events in Eastern Europe have worked out to the agency's satisfaction, any direct contribution by the radios would be nearly impossible to prove. In any case, whatever the success of the two stations, the CIA intended from the beginning that they play an activist role in the affairs of Eastern Europe—well beyond being simply sources of accurate news. For, in addition to transmitting information to Eastern Europe and harassing the communist governments, RFE and RL have also provided the Clandestine Services with covert assets which could be used against the Soviet Union and Eastern Europe.

The two radio stations, with their large staffs of Eastern European refugees, are a ready-made source of agents, contacts, information, and cover for operations. Among further radio-derived sources of intelligence was the comparatively large number of letters RFE and RL received from their listeners in Eastern Europe. Delivered by mail and by travelers coming to the West, these letters were considered by the agency's clandestine operators to be an intelligence-collection resource. RFE and RL émigré personnel used the letters and other information available to the

stations to prepare written analyses of what was happening in the East. Much of this analysis, however, was thought to be of doubtful value back at CIA headquarters, and was held in low esteem throughout the U.S. intelligence community.

However debatable the direct effect of RFE and RL on events in Eastern Europe, the governments of the communist countries obviously were quite disturbed by the stations. Extensive efforts were made to jam their signals, and by the late 1950s the communist intelligence services were actively trying to discredit the stations and to infiltrate the radios' staffs. In many cases, they succeeded, and by the mid-1960s the general view at CIA headquarters was that the two facilities were widely penetrated by communist agents and that much of the analysis coming out of Munich was based on false information planted by opposition agents. During this same time the spirit of East-West *détente* was growing, and many officers in the CIA thought that RFE and RL had outlived their usefulness. Supporters of the stations were finding it increasingly difficult at budget time to justify their yearly costs. Even the Eastern European governments were showing a declining interest in the stations, and the jamming efforts fell off considerably.

The agency carried out several internal studies on the utility of RFE and RL, and the results in each case favored phasing out CIA funding. But after each study a few old-timers in the CIA, whose connections with the stations went back to their beginnings, would come up with new and dubious reasons why the radios should be continued. The emotional attachment of these veteran operators to RFE and RL was extremely strong. Also defending the stations were those influential personalities, like former N.A.T.O. chief Lucius Clay, CBS president Frank Stanton, and General Motors chairman James Roche, who made up the radios' boards of directors. All of these efforts ran counter to attempts of the CIA's own Planning, Programming and Budgeting Staff to end agency support. Additionally, the CIA's top management appeared reluctant to part with the stations because of a fear that if the $30 to $35 million in annual payments were ended, that money would be irrevocably lost to the CIA. Each internal agency study which called for the end of the CIA's involvement invariably

led to nothing more than yet another study being made.

Thus, bureaucratic inertia, the unwillingness of the USIA to take over the radios' functions, and well-placed lobbying efforts by RFL and RE boards of directors combined to keep CIA funds flowing into both stations through the 1960s. Even when agency financing of the stations became widely known during the 1967 scandal surrounding the CIA's penetration and manipulation of the National Student Association, the agency did not reduce its support. In the aftermath of that scandal, President Johnson's special review group, the Katzenbach committee, recommended that the CIA not be allowed to finance "any of the nation's educational or private voluntary organizations." Still, with the approval of the White House, the agency did not let go of RFE or RL.

No change occurred until January 1971, when Senator Clifford Case of New Jersey spoke out against the CIA subsidies to the radios and proposed legislation for open funding.

Case's move attracted quite a bit of attention in the media and it became obvious that the Senator was not going to back down in the face of administration pressure. When the Senate Foreign Relations Committee scheduled hearings on Case's bill and the Senator threatened to call former RFE employees as witnesses, the CIA decided that the time had come to divest itself of the two stations. Open congressional funding became a reality, and by the end of 1971 CIA financial involvement in RFE and RL was officially ended. Whether the agency has also dropped all its covert assets connected with them is not known, but, given past experience, that is not likely. For the time being, the largest threat to the future of RFE and RL would seem to be not Congress, which will probably vote money indefinitely, but the West German government of Willy Brandt. Now that the stations are in the open, Bonn faces pressure from the Eastern European countries to forbid them to broadcast on German soil. (

DELETED

) but he still might at some point accept the argument, as part of an effort to further the East-West *détente*, that RFE and RL represent unnecessary obstacles to improved relations.

Other Propaganda Operations

The CIA has always been interested in reaching and encouraging dissidents in Eastern Europe and the Soviet Union. In the early days of the Cold War, the agency sent its own agents and substantial amounts of money behind the Iron Curtain to keep things stirred up, mostly with disastrous results. In more recent times, operations against Eastern Europe and the U.S.S.R. have become less frequent and less crude. The agency, however, has continued to maintain its contacts with émigré groups in Western Europe and the United States. These groups are sometimes well informed on what is happening in their home countries, and they often provide a conduit for the CIA in its dealings with dissidents in those countries.

(

DELETED

) has found the émigré group to be of only marginal usefulness.

Another organization heavily subsidized by the CIA was the Asia Foundation. Established by the agency in 1956, with a carefully chosen board of directors, the foundation was designed to promote academic and public interest in the East. It sponsored scholarly research, supported conferences and symposia, and ran academic exchange programs, with a CIA subsidy that reached $8 million dollars a year. While most of the foundation's activities were legitimate, the CIA also used it, through penetrations among the officers and members, to fund anti-communist academicians in various Asian countries, to disseminate throughout Asia a negative vision of mainland China, North Vietnam, and North Korea, and to recruit foreign agents and new case officers. Although the foundation often served as a cover for clandestine operations, its main purpose was to promote the spread of ideas which were anticommunist and pro-American—sometimes subtly and sometimes stridently.

The focus of the Asia Foundation's activities was overseas, but the organization's impact tended to be greater in the American academic community than in the Far East. Large numbers of American intellectuals participated in foundation programs, and they—usually unwittingly—contributed to the popularizing of CIA ideas about the Far East. Designed—and justified at budget time—as an overseas propaganda operation, the Asia Foundation also was regularly guilty of propagandizing the American people with agency views on Asia.

The agency's connection with the Asia Foundation came to light just after the 1967 exposure of CIA subsidies to the National Student Association. The foundation clearly was one of the organizations which the CIA was banned from financing and, under the recommendations of the Katzenbach committee, the decision was made to end CIA funding. A complete cut-off after 1967, however, would have forced the foundation to shut down, so the agency made it the beneficiary of a large "severance payment" in order to give it a couple of years to develop alternative sources of fund-

ing. Assuming the CIA has not resumed covert financing, the Asia Foundation has apparently made itself self-sufficient by now.

During the 1960s the CIA developed proprietary companies of a new type for use in propaganda operations. These proprietaries are more compact and more covert than relatively unwieldy and now exposed fronts like the Asia Foundation and Radio Free Europe. (

DELETED

) More and more, as the United States cuts back its overt aid programs and withdraws from direct involvement in foreign countries, the agency will probably be called upon to carry out similar missions in other nations.

The CIA has also used defectors from communist governments for propaganda purposes—a practice which has had more impact in this country than overseas. These defectors, without any prodding by the CIA, would have interesting stories to tell of politics and events in their homelands, but almost all are immediately taken under the CIA's control and subjected to extensive secret debriefings at a special defector reception center near Frankfurt, West Germany, or, in the cases of particularly knowledgeable ones, at agency "safe houses" in the United States. In return for the intelligence supplied about the defector's former life and work, the CIA usually takes care of his resettlement in the West, even providing a new identity if necessary. Sometimes, after the lengthy debriefing has been finished, the agency will encourage—and will help—the defector to write articles or books about his past life. As he may still be living at a CIA facility or be dependent on the agency for his livelihood, the defector would be extremely reluctant to jeopardize his future by not cooperating. The CIA does not try to alter the defector's writings drastically; it simply influences him to leave out certain information because of security considerations, or because the thrust of the information runs counter to existing American policy. The inclusion of information justifying U.S. or CIA practices is, of course, encouraged, and the CIA will provide whatever literary assistance is needed by the defector. While such books tend to show the communist intelligence services as diabolical and unprincipled organs (which they are), almost never do these books describe triumphs by the opposition services over the CIA. Although the other side does indeed win on occasion, the agency would prefer that the world did not know that. And the defector dependent on the CIA will hardly act counter to its interests.

In helping the defector with his writing, the agency often steers him toward a publisher. Even some of the public-relations aspects of promoting his book may be aided by the CIA, as in the case of Major Ladislav Bittman, a Czech intelligence officer who defected in 1968. Prior to the 1972 publication of his book, *The Deception Game,* Bittman was interviewed by the *Wall Street*

Journal, which quoted him on U.S. intelligence's use of the disinformation techniques. "It was our opinion," the former Czech operative said, "that the Americans had more effective means than this sort of trickery—things such as economic-aid programs—that were more influential than any black propaganda operation."

While Bittman may well have been reflecting attitudes held by his former colleagues in Czech intelligence, his words must be considered suspect. The Czechs almost certainly know something about the CIA's propaganda and disinformation programs, just as the CIA knows of theirs. But Bittman's statement, taken along with his extensive descriptions of Czech and Russian disinformation programs, reflects exactly the image the CIA wants to promote to the American public—that the communists are always out to defraud the West, while the CIA, skillfully uncovering these deceits, eschews such unprincipled tactics.

To the CIA, propaganda through book publishing has long been a successful technique. In 1953 the agency backed the publication of a book called *The Dynamics of Soviet Society,* which was written by Walt Rostow, later President Johnson's Assistant for National Security Affairs, and other members of the staff of the Center for International Studies at the Massachusetts Institute of Technology. The center had been set up with CIA money in 1950, and this book was published in two versions, one classified (for the CIA and government policymakers) and the other unclassified (for the public). Both versions, except in some minor details, promoted the thesis that the Soviet Union is an imperialistic power bent on world conquest, and that it is the responsibility of the United States to blunt the communist menace.

Most CIA book operations, however, are more subtle and clandestine. A former CIA official who specialized in Soviet affairs recalls how one day in 1967 a CIA operator on the Covert Action Staff showed him a book called *The Foreign Aid Programs of the Soviet Bloc and Communist China* by a German named Kurt Muller. The book looked interesting to the Soviet expert, and he asked to borrow it. The Covert Action man replied, "Keep it. We've got hundreds more downstairs." Muller's book was some-

thing less than an unbiased treatment of the subject; it was highly critical of communist foreign assistance to the Third World. The Soviet specialist is convinced that the agency had found out Muller was interested in communist foreign-aid programs, encouraged him to write a book which would have a strong anti-communist slant, provided him with information, and then helped to get the book published and distributed.

Financing books is a standard technique used by all intelligence services. Many writers are glad to write on subjects which will further their own careers, and with a slant that will contribute to the propaganda objectives of a friendly agency. Books of this sort, however, add only a false aura of respectability and authority to the information the intelligence agency would like to see spread —even when that information is perfectly accurate—because they are by definition restricted from presenting an objective analysis of the subject under consideration. And once exposed, both the writer and his data become suspect. (

DELETED

)

Spies, however, do not keep journals. They simply do not take that kind of risk, nor do they have the time to do so while they are leading double lives.

(

DELETED

DELETED

) Allen Dulles seemed to be rubbing salt in their wounds when he wrote in *The Craft of Intelligence* that the Penkovsky defection had shaken the Soviet intelligence services with the knowledge that the West had located Russian officials willing to work "in place for long periods of time," and others who "have never been 'surfaced' and [who] for their own protection must remain unknown to the public."

And, of course, the publication of *The Penkovsky Papers* opened the Soviets up to the embarrassment of having the world learn that the top level of their government had been penetrated by a Western spy. Furthermore, Penkovsky's success as an agent made the CIA look good, both to the American people and to the rest of the world. Failures such as the Bay of Pigs might be forgiven and forgotten if the agency could recruit agents like Penkovsky to accomplish the one task the CIA is weakest at—gathering intelligence from inside the Soviet Union or China.

The facts were otherwise, however. **In the beginning, Penkovsky was not a CIA spy. He worked for British intelligence. He had tried to join the CIA in Turkey, but he had been turned down, in large part because the Soviet Bloc Division of the Clandestine Services was overly careful not to be taken in by KGB provocateurs and double agents.** To the skittish CIA operators, Penkovsky seemed too good to be true, especially in the period following the Burgess-McLean catastrophe. The CIA had also suffered several recent defeats at the hands of the KGB in Europe, and it was understandably reluctant to be duped again.

Penkovsky, however, was determined to spy for the West, and in 1960 he made contact with British intelligence, which eventually recruited him. The British informed the CIA of Penkovsky's availability and offered to conduct the operation as a joint project. **CIA operators in Moscow and elsewhere participated in the elaborated clandestine techniques used to receive information from Penkovsky and to debrief the Soviet spy on his visits to Western Europe.** (

DELETED
)

The Penkovsky Papers was a best-seller around the world, and especially in the United States. Its publication certainly caused discomfort in the Soviet Union. (

DELETED

)

Richard Helms years later again referred to Penkovsky in this vein, although not by name, when he claimed in a speech before the American Society of Newspaper Editors that "a number of well-placed and courageous Russians . . . helped us" in uncovering the Soviet move. **One person taken in by this deception was** Senator Milton Young of North Dakota, who serves on the CIA oversight subcommittee. In a 1971 Senate debate on cutting the intelligence budget, the Senator said, "And if you want to read something very interesting and authoritative where intelligence is concerned, read the Penkovsky papers . . . this is a very interesting story, on why the intelligence we had in Cuba was so important to us, and on what the Russians were thinking and just how far they would go."

Yet the CIA intelligence analysts who were working on the Cuban problem at the time of the missile crisis and preparing the

agency's intelligence reports for the President up to and after the discovery of the Soviet missiles saw no such information from Penkovsky or any other Soviet spy. The key intelligence that led to the discovery of the missiles came from the analysis of satellite photography of the U.S.S.R., Soviet ship movements, U-2 photographs of Cuba, and information supplied by Cuban refugees. Penkovsky's technical background information, provided well before the crisis, was of some use—but not of major or critical importance.

Several scholars of the Soviet Union have independently characterized *The Penkovsky Papers* as being partly bogus and as not having come from Penkovsky's "journal." The respected Soviet expert and columnist for the *Manchester Guardian* and the *Washington Post,* Victor Zorza, wrote that "the book could have been compiled only by the Central Intelligence Agency." Zorza pointed out that Penkovsky had neither the time nor the opportunity to have produced such a manuscript; that the book's publisher (Doubleday and Company) and translator (Peter Deriabin, himself a KGB defector to the CIA) both refused to produce the original Russian manuscript for inspection; and that *The Penkovsky Papers* contained errors of style, technique, and fact that Penkovsky would not have made.

British intelligence also was not above scoring a propaganda victory of its own in the Penkovsky affair. Penkovsky's contact officer had been MI-6's Greville Wynne, who, working under the cover of being a businessman, had been arrested at the same time as Penkovsky and later exchanged for the Soviet spy Gordon Lonsdale. **When Wynne returned to Britain, MI-6 helped him** write a book about his experiences, called *Contact on Gorky Street.* British intelligence wanted the book published in part to make some money for Wynne, who had gone through the ordeal of a year and a half in Soviet prisons, but the MI-6's main motive was to counteract the extremely unfavorable publicity that had been generated by the defection of its own senior officer, Harold "Kim" Philby, in 1963, and the subsequent publication of his memoirs prepared under the auspices of the KGB.

Interestingly, nowhere in *Contact on Gorky Street* does Wynne cite the help he received from the CIA. The reason for this omission could have been professional jealousy on the part of British intelligence, good British manners (i.e., not mentioning the clandestine activities of a friendly intelligence service), or most likely, an indication of the small role played by the CIA in the operation.

Another book-publishing effort in which the CIA may or may not have been involved—to some degree—was *Khrushchev Remembers*, and the second volume of Khrushchev memoirs scheduled for publication this year. While these autobiographical and somewhat self-serving works unquestionably originated with the former Soviet premier himself, there are a number of curious circumstances connected with their transmission from Moscow to Time Inc. in New York, and to its book-publishing division, Little, Brown and Company. Time Inc. has been less than forthcoming about how it gained access to the 180 hours of taped reminiscences upon which the books are based, and how the tapes were taken out of the U.S.S.R. without the knowledge of the Soviet government or the ubiquitous and proficient KGB. The whole operation—especially its political implication—was simply too important to have been permitted without at least tacit approval by Soviet authorities. Unlike Alexander Solzhenitsyn, Khrushchev was subsequently neither denounced nor exiled by Moscow's all-powerful party chiefs.

Most of the explanations offered by Time Inc. to clarify the various mysteries involved in this episode have a slightly disingenuous air. They may be true, but a number of highly regarded American and British scholars and intelligence officers dealing with Soviet affairs find them difficult to accept in toto. Why, for example, did Time Inc. find it necessary to take the risky step of sending a copy of the bound galleys of the book to its Moscow bureau—secretly via Helsinki—before it was published? The complete story of the Khrushchev memoirs, in short, may never be publicly known. And if it is, it may turn out to be another example of secret U.S.-Soviet cooperation, of two hostile powers giving wide circulation to information that each wants to see published, while

collaborating to keep their operations away from the eyes of the general public on both sides. After all, the publication of the first volume, in 1971 had a relatively happy effect—it supported Moscow's anti-Stalinists, and in turn increased the prospects for detente.

SEVEN

Espionage and Counterespionage

The soul of the spy is somehow
the model of us all.

—JACQUES BARZUN

Intelligence agencies, in the popular view, are organizations of glamorous master spies who, in the best tradition of James Bond, daringly uncover the evil intentions of a nation's enemies. In reality, however, the CIA has had comparatively little success in acquiring intelligence through secret agents. This classical form of espionage has for many years ranked considerably below space satellites, code-breaking, and other forms of technical collection as a source of important foreign information to the U.S. government. Even open sources (the press and other communications media) and official channels (diplomats, military attachés, and the like) provide more valuable information than the Clandestine Services of the CIA. Against its two principal targets, the Soviet Union and Communist China, the effectiveness of CIA spies is virtually nil. With their closed societies and powerful internal-security organizations, the communist countries have proved practically impenetrable to the CIA.

To be sure, the agency has pulled off an occasional espionage coup, but these have generally involved "walk-ins"—defectors who take the initiative in offering their services to the agency. Remember that in 1955, when Oleg Penkovsky first approached CIA operators in Ankara, Turkey, to discuss the possibility of becoming an agent, he was turned away, because it was feared that he might be a double agent. Several years later, he was recruited by bolder British intelligence officers. Nearly all of the other Soviets and Chinese who either spied for the CIA or defected to the West did so without being actively recruited by America's leading espionage agency.

Technically speaking, anyone who turns against his government is a defector. A successfully recruited agent or a walk-in who offers his services as a spy is known as a defector-in-place. He has not yet physically deserted his country, but has in fact defected politi-

cally in secret. Refugees and émigrés are also defectors, and the CIA often uses them as spies when they can be persuaded to risk return to their native lands. In general, a defector is a person who has recently bolted his country and is simply willing to trade his knowledge of his former government's activities for political asylum in another nation; that some defections are accompanied by a great deal of publicity is generally due to the CIA's desire to obtain public approbation of its work.

Escapees from the U.S.S.R. and Eastern Europe are handled by the CIA's defector reception center at Camp King near Frankfurt, West Germany. There they are subjected to extensive debriefing and interrogation by agency officers who are experts at draining from them their full informational potential. Some defectors are subjected to questioning that lasts for months; a few are interrogated for a year or more.

A former CIA chief of station in Germany remembers with great amusement his role in supervising the lengthy debriefing of a Soviet lieutenant, a tank-platoon commander, who fell in love with a Czech girl and fled with her to the West after the Soviet invasion of Czechoslovakia in 1968. The ex-agency senior officer relates how he had to play marriage counselor when the couple's relationship started to sour, causing the lieutenant to lose his willingness to talk. By saving the romance, the chief of station succeeded in keeping the information flowing from the Soviet lieutenant. Although a comparatively low-level Soviet defector of this sort would seem to have small potential for providing useful intelligence, the CIA has had so little success in penetrating the Soviet military that the lieutenant underwent months of questioning. Through him, agency analysts were able to learn much about how Soviet armor units, and the ground forces in general, are organized, their training and tactical procedures, and the mechanics of their participation in the build-up that preceded the invasion of Czechoslovakia. This was hardly intelligence of strategic importance, but the CIA's Clandestine Services have no choice but to pump each low-level Soviet defector for all he is worth.

The same former chief of station also recalls with pride the defection of Yevgeny Runge, a KGB illegal (or "deep cover"

agent) in late 1967. Runge, like the more infamous Colonel Rudolf Abel from Brooklyn and Gordon Lonsdale of London, was a Soviet operator who lived for years under an assumed identity in West Germany. Unlike his colleagues, however, he was not exposed and arrested. Instead, Runge defected to the CIA when he lost interest in his clandestine work. According to the ex-agency official, Runge was of greater intelligence value to the U.S. government than Penkovsky. This assessment, however, is highly debatable because Runge provided no information which the CIA's intelligence analysts found to be useful in determining Soviet strategic capabilities or intentions. On the other hand, the KGB defector did reveal much concerning the methods and techniques of Soviet clandestine intelligence operations in Germany. To CIA operators who have been unsuccessful in penetrating the Soviet government and who have consequently become obsessed with the actions of the opposition, the defection of an undercover operator like Runge represents a tremendous emotional windfall, and they are inclined to publicize it as an intelligence coup.

Once the CIA is satisfied that a defector has told all that he knows, the resettlement team takes over. The team's objective is to find a place for the defector to live where he will be free from the fear of reprisal and happy enough neither to disclose his connections with the CIA nor, more important, to be tempted to return to his native country. Normally, the team works out a cover story for the defector, invents a new identity for him, and gives him enough money (often a lifetime pension) to make the transition to a new way of life. The most important defectors are brought to the United States (either before or after their debriefing), but the large majority are permanently settled in Western Europe, Canada, or Latin America.*

The defector's adjustment to his new country is often quite difficult. For security reasons, he is usually cut off from any contact with his native land and, therefore, from his former friends and those members of his family who did not accompany him into

---

* On occasion, a defector will be hired as a contract employee to do specialized work as a translator, interrogator, counterintelligence analyst, or the like, for the Clandestine Services.

exile. He may not even know the language of the country where he is living. Thus, a large percentage of defectors become psychologically depressed with their new lives once the initial excitement of resettlement wears off. A few have committed suicide. To try to keep the defector content, the CIA assigns a case officer to each one for as long as is thought necessary. The case officer stays in regular contact with the defector and helps solve any problems that may arise. With a particularly volatile defector, the agency maintains even closer surveillance, including telephone taps and mail intercepts, to guard against unwanted developments.

In some instances, case officers will watch over the defector for the rest of his life. More than anything else, the agency wants no defector to become so dissatisfied that he will be tempted to return to his native country. Of course, redefection usually results in a propaganda victory for the opposition; of greater consequence, however, is the fact that the redefector probably will reveal everything he knows about the CIA in order to ease his penalty for having defected in the first place. Moreover, when a defector does return home, the agency has to contend with the nagging fear that all along it has been dealing with a double agent and that all the intelligence he revealed was part of a plot to mislead the CIA. The possibilities for deception in the defector game are endless, and the communist intelligence services have not failed to take advantage of them.

Bugs and Other Devices

Strictly speaking, classical espionage uses human beings to gather information; technical espionage employs machines, such as photographic satellites, long-range electronic sensors, and communications-intercept stations. Technical collection systems were virtually unknown before World War II, but the same technological explosion which has affected nearly every other aspect of modern life over the last twenty-five years has also drastically changed the intelligence trade. Since the war, the United States has poured tens of billions of dollars into developing ever more advanced machines to keep track of what other countries—especially communist

countries—are doing. Where once the agent sought secret information with little support beyond his own wits, he now is provided with a dazzling assortment of audio devices, miniaturized cameras, and other exotic tools.

Within the CIA's Clandestine Services, the Technical Services Division (TSD) is responsible for developing most of the equipment used in the modern spying game. Some of the paraphernalia is unusual: a signal transmitter disguised as a false tooth, a pencil which looks and writes like an ordinary pencil but can also write invisibly on special paper, a bizarre automobile rear-view mirror that allows the driver to observe not the traffic behind but the occupants of the back seat instead. Except for audio devices, special photographic equipment, and secret communications systems, there is in fact little applicability for even the most imaginative tools in real clandestine operations.

Secret intelligence services in past times were interested only in recruiting agents who had direct access to vital foreign information. Today the CIA and other services also search for the guard or janitor who is in a position to install a bug or a phone tap in a sensitive location. Even the telephone and telegraph companies of other countries have become targets for the agency. In addition to the foreign and defense ministries, the CIA operators usually try to penetrate the target nation's communications systems—a task which is on occasion aided by American companies, particularly the International Telephone and Telegraph Company. Postal services also are subverted for espionage purposes.

Most agency operators receive training in the installation and servicing of bugs and taps, but the actual planting of audio surveillance devices is usually carried out by TSD specialists brought in from headquarters or a regional operational support center, like (**DELETED**). The more complex the task, the more likely it is that headquarters specialists will be utilized to do the job. On some operations, however, agents will be specially trained by TSD experts, or even the responsible case officer, in the skills of installing such equipment.

Audio operations vary, of course, in complexity and sensitivity —that is, in risk potential. A classic, highly dangerous operation

calls for a great deal of planning, during which the site is surveyed in extensive detail. Building and floor plans must be acquired or developed from visual surveillance. The texture of the walls, the colors of interior paints, and the like must be determined. Activity in the building and in the room or office where the device is to be installed must be observed and recorded to ascertain when the area is accessible. The movements of the occupants and any security patrols must be also known. When all this has been accomplished, the decision is made as to where and when to plant the bug. Usually, the site will be entered at night or on a weekend and, in accordance with carefully pre-planned and tightly timed actions, the audio device will be installed. High-speed, silent drills may be used to cut into the wall, and after installation of the bug, the damage will be repaired with quick-drying plaster and covered by a paint exactly matching the original. The installation may also be accomplished from an adjoining room, or one above or below (if a ceiling or floor placement is called for).

The agency's successes with bugs and taps have usually been limited to the non-communist countries, where relatively lax internal-security systems do not deny the CIA operations the freedom of movement necessary to install eavesdropping devices. **A report on clandestine activities in Latin America during the 1960s by the CIA Inspector General, for example, revealed that a good part of the intelligence collected by the agency in that region came from audio devices. In quite a few of the Latin nations, the report noted, the CIA was regularly intercepting the telephone conversations of important officials and had managed to place bugs in the homes and offices of many key personnel, up to and including cabinet ministers. In some allied countries the agency shares in the information acquired from audio surveillance conducted by the host intelligence service, which often receives technical assistance from the CIA for this very purpose—and may be penetrated by the CIA in the process.**

Audio devices are fickle. As often as not, they fail to work after they have been installed, or they function well for a few days, then suddenly fall silent. Sometimes they are quickly discovered by the local security services, or, suspecting that a room

may be bugged, the opposition employs effective countermeasures. The Soviet KGB has the habit of renting homes and offices in foreign countries and then building new interior walls, floors, and ceilings covering the original ones in key rooms—thus completely baffling the effectiveness of any bugs that may have been installed. The simplest way to negate audio surveillance—and it is a method universally employed—is to raise the noise level in the room by constantly playing a radio or a hi-fi set. The music and other extraneous noises tend to mask the sounds of the voices that the bug is intended to capture; unlike the human ear, audio devices cannot distinguish among sounds.

CIA technicians are constantly working on new listening devices in the hope of improving the agency's ability to eavesdrop. Ordinary audio equipment, along with other clandestine devices, are developed by the Technical Services Division. In addition to espionage tools, the TSD devises gadgets for use in other covert activities, such as paramilitary operations. Plastic explosives, incapacitating and lethal drugs, and silent weapons—high-powered crossbows, for example—are designed and fabricated for special operations. The more complex or sophisticated instruments used by the CIA's secret operators are, however, produced by the agency's Directorate of Science and Technology. This component also assists other groups within the CIA engaging in clandestine research and development. (

DELETED

) The D/S & T, furthermore, assists the Office of Communications in devising new and improved methods of communications intercept and security countermeasures.

Although the experts in the Science and Technology Directorate have done much outstanding work in some areas—for example, overhead reconnaissance—their performance in the audio field for clandestine application is often less than satisfactory. One such device long under development was a laser beam which could be

aimed at a closed window from outside and used to pick up the vibrations of the sound waves caused by a conversation inside the room. This system was successfully tested in the field—in West Africa—but it never seemed to function properly elsewhere, except in the United States. Another (

DELETED

)

When CIA operators are successful in planting a bug or making a tap, they send the information thus acquired back to the Clandestine Services at headquarters in Langley with the source clearly identified. However, when the Clandestine Services, in turn, pass the information on to the intelligence analysts in the agency and elsewhere in the federal government, the source is disguised or the information is buried in a report from a real agent. For example, the Clandestine Services might credit the information to "a source in the foreign ministry who has reported reliably in the past" or "a Western businessman with wide contacts in the local government." In the minds of the covert operators, it is more important to protect the source than to present the information straightforwardly. This may guarantee "safe" sources, but it also handicaps the analysts in making a confident judgment of the accuracy of the report's content.*

* This withholding of information within the government for security reasons is not a new phenomenon in the intelligence business. The joint congressional committee investigating the Japanese attack on Pearl Harbor found that "the fact the Japanese codes had been broken was regarded as of

(

DELETED

---

more importance than the information obtained from decoded traffic. The result of this rather specious premise was to leave large numbers of policy-making and enforcement officials in Washington completely oblivious of the most pertinent information concerning Japan."

DELETED

DELETED

)

The fertile imaginations of the S&T Directorate experts during the following years produced many more unique collection schemes aimed at solving the mysteries of China's strategic missile program. Most eventually proved to be unworkable, and at least one entailed a frighteningly high-risk potential. The silliest of all, however, called for the creation of a small one-man airplane that could theoretically be packaged in two large suitcases. In concept, an agent along with the suitcases would somehow be infiltrated into the denied area, where, after performing his espionage mission, he would assemble the aircraft and fly to safety over the nearest friendly border. Even the chief of the Clandestine Services refused to have anything to do with this scheme, and the project died on the drawing boards.

(

DELETED

DELETED

)

The technical difficulties involved in the (**DELETED**) system and the (**DELETED**) device were too great and too time-consuming for either to be fully developed by their inventors before improvements in intelligence-satellite surveillance programs were achieved. Other clandestine collection devices—a few more sensibly contrived, but most of dubious value—were also developed by the agency's technicians and may now be in operation. The CIA's technical experts often feel compelled to build exotic systems only because of the mechanical challenge they pose. Such efforts might be justified by an intelligence requirement; unfortunately, too many intelligence requirements are not honestly based on the needs of the policy-makers but are instead generated by and for the CIA and the other intelligence-community members alone.

The Technical Collection Explosion

While technology has increasingly tended to mechanize classical espionage, its most important impact on the intelligence trade has been in large-scale collection—satellites, long-range sensors, and the interception of communications. These technical espionage systems have become far and away the most important sources of information on America's principal adversaries. Overhead-reconnaissance programs have provided much detailed information on Soviet and Chinese missile programs, troop movements, and other military developments. They have also produced valuable information regarding North Vietnamese infiltration of South Vietnam and North Korean military preparations against South Korea. And such collection has frequently contributed to the U.S. government's knowledge of events in the Middle East.

As technical collection becomes more refined, classical spies have, of course, become nearly obsolete in clandestine operations against the more important target countries. So, too, has the shift to technical espionage caused America's intelligence costs to skyrocket to more than $6 billion yearly. Not only are classical spies relatively cheap, but technical collection systems, producing incredible amounts of information, require huge numbers of people to process and analyze this mass of raw data.

In terms of money spent and personnel involved, the CIA is very much a **junior partner to the Pentagon in the technical-espionage field. The Defense Department has an overall intelligence budget of about $5 billion a year, some 75 to 80 percent of which is spent on technical collection and processing. The CIA's technical programs, however, amount to no more than $150 million yearly. (This is exclusive of several hundred million in funds annually supplied by the Pentagon for certain community-wide programs, such as satellite development, in which the agency shares.) Similarly, there are tens of thousands of people—both military and civilian—working for the Defense Department in the technical fields, whereas the CIA only has about 1,500 such personnel.**

Still, the agency has made a substantial contribution to research

and development in technical espionage. Over the years, CIA scientists have scored major successes by developing the U-2 and **SR-71** spy planes, in perfecting the first workable photographic-reconnaissance satellites, and in producing outstanding advances in stand-off, or long-range, electronic sensors, such as over-the-horizon radars and stationary satellites. A good part of these research and operating costs have been funded by the Pentagon, and in several instances the programs were ultimately converted into joint CIA-Pentagon operations or "captured" by the military services.

America's first experience in technical espionage came in the form of radio intercepts and code-breaking, an art known as communications intelligence (COMINT). Although Secretary of State Henry Stimson closed down the cryptanalytical section of the State Department in 1939 with the explanation that "gentlemen do not read each other's mail," COMINT was revived, and played an important part in U.S. intelligence activities during World War II. In the immediate postwar period this activity was initially reduced, then expanded once again as the Cold War intensified. In 1952 the President, by secret executive order, established the National Security Agency (NSA) to intercept and decipher the communications of both the nation's enemies and friends and to ensure that U.S. codes were secure from similar eavesdropping. The NSA, though placed under the control of the Defense Department, soon established an independent bureaucratic identity of its own—and at present has a huge budget of well over a billion dollars per annum and a workforce of some 25,000 personnel.

Before the NSA can break into and read foreign codes and ciphers, it must first intercept the encoded and encrypted messages of the target country. To make these intercepts, it must have listening posts in locations where the signal waves of the transmitters that send the messages can be acquired. Radio traffic between foreign capitals and embassies in Washington can be easily picked off by listening equipment located in suburban Maryland and Virginia, but communications elsewhere in the world are not so easily intercepted. Thus, the NSA supports hundreds of listening

posts around the globe, such posts usually being operated by other U.S. government agencies. Most commonly used to run the NSA's overseas facilities are the armed services' cryptological agencies: the Army Security Agency, the Navy Security Service, and the Air Force Security Agency. These three military organizations come under the NSA's policy coordination; the messages they intercept are sent back to NSA headquarters at Fort Meade, Maryland, near Washington.

Perhaps the most controversial NSA base (operated by the Army) is at (**DELETED**) in (**DELETED**). A Senate subcommittee investigating American commitments abroad, chaired by Stuart Symington, revealed in 1970 that this heretofore secret facility had been secured from the Haile Selassie regime in return for hundreds of millions of dollars in military and economic assistance—without most members of Congress ever being aware of its existence. The Symington subcommittee also discovered a similar NSA facility (operated by the Navy) at (**DELETED**) in (**DELETED**) which also had been kept secret from Congress. Both these bases have been used to intercept communications from the Middle East and Africa, and both required the U.S. government to offer an implicit—but secret—commitment to the host government.

(

DELETED

)

Although the NSA engineered some successes against the Eastern European countries and Communist China in its early days, for at least the last fifteen years it has been completely unable to break into the high-grade cipher systems and codes of these nations. Against such major targets, the NSA has been reduced to reading comparatively unimportant communications between low-level military components and the equally inconsequential routine exchanges between low-grade bureaucrats and economic planners. This is far short of learning the Soviet Union's or China's most vital secrets. (

DELETED

).* One such benefit is derived from traffic analysis, the technique by which the NSA gleans some useful information through the study of communication patterns. A principal assistant of the NSA Director observed at the same meeting that another justification for the agency's continuing programs against the Soviets and Chinese is the hope that "maybe we'll get a break sometime, like the *Pueblo*." He was, of course, referring to the capture in 1968 of the NSA spy ship by North Korea. Much of the *Pueblo*'s cryptological machinery was seized intact by the North Koreans and probably turned over to the Soviets. While these

---

* David Kahn, author of the definitive work on modern cryptology, *The Code Breakers*, explained in the June 22, 1973, *New York Times* why NSA has had and will continue to have so little luck with reading advanced communications systems like the Soviets': "Cryptology has advanced, in the last decade or so, to systems that, though not unbreakable in the absolute, are unbreakable in practice. They consist essentially of mathematical programs for computer-like cipher machines. They engender so many possibilities that, even given torrents of intercepts, and scores of computers to batter them with, cryptanalysts could not reach a solution for thousands of years. Moreover, the formulas are so constructed that even if the cryptanalyst has the ideal situation—the original plain text of one of the foreign cryptograms— he cannot recreate the formula by comparing the two and then use it to crack the next message that comes along."

machines were not associated with the highest-grade U.S. military or diplomatic systems, the Soviets would have been able to use them to read messages previously sent through certain American military channels and intercepted and stored by the Soviets. The NSA has for many years been recording and storing not-yet-"broken" Soviet and Chinese messages, and can presume the same has been done with American communications; for our part, there are literally boxcars and warehouses full of incomprehensible tapes of this sort at NSA's Fort Meade headquarters.

As with so many other parts of the American intelligence apparatus, the NSA has had considerably more success operating against the Third World countries and even against some of our allies. With what is reportedly the largest bank of computers in the world and thousands of cryptanalysts, the NSA has had little trouble with the codes and ciphers of these nations. Two of the highly secret agency's young officers, William Martin and Bernon Mitchell, who defected to the Soviet Union in 1960, mentioned thirty to forty nations whose systems the NSA could read. In addition, Martin and Mitchell told of a practice under which the NSA provided encoding and cryptographic machines to other nations, then used its knowledge of the machinery to read the intercepted messages of these countries. This practice still flourishes.

One of the countries that Martin and Mitchell specifically named as being read by the NSA at that time was Egypt—the United Arab Republic. After making their revelation at a Moscow press conference, (

DELETED

DELETED

) The Soviets prob-
ably were, too. (

DELETED

)
A "break," in the terminology of the cryptanalyst, is a success
scored not through deciphering skill, but because of an error on the
part of another country's communications clerks or, on rare occasions, a failure in the cipher equipment. A few years ago, a new
code clerk arrived at a foreign embassy in Washington and promptly
sent a message "in the clear" (i.e., unenciphered), to his Foreign
Ministry. Realizing that he should have encrypted the transmission,
he sent the same message again, but this time in cipher. With the
"before and after" messages in hand, the NSA had little difficulty
thereafter, of course, reading that country's secret communications.
Malfunctioning or worn-out cryptographic equipment results in
triumphs for the NSA by unintentionally establishing repetitious
patterns which detract from the random selections that are vital to

sophisticated ciphers. A rough analogy would be a roulette wheel which, because of poor construction or excessive wear, develops certain predictable characteristics discernible to a keen observer who is then able to take advantage because of his special knowledge.

Another type of break comes as a result of a physical (rather than cerebral) attack on another country's communications system. The attack may be a clandestine operation to steal a code book or cipher system, the suborning of a communications clerk, or the planting of an audio device in an embassy radio room. Within the CIA's Clandestine Services, a special unit of the Foreign Intelligence (i.e., espionage) Staff specializes in these attacks.* When it is successful, the information it acquires is sent to the NSA to help that agency with its COMINT efforts.

In 1970, NSA Director Admiral Noel Gayler and his top deputies admitted privately that a good part of the NSA's successes came from breaks, and they emphasized that the agency was extremely adept at exploiting these non-cryptanalytical windfalls. Nevertheless, breaks are never mentioned in the authorized U.S. government "leaks" concerning the NSA's activities that from time to time appear in the press. In its controlled revelations to the public, the NSA deliberately tries to create the impression that it is incredibly good at the art of deciphering secret foreign communications and that its triumphs are based purely on its technical skills. (

DELETED

---

* This approach apparently appealed to President Nixon when he approved the 1970 Huston plan for domestic espionage which surfaced during the Watergate scandal. The plan called for breaking into foreign embassies in Washington because it would be "possible by this technique to secure the material with which the NSA can crack foreign cryptographic codes. We spend millions of dollars attempting to break these codes by machines. One surreptitious entry can do the job successfully at no dollar cost." While the Huston plan might have been effective against Third World countries with unsophisticated cryptological systems, it was unlikely to score any significant gains against major powers—even if there had been any successful break-ins. David Kahn explains why: "Codebooks could be photographed, [because] today's cipher secrets reside in electronic circuits, some of them integrated on a pinhead, some of them embodied in printed-circuit boards with up to fifteen layers."

DELETED

)

A side effect of the NSA's programs to intercept diplomatic and commercial messages is that rather frequently certain information is acquired about American citizens, including members of Congress and other federal officials, which can be highly embarrassing to those individuals. This type of intercepted message is handled with even greater care than the NSA's normal product, which itself is so highly classified that a special security clearance is needed to see it. Such information may, for example, derive from a Senator's conversation with a foreign ambassador in Washington who then cables a report of the talk to his Foreign Ministry.

A more serious embarrassment happened in 1970 during the course of delicate peace talks on the Middle East. A State Department official had a conversation about the negotiations with an Arab diplomat who promptly reported what he had been told to his government. His cable disclosed that the State Department man had either grossly misstated the American bargaining position or

the diplomat had badly misunderstood what had been told him. In any case, high State Department officers were quite disturbed about the misrepresented position and the incident did not reflect well on the competence of the American official in the eyes of his superiors.

Not even the CIA is immune to such prying by the NSA. On one occasion the Director of Central Intelligence was supplied with an intercepted message concerning his deputy. According to this message, a transmission from a Western European ambassador to his Foreign Office, the CIA's number-two man had a few evenings earlier at a dinner party hosted by the ambassador indiscreetly opined on several sensitive U.S. policy positions. The ambassador's interpretation of the conversation was contradicted by the Deputy Director—to the apparent satisfaction of the DCI—and the matter was quietly dropped.

Some NSA-intercepted communications can cause surprising problems within the U.S. government if they are inadvertently distributed to the wrong parties. When particularly sensitive foreign-policy negotiations are under way which may be compromised internally by too much bureaucratic awareness, the White House's usual policy has been to issue special instructions to the NSA to distribute messages mentioning these negotiations only to Henry Kissinger and his immediate staff.

The FBI operates a wiretap program against numerous foreign embassies in Washington which, like some of the NSA intercept operations, also provides information about Americans. In cooperation with the **Chesapeake and Potomac Telephone Company (a Bell subsidiary)**, FBI agents regularly monitor the phones in the offices of all communist governments represented here; on occasion, the embassies of various non-communist countries have their phones tapped, especially when their nations are engaged in negotiations with the U.S. government or when important developments are taking place in these countries. (

DELETED

DELETED

)
Wiretaps on foreign embassies, justified on the grounds of preserving national security, must be approved by the State Department before they are installed by the FBI. As it is often State which requests the FBI to activate the listening devices, approval is almost always given. The transcripts of such conversations are never marked as having come from wiretaps, but instead carry the description "from a source who has reported reliably in the past." Such reliable "sources" include State Department officials themselves—the CIA has, on occasion, intercepted communications between American ambassadorial officials and their colleagues in Washington.

In the way of background, it should be understood that CIA communications clerks handle nearly all classified cables between American embassies and Washington—for both the CIA and the State Department. To have a separate code room for each agency in every embassy would be a wasteful procedure, so a senior CIA communications expert is regularly assigned to the administrative part of the State Department in order to oversee CIA's communicators who work under State cover. In theory, CIA clerks are not supposed to read the messages they process for State, but any code clerk who wants to have a successful career quickly realizes that his promotions depend on the CIA and that he is well advised to show the CIA station chief copies of all important State messages. The State Department long ago implicitly recognized that its most secret

cables are not secure from CIA inspection by setting up special communications channels which supposedly cannot be deciphered by the CIA.

When in 1968 Ambassador to Iran Armin Meyer ran into troubles with the CIA station chief in Teheran, Meyer switched his communications with State in Washington to one of these "secure" channels, called "Roger." But the CIA had nonetheless figured out a way to intercept his cables and the replies he received from Washington; the CIA Director thus received a copy of each intercepted cable. Written on top of each cable was a warning that the contents of the cable should be kept especially confidential because State was unaware that the CIA had a copy.

Satellites and Other Systems

The most important source of technical intelligence gathered by the U.S. is that collected by photographic and electronic reconnaissance satellites. **Most are launched into north-south orbits designed to carry them over such targets as the U.S.S.R. and China with maximum frequency** as they circle around the earth. Others are put into orbits synchronized with the rotation of the globe, giving the illusion that they are stationary. **All satellite programs come under the operational authority of the National Reconnaissance Office (NRO), a component of the Secretary of the Air Force's office. The NRO spends well over a billion dollars every year for satellites and other reconnaissance systems. While the Defense Department provides all the money, policy decisions on how the funds will be allocated are made by the Executive Committee for Reconnaissance, consisting of the Assistant Secretary of Defense for Intelligence, the Director of Central Intelligence, and the Assistant to the President for National Security Affairs. Requirements for satellite collection are developed by the U.S. Intelligence Board (USIB), which is chaired by the Director of Central Intelligence and whose members are the heads of all other intelligence agencies. A special committee of the USIB designates the specific targets each satellite will cover.**

Employing high-resolution and wide-angle cameras, the photo-

graphic satellites have for years provided voluminous and detailed information on Soviet and Chinese military developments and other matters of strategic importance; conversely, except for special cases such as the Arab-Israeli situation, there has been little reason to apply satellite reconnaissance against other, less powerful countries.

Some photographic satellites are equipped with color cameras for special missions, and some even carry infrared sensing devices which measure heat emissions from ground targets, to determine, for example, if a site is occupied or what the level of activity is at certain locations. There are satellites that have television cameras to speed up the delivery of their product to the photo interpreters who analyze, or read out, the film packages of the spies in the sky. But, good as they are, photographic satellites have inherent limitations. They cannot see through clouds, nor can they see into buildings or inside objects.

In addition to photographic satellites, U.S. intelligence possesses a wide array of other reconnaissance satellites which perform numerous electronic sensing tasks. These satellites collect data on missile testing, on radars and the emissions of other high-power electronic equipment, and on communications traffic. Electronic satellites are in some cases supported by elaborate ground stations, both in friendly foreign countries and in the United States, that feed targeting directions to the sensors, receive the collected data from the satellites, and transmit the processed data to the intelligence agencies in Washington. (

DELETED

)

Until satellites became operational in the early 1960s, spy planes and ships were valuable sources of information, serving as supplements to the product of the NSA, then the best material available to U.S. intelligence. Air Force and CIA aircraft frequently flew along the perimeters of the communist countries and even over their territory in search of badly needed electronic and photographic information. Spy ships operated by the Navy—like the *Pueblo*—sailed along the coasts listening in on communications and other

electronic signals. Although these programs were considered to be great successes by the intelligence community, occasional blunders such as the 1959 U-2 affair and the Tonkin Gulf incident in 1964 (the two U.S. destroyers "torpedoed" by North Vietnamese boats were on a clandestine spy mission) had a serious and detrimental effect on world politics. Aggressive technical intelligence-collection efforts have also led to the capture of the *Pueblo*, the Israeli attack on the *Liberty* in 1967, and shoot-downs of RB-47s by the Soviets, and of EC-121s and several U-2s by the Chinese.

Despite the risks incurred by such provocative collection actions in the name of intelligence, the Pentagon continues to sponsor these now obsolete programs. Satellites and long-range stand-off (i.e., non-penetrating) systems have deeply reduced, if not eliminated, the need for spy flights and cruises. But the armed services have spent billions of dollars to develop the spy planes and ships (just as the CIA and the NSA have invested in outmoded listening posts ringing the U.S.S.R. and China); consequently, there has been a stubborn bureaucratic reluctance to take these collectors out of service. The "drone"—pilotless aircraft—flights over China, for example, were continued even after the Chinese started shooting them down on a regular and embarrassing basis, and after they had proven nearly useless. State Department reconnaissance intelligence experts insisted that the Air Force maintained the drone activity, even though the information thus gathered was of marginal value, because it had nowhere else to use such spy equipment. Similarly, Air Force SR-71s have continued to fly over North Korea despite that country's lack of meaningful intelligence targets. With the Soviet Union declared off bounds for secret overflights since 1960, and China since 1971, the Air Force can devise no other way of justifying the operational need for these aircraft.

(

DELETED

DELETED

)

Clearly, the prevailing theology in the U.S. intelligence community calls for the collection of as much information as possible. Little careful consideration is given to the utility of the huge amounts of material so acquired. The attitude of "collection for collection's sake" has resulted in mountains of information which can only overwhelm intelligence analysts charged with interpreting it. Further, such material contributes little to the national requirements, though it may prove interesting to certain highly specialized analysts, particularly in the Pentagon. There has been little coordination between the managers of the various technical espionage programs, and even less between the collectors and the policymakers. Each of the many agencies which carry out such programs has a vested bureaucratic interest in keeping its particular system in being, and the extreme compartmentalization of the operations has made it almost impossible for the programs to be evaluated as a whole. Former CIA Director Helms failed almost completely in his assigned mission of bringing a more rational and coordinated approach to the myriad technical espionage systems. It is not likely that his successors will do much better. No CIA Director has ever been able to manage the intelligence community.

Despite the roughly $5 billion already being spent each year on technical systems and on processing the great amounts of data collected, there remains significant pressure within the intelligence community to collect still more information. (

DELETED

) This secrecy is unquestionably needed to protect the actual workings of the system, but then the operation of the ABM was no less classified, and the national security did not seem to be injured by the ABM debate in Congress. However, the very word "intelligence" seems to make our legislators bow and genuflect. They have in the past bestowed virtual blank checks on the various intelligence agencies, allowing these organizations to do practically anything they desired. The Soviets have a fairly clear idea of the functions performed by American satellites and other collection systems; there would seem to be little practical reason why the Congress and the American people must be kept completely in the dark.

Furthermore, technical espionage of any kind has a limited value. It can identify and measure missile development and troop movements, but it cannot tell what foreign leaders are planning to do with those missiles and troops. In 1968 the U.S. intelligence community had a relatively clear picture of the Soviet preparations for military action against Czechoslovakia; it had no means whatever of knowing whether or not an actual attack would be made. That kind of information could have been provided only by a human spy inside the Kremlin, and the CIA had none of those, and small prospect for recruiting any. The United States knew what *could* happen, but intelligence consumers have an insatiable appetite for knowledge of what *will* happen. Their clamoring makes for more and bigger collection systems to attempt to satisfy their demands.

Counterespionage

Counterespionage, the clandestine warfare waged between rival intelligence agencies, is usually referred to more delicately in the spy business as counterintelligence. Essentially, it consists of preventing the opposition from penetrating your own secret service while at the same time working to penetrate the opposition's—to learn what he is planning against you. As practiced by the CIA and the Soviet KGB, counterespionage is a highly complex and devious activity. It depends on cunning entrapments, *agents provocateurs,* spies and counterspies, double and triple crosses. It is the stuff that spy novels are made of, with limitless possibilities for deception and turns of plot.

While foreign intelligence organizations with longer histories have traditionally emphasized counterespionage, U.S. intelligence was slow to develop such a capability. To Americans during World War II and immediately thereafter, counterespionage meant little more than defensive security measures such as electrified fences, watchdogs, and codes. The obscure subtleties and intricate conspiracies of counterespionage seemed alien to the American character and more suited to European back alleys and the Orient Express. But the demands of the Cold War and the successes scored by the KGB in infiltrating Western intelligence services gradually drew the CIA deeply into the counterespionage game.

Primary responsibility for U.S. internal security rests with the FBI, but inevitably there has been friction between the agency and the bureau in their often overlapping attempts to protect the nation against foreign spies. In theory, the CIA cooperates with the FBI in counterespionage cases by handling the overseas aspects and letting the bureau take care of all the action within the United States. In actual fact, the agency tends to keep within its own control, even domestically, those operations which are designed to penetrate opposition intelligence services; the basically defensive task of preventing the Soviets from recruiting American agents in the United States is left to the FBI. While the FBI also on occasion goes on the offensive by trying to recruit foreign intelligence agents,

the bureau's first inclination seems to be to arrest or deport foreign spies rather than to turn them, as the CIA tries to do, into double agents. This fundamental difference in approach limits the degree of FBI-CIA cooperation in counterespionage and confirms the general view within the agency that FBI agents are rather un-imaginative police-officer types, and thus incapable of mastering the intricacies of counterespionage work. (The FBI, on the other hand, tends to see CIA counterintelligence operators as dilettantes who are too clever for their own good.) Although the CIA has had almost no success in penetrating the Soviet and other opposition services, it nonetheless continues to press for additional operational opportunities in the United States, claiming that the FBI is not sophisticated enough to cope with the KGB.

Within the CIA, the routine functions of security—physical protection of buildings, background investigations of personnel, lie-detector tests—are assigned to the Office of Security, a com-ponent of the housekeeping part of the agency, the M&S Direc-torate. Counterespionage policy and some actual operations ema-nate from the Counterintelligence (CI) Staff of the Clandestine Services. As with the bulk of espionage activities, however, most operations are carried out by the area divisions (Far East, Western Hemisphere, etc.), which are also responsible. The area divisions tend to see espionage value or information-gathering value in coun-terespionage operations, which are referred to in CIA files as joint FI/CI projects—FI (Foreign Intelligence) being the Clan-destine Services' euphemism for espionage.

Almost every CIA station or base overseas has one or more officers assigned to it for counterespionage purposes. The first priority for these counterspy specialists is to monitor agency espi-onage and covert-action operations to make sure that the opposition has not penetrated or in some other way compromised the activity. All reports submitted by CIA case officers and their foreign agents are carefully studied for any indication of enemy involvement. The counterintelligence men know all too well that agents, wittingly or unwittingly, can be used by the KGB as deceptions to feed false information to the CIA, or employed as provocations to disrupt carefully laid operational plans. Foreign agents can also be pene-

trations, or double agents, whose task it is to spy on the CIA's secret activities. When a double agent is discovered in an operation, consideration is given to "turning" him—that is, making him a triple agent. Or perhaps he can be unwittingly used to deceive or provoke the opposition.

If a KGB officer tries to recruit a CIA staff employee, the counterespionage experts may work out a plan to entrap the enemy operator, then publicly expose him or attempt to "turn" him. Or they may encourage the agency employee to pretend to cooperate with the Soviets in order to learn more about what kind of information the KGB wants to collect, to discover more about KGB methods and equipment, or merely to occupy the time and money of the KGB on a fruitless project. CIA counterespionage specialists do not necessarily wait for the KGB to make a recruitment effort, but instead may set up an elaborate trap, dangling one of their own as bait for the opposition.

Further, beyond safeguarding the CIA's own covert operations, counterespionage officers actively try to penetrate the opposition services. Seeking to recruit agents in communist and other intelligence services, they hope both to find out what secret actions the opposition is planning to take against the CIA, and to thwart or deflect those initiatives.

Counterespionage, like covert action, has become a career specialty in the CIA; some clandestine operators do no other type of work during their years with the agency. These specialists have developed their own clannish subculture within the Clandestine Services, and even other CIA operators often find them excessively secretive and deceptive. The function of the counterespionage officers is to question and verify every aspect of CIA operations; taking nothing at face value, they tend to see deceit everywhere. In an agency full of extremely mistrustful people, they are the professional paranoids.*

* It is commonly thought within the CIA that the Counterintelligence Staff operates on the assumption that the agency—as well as other elements of the U.S. government—is penetrated by the KGB. The chief of the CI Staff is said to keep a list of the fifty or so key positions in the CIA which are most likely to have been infiltrated by the opposition, and he reportedly keeps the persons in those positions under constant surveillance. Some CIA

Many experienced CIA operators believe that counterespionage operations directed against opposition services receive a disproportionate amount of attention and resources within the Clandestine Services, for even if a spy were recruited in the KGB (which almost never happens), he would likely be of less intelligence value than a penetration at a similar level elsewhere in the Soviet government or Communist Party. To be sure, the spy could probably provide the CIA with some information on foreign agents working for the KGB, perhaps the type of intelligence received from them and other foreign sources, and maybe a few insights into KGB operations against the United States and other countries. But he would know little about the intentions of the Soviet leadership or Moscow's military and nuclear secrets—the most crucial information of all to those officials responsible for looking after the national security of the United States. The KGB officer, like most clandestine operators, is usually better versed on developments in foreign countries than those in his own nation. Although it is interesting to know what the KGB operators know and how they acquired their knowledge, that in itself is of little significance in achieving U.S. intelligence goals. The justification for the counterintelligence effort, although usually couched in intricate, sophisticated argument, amounts to little more than "operations for operations' sake." Admittedly, there can occasionally be a positive intelligence windfall from a counterespionage operation; an agent recruited in a foreign service may have access to information on his own government's secret policies and plans. Penkovsky, who was in Soviet military intelligence (GRU), provided his British and American case officers with reams of documents concerning the Soviet armed forces and their advanced weapons-development programs, in addition to clandestine operational information and doctrine. Agents working for other foreign services have from time to time made similar, although less valuable, contributions. But the CIA's preoccupation with this type of clandestine operation, often to the

---

officers speculate—and a few firmly believe—that the only way to explain the poor performance in recruiting Soviet agents—and conducting classical intelligence operations in general against the U.S.S.R.—is that KGB penetrations inside the agency have been for years sending back advance warnings.

exclusion of a search for more important secrets, is at least questionable.

Within the Clandestine Services, the Soviet Bloc (SB) Division, quite obviously, is the most counterespionage-oriented of all the area divisions. The rationale generally given for this emphasis is that it is nearly impossible to recruit even the lowest-level spy in the U.S.S.R. because of the extremely tight internal-security controls in force there. Among the few Soviets who can, however, move about freely despite these restrictions are KGB and other intelligence officers. They are, furthermore, part of that small group of Soviet officials who regularly come in contact with Westerners (often searching for their own recruits). And they are among those officials most likely to travel outside the Soviet Union, where recruitment approaches by CIA operators (or induced defections) can more easily be arranged. Being the most accessible and least supervised of all Soviet citizens, KGB officers are, therefore, potentially the most recruitable.

Outside the Soviet Union, according to the SB Division's rationale, recruitment of non-KGB agents is almost as difficult as in the U.S.S.R. Most other Soviets, including the highest officials, are usually under KGB surveillance; they travel or live in groups, or are otherwise unreachable by the agency's clandestine operators. Once again, it is only the opposition intelligence officer who has the freedom of movement which allows for secret contact with foreigners. The division's efforts are therefore concentrated on seeking out potential agents among the KGB.

There is much truth in the Soviet Bloc Division's view of this operational problem, but the fact that the agency's operators have recruited *no* high-level Soviet spies and induced almost *no* significant defections from the U.S.S.R. in well over a decade raises serious questions concerning the CIA's competence as a clandestine intelligence organization. In fact, since the early 1960s there have been practically no CIA attempts to recruit a Soviet agent, and only a handful of defection inducements; Oleg Penkovsky, it must be remembered, was turned away when he first tried to defect.

To be sure, there is reason for extreme care. Most Soviet de-

fectors who bolt to the West are greeted by the agency with great caution because they may be KGB deceptions or provocations. The clandestine operators are so unsure of their ability to evaluate the intentions and establish the legitimacy of most defectors that the CIA has set up an inter-agency committee within the U.S. intelligence community to review all defector cases. This bureaucratic layering not only works to reduce the number of defectors accepted by the U.S. government (perhaps wisely), but also serves to spread the blame if mistakes are made.

Despite the CIA's extreme caution, however, a few defectors, some of them KGB undercover officers, have managed to accomplish their goal of escaping and establishing, as it is known in the clandestine trade, their *bona fides,* in spite of the agency's doubts. Svetlana Stalin succeeded simply because the CIA officers on the scene in India, with the encouragement of Ambassador Chester Bowles, refused to be held back by the SB Division's bureaucratic precautions.

It has been well established that the CIA cannot spy, in the classical sense, against its major target, the Soviet Union. Nor does the CIA seem to be able to conduct effective counterespionage (in the offensive aspect) against the Soviets. It even has difficulty dealing with the gratuitous opportunities presented by walk-ins and defectors. Much of this obviously can be attributed to the inherent difficulties involved in operating in a closed society like the U.S.S.R.'s, and against a powerful, unrelenting opposition organization like the KGB; and some of the lack of success can, too, be explained by the CIA's incompetence. But there is more to the failure against the Soviet target than insurmountable security problems or ineptitude. The CIA's Clandestine Services are, to a large extent, fearful of and even intimidated by the Soviet KGB because they have so frequently been outmaneuvered by it.

Most Soviet spying successes against the major Western powers have involved penetrations of their intelligence services. The KGB, with its origins in the highly conspiratorial czarist secret police, has often appeared to professional observers to be more adept at

penetrating foreign intelligence organizations than in recruiting ordinary spies.

Most notorious among the KGB's infiltrations of Western intelligence (at least those that have been discovered) was Harold "Kim" Philby, who spied for Moscow for over twenty years while a very high-ranking official of Britain's MI-6.* There have been several other highly damaging KGB penetrations of British intelligence, French and German intelligence, and the services of most of the smaller N.A.T.O. countries. And KGB agents have been uncovered on several occasions in U.S. intelligence agencies, including the National Security Agency, several of the military security agencies, and the intelligence section of the Joint Chiefs of Staff.

But as far as is publicly known, no career officer of the CIA has ever been proved to be an enemy spy. There have been some odd dismissals of clandestine officers from time to time for reasons that have smacked of more than mere incompetence or corruption, but none of these has ever officially been designated as a penetration. On the other hand, foreign agents recruited by the agency have sometimes been found to be working for an opposition service. Whenever such a penetration is discovered in a CIA operation, the agency's counterespionage specialists compile a damage report assessing how much information has been revealed to the subject and the possible repercussions of such disclosures on other CIA activities. Similarly, agency counterespionage officers participate in the preparation of damage reports when a penetration is exposed elsewhere in the U.S. intelligence community.

One such report was prepared in cooperation with the Defense Department in 1966 when Lieutenant Colonel W. H. Whalen, a U.S. Army intelligence officer working for the Joint Chiefs of Staff, was arrested as a KGB spy. The investigation disclosed that Whalen had had access to almost all the U.S. national intelligence

---

* In his memoirs (unquestionably full of KGB disinformation) Philby expressed little professional respect for the CIA's talents in counterespionage. But he did admit that it was an agency officer (ironically, an ex-FBI agent) who ultimately saw through his masquerade and was responsible for exposing him to British authorities.

estimates of Soviet strategic military capabilities during the "missile gap" controversy several years earlier. Evidently, he had delivered copies of these top-secret documents to his KGB employers.

However, the results of Whalen's actions were, upon examination, as surprising as they were discouraging to U.S. intelligence. A principal reason why CIA and Pentagon analysts believed there was a missile gap during the late 1950s and early 1960s was the numerous references in speeches made at the time by Khrushchev and other Soviet leaders alluding to the development and deployment of Soviet long-range nuclear missiles. These announcements, carefully timed to correspond to the progressive phases of intercontinental ballistic missile research, testing, production, and operational introduction to the armed forces, were studied in great detail by the Kremlin-watchers of the U.S. intelligence community. Learning from American scientists working on U.S. missile programs what was technically feasible in the field of ICBM development, and having already witnessed the startling demonstration of Soviet space technology demonstrated in the launching of Sputnik, the intelligence analysts assumed the worst—that the Soviets were well ahead of the United States in the missile race. The analysts noted in their estimates that the statements of the Soviet leaders were a significant factor in making this judgment.

Neither the U-2 reconnaissance flights nor the first missions of American photographic satellites confirmed the fears of the analysts, but the U.S. government took no chances, and pressed fervently ahead with its own strategic strike programs, especially the Minuteman ICBM and the Polaris submarine. By 1963 it was abundantly evident that the only "missile gap" which existed was in America's favor, created by the rapid deployment of U.S. systems. Khrushchev and his colleagues had deliberately attempted to mislead by cleverly implying a nuclear attack capability which the Soviet Union did not possess; apparently, they were somewhat encouraged by those U.S. intelligence estimates secretly provided by Colonel Whalen which showed how worried U.S. officials were by the Soviet bluff. But even though deception was

at first successful, in that U.S. officials believed the Soviet claims, it ultimately backfired as the United States chose to accelerate its own missile-development programs, thereby placing the Soviet Union in a position of still greater strategic disadvantage than before.

Perhaps an even greater service which Colonel Whalen unintentionally performed for his country while spying for the KGB came during the Berlin crisis of 1961. At that time, in addition to building the wall to separate the east and west portions of the city, the East Germans attempted, with obvious Soviet support, to reduce access to Berlin from West Germany. The U.S. intelligence estimate was that the communists were toughening and unlikely to back down. This gloomy but influential estimate was passed to the KGB by Colonel Whalen, probably along with other information that the United States would stand absolutely firm. When the Soviets suddenly and unexpectedly eased their position, both the White House and the intelligence community, although pleased, were confused by Moscow's turnabout. Only years later, during the preparation of the Whalen damage report, did the analysts get a better idea why their original estimates of Soviet behavior had proved to be wrong in 1961. With the benefit of hindsight, the analysts reasoned: The Soviet leaders had decided to ease their stand when they realized the U.S. government would not back down, *despite* the estimate of Soviet intransigence. Apparently afraid they might be on the verge of provoking a major military conflict, the Soviets abruptly softened their demands.

The unexpected benefits to the U.S. government stemming from the Whalen penetration, while clearly fortuitous, are not unique in clandestine operations. In 1964 it was learned that the American embassy in Moscow had been thoroughly bugged by the KGB. Scores of Soviet audio devices were found throughout the building. Counterespionage and security specialists determined that the equipment had been installed in 1952 when the embassy had been renovated, and that the bugs had been operational for roughly twelve years. The damage report asserted that during this entire period—at the height of the Cold War—Soviet intelligence had

probably intercepted every diplomatic cable between Washington and the embassy. (

DELETED

)

U.S. suspicions about the Soviet eavesdropping were apparently aroused early in 1964 when Nikita Khrushchev made a remark to Ambassador Foy Kohler about Kohler's role in blocking the shipment to the Soviet Union of steel for an important pipeline. Taken in context, Khrushchev's remark indicated to Kohler that there was a leak somewhere in American security. Kohler started a massive investigation and, within a month or two, found forty-odd bugs embedded in walls throughout the embassy. Although Kohler would later claim there was no connection between the discovery of the bugs and the investigation he ordered after his conversation with Khrushchev, the timing would seem to indicate otherwise.

(

DELETED

)

Today the likelihood of the KGB eavesdropping on the activities in an embassy code room is extremely remote. Most State Department communications overseas are handled by the CIA. **The machines and other equipment are cushioned and covered to mute the sounds emanating from them. The rooms themselves are**

encased in lead and rest on huge springs that further reduce the internal noises. Resembling large camping trailers, the code rooms now are normally located deep in the concrete basements of embassy buildings. Access to them by sound-sensitive devices is, for all practical purposes, impossible.

The CIA's counterespionage operators not only try to recruit secret agents in opposition services like the KGB; they also work against the so-called friendly or allied services. Off bounds for the most part—in principle, at least—are the intelligence agencies of the English-speaking countries, among which there is a kind of unwritten agreement not to spy on each other. (

DELETED

DELETED

)

Attempts are made by the Intelligence Directorate to restrict the dissemination of highly classified analysis to foreign intelligence services, but for the most part these are limited to relatively minor deletions of references to collection sources. In some instances, the practice involves simply cutting out with a razor a few words here and there from the text of, say, a National Intelligence Estimate on Soviet missile capabilities. Usually this is done on only a few documents being given to the British or other English-speaking services. (

DELETED

DELETED

DELETED

)

Domestic Operations

On December 17, 1972, the *New York Times* revealed that the CIA had secretly provided training to fourteen New York City policemen. At the time, agency spokesman Angus Thuermer acknowledged that other American police departments had received "similar courtesies," but he would not specify how many. Thuermer said to the *Times*, "I doubt very much that [CIA officials] keep that kind of information." But New York Congressman Edward Koch persisted in seeking precisely "that kind of information" from the agency. On January 29, 1973, the CIA's Legislative Counsel, John Maury (himself a longtime clandestine operator and former station chief in Greece), admitted to Koch that "less than fifty police officers all told, from a total of about a

dozen city and county police forces, have received some sort of Agency briefing within the past two years." But again the CIA was being less than forthcoming, for its police training (which consisted of much more than a "briefing") had been going on for considerably more than the two years cited by the CIA—at least since 1967, when Chicago police received instruction at both the agency's headquarters and at "The Farm" in southeastern Virginia. When queried by newspaper reporters in 1973, police authorities in Chicago denied that any of their men had received any such agency training. But Richard Helms, then recently departed as Director, specifically told a secret session of the Senate Foreign Relations Committee at the beginning of February that Chicago police had been included in the agency training effort, and his disclosure subsequently leaked out to the press.

It was significant that when the CIA publicly owned up to training sessions in Maury's letter to Koch, the only time period mentioned was "the past two years"; it was likely true that in "the past two years" fewer than fifty officers from a dozen localities had been trained. But if the CIA had confessed to the full extent of its pre-1971 police-training activities, the figures would have been much larger. More important, the agency could not have justified its domestic police-training program, as it did, on the grounds that a provision of the Omnibus Crime Control and Safe Streets Act of 1968 encouraged federal law-enforcement agencies to assist local forces. That law was not passed until June 1968, well after the CIA training had started. Of course, once the agency had been shown to have carried out this domestic activity, it needed such a justification or excuse: the National Security Act of 1947 had forbidden it to exercise any "police, subpoena, law-enforcement powers, or internal security functions."

The tactics used by the CIA to cover its tracks in this instance were typical of the kind of deception that the agency has generally used to conceal its numerous activities inside the United States. The subject of domestic operations is a particularly sensitive one in the CIA, and probably no other program is handled with greater secrecy.

CIA training of local police departments may seem like a rela-

tively harmless activity, but it does raise several questions. Why did the agency at first try to cover up and then mislead Congress, the press, and the public about its activity? Why could the same training not have been given by the FBI, which maintains facilities and has legal authorization for that purpose? (Helms told the Foreign Relations Committee that the police requested CIA assistance because the agency's techniques in keeping intelligence files and in performing certain kinds of surveillance were more advanced than the FBI's.) And why have subsequent CIA Directors James Schlesinger and William Colby not specifically ruled out any future police training, even after the press and the Congress have raised the questions of illegality and impropriety?

None of these questions has an obvious answer. In general, however, the CIA does not like to admit that it has been doing something it shouldn't have, and deceptive public statements by the agency are as much a standard reflex action as an indication that something particularly unsavory has occurred. Another explanation might be that during those days in December 1972 and January 1973 when the police-training incident was being exposed, the Watergate cover-up had not yet come unglued and the CIA might have been trying to keep investigators away from its domestic activities. A few months later, of course, the press would discover, and various public officials would reveal, that Richard Helms had been "most cooperative and helpful" in helping to organize the top-secret White House plan for domestic surveillance and intelligence collection; that the CIA had provided "technical" assistance to the White House plumbers in their 1971 burglary of the office of Daniel Ellsberg's psychiatrist; that the agency maintained "safe houses" in the heart of Washington where E. Howard Hunt was clandestinely provided with CIA-manufactured false documents, a disguise, a speech-altering device, and a camera fitted into a tobacco pouch; that five of the seven Watergate burglars were ex-CIA employees, and one was still on the payroll and regularly reporting to an agency case officer; that in the week after the break-in at the Democratic Party's headquarters, high White House officials tried to involve the agency directly in the Watergate cover-up; and, perhaps most significantly, that top

CIA officials remained silent, even in secret testimony before congressional committees, about the illegal activities they knew had taken place. In fact, Helms' answers to the Senate Foreign Relations Committee's questions on Watergate in February and March 1973 proved to be so evasive and misleading, particularly as subsequent disclosures were made, that the *Washington Post*'s Laurence Stern wrote on July 10 of the same year "that the word perjury was being uttered in Senate offices by those who were privy to the secret testimony given by Helms. . . ."

At a February 7 hearing, for example, New Jersey's Senator Clifford Case told Helms it had come to his attention that in 1969 or 1970 the White House had asked the various government intelligence agencies to pool resources to learn more about the anti-war movement. "Do you know anything," Case asked Helms, "about any activity on the part of the CIA in that connection? Was it asked to be involved?" Helms replied, "I don't recall whether we were asked, but we were not involved because to me that was a clear violation of what our charter was." Case persisted, "What do you do in a case like that? Suppose you were?" Helms answered, "I would simply go to explain to the President this didn't seem advisable." Case: "That would end it?" Helms: "Well, I think so, normally."*

But the facts and suspicions to emerge from the Senate Watergate hearings during the following months suggested that this is not at all the way such matters are worked out behind the scenes in the executive branch of the government, raising still more questions as to the reliability of the CIA's clandestine leadership—and the agency's role in U.S. domestic intelligence operations.

* Four months later a memorandum written by former White House aide Tom Charles Huston leaked to the *New York Times*. It outlined a program for domestic surveillance of U.S. citizens that had been approved by President Nixon on July 15, 1970, and then rescinded by him five days later. Huston noted a series of meetings with top officials of the FBI, the CIA, the DIA, the NSA, and the service intelligence agencies, and said, "I went into this exercise fearful that CIA would refuse to cooperate. In fact, Dick Helms was most cooperative and helpful." According to the Huston memorandum, the authenticity of which has been confirmed by the White House, the CIA was slated to be a full participating member.

The CIA and the FBI

The CIA has always conducted clandestine operations within the United States, although for the most part these have been related to its overseas activities or their support. It was for this purpose that the agency originally established, a number of years ago, a special component of the Clandestine Services, the Domestic Operations Division. But the separation between foreign-oriented covert operations and those considered essentially domestic is often vague and confusing in the intelligence business. Thus, over the years there has been constant bureaucratic friction between the CIA and the FBI, which has primary responsibility for internal security. Compromises and other working arrangements have had to be evolved, allowing the CIA a certain operational latitude within the U.S.A. and giving the bureau in return special privileges abroad in the agency's sphere of responsibility.

The Domestic Operations Division (DOD), with a staff of a few hundred people and an annual budget of up to $10 million, is a well-established part of the Clandestine Services. Divisional headquarters for Domestic Operations is not at the main CIA installation at Langley, but in an office building on downtown Washington's Pennsylvania Avenue, within two blocks of the White House. This is also the Washington "station," and its subordinate "bases" are situated in major American cities. These offices are separate from the agency's other facilities for routine personnel-recruiting and overt contact with American overseas travelers. The "secret" DOD offices serve as springboards for the Clandestine Services' covert operations in American cities.

The DOD is surrounded by extreme secrecy, even by CIA standards, and its actual functions are shrouded in mystery. The extent of the agency's unwillingness to discuss the Domestic Division could be seen when the CIA officer preparing the agency's annual budget request to Congress in 1968 was pointedly told by the Executive Director not to include anything about the DOD in the secret briefing to be given to the Senate and House appropriations committees. In at least one other instance, Director Helms was

specifically asked in a secret congressional session about the "Domestic Operations Division." In his answer to the unsuspecting legislators, he described the functions of the "Domestic Contact Service"—the overt agency office that recruits American travelers to be unofficial CIA eyes and ears abroad—which at the time was a completely separate entity housed outside the Clandestine Services.

The Domestic Division's task, like all agency clandestine area divisions, is the collection of covert intelligence and the conduct of other secret operations—but in this instance inside the United States. It operates some of the espionage programs aimed against foreign students and other visitors to the United States, but by no means all of them. Recruitment of a Soviet diplomat at the United Nations or in Washington would fall under the Clandestine Services' Soviet Bloc Division. Programs with Cuban-Americans in Florida would be handled by the Western Hemisphere Division, the Covert Action Staff, or the Special Operations (paramilitary) Division—depending on the agent's intended role.

There is a relatively widespread feeling among observers of the CIA's Clandestine Services that the DOD would like to do more on the American scene than it apparently has up to now. It is also believed that if the Nixon administration's domestic-security plan of 1970 and the related surveillance of American dissidents had ever been put into operation—which the White House has denied but various press accounts have suggested—the DOD probably would have become deeply involved. The rationale used by the CIA would most likely have been the same one mentioned by Director Colby at his confirmation hearing: that the agency can rightfully spy on Americans "involved with foreign institutions." To the mistrustful minds of the Clandestine Services, the problems caused in the United States by dissidents, civil-rights activists, and anti-war protesters certainly conjured up the specter of foreign influences. After all, the covert officers reasoned, the dissident political groups in the United States were obviously receiving financial support from somewhere, and the sources could be foreign. The clandestine operators familiar with the CIA's secret efforts to aid and strengthen anti-government groups in Eastern Europe and elsewhere easily calculated that somehow the communist countries were now get-

ting even by using American groups to stir up trouble in the United States. CIA support for dissident movements in Eastern Europe never made any less real the source of their grievances, but that did not prevent the agency from using them to put pressure on the Soviet government and perhaps even to divert Moscow's attention from its struggle with the West. And in the late 1960s and early 1970s American dissidents were certainly causing difficulties for the U.S. government. Since the Clandestine Services knew it had exploited similar circumstances in Eastern Europe, its operators naturally looked for KGB involvement in the United States.*

The Johnson White House, however, had chosen not to involve the CIA deeply in domestic clandestine operations at the time when it first asked, back in the beginnings of the anti-war movement. The Domestic Operations Division was given only a small piece of the action—namely, to increase its surveillance of the movement, and its activities against direct foreign involvement in the movement. The FBI, too, was instructed to expand its domestic political-intelligence capabilities. But the lion's share of the responsibility in the matter was given to the Pentagon—in particular, the Army—apparently under a newly discovered, but outdated, emergency law granting the President special power to utilize the military and take whatever measures he deemed necessary to put down domestic unrest and conspiracies. Literal legal justification probably was not the sole reason why Army intelligence was assigned as the main instrument with which to attack the domestic targets; size was another consideration. Neither the CIA nor the FBI had the manpower for an all-out clandestine offensive against the radicals. Nor did either have available large numbers of young intelligence personnel who could actually penetrate the movement. But Army Intelligence soon blundered, and its domestic surveillance programs were exposed in January 1970 by ex-agent Christopher Pyle, writing in the *Washington Monthly*. During the following year the military services were forced to withdraw from their massive

---

* Clandestine Services had sympathizers everywhere. H. R. Haldeman, in a secret memo made public during the Senate Watergate hearings: "We need our people to put out the story on the foreign or Communist money that was used in support of demonstrations against the President in 1972."

attack against domestic dissidents; the field was once again left to the "professionals"—the FBI and the CIA.

This situation, however, soon resulted in an open break between the agency and the bureau. The *New York Times* attributed the split, in late 1971, to a minor event involving jurisdictional control over the handling of an informant/agent in Denver, Colorado. But shortly afterward Sam Papich, the FBI's officer in charge of liaison with the CIA, and a member of J. Edgar Hoover's immediate staff, was dismissed by the bureau chief. And only weeks later William Sullivan, head of the FBI's Division of Internal Security, the bureau's representative on the U.S. Intelligence Board, and a good friend of the CIA, was locked out of his office and fired by Hoover.

In the aftermath of the troubles at the FBI, the press carried a series of reports of Hoover's and the bureau's incompetence. Some comments, attributed to "authoritative sources" in the intelligence community, accused the FBI of having done a poor job of protecting the nation's internal security in recent years. These same sources also noted that the bureau had uncovered only a handful of foreign spies in the United States during the past several years, and described the FBI as lacking in the "sophisticated" approach to modern counterespionage. Such statements, in substance and in phraseology, clearly originated with, or were inspired by, the CIA.

What the public was unaware of at the time, however, was that since 1970—long before the open CIA-FBI split—the White House had been planning to expand domestic intelligence operations. And while the CIA had gone along with and encouraged the secret policy, the FBI had resisted it. It was, in fact, Hoover's personal refusal to support the new policy that resulted in the collapse of the White House plan. And it was in these circumstances that a paranoid President then established the infamous "plumbers" squad, with which the CIA was evidently quite willing to cooperate —and with which the FBI seems to have been reluctant to become involved.

When CIA Director William Colby was asked at his Senate confirmation hearings, in the fall of 1973, what he believed to be the proper scope of CIA activities within the United States, his first

response was "We obviously have to run a headquarters here; we have to recruit people for our staffs, and so forth, and we have to conduct investigations on those people. . . ." No one disputes the need for the agency to conduct certain routine administrative business within the United States, but few people realize that what the "headquarters" needs to be "run" includes dozens of buildings in the Washington area alone, large training facilities at several locations in Virginia, a paramilitary base in North Carolina, secret air bases in Nevada and Arizona, communications and radio intercept bases around the country, scores of "dummy" commercial organizations and airlines, operational offices in more than twenty major cities, a huge arms warehouse in the Midwest, and "safe houses" for secret rendezvous in Washington and other cities. While most of these are oriented toward foreign operations, some are used full- or part-time for purely domestic activities.

Colby continued: "We have to contract with a large number of American firms for the various kinds of equipment that we might have need for abroad." Again, this is on the surface a legitimate function. The CIA every year purchases tens of millions of dollars' worth of goods from domestic companies—everything from office supplies to esoteric espionage equipment. But Colby carefully left out any mention of those other "purchases"—the services provided for by the CIA's contractual relationships with universities, "think tanks," and individual professors.

Many of these came to light in the winter of 1967 after *Ramparts* first revealed the CIA subsidization of the National Student Association and as exposure followed exposure Richard Helms asked his Executive Director to report back to him exactly what the CIA was doing on American campuses. The Executive Director quickly found that he had no easy task before him, since nearly every agency component had its own set of programs with one or more American universities and there was no central office in the CIA which coordinated or even kept track of these programs. A special committee was formed to compile a report, and its staff officers spent weeks going from office to separate office to put together the study.

The committee compiled data on the hundreds of college professors who had been given special clearances by the agency's Office

of Security to perform a wide variety of tasks for different CIA components. The Intelligence Directorate, for example, had a corps of consultants on campus who did historical and political research, much like normal scholars, with the difference that they were almost never permitted to publish their findings; in a few instances, that rule was suspended on condition that the source of their funding was not identified, and if the work neatly coincided with a prevailing CIA propaganda line.

Similarly, the Directorate of Science and Technology employed individual professors, and at times entire university departments or reseach institutes, for its research and development projects. (This apart from the millions of dollars of work the S&T Directorate contracted out every year to private companies and "think tanks.") Research of this type included the development (

DELETED

) commonly used).

In many cases, the CIA's research involvement on the campuses went much deeper than simply serving as the patron of scholarly work. In 1951, CIA money was used to set up the Center for International Studies at the Massachusetts Institute of Technology. A key figure at the MIT Center was Walt Rostow, a political scientist with intelligence ties dating back to OSS service during World War II who later became President Johnson's Assistant for National Security Affairs. In 1952, Max Millikan, who had been Director of the CIA's Office of National Estimates, became head of the center. This linkage between the CIA and research institutions on campus and in the private sector became standard practice in later years, just as it did for the Pentagon. But whereas the Pentagon's procedures could to some extent be monitored by the Congress and the public, the CIA set up and subsidized its own "think tanks" under a complete veil of secrecy. When in 1953 the MIT Center published *The Dynamics of Soviet Society,* a book by Rostow and his colleagues, there was no indication to the

reader that the work had been financed by CIA funds and that it reflected the prevailing agency view of the Soviet Union. MIT cut off its link with the center in 1966, but the link between the center and the CIA remained, and the agency has continued to subsidize a number of similar, if smaller, research facilities around the country.

The compilers of the 1967 study on CIA ties to the academic community also found that the Clandestine Services had their own research links with universities, for the purpose of developing better espionage tools (listening devices, advanced weapons, invisible inks, etc.). But for the covert operators, research was not the primary campus interest. To the Clandestine Services the universities represented fertile territory for recruiting espionage agents. Most large American colleges enrolled substantial numbers of foreign students, and many of these, especially those from the Third World, were (and are) destined to hold high positions in their home countries in a relatively few years. They were much easier to recruit at American schools—when they might have a need for money, where they could be easily compromised, and where foreign security services could not interfere—than they would be when they returned home. To spot and evaluate these students, the Clandestine Services maintained a contractual relationship with key professors on numerous campuses. When a professor had picked out a likely candidate, he notified his contact at the CIA and, on occasion, participated in the actual recruitment attempt. Some professors performed these services without being on a formal retainer. Others actively participated in agency covert operations by serving as "cut-outs," or intermediaries, and even by carrying out secret missions during foreign journeys.

The Clandestine Services at times have used a university to provide cover or even assist in a covert operation overseas. The best-known case of this sort was exposed in 1966 when *Ramparts* revealed that Michigan State University had been used by the CIA from 1955 to 1959 to run a covert police-training program in South Vietnam. The agency had paid $25 million to the university for its service, and five CIA operators were concealed in the program's staff.

The 1967 study on the CIA's ties with American universities covered all the activities described above, but the staff officer responsible for preparing it **was told that no research program concerning the use of drugs was to be mentioned in the report.***

The final study that the Executive Director presented to Director Helms was several inches thick, but the man who wrote it was still not sure that it was complete, less because he feared having overlooked some particular CIA component or proprietary organization which had its own university program than because he suspected that information had been withheld from him, particularly by the covert operators.

Because of its sensitivity, only one copy of the study was made, and it was turned over to the Director. Helms reviewed it and agreed with its conclusion: that all the CIA's campus activities were valuable to the agency and should be continued, except for a few individual contracts that had become outdated or too exposed. In the end, there was selective pruning of these programs, but essentially the CIA's activities with and at the universities continued as they had before the NSA scandal broke. They do so today.

The lone copy of the study was placed in the CIA Executive Director's safe for future reference. Within a few weeks after Helms' review, the report had to be pulled out; a controversy had erupted at a Midwestern university over alleged contracts between a certain professor and the CIA. When the study was consulted to find out if the allegations were correct, neither the professor nor the program he was associated with was listed anywhere in the bulky document. There was a collective sigh of relief in the agency's executive suite and some mumbling about irresponsible students making ridiculous charges. Shortly thereafter, however, the Director's staff found out that the exposed professor was genuine and had telephoned his CIA contact to discuss how he should react to the charges. He was told to get a teaching job elsewhere—and he did.

---

* **The agency's interest in drugs was more than a passing one; one officer was assigned to travel all over Latin America, buying up all sorts of hallucinatory drugs which might have some application to intelligence activities and operations.**

Soon after, another incident occurred. (

DELETED

)

Returning to Director Colby's explanation of the CIA's domestic activities:

> We also, I believe quite properly, can collect foreign intelligence in the United States, including the requesting [*sic*] American citizens to share with their Government certain information they may know about foreign situations, and we have a service that does this, and I am happy to say a very large number of American citizens have given us some information. We do not pay for that information. We can protect their proprietary interest and even protect their names if necessary, if they would rather not be exposed as the source of that information.

What Colby was referring to was the Domestic Contact Service (DCS). The DCS's primary function has traditionally been to collect intelligence from Americans without resorting to covert methods. Until early 1973 the DCS was part of the CIA's Intelligence Directorate, the overt analytical part of the agency. The DCS's normal operating technique is to establish relationships with businessmen, scholars, tourists, and other travelers who have made trips abroad, usually to Eastern Europe or China. These people are asked to provide information voluntarily about what they have seen or heard on their journeys. Most often they are contacted by the agency after they have returned home, but occasionally, if the CIA hears that a particular person plans to visit, say, a remote part of the Soviet Union, the DCS will get in touch in advance and ask

the traveler to seek out information on certain targets. In the past the DCS has, however, shied away from assigning specific missions, since the travelers are not professional spies and may easily be arrested if they take their espionage roles too seriously.

On several occasions over the years, the Clandestine Services have expressed an interest in assuming control of the DCS—with the argument that in the interest of efficiency all CIA intelligence collection by human sources should be run out of the same directorate. During the late 1960s the Clandestine Services were specifically rebuffed after a crude takeover attempt, but as a compromise measure Director Helms allowed clandestine operators to be assigned to the DCS in order to better coordinate intelligence collection. The DCS itself remained under the Intelligence Directorate. But in early 1973 Director James Schlesinger approved the transfer of the DCS to the Clandestine Services. Although there was no public notice of this change and travelers were not informed they were now dealing with the CIA's clandestine operators, Senator William Proxmire somehow got the word and told the Senate on August 1, 1973, that he was "particularly disturbed" by the shift. "Mr. Colby says," Proxmire explained, "that this is to improve the coordination of its collection activities with those of the Agency abroad. I find this disturbing because of the possibility that the DCS, which has a good reputation, may now become 'tainted' by the covert side of the Agency."

Again, Colby at the Senate hearing:

> We also, I believe, have certain support activities that we must conduct in the United States in order to conduct foreign intelligence operations abroad; certain structures are necessary in this country to give our people abroad perhaps a reason for operating abroad in some respects so that they can appear not as CIA employees but as representatives of some other entity.

Here Colby was undoubtedly talking about the CIA's training facilities, weapons warehouses, secret arrangements with U.S. companies to employ "deep cover" CIA operators, covert dealings

with arms dealers, and other back-up activities necessary to support paramilitary operations and other clandestine doings overseas. He may also have been referring to the CIA's use of American foundations, labor unions, and other groups as fronts to fund covert-action programs overseas, or to the proprietary corporations which operate for the CIA around the world. In this last category are the complex web of agency-owned airlines—Air America, Air Asia, Civil Air Transport, Southern Air Transport, Intermountain Aviation, (**DELETED**)—all of which have headquarters in the United States, and some of which maintain extensive facilities here. These airlines are run in direct competition with private companies, receive charter contracts from the U.S. government, and often operate domestically, in addition to taking on secret missions for the CIA abroad. (

DELETED

) All these companies—and others not yet revealed—do much more than provide cover for CIA employees, as Colby implied. They represent businesses worth hundreds of millions of dollars that can be used in all manner of operations by the CIA both at home and overseas.

Colby concluded:

> Lastly, I think that there are a number of activities in the United States where foreign intelligence can be collected from foreigners, and as long as there is foreign intelligence, I think it is quite proper that we do this.

In this instance Colby was referring in part to the CIA's efforts to recruit foreign students on American campuses, and a similar program, operated with the cooperation of military intelligence, to suborn foreign military officers who come to the United States for training. But the CIA also targets other foreign visitors to the U.S. —businessmen, newsmen, scholars, diplomats, U.N. delegates and employees, even simple tourists. It is specifically for the recruit-

ment and handling of foreign agents that the CIA maintains safe houses in Washington, New York, and other cities.

Another group of Americans who are very much targets of the CIA are recent immigrants. Almost from the moment Fidel Castro took power in 1959, CIA operators have worked closely with Cuban exiles, particularly in Florida. Most of the recruiting and some of the training for the agency's abortive invasion of the island in 1961 took place in the Miami area. Even after that fiasco the CIA has continued to use Cuban-Americans (few as celebrated as "retained" agent—and Watergate burglar—Eugenio Martinez) to carry out guerrilla operations against the Castro government. It has also been quite active among Eastern European émigrés in the United States. In November 1964, Eerik Heine, an Estonian refugee living in Canada, sued for slander another Estonian named Juri Raus, a resident of Hyattsville, Maryland. Raus, who was American national commander of the Legion of Estonian Liberation, was alleged to have denounced Heine as an agent of the KGB. Raus' defense in court was based not on the specifics of the case but on an affidavit submitted by then CIA Deputy Director Richard Helms stating that Raus was a CIA agent and had spoken out against Heine among Estonian-Americans under direct agency orders. Helms submitted two more affidavits to the court stating that the CIA had further ordered Raus not to testify in court, but explaining he had said what he had "to protect the integrity of the Agency's foreign intelligence sources." The federal judge, Roszel C. Thomsen, ruled in the CIA's favor and did not accept the plaintiff's contention that even if the agency had ordered that the alleged slander be committed, it had no power to do so under the National Security Act of 1947, which forbade the CIA to exercise any "internal security functions."

In his decision, Judge Thomsen wrote:

It is reasonable that émigré groups from behind the Iron Curtain would be a valuable source of information as to what goes on in their homeland. The fact that the intelligence source is located in the United States does not make it an "internal security function" over which the CIA has no authority. The

court concludes that activities by the CIA to protect its foreign intelligence sources located in the United States are within the power granted by Congress to the CIA.

By extension, it might also be argued that any "foreign intelligence source" located in the United States, émigré or not, is fair game for the CIA. Clearly, American citizens traveling abroad are eligible; clearly, researchers in universities are eligible; and if the agency can come up with a reason—such as the threat of "foreign influence" in American politics—then everyone's eligible. And that eligibility extends not only to the honor of being consulted, cajoled, and financed, but to the privilege of being investigated, suborned, or whatever else the covert operators might wish to do.

PART III

EIGHT

The Clandestine Mentality

The greatest dangers to liberty
lurk in insidious encroachment
by men of zeal, well-meaning
but without understanding.

—JUSTICE BRANDEIS, 1928

The nation must to a degree take
it on faith that we too are
honorable men devoted to her
service.

—CIA DIRECTOR HELMS, 1971

T HE man who masterminded and oversaw the CIA's clandestine operations in Indochina during much of the 1960s was William Colby. He is a trim, well-groomed Princeton and Columbia Law School graduate who, if he were taller, might be mistaken for a third Bundy brother. He started in the intelligence business during World War II with the Office of Strategic Services. His field assignments included parachuting into German-occupied France and Norway to work with the anti-Nazi underground movements, during which he showed a remarkable talent for clandestine work. After the war he joined the newly formed CIA and rose rapidly through its ranks, becoming an expert on the Far East. From 1959 until 1962 he served as the CIA's chief of station in Saigon. In 1962 he was named head of the Far East Division of the Clandestine Services.

In this position Colby presided over the CIA's rapidly expanding programs in Southeast Asia. Under his leadership (but always with White House approval) the agency's "secret" war in Laos was launched, and more than 30,000 Meo and other tribal warriors were organized into the CIA's own Armée Clandestine. Colby's officers and agents directed—and on occasion participated in—the battles against the Pathet Lao, in bombing operations by the **CIA's proprietary** company Air America, and in commando-type raids into China and North Vietnam, well before Congress had passed the Gulf of Tonkin Resolution.

Colby seemed to keep the secret operation always under tight control. His colleagues in the CIA marveled at his ability to run all the agency's activities in Laos with no more than forty or fifty career CIA officers in the field. There were, to be sure, several thousand other Americans supporting the CIA effort, but these were soldiers of fortune or pilots under contract to the agency, not

career men. From the CIA's point of view, the war in Laos was cheap (costing the agency only $20 to $30 million a year) and well managed.* The number of Americans involved was small enough that a relatively high degree of secrecy could be maintained. In contrast to the tens of thousands of Laotians who died in the war, few Americans were killed, and those who were casualties were not CIA career officers but rather mercenaries, contract officers, and personnel of the agency's air proprietaries. The agency considered Laos to be a very successful operation. And Colby received much of the credit for keeping things under control.

The agency's clandestine activities in Vietnam were not so well organized, concealed, or successful as its Laotian operation. In the mid-1960s the CIA was swept along with the rest of the U.S. government into launching huge programs designed to support the war effort. The agency would have preferred to run relatively small, highly secret operations (or to have had complete control of covert action), but the stiffer and stiffer demands of the Johnson administration made this impossible. Thus, if the President wanted a larger contribution from the CIA, the CIA would contribute. In 1965 Colby, still stationed in Washington, oversaw the founding in Vietnam of the agency's Counter Terror (CT) program. In 1966 the agency became wary of adverse publicity surrounding the use of the word "terror" and changed the name of the CT teams to the Provincial Reconnaissance Units (PRUs). Wayne Cooper, a former Foreign Service officer who spent almost eighteen months as an advisor to South Vietnamese internal-security programs, described the operation: "It was a unilateral American program, never recognized by the South Vietnamese government. CIA representatives recruited, organized, supplied, and directly paid CT teams, whose function was to use Viet Cong techniques of terror—assassination, abuses, kidnappings and intimidation—against the Viet Cong leadership." Colby also supervised the establishment of a network of Provincial Interrogation Centers. One of these centers was constructed, with agency funds,

---

* The full cost of the war was actually closer to a half-billion dollars a year, but most of this was funded by other agencies—the Defense Department and AID.

in each of South Vietnam's forty-four provinces. An agency operator or contract employee directed each center's operations, much of which consisted of torture tactics against suspected Vietcong, such torture usually carried out by Vietnamese nationals.

In 1967 Colby's office devised another program, eventually called Phoenix, to coordinate an attack against the Vietcong infrastructure among all Vietnamese and American police, intelligence, and military units. Again CIA money was the catalyst. According to Colby's own testimony in 1971 before a congressional committee, 20,587 suspected Vietcong were killed under Phoenix in its first two and a half years.* Figures provided by the South Vietnamese government credit Phoenix with 40,994 VC kills.

Also in 1967, President Johnson sent Robert Komer, a former agency employee who had joined the White House staff, to Vietnam to head up all the civilian and military pacification programs. In November of that year, while Komer was in Washington for consultation, the President asked him if there was anything he needed to carry out his assignment. Komer responded that he certainly could use the services of Bill Colby as his deputy. The President replied that Komer could draft anybody he chose. A year later Colby succeeded Komer as head of the pacification program, with the rank of ambassador. The longtime clandestine officer had ostensibly resigned from the CIA to become a State Department employee.

One of Colby's principal functions was to strengthen the Vietnamese economy in order to improve the lot of the average Vietnamese peasant, and thereby make him less susceptible to Vietcong appeals and more loyal to the Thieu government. To win over the peasants, Colby insisted that corruption within the Saigon govern-

* Even Colby has admitted that serious abuses were committed under Phoenix. Former intelligence officers have come before congressional committees and elsewhere to describe repeated examples of torture and other particularly repugnant practices used by Phoenix operatives. However, according to David Wise, writing in the *New York Times Magazine* on July 1, 1973, "Not one of Colby's friends or neighbors, or even his critics on the Hill, would, in their wildest imagination, conceive of Bill Colby attaching electric wires to a man's genitals and personally turning the crank. *'Not Bill Colby . . . He's a Princeton man.'* "

ment had to be greatly reduced. At one point he even proposed a systematic campaign called the "Honor the Nation" program, which was to be an attack on illegal practices at all levels of Vietnamese society. At that time Colby was well aware that black-market trafficking in money was one of the biggest corruption problems in Vietnam. All U.S. personnel in Vietnam were under strict orders not to buy Vietnamese piasters on the black market, and a number of Americans had either been court-martialed by the military or fired by their civilian agencies for violating these orders. But Colby also knew that for many years the CIA had been obtaining tens of millions of dollars in piasters on the black market, either in Hong Kong or in Saigon. In this way the agency could get two to three times as much buying power for its American dollars. Additionally, the Clandestine Services claimed, black-market piasters were untraceable and thus ideal for secret operations.* Although from a strict budgetary point of view the agency's currency purchases were sound fiscal policy, they directly violated both Vietnamese law and U.S. official policy. Moreover, the purchases helped to keep alive the black market which the U.S. government was professedly working to stamp out.

During the mid-1960s while Colby was still in Washington, the Bureau of the Budget learned that the CIA budget for Vietnam provided for dollar expenditures figured at the legal exchange rate. Since in truth the agency was buying its piasters on the black market, it actually had two to three times more piasters to spend in Vietnam than its budget showed. The Bureau of the Budget then insisted that all figures be listed at the actual black-market rate, so at least examiners of the agency's budget in Washington would have a true idea of how much money the CIA was spending. The bureau then also tried to cut U.S. government costs by having the CIA buy piasters for *other* agencies on the black market. The agency was unenthusiastic about this idea and managed to avoid doing it, not because massive black-market purchases would have

* Given more than 500,000 Americans in Vietnam, all using Vietnamese piasters, and a chaotic Vietnamese banking system, the CIA could of course have obtained untraceable or "sterile" money without resorting to the black market.

negated the government's avowed efforts to support the piaster, but because the agency did not want the secrecy of its money-exchange operations disturbed.

Compared to other aspects of the Vietnam war, the CIA's use of the black market is not a major issue. It simply points up the fact that the CIA is not bound by the same rules that apply to the rest of the government. The Central Intelligence Agency Act of 1949 makes this clear: "The sums made available to the Agency may be expended without regard to the provisions of law and regulations relating to the expenditures of Government."*

Thus, a William Colby can, with no legal or ethical conflict, propose programs to end corruption in Vietnam while at the same time condoning the CIA's dubious money practices. And extending the concept of the agency's immunity to law and morals, a Colby can devise and direct terror tactics, secret wars, and the like, all in the name of democracy. This is the clandestine mentality: a separation of personal morality and conduct from actions, no matter how debased, which are taken in the name of the United States government and, more specifically, the Central Intelligence Agency.

When Colby left his post as deputy ambassador to Vietnam in 1971, the CIA immediately "rehired" him, and Director Helms appointed him Executive Director-Comptroller, the number-three position in the agency. When James Schlesinger took over the agency in early 1973, he made Colby chief of the Clandestine Services. In May 1973, at the height of the personnel shake-ups caused by the Watergate affair, President Nixon moved Schlesinger to the Defense Department and named Colby to head the CIA. Thus, after about four months under the directorship of the outsider Schlesinger, control of the agency was again in the hands of a clandestine operator.

Senator Harold Hughes, for one, expressed grave reservations about Colby's appointment as CIA Director in a Senate speech on

---

* The CIA in Vietnam even escaped the Johnson administration's worldwide edict that all cars purchased by the American government would be of American manufacture. While State Department and AID personnel were forced to navigate Saigon's narrow streets in giant Chevrolets and Plymouths, the agency motorpool was full of much smaller and more practical Japanese Toyotas.

August 1, 1973: "I am fearful of a man whose experience has been so largely devoted to clandestine operations involving the use of force and manipulation of factions in foreign governments. Such a man may become so enamored with these techniques that he loses sight of the higher purposes and moral constraints which should guide our country's activities abroad."

Deeply embedded within the clandestine mentality is the belief that human ethics and social laws have no bearing on covert operations or their practitioners. The intelligence profession, because of its lofty "natural security" goals, is free from all moral restrictions. There is no need to wrestle with technical legalisms or judgments as to whether something is right or wrong. The determining factors in secret operations are purely pragmatic: Does the job need to be done? Can it be done? And can secrecy (or plausible denial) be maintained?

One of the lessons learned from the Watergate experience is the scope of this amorality and its influence on the clandestine mentality. E. Howard Hunt claimed that his participation in the Watergate break-in and the other operations of the plumbers group was in "what I believed to be the . . . the best interest of my country." In this instance, at least, we can accept Hunt as speaking sincerely. He was merely reflecting an attitude that is shared by most CIA operators when carrying out the orders of their superiors.

Hunt expanded on this point when interrogated before a federal grand jury in April 1973 by Assistant U.S. Attorney Earl Silbert.

SILBERT: Now while you worked at the White House, were you ever a participant or did you ever have knowledge of any other so-called "bag job" or entry operations?

HUNT: No, sir.

SILBERT: Were you aware of or did you participate in any other what might commonly be referred to as illegal activities?

HUNT: Illegal?

SILBERT: Yes, sir.

HUNT: I have no recollection of any, no, sir.

SILBERT: What about clandestine activities?

HUNT: Yes, sir.

SILBERT: All right. What about that?

HUNT: I'm not quibbling, but there's quite a difference between something that's illegal and something that's clandestine.

SILBERT: Well, in your terminology, would the entry into Mr. Fielding's [Daniel Ellsberg's psychiatrist] office have been clandestine, illegal, neither or both?

HUNT: I would simply call it an entry operation conducted under the auspices of competent authority.

Within the CIA, similar activities are undertaken with the consent of "competent authority." The Watergate conspirators, assured that "national security" was at stake, did not question the legality or the morality of their methods; nor do most CIA operators. Hundreds if not thousands of CIA men have participated in similar operations, usually—but not always—in foreign countries; all such operations are executed in the name of "national security." The clandestine mentality not only allows it; it veritably *wills* it.

In early October, 1969, the CIA learned through a secret agent that a group of radicals was about to hijack a plane in Brazil and escape to Cuba. This intelligence was forwarded to CIA headquarters in Langley, Virginia and from there sent on an "eyes only" basis to Henry Kissinger at the White House and top officials of the State Department, the Defense Department, and the National Security Agency. Within a few days, on October 8, the same radicals identified in the CIA report commandeered at gunpoint a Brazilian commercial airliner with 49 people aboard, and after a refueling stop in Guyana, forced the pilot to fly to Havana. Neither the CIA nor the other agencies of the U.S. government which had advance warning of the radicals' plans moved to stop the crime from being committed, although at that time the official policy of the United States —as enunciated by the President—was to take all possible measures to stamp out aerial piracy.

Afterwards, when officials of the State Department questioned their colleagues in the CIA on why preventive measures had not been taken to abort the hijacking, the agency's clandestine opera-

tors delayed more than a month before responding. During the interim, security forces in Brazil succeeded in breaking up that country's principal revolutionary group and killing its leader, Carlos Marighella. Shortly after the revolutionary leader's death on November 4, the CIA informally passed word back to the State Department noting that if any action had been taken to stop the October skyjacking, the agency's penetration of the radical movement might have been exposed and Marighella's organization could not have been destroyed. While it was never quite clear whether the agent who alerted the clandestine operators to the hijacking had also fingered Marighella, that was the impression the CIA tried to convey to the State Department. The agency implied it had not prevented the hijacking because to have done so would have lessened the chances of scoring the more important goal of "neutralizing" Marighella and his followers. To the CIA's clandestine operators, the end—wiping out the Brazilian radical movement—apparently had justified the means, thus permitting the hijacking to take place and needlessly endangering forty-nine innocent lives in the process.

During the last twenty-five years American foreign policy has been dominated by the concept of containing communism; almost always the means employed in pursuit of "national security" have been justified by the end. Since the "free world" was deemed to be under attack by a determined enemy, sincere men in the highest government posts believed—and still do believe—that their country could not survive without resorting to the same distasteful methods employed by the other side. In recent years the intensity of the struggle has been reduced as monolithic communism has split among several centers of power; as a result, there have been tactical changes in America's conduct of foreign affairs. Yet the feeling remains strong among the nation's top officials, in the CIA and elsewhere, that America is responsible for what happens in other countries and that it has an inherent right—a sort of modern Manifest Destiny—to intervene in other countries' internal affairs. Changes may have occurred at the negotiating table, but not in the planning arena; intervention—either military or covert—is still the rule.

To the clandestine operations of the CIA, nothing could be more normal than the use of "dirty tricks" to promote the U.S. national interest, as they and their agency determine it. In the words of former Clandestine Services chief Richard Bissell, CIA men "feel a higher loyalty and . . . they are acting in obedience to that higher loyalty." They must be able to violate accepted standards of integrity and decency when the CIA's objectives so demand. Bissell admitted in a 1965 television interview that agency operators at times carried out actions which "were contrary to their moral precepts" but they believed "the morality of . . . cold war is so infinitely easier than the morality of almost any kind of hot war that I never encountered this as a serious problem."

Perhaps as a consequence of the confused morality that guides him, a clandestine operator is dedicated to the utmost secrecy. Convicted Watergate burglar Bernard Barker, who long worked with and for the agency, described these operators in a September 1972 *New York Times* interview: "They're anonymous men. They hate publicity; they get nervous with it. They don't want to be spoken of. They don't even want to be known or anything like that." And nearly always accompanying this passion for secrecy comes an obsession with deception and manipulation. These traits, developed in the CIA's training programs, are essential elements for success in the operator's career. He learns that he must become expert at "living his cover," at pretending he is something he is not. Agency instructors grade the young operators on how well they can fool their colleagues. A standard exercise given to the student spies is for one to be assigned the task of finding out some piece of information about another. Since each trainee is expected to maintain a false identity and cover during the training period, a favorite way to coax out the desired information is to befriend the targeted trainee, to win his confidence and make him let down his guard. The trainee who gains the information receives a high mark; his exploited colleague fails the test. The "achievers" are those best suited, in the view of the agency, for convincing a foreign official he should become a traitor to his country; for manipulating that

official, often against his will; and for "terminating" the agent when he has outlived his usefulness to the CIA.

Operating with secrecy and deception gradually becomes second nature to the clandestine operator as his early training progresses and he moves into an actual field assignment. The same habits may at times carry over into his dealings with his colleagues and even his family. Most operators see no inconsistency between an upstanding private life and immoral or amoral work, and they would probably say that anyone who couldn't abide the dichotomy is "soft." The double moral standard has been so completely absorbed at the CIA that Allen Dulles once stated, "In my ten years with the Agency I only recall one case of many hundreds where a man who had joined the Agency felt some scruples about the activities he was asked to carry on." Even today Dulles' estimate would not be far off.

As much as the operator believes in the rightness of his actions, he is forced to work in an atmosphere that is potentially demoralizing. He is quite often on the brink of the underworld, or even immersed in it, and he frequently turns to the least savory types to achieve his goals. Criminals are useful to him, and are often called upon by him, when he does not want to perform personally some particularly distasteful task or when he does not want to risk any direct agency involvement in his dirty work. And if the clandestine operator wants to use attractive young women to seduce foreign officials, he does not call on female CIA employees. Instead he hires local prostitutes, or induces foreign girls to assume the seductress's role, hoping to use his women to ferret information out of targeted opponents and to blackmail them into cooperating with the CIA.

Other CIA men regularly deal with black-marketeers to purchase "laundered" currency. The agency cannot very well subsidize a political party in South Vietnam or buy labor peace on the Marseilles docks with money that can be traced back to the CIA. Thus, CIA "finance officers" permanently assigned to Hong Kong, Beirut, and other international monetary centers frequently turn to the world's illegal money changers to support agency clandestine operations. "Sterile" weapons for CIA paramilitary activities are

obtained in the same fashion from the munitions merchants who will provide arms to anyone able to pay the price. And when untraceable troops are needed to assist a CIA-sponsored revolution or counter-revolution, the agency will put out the word in such mercenary centers as Brussels, Kinshasa, and Saigon that it is hiring soldiers of fortune willing to support any cause for a price.

Yet there are certain standards the CIA's clandestine operator must maintain in order to hold on to his job and the respect of his colleagues. By the agency's code, he is not supposed to profit personally from his activities. If he were involved in narcotics traffic for his own gain, he would probably be fired for having been "corrupted by the trade." But if the same CIA man were involved in narcotics traffic because he was using his narcotics connections to blackmail a Soviet official, he would be considered by his colleagues to be doing his work well.

While the CIA has never trafficked in dope as a matter of official policy, its clandestine personnel have used this trade—as they have used almost every other criminal activity known to man—in the pursuit of their goals. In Laos the CIA hoped to defeat the Pathet Lao and North Vietnamese (and, thus, "stop communism"); for that purpose, it was willing to supply guns, money, and training to the Meo tribe, the part of the Laotian population most eager to fight for the agency. The CIA was willing to overlook the fact that the Meos' primary cash crop was opium and that they continued to sell the drug during most of the years that they participated in the "secret" war as the "cutting edge" of the anti-communist force in Laos. While the planes of the **CIA proprietary airline,** Air America, were on occasion used to carry opium and while some of the highest military officers supported by the agency were also the kingpins of the drug trade, the agency could still claim that it did not officially sanction these activities. But not until the heroin traffic from Southeast Asia was perceived as a major American problem a few years ago did the CIA make any serious effort to curb the flow of the drug, for it mattered not what sort of people the Meo were—what mattered was what they were willing and able to do for the CIA. The agency would hire Satan himself as an agent if he could help guarantee the "national security."

The key to a successful espionage operation is locating and using the right agent. There are seven basic areas of agent relations— spotting, evaluation, recruiting, testing, training, handling, and termination. Each deserves extended examination.

Spotting: This is the process of identifying foreigners or other persons who might be willing to spy for the CIA.

The agency operator mingles as much as possible with the native population in the country to which he is assigned, hoping to spot potential agents. He normally concentrates on officials in the local government, members of the military services, and representatives of the intelligence agencies of the host country. People in other professions, even if recruitable, usually do not have access to the kind of strategic or high-level information which the CIA is seeking. Most operators work out of the local U.S. embassy; their diplomatic cover allows a convenient approach to their target groups through the myriad of officials and social contacts that characterize the life of a diplomat, even a bogus one serving the CIA. Some agency officers pose as military men or other U.S. government representatives—officials of the AID, the USIA, and other agencies. In addition to official cover, the CIA sometimes puts officers under "deep cover" as businessmen, students, newsmen, or missionaries.

The CIA operator is constantly looking for indications of vulnerability on the part of potential foreign agents. The indicators may come from a casual observation by the operator at a cocktail party, gossip picked up by his wife, suggestions from already recruited agents, or assistance furnished—wittingly or unwittingly —by a genuine American diplomat or businessman. The CIA operator receives instruction, based on studies made by agency specialists or American college professors under contract to the CIA, on what kinds of people are most susceptible to the intrigues and strategies of clandestine life. Obviously, the personality of the potential spy varies from country to country and case to case, but certain broad categories of preferable and susceptible agent types have been identified. The most sought-after informants are foreign officials who are dissatisfied with their country's policies and who

look to the United States for guidance. People of this sort are much more likely to become loyal and dedicated agents than those whose primary motivation is monetary. Money certainly can go a long way in obtaining information, especially in the Third World, but the man who can be bought by the CIA is also a relatively easy mark for the opposition. On the other hand, the agent who genuinely believes that what he is doing has a higher purpose will probably not be vulnerable to approaches from the KGB or other opposition services, and he is less likely to be plagued by the guilt and the accompanying psychological deterioration which frequently hamper the work of spies. The ideological "defector in place" is the prize catch for CIA operators. Other likely candidates for spying are officials who have expensive tastes which they cannot satisfy from their normal incomes, or those with an obviously uncontrollable weakness for women, other men, alcohol, or drugs.

The operator does not always search for potential agents among those who are already working in positions of importance. He may take someone who in a few years may move into an important assignment (with or without a little help from the CIA). Students are considered particularly valuable targets in this regard, especially in Third World countries where university graduates often rise to high-level governmental positions only a few years after graduation. In Latin American and African countries the agency puts special emphasis on seeking agents in the armed forces, since so many of these nations are ruled or controlled by the military. Hence, the "cleared" professors on the CIA's payroll at American universities with substantial foreign enrollments, and military training officers at such places as the field command school at Fort Leavenworth, Kansas, are prime recruiters.

In the communist countries, as we have said, agency operators tend to focus on members of the opposition intelligence services in their search for secret agents.

Evaluation: Once a potential spy has been spotted, the agency makes a thorough review of all information available on him to decide whether he is, or someday will be, in a position to provide useful intelligence. The first step in the evaluation process is to run a "namecheck," or trace, on the person, using the CIA's exten-

sive computerized files located at headquarters in Langley. This data bank was developed by International Business Machines exclusively for the CIA and contains information on hundreds of thousands of persons. Any relevant biographical information on the potential agent found in the files is cabled back to the field operator, who meanwhile continues to observe the prospect and makes discreet inquiries about his background, personality, and chances for advancement. The prospect will probably be put under surveillance to learn more of his habits and views. Eventually a determination will be made as to the prospect's probable motivation (ideological, monetary, or psychological) for becoming a spy. If he hasn't any such motivation, the CIA searches for ways—blackmail and the like—of pressuring him. At the same time, the case officer must determine if the prospect is legitimate or if he is an enemy plant—a provocation or a double agent. Some member of the CIA team, perhaps the original spotter, will attempt to get to know the potential agent on a personal basis and win his confidence.

Recruiting: At the conclusion of the evaluation period, which can last weeks or months, CIA headquarters, in consultation with the field component, decides whether or not the prospective agent should be approached to spy for the agency. Normally, if the decision is affirmative, a CIA outsider will approach the prospect. Neither the spotter nor the evaluator nor, for that matter, any member of the local agency team will generally be used to make the recruitment "pitch"; if something goes wrong, the individual being propositioned will therefore be unable to expose any of the CIA operators. As a rule, the CIA officer giving the pitch is furnished with a false identity and given an agency-produced fake American passport. The "pitchman" can quickly slip out of the country in case of trouble.

Once the recruiter is on the scene, agency operators will concoct a meeting between him and the prospective agent. The pitchman will be introduced to the target under carefully prearranged—and controlled—circumstances, allowing the operator who made the introduction to withdraw discreetly, leaving the recruiter alone with the potential agent. Steps also will have been taken to provide the recruiter with an escape route in the event that the pitch should

backfire. If he is clever in his approach, the recruiter makes his pitch subtly, without any overt statements to reveal his true purpose or affiliation with the agency.

If the potential agent has previously voiced opposition to his government, the recruiter is likely to begin with an appeal to the man's patriotic obligations and higher ideological inclinations. Ways by which he could aid his country and its people through secret cooperation with a benevolent foreign power will be suggested. If, on the other hand, the prospect is deemed susceptible to money, the recruiter probably will play to this point, emphasizing that he knows of ways for the right individual to earn big money— quickly and easily. If the subject is interested in power, or merely has expensive habits to satisfy (sex, drugs, and so forth), if he wants to defect from his country, or simply wishes to get away from his family and social situation, the recruiter will attempt to concentrate his efforts on these human needs, all the time offering suggestions as to how they may be met through cooperation with "certain parties." People volunteer or agree to spy on their governments for many reasons. It is the task of the recruiter to determine what reason—if one exists—is most likely to motivate the potential agent.

If the agency has concluded that the prospect is vulnerable to blackmail, thinly veiled threats of exposure will be employed during the pitch. In some cases, however, the recruiter may directly confront the potential agent with the evidence which could be used to expose him, in an effort to shock him into accepting the recruitment pitch. And in all cases the meeting between the recruiter and the prospect will be monitored either by audio surveillance (i.e., a tape recording) or some other method—photographs, fingerprints, or anything which will produce evidence that can later be used to incriminate the prospect. If not at first susceptible to blackmail, the prospect who wittingly or unwittingly entertains a recruitment pitch may afterward find himself entrapped by evidence which could be employed to ruin his career or land him in jail.

After the prospect accepts the CIA's offer, or yields to blackmail, the recruiter will go into the details of the arrangement. He may offer an agent with high potential $500 to $1,000 a month, say,

partly in cash but mostly by deposit in an escrow account at some American or Swiss bank. He will try to keep the direct non-escrow payments as low as possible: first, to prevent the man from going on a spending spree which could attract the unwanted attention of the local security service, and, second, to strengthen his hold over the spy. The latter reason is particularly important if the agent is not ideologically motivated. The recruiter may pledge that the CIA will guarantee the safety of the agent or his family, in case of difficulties with the local police, and he may promise a particularly valuable agent a lifelong pension and even American citizenship.

The fulfillment of such pledges varies greatly, depending on the operational situation and the personality of the CIA case officer in charge. Some are cynical, brutal men whose word, in most instances, is absolutely worthless. Others, though, will go to extraordinary lengths to protect their agents. In the early 1960s in Syria, one CIA man endangered his life and that of a trusted colleague to exfiltrate an agent who had been "rolled up" (i.e., captured) by the local security service, tortured, and forced to confess his complicity in the CIA's operations there. Although the agent, rendered a physical and mental wreck, was no longer of any use to the CIA, the two operators put him in the trunk of a private automobile and drove him to a nearby country—and safety.

The recruiter will try to get the new agent, upon agreeing to work for the CIA, to sign a piece of paper that formally and evidentially connects him with the agency, a paper which can later be used to threaten a recalcitrant agent with exposure, should he balk at continuing to work for the CIA.

The recruiter's last function is to set up a meeting between the new agent and the CIA operator stationed in that country who will serve as his case officer. This will often involve the use of prearranged recognition signals. One technique, for example is to give the agent a set of unusual cufflinks and tell him that he will soon be approached by a man wearing an identical pair. Another is to set up an exchange of code words which the case officer can later use to identify himself to the agent. When all this is accomplished, the recruiter breaks off the meeting and as soon as possible thereafter leaves the country.

When the recruitment pitch doesn't work, (

DELETED

DELETED

) meeting with a potential agent/defector in a local "gasthaus" only to find that the occupants of the nearby tables were not Viennese but rather members of a KGB goon squad. In that instance, when fighting erupted, he managed to escape by fleeing to the men's room and ignominiously crawling to safety through the window above the toilet.

Testing: Once an agent has been recruited, his case officer immediately tests his loyalty and reliability. He will be given certain tasks to carry out which, if successfully performed, will establish his sincerity and access to secret information. The agent may be asked, for example, to collect information on a subject about which, unknown to him, the agency has already acquired a great deal of knowledge. If his reporting does not jibe with the previous intelligence, he is likely to be either a double agent attempting to mislead his case officer or a poor source of information clumsily trying to please his new employer. When feasible, the agent's performance will be carefully monitored during the testing period through discreet surveillance.

In addition, the new agent will almost certainly be required to take a lie-detector test. CIA operators place heavy reliance on the findings of a polygraph machine—referred to as the "black box"—in their agent operations. Polygraph specialists are available from headquarters and several of the agency's regional support centers to administer the tests on special assignment. According to one

such specialist, testing foreign agents calls for completely different skills than questioning Americans under consideration for career service with the CIA. He found Americans to be normally straightforward and relatively predictable in their responses to the testing, making it comparatively simple to isolate someone who is not up to the agency's standards. But testing foreign agents, he says, is much more difficult. Adjustments must be made to allow for cultural differences, and for the fact that the subject is engaging in clearly illegal and highly dangerous secret work. An ideologically motivated agent, furthermore, may be quite emotional and thus unusually difficult to "read," or evaluate, from the machine's measurements. One spying solely for monetary gain or to satisfy some private vice may be impossible to read because there is no way of gauging his moral limits. Congenital liars, psychopaths, and users of certain drugs can frequently "beat the black box." According to the polygraph expert, a decision on the agent's reliability and sincerity is, therefore, based as much on the intuition of the tester as on the measurements of the machine. The agent, however, is led to believe that the black box is infallible, so if he is neither a well-trained double agent nor clinically abnormal, he will more than likely tell the truth.

Training: When the agent has completed the testing process, he is next given instruction in the special skills required for his new work as a spy. The extent, location, and specific nature of the training varies according to the circumstances of the operation. In some instances the secret instruction is quite thorough; in other cases the logistics of such training are nearly impossible to handle, and consequently there is virtually none. In such circumstances the agent must rely on his instinct and talents and the professionalism of his case officer, learning the ways of clandestine life as the operation develops.

When training can be provided to an agent, he will be taught the use of any equipment he may need—a miniature camera for photographing documents, for example. He will be instructed in one of several methods of covert communications—secret writing, coded or encrypted radio transmissions, or the like. He will also learn the use of clandestine contacts. And he will be given training

in security precautions, such as the detection and avoidance of surveillance.

Depending upon the agent's availability, however, and his estimated worth in the eyes of the Clandestine Services, he may receive only a few short lessons from his case officer on how to use an audio device or how to communicate with the agency through a series of cut-outs. Or he may be asked to invent a cover story to give to his family and his employer that will allow him to spend several days or even a couple of weeks at an agency safe house, learning the art of espionage. He may even seek an excuse to leave the country so he can receive instruction at a CIA facility in another nation, where he is much less likely to be observed by his country's security service. Or he may even be brought to the United States for training, constantly monitored while here by the CIA Office of Security. Special training facilities for foreign recruits, isolated from all other activities, exist at **Camp Peary— "The Farm"—in southern Virginia.**

While the tradecraft taught to the agent is unquestionably useful, the instruction period also serves as an opportunity for his case officer and the other instructors to motivate him and increase his commitment to the CIA's cause. The agent is introduced to the clandestine proficiency and power of the agency. He sees its tightly knit professional camaraderie. He learns that although he is abandoning his former way of life, he now has a chance for a better one. Good work on his part will be rewarded with political asylum; the government he is rejecting may even be replaced by a superior one. Thus his allegiance to his new employer is further forged. It is the task of the case officer to maintain this attitude in the mind of his agent.

Handling: Successful handling of an agent hinges on the strength of the relationship that the case officer is able to establish with his agent. According to one former CIA operator, a good case officer must combine the qualities of a master spy, a psychiatrist, and a father confessor.

There are two prevailing views within the CIA's Clandestine Services on the best way to handle, or run, an agent. One is the "buddy" technique, in which the case officer develops a close

personal relationship with his agent and convinces him that they are working together to attain an important political goal. This approach can provide a powerful motivating force, encouraging the agent to take great risks for his friend. Most senior operators believe, however, that the "buddy" technique leads to the danger of the case officer forming an emotional attachment to his agent, sometimes causing the CIA man to lose his professional objectivity. At the other end of the agent-handling spectrum is the "cynical" style, in which the operator, while feigning personal concern for the agent, actually deals with him in a completely callous manner—one that may border on ruthlessness. From the beginning, this case officer is interested only in results. He drives the agent to extremes in an attempt to achieve maximum operational performance. This method, too, has it drawbacks: once the agent senses he is merely being exploited by his case officer, his loyalty can quickly evaporate.

Agents are intricate and, often, delicately balanced individuals. The factors which lead them into the clandestine game are many and highly complex. The stresses and pressures under which they must function tend to make such men volatile, often unpredictable. The case officer, therefore, must continually be alert for any sign that his agent is unusually disturbed, that he may not be carrying out his mission. The operator must always employ the right mixture of flattery and threats, ideology and money, emotional attachment and ruthlessness to keep his agent actively working for him.

With the Soviet Oleg Penkovsky, his British and CIA handlers found that flattery was a particularly effective method of motivation. Although he preferred British manners, Penkovsky greatly admired American power. Accordingly, he was secretly granted U.S. citizenship and presented with his "secret" CIA medal. As a military man, he was quite conscious of rank; consequently, he was made a colonel in the U.S. Army to show him that he suffered no loss of status because of his shift in allegiance.

On two occasions while Penkovsky was an active spy, he traveled outside the U.S.S.R. on official duty with high-level delegations attending Soviet-sponsored trade shows. Both times, first

in London and then in Paris, he slipped away from his Soviet colleagues for debriefing and training sessions with British and American case officers. During one of the London meetings, he asked to see his U.S. Army uniform. None of the CIA men, nor any of the British operators, had anticipated such a request. One quick-thinking officer, however, announced that the uniform was at another safe house and that driving there and bringing it back for Penkovsky to see would take a while. The spy was temporarily placated, and a CIA case officer was immediately dispatched to find a colonel's uniform to show to the agent. After scurrying around London for a couple of hours in search of an American Army colonel with a build similar to Penkovsky's, the operator returned triumphantly to the debriefing session just as it was concluding—uniform in hand. Penkovsky was pleased.

Months later, in Paris, the CIA operators were better prepared. A brand-new uniform tailored to Penkovsky's measurements was hung in a closet in a room adjacent to where he was being debriefed, and he inspected it happily when the meeting was concluded.

In the 1950s the CIA recruited an Eastern European intelligence officer in Vienna whose motivation, like Penkovsky's, was essentially ideological. While he was promised a good salary (and a comfortable pension upon the completion of the operation, at which time he would formally defect to the United States), his case officer avoided making any direct payments to him in Vienna in order not to risk attracting the opposition's attention to him. The agent well understood the need for such precautions, yet after he had been spying for a while, he shocked his case officer one day by demanding a fairly substantial amount of cash. He refused to say why he wanted the money, but it was obvious to his case officer that the agent's continued good work for the agency was contingent on getting the money he had requested. After consultations with the local CIA station chief and with headquarters, it was finally decided that the risk must be taken and the agent was given the money, with the hope that he would not do something outlandish or risky with it. Agency operators then put him under surveillance to learn what he was up to. To their consternation,

they discovered him the following weekend on the Danube River cruising back and forth in a motorboat which he had just bought. A few days afterward his case officer confronted him and demanded that he get rid of the boat, for it was not something a man of his ostensibly austere circumstances could possibly have purchased on his own salary. The agent agreed, casually explaining that ever since he was a small boy he had wanted to own a motorboat. Now that yearning was out of his system and he was quite willing to give up the boat.

Another Eastern European, who spied briefly for the CIA years later, refused all offers of pensions and political asylum in the West. He wanted only Benny Goodman records.

One of the biggest problems in handling an agent is caused by the changeover of case officers. In keeping with the CIA's policy of employing diplomatic and other forms of official cover for most of its operators serving abroad, case officers masquerading as U.S. diplomats, AID officials, Department of Defense representatives, and the like, must be transferred every two to four years to another foreign country or to Washington for a headquarters assignment, as is customary with genuine American officials. A departing case officer introduces his replacement to all his agents before he leaves, but often the agents are initially reluctant to deal with a new man. Having developed an acceptable working relationship with one case officer, they usually are not eager to change to another. Their reluctance is often heightened by the agency's practice of assigning young case officers to handle already proven agents. In this way, junior operators can gain experience with agents who, as a rule, do not need as much professional guidance or sympathetic "hand-holding" as newly recruited ones. Most agents, however, feel that dealing with an inexperienced officer only increases the risks of compromise. All in all, making the changeover can be quite sticky, but it is almost always accomplished without permanent damage to the operation. If persuasion and promises are not adequate to retain the agent's loyalty, threats of blackmail usually are. The agency precaution of amassing incriminating evidence—secret contracts, signed payment receipts, tape recordings, and photographs—generally will convince even

the most reluctant agent to see things the CIA's way.

In certain highly sensitive operations the problem of case-officer changeover is avoided in deference to the wishes of a particularly highly placed agent. The potential damage to the operator's cover by his prolonged service in a given country is considered of less importance than the maintenance of the delicate relationship he has developed with the agent. Similarly, in those situations where a (

DELETED

) the agency officer may serve as many as six or eight years on the operation before being replaced. And when he is eventually transferred to another post, great care is taken to select a replacement who will be acceptable to the friendly chief of state.

Termination: All clandestine operations ultimately come to an end. Those dependent upon agent activities have a short life expectancy and often conclude suddenly. The agent may die of natural causes or by accident—or he may be arrested and imprisoned, even executed. In any such event, the sole consideration of the CIA operators on the scene is to protect the agency's interests, usually by covering up the fact that the individual was a secret agent of the U.S. government. Sometimes, however, the agency itself must terminate the operation and dispose of the agent. The decision to terminate is made by the CIA chief of station in the country where the operation is in progress, with the approval of agency headquarters. The reason for breaking with an agent may be simply his loss of access to the secrets that the CIA is interested in acquiring; more complicated is emotional instability, lack of personal trustworthiness endangering the operation, or threat of imminent exposure and arrest. Worst of all, there may be a question of political unreliability—it may be suspected that the man is, or has become, a double agent, provocation, or deception controlled by an opposition intelligence service.

The useless or unstable agent can usually be bought off or, if necessary, successfully threatened. A reliable or useful agent in danger of compromise or exposure to the opposition, or an agent who has fulfilled his agreement as a spy and has performed well,

can be resettled in another country, provided with the necessary funds, even assisted in finding employment or, at least, retraining for a new profession. In those cases where the agent has contributed an outstanding service to the CIA at great personal risk, particularly if he burned himself out in so doing, he will be brought to the United States for safe resettlement. The Director of Central Intelligence, under the CIA Act of 1949, can authorize the "entry of a particular alien into the United States for permanent residence . . . in the interest of national security or the furtherance of the national intelligence mission." The agent and his family can be granted "permanent residence without regard to their inadmissibility under the immigration or any other laws and regulations."

Resettlement, however, does not always go smoothly. And sometimes this is the fault of the CIA. In the late 1950s, when espionage was still a big business in Germany, former agents and defectors were routinely resettled in Canada and Latin America. The constant flow of anti-communist refugees to those areas was too much for the agency's Clandestine Services to resist. **From time to time, an active agent would be inserted into the resettlement process. But the entire operation almost collapsed when, within a matter of months, both Canadian and Brazilian governments discovered that the CIA was using it as a means to plant operating agents in their societies.**

Not all former agents are willing to be resettled in the United States, especially not on the CIA's terms. In the 1960s a high-ranking Latin American official who had been an agent for years was forced for internal political reasons to flee his native country. He managed to reach Mexico City, where agency operators again made contact with him. In consideration of his past services, the agency was willing to arrange for his immigration to the U.S. under the 1949 CIA law if he would sign an agreement to remain quiet about his secret connection with the U.S. government and not become involved in exile political activities in this country. The Latin American, who had ambitions to return triumphantly to his native country one day, refused to forgo his right to plot against his enemies back home, and wanted residence in the

United States without citizenship, thus presenting the CIA with a difficult dilemma. As long as the former agent remained unhappy and frustrated in Mexico City, he represented a threat that his relationship with the agency and those of the many other CIA penetrations of his government which he knew about might be exposed. As a result, CIA headquarters in Langley sent word to the station in Mexico City that the ex-agent could enter the country without the usual preconditions. The agency's top officials hoped that he could be kept under reasonable control and prevented from getting too deeply involved in political activities which would be particularly embarrassing to the U.S. government.

It is only logical to believe that there are instances when termination requires drastic action on the part of the operators. Such cases are, of course, highly sensitive and quite uncommon in the CIA. But when it does become necessary to consider the permanent elimination of a particularly threatful agent, the final decision must be made at the highest level of authority, by the Director of Central Intelligence. With the exception of special or paramilitary operations, physical violence and homicide are not viewed as acceptable clandestine methods—unless they are acceptable to the Director himself.

Two aspects of clandestine tradecraft which have particular applicability to classical espionage, and to agent operations in general, are secret communications and contacts. The case officer must set up safe means of communicating with his agent; otherwise, there will be no way of receiving the information that the agent is stealing, or of providing him with instructions and guidance. In addition to a primary communication system, there will usually be an alternate method for use if the primary system fails. From time to time, different systems will be employed to reduce the chances of compromising the operation. As with most activities in the intelligence game, there are no hard and fast rules governing communication with secret agents. As long as the methods used are secure and workable, the case officer is free to devise any means of contact with his agent that is suitable to the operational situation.

Many agents want to pass on their information verbally to the case officer. From their point of view, it is both safer and easier than dealing with official papers or using spy equipment, either of which could clearly incriminate them if discovered by the local authorities. The CIA, however, prefers documents. Documents can be verified, thus establishing the agent's reliability. They can be studied and analyzed in greater detail and with more accuracy by the intelligence experts at headquarters. In the Penkovsky case, for example, the secret Soviet documents he provided were far more valuable than his personal interpretations of events then occurring in Moscow's military circles.

On the other hand, some agents want to have as little personal contact as possible with their case officers. Each clandestine meeting is viewed as an invitation to exposure and imprisonment, or worse. Such agents would prefer to communicate almost exclusively through indirect methods or even by mechanical means (encoded or encrypted radio messages, invisible ink, micro-dots, and so on). But the CIA insists on its case officers having personal contact with their agents, except in exceptionally risky cases. Periodically, the spy's sincerity and level of motivation must be evaluated in face-to-face meetings with the operator.

Each time the case officer has a personal contact with his agent, there is the danger that the two will be observed by the local security forces, or by a hostile service such as the KGB. To minimize the risk of compromise, indirect methods of contact are employed most of the time, especially for the passing of information from the agent to the operator. One standard technique is the use of a cut-out, an intermediary who serves as a go-between. The cut-out may be witting or unwitting; he may be another agent; he may even reside in another country. Regardless, his role is to receive material from either the agent or the case officer and then relay it to the other, without being aware of its substance.

Another technique is the dead-drop, or dead-letter drop. This is a kind of secret post-office box such as a hollow tree, the underside of a park bench, a crevice in an old stone wall—any natural and unlikely repository that can be utilized for transferring materials. (One of the dead-drops used in the Penkovsky opera-

tion was the space behind the steam-heat radiator in the entry of an apartment building in Moscow.) The agent simply deposits his material in the dead-drop at a prearranged time; later it is "serviced" by the case officer or a cut-out engaged for this purpose.

Still another frequently used technique is that of the brush contact, in which the agent and his case officer or a cut-out meet in passing at some prearranged public place. The agent may encounter his contact, for example, on a crowded subway platform, in a theater lobby, or perhaps on a busy downtown street. Acting as if they are strangers, the two will manage to get close together for a moment, long enough for one to slip something into the other's hand or pocket. Or they may quickly exchange newspapers or briefcases. Such a contact is extremely brief as well as surreptitious, and usually it is quite secure if well executed.

Although the case officer makes frequent use of indirect contacts, he still must arrange personal meetings with his agent from time to time. Whenever there is a clandestine meeting—on a bus, in a park, at a restaurant—other CIA operators keep watch as a precaution against opposition monitoring or interference. This is known in the covert business as countersurveillance. The case officer works out safe and danger signals in advance of each rendezvous with both the agent and the countersurveillance team. In this way, the operator, the agent, or any member of the team can signal to the others to proceed with the meeting or to avoid or break off contact if something seems out of the ordinary. Safe houses (CIA-maintained residences) are also used for meetings with agents, especially if there is a lot to be discussed. A safe house has the advantage of providing an atmosphere where the agent and the case officer can relax and talk freely without fear of surveillance, but the more frequently one location is used, the more likely it is to be discovered by the opposition. The need for secrecy can keep the clandestine operator busy; but it is a need on which the clandestine operator thrives.

Agency Culture

A few years ago *Newsweek* magazine described the CIA as the most secretive and tightly knit organization (with the possible exception of the Mafia) in American society. The characterization is something of an overstatement, but it contains more than a kernel of truth. In its golden era, during the height of the Cold War, the agency did possess a rare *élan*; it had a staff of imaginative and daring officers at all levels and in all directorates. But over the years the CIA has grown old, fat, and bureaucratic. The *esprit de corps* and devotion to duty its staff once had, setting the agency apart from other government departments, has faded, and to a great degree it has been replaced by an outmoded, doctrinaire approach to its missions and functions. The true purpose of secrecy—to keep the opposition in the dark about agency policies and operations—has been lost sight of. Today the CIA often practices secrecy for secrecy's sake—and to prevent the American public from learning of its activities. And the true purpose of intelligence collection—to monitor efficiently the threatening moves of international adversaries—has been distorted by the need to nourish a collective clandestine ego.

After the U.S. invasion of Cambodia in 1970, a few hundred CIA employees (mostly younger officers from the Intelligence and Science and Technology directorates, *not* the Clandestine Services) signed a petition objecting to American policies in Indochina. Director Richard Helms was so concerned about the prospect of widespread unrest in the agency's ranks and the chance that word of it might leak out to the public that he summoned all the protesters to the main auditorium and lectured them on the need to separate their personal views from their professional duties. At the same time, similar demonstrations on the Cambodian issue were mounted at the State Department and other government agencies. Nearly every newspaper in the country carried articles about the incipient rebellion brewing in the ranks of the federal bureaucracy. The happenings at the CIA, which were potentially

the most newsworthy of all, were, however, never discovered by the press. In keeping with the agency's clandestine traditions, CIA employees had conducted a secret protest.

To agency personnel who had had the need for secrecy drilled into them from their moment of recruitment, there was nothing strange about keeping their demonstration hidden from public view. Secrecy is an absolute way of life at the agency, and while outsiders might consider some of the resulting practices comical in the extreme, the subject is treated with great seriousness in the CIA. Training officers lecture new personnel for hours on end about "security consciousness," and these sessions are augmented during an employee's entire career by refresher courses, warning posters, and even the semi-annual requirement for each employee to review the agency's security rules and to sign a copy, as an indication it has been read. As a matter of course, outsiders should be told absolutely nothing about the CIA and fellow employees should be given only that information for which they have an actual "need to know."*

CIA personnel become so accustomed to the rigorous security precautions (some of which are indeed justified) that they easily accept them all, and seldom are caught in violations. Nothing could be more natural than to work with a telephone book marked SECRET, an intentionally incomplete telephone book which lists no one working in the Clandestine Services and which in each semi-annually revised edition leaves out the names of many of the people employed by the overt directorates, so if the book ever falls into unauthorized hands, no enterprising foreign agent or reporter will be able to figure out how many people work at CIA headquarters, or even how many work in non-clandestine jobs. Those temporarily omitted can look forward to having their names appear in the next edition of the directory, at which time others are selected for telephonic limbo. Added to this confusion is the

---

* The penchant for secrecy sometimes takes on an air of ludicrousness. Secret medals are awarded for outstanding performance, but they cannot be worn or shown outside the agency. Even athletic trophies—for intramural bowling, softball, and so on—cannot be displayed except within the guarded sanctuary of the headquarters building.

fact that most agency phone numbers are regularly changed for security reasons. Most employees manage to keep track of commonly called numbers by listing them in their own personal desk directories, although they have to be careful to lock these in their safes at night—or else risk being charged with a security violation. For a first violation the employee is given a reprimand and usually assigned to several weeks of security inspection in his or her office. Successive violations lead to forced vacation without pay for periods up to several weeks, or to outright dismissal.

Along with the phone books, all other classified material (including typewriter ribbons and scrap paper) is placed in these safes whenever an office is unoccupied. Security guards patrol every part of the agency at roughly half-hour intervals in the evening and on weekends to see that no secret documents have been left out, that no safes have been left unlocked, and that no spies are lurking in the halls. If a guard finds any classified material unsecured, both the person who failed to put it away and the person within the office who was assigned to double-check the premises have security violations entered in their personnel files.

These security precautions all take place inside a headquarters building that is surrounded by a twelve-foot fence topped with barbed wire, patrolled by armed guards and police dogs, and sealed off by a security check system that guarantees that no one can enter either the outer perimeter or the building itself without showing proper identification. Each CIA employee is issued a laminated plastic badge with his picture on it, and these must not only be presented to the guards on entry, but be kept constantly in view within the building. Around the edges of the badge are twenty or so little boxes which may or may not be filled with red letters. Each letter signifies a special security clearance held by the owner. Certain offices at the CIA are designated as restricted, and only persons holding the proper clearance, as marked on their badges, can gain entry. These areas are usually guarded by an agency policeman sitting inside a glass cage, from which he controls a turnstile that forbids passage to unauthorized personnel. Particularly sensitive offices are protected, in addition to the guarded

turnstile, by a combination or cipher lock which must be opened by the individual after the badge is inspected.

Even a charwoman at the CIA must gain security clearance in order to qualify for the badge that she, too, must wear at all times; then she must be accompanied by an armed guard while she cleans offices (where all classified material has presumably already been locked up). Some rooms at the agency are considered so secret that the charwoman and her guard must also be watched by someone who works in the office.

The pervasive secrecy extends everywhere. Cards placed on agency bulletin boards offering items for sale conclude: "Call Bill, extension 6464." Neither clandestine nor overt CIA employees are permitted to have their last names exposed to the scrutiny of their colleagues, and it was only in 1973 that employees were allowed to answer their phones with any words other than those signifying the four-digit extension number.

Also until recent years all CIA personnel were required to identify themselves to non-agency people as employees of the State or Defense Department or some other outside organization. Now the analysts and technicians are permitted to say they work for the agency, although they cannot reveal their particular office. Clandestine Service employees are easily spotted around Washington because they almost always claim to be employed by Defense or State, but usually are extremely vague on the details and unable to furnish an office address. They do sometimes give out a phone number which corresponds to the correct exchange for their cover organization, but these extensions, through some deft wiring, ring in Langley.

The headquarters building, located on a partially wooded 125-acre tract eight miles from downtown Washington, is a modernistic fortress-like structure. Until the spring of 1973 one of the two roads leading into the secluded compound was totally unmarked, and the other featured a sign identifying the installation as the Bureau of Public Roads, which maintains the Fairbanks Highway Research Station adjacent to the agency.

Until 1961 the CIA had been located in a score of buildings scattered all over Washington. One of the principal justifications for the $46 million headquarters in the suburbs was that considerable expense would be saved by moving all employees under one roof. But in keeping with the best-laid bureaucratic plans, the headquarters building, from the day it was completed, proved too small for all the CIA's Washington activities. The agency never vacated some of its old headquarters buildings hidden behind a naval medical facility on 23rd Street Northwest in Washington, and its National Photo Interpretation Center shares part of the Navy's facilities in Southeast Washington. Other large CIA offices located downtown include the Domestic Operations Division, on Pennsylvania Avenue near the White House.

And in Washington's Virginia suburbs there are even more CIA buildings outside the headquarters complex. An agency training facility is located in the Broyhill Building in Arlington, and the CIA occupies considerable other office space in that county's Rosslyn section. Also at least half a dozen CIA components are located in the Tyson's Corner area of northern Virginia, which has become something of a mini-intelligence community for technical work due to the presence there of numerous electronics and research companies that do work for the agency and the Pentagon.

The rapid expansion of CIA office space in the last ten years did not happen as a result of any appreciable increase in personnel. Rather, the technological explosion, coupled with inevitable bureaucratic lust for new frontiers, has been the cause. As Director, Richard Helms paid little attention to the diffusion of his agency until one day in 1968 when a CIA official mentioned to him that still one more technical component was moving to Tyson's Corner. For some reason this aroused Helms' ire, and he ordered a study prepared to find out just how much of the agency was located outside of headquarters. The completed report told him what most Washington-area real-estate agents already knew, that a substantial percentage of CIA employees had vacated the building originally justified to Congress as necessary to put all personnel under one roof. Helms decreed that all future moves

would require his personal approval, but his action slowed the exodus only temporarily.

When the CIA headquarters building was being constructed during the late 1950s, the subcontractor responsible for putting in the heating and air-conditioning system asked the agency how many people the structure was intended to accommodate. For security reasons, the agency refused to tell him, and he was forced to make his own estimate based on the building's size. The resulting heating system worked reasonably well, while the air-conditioning was quite uneven. After initial complaints in 1961, the contractor installed an individual thermostat in each office, but so many agency employees were continually readjusting their thermostats that the system got worse. The M&S Directorate then decreed that the thermostats could no longer be used, and each one was sealed up. However, the M&S experts had not considered that the CIA was a clandestine agency, and that many of its personnel had taken a "locks and picks" course while in training. Most of the thermostats were soon unlocked and back in operation.

At this point the CIA took the subcontractor to court to force him to make improvements. His defense was that he had installed the best system he could without a clear indication of how many people would occupy the building. The CIA could not counter this reasoning and lost the decision.

Another unusual feature of the CIA headquarters is the cafeteria. It is partitioned into a secret and an open section, the larger part being only for agency employees, who must show their badges to the armed guards before entering, and the smaller being for visitors as well as people who work at the CIA. Although the only outsiders ever to enter the small, dismal section are employees of other U.S. government agencies, representatives of a few friendly governments, and CIA families, the partition ensures that no visitor will see the face of any clandestine operator eating lunch.

The CIA's "supergrades" (civilian equivalents of generals) have their own private dining room in the executive suite, however. There they are provided higher-quality food at lower prices than

in the cafeteria, served on fine china with fresh linens by black waiters in immaculate white coats. These waiters and the executive cooks are regular CIA employees, in contrast to the cafeteria personnel, who work for a contractor. On several occasions the Office of Management and Budget has questioned the high cost of this private dining room, but the agency has always been able to fend off the attacks, as it fends off almost all attacks on its activities, by citing "national security" reasons as the major justification.

Questions of social class and snobbery have always been very important in the CIA. With its roots in the wartime Office of Strategic Services (the letters OSS were said, only half-jokingly, to stand for "Oh So Social"), the agency has long been known for its concentration of Eastern Establishment, Ivy League types. Allen Dulles, a former American diplomat and Wall Street lawyer with impeccable connections and credentials, set the tone for an agency full of Roosevelts, Bundys, Cleveland Amory's brother Robert, and other scions of America's leading families. There have been exceptions, to be sure, but most of the CIA's top leaders have been white, Anglo-Saxon, Protestant, and graduates of the right Eastern schools. While changing times and ideas have diffused the influence of the Eastern élite throughout the government as a whole, the CIA remains perhaps the last bastion in official Washington of WASP power, or at least the slowest to adopt the principle of equal opportunity.

It was no accident that former Clandestine Services chief Richard Bissell (Groton, Yale, A.B., Ph.D., London School of Economics, A.B.) was talking to a Council on Foreign Relations discussion group in 1968 when he made his "confidential" speech on covert action. For the influential but private Council, composed of several hundred of the country's top political, military, business, and academic leaders, has long been the CIA's principal "constituency" in the American public. When the agency has needed prominent citizens to front for its proprietary companies or for other special assistance, it has often turned to Council members. Bissell knew that night in 1968 that he could talk freely and

openly about extremely sensitive subjects because he was among "friends." His words leaked out not because of the indiscretion of any of the participants, but because of student upheavals at Harvard in 1971.

It may well have been the sons of CFR members or CIA officials who ransacked the office housing the minutes of Bissell's speech, and therein lies the changing nature of the CIA (and the Eastern Establishment, for that matter). Over the last decade the attitudes of the young people, who in earlier times would have followed their fathers or their fathers' college roommates into the CIA, have changed drastically. With the Vietnam war as a catalyst, the agency has become, to a large extent, discredited in the traditional Eastern schools and colleges. And consequently the CIA has been forced to alter its recruiting base. No longer do Harvard, Yale, Princeton, and a few other Eastern schools provide the bulk of the agency's professional recruits, or even a substantial number.

For the most part, Ivy Leaguers do not want to join the agency, and the CIA now does its most fruitful recruiting at the universities of middle America and in the armed forces. While the shift unquestionably reflects increasing democratization in American government, the CIA made the change not so much voluntarily as because it had no other choice if it wished to fill its ranks. If the "old boy" network cannot be replenished, some officials believe, it will be much more difficult to enlist the aid of American corporations and generally to make use of influential "friends" in the private and public sectors.

Despite the comparatively recent broadening of the CIA's recruiting base, the agency is not now and has never been an equal-opportunity employer. The agency has one of the smallest percentages—if not *the* smallest—of blacks of any federal department. The CIA's top management had this forcefully called to their attention in 1967 when a local civil-rights activist wrote to the agency to complain about minority hiring practices. A study was ordered at that time, and the CIA's highest-ranking black was found to be a GS-13 (the rough equivalent of an Army major). Altogether, there were fewer than twenty blacks among the CIA's approximately **12,000** non-clerical employees, and even the pro-

portion of black secretaries, clerks, and other non-professionals was considerably below that of most Washington-area government agencies. One might attribute this latter fact to the agency's suburban location, but blacks were notably well represented in the guard and char forces.

Top officials seemed surprised by the results of the 1967 study because they did not consider themselves prejudiced men. They ordered increased efforts to hire more blacks, but these were not particularly successful. Young black college graduates in recent years have shied away from joining the agency, some on political grounds and others because of the more promising opportunities available in the private sector. Furthermore, the CIA recruiting system could not easily be changed to bring in minorities. Most of the "spotting" of potential employees is done by individual college professors who are either friends or consultants of the agency, and they are located on predominantly white campuses where each year they hand-pick a few carefully selected students for the CIA.

The paucity of minority groups in the CIA goes well beyond blacks, however. In 1964 the agency's Inspector General did a routine study of the Office of National Estimates (ONE). The Inspector found no black, Jewish, or women professionals, and only a few Catholics. ONE immediately took steps to bring in minorities. One woman professional was hired on a probationary basis, and one black secretary was brought in. When the professional had finished her probation, she was encouraged to find work elsewhere, and the black secretary was given duties away from the main ONE offices—out of sight in the reproduction center. ONE did bend somewhat by hiring a few Jews and some additional Catholics.

There are extremely few women in high-ranking positions in the CIA, but, of course, the agency does employ women as secretaries and for other non-professional duties. As is true with all large organizations, there is a high turnover in these jobs, and the agency each year hires a thousand or more new applicants. In a search for suitable candidates, CIA recruiters concentrate on recent high-school graduates from the mostly white small towns and cities of Virginia and the neighboring states, Maryland, West Virginia, and Pennsylvania. Washington, with its overwhelming black majority,

supplies comparatively few of the CIA's secretaries. Over the years the recruiters have established good contacts with high-school guidance counselors and principals in the nearby states, and when they make their annual tour in search of candidates, interested girls are steered their way, with several from the same class often being hired at the same time. When the new secretaries come to CIA headquarters outside of Washington, they are encouraged to live in agency-selected apartments in the Virginia suburbs, buildings in which virtually all the tenants are CIA employees.

Security considerations play a large part in the agency's lack of attention to urban areas in its secretarial recruiting. All agency employees must receive full security clearances before they start work. This is a very expensive process, and women from small towns are easier and cheaper to investigate. Moreover, the CIA seems actually to prefer secretaries with the All-American image who are less likely to have been "corrupted" or "politicized" than their urbanized sisters.

Agency secretaries, as well as all other personnel, must pass lie-detector tests as a condition of employment. Then they periodically —usually at five-year intervals or when they return from overseas assignments—must submit themselves again to the "black box." The CIA, unlike most employers, finds out nearly everything imaginable about the private lives of its personnel through these polygraph tests. Questions about sex, drugs, and personal honesty are routinely asked along with security-related matters such as possible contacts with foreign agents. The younger secretaries invariably register a negative reading on the machine when asked the standard: "Have you ever stolen government property?" The polygraph experts usually have to add the qualifying clause, "not including pens, pencils, or minor clerical items."

Once CIA recruits have passed their security investigations and lie-detector tests, they are given training by the agency. Most of the secretaries receive instruction in the Washington area, such instruction focusing on the need for secrecy in all aspects of the work. Women going overseas to type and file for their CIA bosses are given short courses in espionage tradecraft. A former secretary reported that the most notable part of her field training in the late

1960s was to trail an instructor in and out of Washingon department stores.*

The agency's professionals, most of them (until the 1967 NSA disclosures) recruited through "friendly" college professors, receive much more extensive instruction when they enter the CIA as career trainees (CTs). For two years they are on a probationary status, the first year in formal training programs and the second with on-the-job instruction. The CTs take introductory courses at a CIA facility, known as the Broyhill Building, in Arlington, Virginia, in subjects such as security, the organization of the agency and the rest of the intelligence community, and the nature of international communism. Allen Dulles, in his days as Director, liked to talk to these classes and tell them how, as an American diplomat in Switzerland during World War I, he received a telephone call from a Russian late on a Saturday morning. The Russian wanted to talk to a U.S. government representative immediately, but Dulles had a date with a young lady, so he declined the offer. The Russian turned out to be Nikolai Lenin, and Dulles used the incident to urge the young CTs always to be alert to the possible importance of people they meet in their work.

Afterward, CTs go to "The Farm," the establishment near Williamsburg that is disguised as a Pentagon research-and-testing facility and indeed resembles a large military reservation. Barracks, offices, classrooms, and an officers' club are grouped around a central point. Scattered over its 480 mostly wooded acres are weapons ranges, jump towers, and a simulated closed border of a mythical communist country. Away from these facilities are heavily guarded and off-limits sites, locations used for super-secret projects such as debriefing a recent defector, planning a special operation, or training an important foreign agent who will be returning to his native country to spy for the CIA.

As part of their formal clandestine training at "The Farm," the CTs are regularly shown Hollywood spy movies, and after the performance they collectively criticize the techniques used in the

---

* This woman's training proved useful, however, when in her first post abroad, ostensibly as an embassy secretary, she was given the mission of surveilling an apartment building in disguise as an Arab woman.

films. Other movies are also used, as explained by the former clandestine operator who wrote about his experience in the April 1967 *Ramparts*:

> We were shown Agency-produced films depicting the CIA in action, films which displayed a kind of Hollywood flair for the dramatic that is not uncommon inside the Agency. A colleague who went through a 1963 training class told of a film on the U-2 episode. In his comments prefatory to the film, his instructor intimated that President Eisenhower "blew his cool" when he did not continue to deny that the U-2 was a CIA aircraft. But no matter, said the instructor, the U-2 was in sum an Agency triumph, for the planes had been overflying Soviet territory for at least five years. During this time the Soviet leaders had fumed in frustration, unable to bring down a U-2 on the one hand, and reluctant to let the world know of their inability on the other. The photography contained in the film confirmed that the "flying cameras" had accomplished a remarkable job of reconnaissance. When the film ended and the lights came on, the instructor gestured toward the back of the room and announced: "Gentlemen, the hero of our film." There stood Francis Gary Powers. The trainees rose and applauded.

All the CTs receive some light-weapons training, and those destined for paramilitary duties receive a full course which includes instruction in explosives and demolition, parachute jumps, air and sea operations, and artillery training. This paramilitary training is also taken by the contract soldiers (who greatly resent being called "mercenaries") who have been separately recruited for special operations. They join the CTs for some of the other courses, but generally tend to avoid the younger and less experienced recent college graduates who make up the bulk of the CT ranks. Many of these mercenaries and a few of the CTs continue on for an advanced course in explosives and heavy weapons given at a CIA training facility in North Carolina. Postgraduate training in paramilitary operations is conducted at Fort Bragg in North Carolina and at Fort Gulick in the Panama Canal Zone.

Fringe Benefits

Although agency personnel hold the same ratings and receive the same salaries as other government employees, they do not fall under Civil Service jurisdiction. The Director has the authority to hire or fire an employee without any regard to normal governmental regulations, and there is no legal appeal to his decisions. In general, however, it is the CIA's practice to take extremely good care of the people who remain loyal to the organization. There is a strong feeling among agency management officials that they must concern themselves with the welfare of all personnel, and this feeling goes well beyond the normal employer-employee relationship in the government or in private industry. To a certain extent, security considerations dictate this attitude on the part of management, since an unhappy or financially insecure employee can become a potential target for a foreign espionage agent. But there is more to it than that. Nearly everyone seems to believe: *We're all in this together and anyone who's on the team should be taken care of decently.* The employees probably feel a higher loyalty to the CIA than members of almost any other agency feel for their organization. Again, this is good for security, but that makes the sentiments no less real.

Some of the benefits for agency personnel are unique in the federal bureaucracy. For example, the CIA operates a summer intern program for college students. Unlike other government agencies which have tried to hire disadvantaged and minority youngsters, the CIA's program is only for the sons and daughters of agency employees. Again the justification is security and the expense of clearing outsiders, but it is a somewhat dubious claim since the State Department manages to clear all its interns for "top secret" without significant expense or danger to security.

If a CIA employee dies, an agency security officer immediately goes to his or her house to see that everything is in order for the survivors (and, not incidentally, to make sure no CIA documents have been taken home from the office). If the individual has been living under a cover identity, the security officer ensures that the

cover does not fall apart with the death. Often the security man will even help with the funeral and burial arrangements.

For banking activities, CIA employees are encouraged to use the agency's own credit union, which is located in the headquarters building. The union is expert in giving loans to clandestine operators under cover, whose personal-background statements are by definition false. In the rare instance when an employee forfeits on a loan, the credit union seldom prosecutes to get back the money: that could be a breach of security. There is also a special fund, supported by annual contributions from agency officers, to help fellow employees who accidentally get into financial trouble.

The credit union also makes various kinds of insurance available to CIA employees. Since the agency does not wish to give outsiders any biographical information on its personnel, the CIA provides the insuror with none of that data that insurance companies normally demand, except age and size of policy. The agency certifies that all facts are true—even that a particular employee has died—without offering any proof. Blue Cross, which originally had the agency's health-insurance policy, demanded too much information for the agency's liking, and in the late 1950s the CIA switched its account to the more tolerant Mutual of Omaha. Agency employees are even instructed not to use the airplane-crash insurance machines available at airports, but to purchase such insurance from the credit union.

Attempts are made even to regulate the extracurricular activities of agency employees—to reinforce their attachment to the organization and, of course, for security reasons. An employee-activity association (incorporated for legal purposes) sponsors programs in everything from sports and art to slimnastics and karate. The association also runs a recreational travel service, a sports and theater ticket service, and a discount sales store. The CIA runs its own training programs for reserve military officers, too. And it has arranged with local universities to have its own officers teach college-level and graduate courses for credit to its employees in the security of its headquarters building.

The CIA can be engagingly paternal in other ways, too. On the whole, it is quite tolerant of sexual dalliance among its em-

ployees, as long as the relationships are heterosexual and not with enemy spies. In fact, the CIA's medical office in Saigon was known during the late 1960s for its no-questions-asked cures of venereal disease, while State Department officers in that city avoided the embassy clinic for the same malady because they feared the consequences to their careers of having VD listed on their personnel records.

In many other ways the CIA keeps close watch over its employees' health. If a CIA officer gets sick, he can go to an agency doctor or a "cleared" outside physician. If he undergoes surgery, he frequently is accompanied into the operating room by a CIA security man who makes sure that no secrets are revealed under sodium-pentathol anesthesia. If he has a mental breakdown, he is required to be treated by an agency psychiatrist (or a cleared contact on the outside) or, in an extreme case, to be admitted to a CIA-sanctioned sanitarium. Although no statistics are available, mental breakdowns seem more common in the agency's tension-laden atmosphere than in the population as a whole, and the CIA tends to have a more tolerant attitude toward mental-health problems and psychiatric therapy than the general public. In the Clandestine Services, breakdowns are considered virtually normal work hazards, and employees are encouraged to return to work after they have completed treatment. Usually no stigma is attached to illness of this type; in fact, a number of senior officers suffered breakdowns while they were in the Clandestine Services and it clearly did not hurt their careers. Ex–Clandestine Services chief Frank Wisner had such an illness, and he later returned to work as the CIA station chief in London.

Many agency officials are known for their heavy drinking—which also seems to be looked upon as an occupational hazard. Again, the CIA is more sympathetic to drinking problems than outside organizations. Drug use, however, remains absolutely taboo.

While the personnel policies and benefits extended by the CIA to its employees can be justified on the grounds of national security and the need to develop organizational loyalty, these tend to have something of a personal debilitating effect on the career officers.

The agency is unconsciously viewed as an omniscient, omnipotent institution—one that can even be considered infallible. Devotion to duty grows to fanaticism; questioning the decisions of the authorities is tantamount to religious blasphemy. Such circumstances encourage bureaucratic insulation and introversion (especially under strong pressures from the outside), and they even promote a perverse, defensive attitude which restricts the individual from keeping pace with significant social events occurring in one's own nation—to say nothing of those evolving abroad. Instead of continuing to develop vision and sensitivity with regard to their professional activities, the career officers become unthinking bureaucrats concerned only with their own comfort and security, which they achieve by catering to the demands of the existing political and institutional leaderships—those groups which can provide the means for such personal ends.

Secret Writings

A number of years ago the CIA established a secret historical library, later a secret internal professional journal, and ultimately began the preparation of the exhaustive secret history of the agency, being written by retired senior officers.

The Historical Intelligence Collection, as the special library is officially known in the CIA, is a fascinating library of spy literature, containing thousands of volumes, fiction and non-fiction, in many languages. The curator, a senior career officer by trade but by avocation a bibliophile of some note, is annually allocated a handsome budget to travel around the world in search of rare books and documents on espionage. Through his efforts, the CIA today possesses probably the most complete compilation of such publications in the world. In recent years the collection has been expanded to include intelligence memorabilia, featuring exhibits of invisible inks, bugs, cameras, and other equipment actually used in certain operations by spies or their handlers.

The CIA's own quarterly trade journal is called *Studies in Intelligence*. Articles in recent years have dealt with subjects ranging from the practical to the theoretical: there have been articles on

how to react when undergoing enemy interrogation; how the National Estimate process works; how to covertly infiltrate and exfiltrate heavily guarded enemy borders. After the Cuban missile crisis the journal ran a debate on whether the CIA had failed to detect the Soviet missiles early enough or had succeeded in time to allow the government to take remedial action.

Some articles are of pure historical interest. In 1970 there was a fascinating account of the successful efforts at the end of World War II of the couturier Count Emilio Pucci, then in the Italian army, to keep out of German hands the diary of Mussolini's Foreign Minister (and son-in-law) Count Ciano, who had earlier been executed by the Duce. Presumably stories of this kind would be of interest to ordinary citizens but *Studies in Intelligence,* while bearing a physical resemblance to many regularly published magazines, is different in one important respect. It is stamped SECRET and is therefore available only to CIA employees and a few selected readers elsewhere in the intelligence community. Even its regular reviews of current spy novels are withheld from the American public.

The most important of the CIA's private literary projects is the massive secret history of the agency that has been in preparation since 1967. Recognizing the irresistible tendency of former intelligence officers to write their memoirs and, thereby, often to embarrass their organizations and their government with their revelations, Director Helms prudently agreed to permit the preparation of an official secret history of the CIA and its clandestine activities. A professor of history from a Midwestern university was hired to to act as coordinator and as a literary/research advisor to those officers who would participate in the project. Retired senior officials were rehired on contract at their former salaries to spend a couple of additional years with the agency putting their recollections down on paper for eventual incorporation in the encyclopedic summary of the CIA's past.

Helms' decision was a master stroke. The history will never be completed, nor will it ever be published. By definition it is a perpetual project and one that can be read only by those who have a clear "need to know"—and they are few indeed. But the writers, the

battle-scarred old hands, have gotten their frustrations out of their systems—with no harm done—and they have been paid, well paid, for their efforts. (Probably better than they could have been had they gone public.) As for the CIA, it, too, is content with the arrangement; for it is *its* arrangement, a pact made among friends and colleagues, one that conveniently shuts out the primary enemy of those possessed of the clandestine mentality—the public.

NINE

Intelligence and Policy

Policy must be based on the best estimate of the facts which can be put together. That estimate in turn should be given by some agency which has no axes to grind and which itself is not wedded to any particular policy.

—ALLEN DULLES

W

ORKMEN had already started to put the White House Christmas decorations in place on a December day in 1969 when the President met in the Cabinet room with the National Security Council. The (

DELETED

) out to the interested parts of the federal government the previous April, bureaucrats had been writing position papers to prepare their chiefs for this meeting. There was sharp disagreement within the government on how hard a line the United States should take with the (

DELETED

) Now the time for decision-making was at hand, and those present included the Vice President, the Secretaries of State and Defense, the Under Secretaries of State and Commerce, the Director of Central Intelligence, a representative of the National Aeronautics and Space Agency (NASA), the Assistant to the President for National Security Affairs, and the Chairman of the Joint Chiefs of Staff.*

The President opened the session by stating that the NSC had before it some very complex problems—complex not only in the usual foreign-policy sense but also in a moral context which, the President noted, concerned a large portion of the American population. Nixon then turned to his DCI, Richard Helms, and said, "Go ahead, Dick."

The NSC meeting had officially begun, and, as was customary,

---

* Admiral Thomas Moorer, the newly named Chairman of the JCS, was attending his first NSC meeting in this capacity. The President noted the occasion by introducing him to all assembled as "Admiral Mormon."

Helms set the scene by giving a detailed briefing on the political and economic background of the countries under discussion. Using charts and maps carried in by an aide, he described recent developments in **southern Africa. (His otherwise flawless performance was marred only by his mispronunciation of "Malagasy" [formerly Madagascar], when referring to the young republic.)**

Next, Henry Kissinger talked about the kind of general posture the United States could maintain toward the (**DELETED**   ) and outlined the specific policy options open to the President. In the case of (

DELETED

.*

---

* Some of the statements were quite revealing. Early in the meeting Secretary of State William Rogers jokingly pointed out, to general laughter in the room, that it might be inappropriate for the group to discuss the sub-

DELETED

) the United States to do so. To what extent Helms' arguments played a part in the presidential decision can be answered only by Richard Nixon himself. But, the following year, at the request of the British, the United States did end its (

DELETED

---

ject at hand, since some of those present had represented southern African clients in earlier law practices. Vice President Spiro Agnew gave an impassioned speech on how the South Africans, now that they had recently declared their independence, were not about to be pushed around, and he went on to compare South Africa to the United States in its infant days. Finally, the President leaned over to Agnew and said gently, "You mean Rhodesia, don't you, Ted?"

DELETED

) was such an estab-
lished factor that it was not even under review at the NSC meeting.

It was quite extraordinary for Helms to speak out to the NSC
about the detrimental effect his agency would suffer if the (
       DELETED   ) since the DCI's normal
role at these sessions is limited to providing the introductory background briefing. As the President's principal intelligence advisor,
his function is to supply the facts and the intelligence community's
best estimate of future events in order to help the decision-makers
in their work. What Helms was saying to the NSC was entirely
factual, but it had the effect of injecting intelligence operations
into a policy decision. In theory at least, the decision-makers are
supposed to be able to choose the most advantageous options *with*
the benefit of intelligence—not *for* the benefit of intelligence.

Analysis v. Operations

Many, but by no means all, intelligence professionals agree that
the primary and, indeed, paramount purpose of the intelligence
process is to produce meaningful, timely information on foreign
developments after a careful analysis of secret and open sources.
The finished product should be balanced in perspective and
objective in presentation. Under no circumstances is intelligence
supposed to advise a particular course of action. The intelligence
function, when properly performed, is strictly an informational
service.

This is the theory, but in actual practice the U.S. intelligence
community has deeply intruded—and continues to—into the policy-
making arena. Perhaps it is unrealistic to expect that a $6 billion
activity with more than 150,000 employees working in over 100
countries would do otherwise. Nevertheless, it should be understood that when someone like Richard Helms publicly declares, as
he did in 1971, "We make no foreign policy," he may be technically
correct in the sense that CIA officials must receive approval from
the White House for their main programs; but he is absolutely

incorrect in leaving the impression that the intelligence community, apart from supplying information, does not have a profound determinative effect on the formulation and carrying out of American foreign policy.

The very existence of the CIA as an instrument for secret intervention in other countries' internal affairs changes the way the nation's highest leaders look at the world. They know that if open political or economic initiatives fail, they can call on the CIA to bail them out. One suspects that the Eisenhower administration might have made more of an effort during its last ten months to prevent relations with Cuba from reaching the breaking point if the President had not already given his approval to the clandestine training of a refugee army to overthrow the Castro regime.

The extreme secrecy in which the CIA works increases the chances that a President will call it into action. He does not have to justify the agency's activities to Congress, the press, or the American people, so, barring premature disclosure, there is no institutional force within the United States to stop him from doing what he wants. Furthermore, the secrecy of CIA operations allows a President to authorize actions in other countries which, if conducted openly, would brand the United States as an outlaw nation. International law and the United Nations charter clearly prohibit one country from interfering in the internal affairs of another, but if the interference is done by a clandestine agency whose operations cannot readily be traced back to the United States, then a President has a much freer hand. He does not even have to worry about adverse public reaction at home or abroad. For example, after Salvador Allende had been elected President of Chile in 1970, President Nixon was asked at a press conference why the United States was willing to intervene militarily in Vietnam to prevent a communist takeover but would not do the same thing in Chile to prevent a Marxist from taking power; he replied that "for the United States to have intervened in a free election and to have turned it around, I think, would have had repercussions all around Latin America that would have been far worse than what happened in Chile." The President failed to mention that he had approved (**DELETED**

DELETED
) but by keeping his action secret, he was able to avoid—at least for the time being—the "adverse political reaction" which he feared. If there had been no CIA to do the job covertly, the U.S. government almost certainly would not have tried to involve itself in the Chilean elections, since it was obviously not willing to own up to its actions.

Clandestine operations can appear to a President as a panacea, as a way of pulling the chestnuts out of the fire without going through all the effort and aggravation of tortuous diplomatic negotiations. And if the CIA is somehow caught in the act, the "deniability" of these operations, in theory, saves a President from taking any responsibility—or blame. Additionally, the CIA is equipped to act quickly in a crisis. It is not hindered nearly as much by a cumbersome bureaucracy as is the Pentagon, and it has proved its ability to move with little advance notice, as it did in the Congo during the early 1960s, to put an "instant air force" into action. And the agency's field personnel do not demand the support facilities of their military colleagues. In Laos forty or fifty career CIA officers assisted by several hundred contractees ran an entire "secret war," whereas the Pentagon, given the same mission, probably would have set up a military-assistance command with thousands of personnel (as it did in Vietnam), at a much greater cost to the United States. Also, CIA operators are much less likely than the military to grouse publicly that political restrictions are forcing them to fight "with one arm tied behind our back," and this makes the agency attractive to a President who has no desire to engage in a running battle with his generals over the tactics to be used in a particular situation.

The CIA does not originate an American commitment to a country. The President and the State Department do that. But once CIA operations are started in a foreign land, the U.S. stake in that nation's future increases. Certainly the American interest would be even larger if the President decided to send in combat troops instead of his covert warriors, but such open intervention would have to be justified publicly. In the 1950s and early 1960s neither President Eisenhower nor President Kennedy wanted to

make such a commitment in Vietnam or Laos. Yet, by using foreign-aid funds and heavy doses of covert operations, they were able to create and then keep alive anti-communist governments in both countries. When these palliatives proved insufficient later in the 1960s, President Johnson chose to send American ground troops into Vietnam and to begin the systematic bombing of Laos by the U.S. Air Force. It might be argued that the CIA's covert operations put off the day when more massive amounts of American power would be needed, but it also might be said that if the agency had not managed to keep the governments in Saigon and Vientiane functioning for such a long time, the United States would never have intervened openly at all.

In neither Vietnam nor Laos was the CIA acting without the approval of the nation's highest policy-makers. Indeed, all the agency's major covert-action operations are approved by the 40 Committee, and the President himself closely reviews this committee's decisions. But even approved clandestine activities have a way of taking on a life of their own, as field operatives loosely interpret the general guidelines that come down from the White House through Langley. By not closely supervising CIA covert operations, the nation's highest leaders have allowed the agency to affect foreign policy profoundly. For example, during the CIA revolt against the leftist Guatemalan regime in 1954, an agency plane bombed a British freighter which was suspected of carrying arms to the embattled government troops. In fact the ship was loaded with coffee and cotton, and, fortunately, no one was injured when only one of the bombs exploded. Richard Bissell admitted to the *New York Times* on April 28, 1966, that the attack on the British vessel was a "sub-incident" that "went beyond the established limits of policy." Bissell continued, "You can't take on operations of this scope, draw boundaries of policy around them and be absolutely sure that those boundaries will not be overstepped."

The CIA got involved in another "sub-incident" while it was training Cuban exiles at secret bases in Guatemala for an invasion of their homeland. In November 1960 a rebellion broke out against the Guatemalan government which had been so gracious

in allowing the agency to use its territory as the jumping-off point for the Cuban operation. The CIA returned the favor by sending its B-26 bombers to help crush the insurgency. It is not clear whether White House permission was given for these attacks, but there was no question that the CIA had again interfered in Guatemalan internal politics—this time to make sure that no new Guatemalan government would oust it from its secret bases. Once embarked on the attempt to overthrow Castro, the agency had become involved in a chain of events which forced it to intervene militarily in a second country to protect its operation against Cuba. The President may have set the original policy, but there was no way he could have known that simply by approving an attack on Cuba he would set in motion agency paramilitary activities against Guatemala.

CIA operations can have another unforeseen effect on American foreign policy: they can subject the country to blackmail if something goes wrong. For instance, within five days after the **CIA** pilot was shot down and captured by Indonesia in 1958, the U.S. government approved the sale for local currency of 37,000 tons of American rice and lifted an embargo on $1 million in small arms and other military equipment. Considering that at that moment the **CIA was actively backing an armed revolution against the Sukarno regime,** these would have been strange actions indeed for the U.S. government to take if it were not extremely concerned about saving the captured pilot.

A somewhat similar incident occurred in Singapore in 1960 after a CIA lie-detector expert was flown into the city to make sure that a locally recruited agent was trustworthy. When the agency technician plugged in his polygraph machine in a hotel room, he blew out all the fuses in the building.* The lie-detector man, a

* (

DELETED

CIA case officer, and the local agent were soon under arrest. The Singapore government and the British, who were in the process of granting Singapore its independence, were both disturbed by the incident. Negotiations then ensued to secure the men's release. According to Singapore Prime Minister Lee Kuan Yew, the U.S. government offered $3.3 million to get them out. Lee claimed that he wanted ten times as much and consequently took nothing. In any case, the two CIA officials were subsequently freed, and the newly installed Secretary of State, Dean Rusk, wrote a secret letter of apology to the Singapore leader. In a 1965 speech Lee mentioned the affair as an example of the type of activity engaged in by the CIA. The State Department issued a routine denial furnished by the CIA—State's press office not realizing the truth of Lee's charges. Lee reacted by publicly producing Rusk's letter of apology, and State was forced to retract its original statement, although it still maintained that no ransom had ever been offered. As well as embarrassing the U.S. government and making headlines around the world, the incident caused the State Department to revamp its internal system for making announcements about intelligence matters. (

DELETED

)

In general the presence of American intelligence facilities in a foreign country can have an important effect on American policy toward that country, especially in the Third World. Closely aligned countries, such as (

DELETED

DELETED

)

DELETED

) But to the less developed countries, the presence of an American installation is both a threat and an opportunity. The threat comes from domestic opposition forces who look on the base as an example of "neo-colonialism" and use it as a weapon against those in power. The opportunity arises out of the fact that the United States will pay dearly for the right to install its eavesdropping equipment and keep it in place—as (**DELETED**
) discovered.
(

DELETED

) Both host governments have been severely criticized by internal forces and neighboring countries for giving the United States a foothold in their nations, but both have been handsomely rewarded in American military and economic assistance well into the hundreds of millions of dollars. While comparatively modest amounts of aid would probably have been supplied even if there had been no bases, the large size of the programs represented, in effect, a direct payment for the intelligence facilities.

Similarly, from 1956 until the end of 1969 the U.S. Air Force operated a huge base near Peshawar in Pakistan which was primarily an intelligence facility. For several years before Francis Gary Powers' abortive flight over the Soviet Union in 1960, the CIA's U-2 planes used Peshawar as a principal takeoff point for reconnaissance flights over and along the edges of the Soviet Union. In addition, (

DELETED

) From the early days of the Eisenhower administration, the United States had allied itself more closely with Pakistan than with India in those two countries' continuing struggle. Yet at least some experts on the region believe that an important factor in the American "tilt" toward Pakistan, at least until the late 1960s, was the desire to hold on to the base at Peshawar.

Another site of large American technical espionage installations is the island of Taiwan. In this instance the United States did

not have to provide the Nationalist Chinese government with much inducement to allow the construction of the facilities, since they were aimed against the Nationalists' archenemy on the mainland and some of the information gathered was shared with the Chiang Kai-shek government. Furthermore, in the fifteen or so years after the Nationalists' expulsion from China, the CIA closely cooperated with Chiang's intelligence service to run covert missions against the mainland, and the Nationalists were so dependent on the United States for their very existence that they were in no position to extract a large payment from the United States for the intelligence bases. Yet, by giving the CIA and the other agencies a free hand to build virtually any kind of facility they chose, the Chiang government made it much more difficult for the United States to disengage from Taiwan and build better relations with China. Many of the most important installations for the surveillance of the mainland are located on the island, and they represent an investment valued in the hundreds of millions of dollars. All American military forces, including those engaged in intelligence work, will have to be removed from Taiwan before the United States meets the Chinese conditions for complete normalization of relations between the two countries.

Recent history is full of other examples of technical espionage programs having a profound effect on U.S. foreign policy. The shoot-down of the U-2 over the Soviet Union in 1960 caused the cancellation of the Eisenhower-Khrushchev summit meeting. The spy ship *Liberty*, while trying to monitor the action during the 1967 Six Day War, moved in too close (because a "warning" message from Washington was misrouted) and was shot up by Israeli planes and boats. Thirty-four Americans were killed. As a result, according to former DIA and CIA staffer Patrick McGarvey in his book *CIA: The Myth and the Madness*, the Joint Chiefs of Staff "proposed a quick, retaliatory air strike on the Israeli naval base which launched the attack." The Chief's recommendation was turned down. McGarvey continues:

The next year the North Koreans seized a similar ship, the *Pueblo*, and interned its crew. Again we were on the brink

of war because of intelligence, the supposed secret arm of government. The JCS again recommended an air strike. The *Pueblo* incident was followed by the shoot-down of a United States reconnaissance plane [a Navy EC-121] off the coast of North Korea a little over a year later. And again JCS wanted to mount an air strike.

There have been other disastrous reconnaissance flights—these over China—that have gone virtually unreported in the American press. Some of these have been mentioned by the New China News Agency, but have apparently been dismissed in the West as communist propaganda. They include the shooting down of several CIA U-2 planes flown by Nationalist pilots and even more U.S. Air Force pilotless "drone" aircraft (the Chinese claim nineteen downed between 1964 and 1969) over the Chinese mainland. American SR-71s also flew regularly over China (and continue to do so over North Korea) until all reconnaissance flights were stopped as a result of Henry Kissinger's first trip to Peking in 1971. At the very time in October 1969 when the United States was trying to resume diplomatic contact with the Chinese, Air Force Intelligence, **with the approval of the 40 Committee**, sent a drone over southern China. On October 28 the New China News Agency reported the downing of "a U.S. imperialist, pilotless, high altitude plane," but (

DELETED

)

Another extremely provocative drone flight was proposed by the Pentagon in the period after the American invasion of Cambodia in 1970. The **mission was approved by the 40 Committee over the strong objections of the State Department** which estimated that roughly one in three of these aircraft would be shot down. (

DELETED

DELETED

)

The official justification for all the espionage missions carried out by intelligence planes and ships is to gather intelligence which helps to protect the national security of the United States. But with literally hundreds of flights and cruises scheduled each month along the borders of and over unfriendly countries, inevitably there are embarrassing failures. That these abortive missions on occasion cause international crises is understood by the policy-makers who rather routinely give their approval, and is presumably figured in as one of the costs of acquiring the intelligence. Yet it is frightening to realize that some of these spying forays could have led—and could in the future lead—to armed conflict. Missions that violate the territorial integrity of foreign countries are clear violations of sovereignty, and any country that shoots at an intruder inside its borders is completely within its legal rights.

While Allen Dulles professed to believe that U.S. foreign policy should be based on intelligence estimates developed by an agency with "no axes to grind and . . . itself . . . not wedded to any particular policy," his actions were not always true to these words. Consequently, he made possible the Bay of Pigs—the classic case of what can happen when intelligence is misused in the carrying out of a clandestine operation.

The problem started on the eve of Fidel Castro's triumphant march into Havana in January 1959 while CIA analysts were preparing a report for the White House stating that the rebels' success was due largely to the corruption of the Batista regime and the resulting popular disgust among the Cuban people. Allen Dulles

personally intervened in the intelligence process and rewrote this report to suit his own political biases. In Dulles' view, Castro's victory was not a natural development that could have been expected in light of the faults of Batista. Dulles' Calvinistic mind may well have seen the hand of the Devil at work, and he predicted that there would be a slaughter in Havana which would put the French Revolution to shame. "Blood will flow in the streets," he wrote passionately in the CIA report to the White House.

For the most part, however, the agency's analysts took a more moderate tone in the months that followed. They stressed that Castro's Cuba, while something of an annoyance, was in no way a direct threat to the security of the United States. The Intelligence Directorate also tried to explain that Castro, despite his socialistic leanings, was fiercely independent and a devout nationalist, much like Indonesia's Sukarno, Egypt's Nasser, and Ghana's Nkrumah— all opponents of Western domination of the Third World but certainly not agents of any international communist conspiracy. Most important for future events, the analysts wrote that, regardless of the emotional reports flowing from Cuban refugees concerning political unrest on the island, Castro appeared to have general support of the populace.

Dulles did not accept this finding of his intelligence analysts, nor did he promote their point of view at the White House. Instead, he seized upon the reporting of the Clandestine Services as more truly reflective of events in Cuba. Dulles had always believed that the field operator was a more reliable judge of events than the intelligence analyst back at headquarters. Prior to Castro's takeover, there had not even been a full-time CIA analyst of Cuban problems in the Intelligence Directorate, and the two that were added after January 1959 never really won Dulles' trust. He preferred to read the assessments of the Clandestine Services' officers, who did their own evaluation of the clandestine reports received from secret agents.

Sometime during late 1959 Dulles decided that the best solution for the Cuban problem would be to invade Cuba with an army of Cuban refugees and to overthrow Castro. He was unquestionably influenced by the reports of the Clandestine Services, which, unlike

those of the Intelligence Directorate, stressed the unpopularity of the Castro regime, its internal frictions, and its economic troubles. In March 1960, President Eisenhower, at Dulles' urging and with Dulles' facts at hand, gave his approval for the CIA to start recruiting and training the ill-fated invasion force. Robert Amory, the Deputy Director of Intelligence, was never officially told that the invasion was in the works so that his experts could analyze the chances of success. Dulles was convinced that Cuba was ripe for an invasion, and as he was the President's chief intelligence advisor, that was that.

When the CIA's military force failed to topple Castro in the spring of 1961, the agency's Intelligence Directorate temporarily gained equal footing with the Clandestine Services. This did not occur because there was any newfound appreciation of the analysts' work but rather because the operators were in a general state of disgrace after the Bay of Pigs. John McCone took over as Director in November 1961, and after rising above his initial distrust of the entire organization, he ultimately saw the need for and the value of high-quality national intelligence.

(

DELETED

)* Castro, whose secret agents had penetrated

---

* Assassination of Castro seemed to have been a recurrent idea in the CIA during these years. E. Howard Hunt claims to have recommended it before the Bay of Pigs, only to be turned down. In November of 1961, President Kennedy mentioned the idea in a private chat with Tad Szulc, then of the *New York Times*. Kennedy asked the newsman, "How would you feel if the United States assassinated Castro?" When Szulc said he thought it was a very poor idea, Kennedy said, "I'm glad you feel that way because suggestions to that effect keep coming to me, and I believe very strongly the United States should not be a party to political assassination." Lyndon Johnson told his former aide Leo Janos, as recounted in a July 1973 *Atlantic* article, "We had been operating a damned Murder, Inc. in the Caribbean." Janos elaborated, "A year or so before Kennedy's death a CIA–backed assassination team had been picked up in Havana. Johnson specu-

the CIA's operations long before the Bay of Pigs, knew perfectly well what the CIA was doing, and the ongoing American attacks against his rule may well have been an important factor in his decision in the spring of 1962 to allow the Soviet Union to install offensive nuclear weapons in his country.

The Cuban missile crisis that developed as a result produced one of the finest hours for the CIA and the intelligence community, although the last National Intelligence Estimate, prepared by the CIA a little over a month before President Kennedy went on nationwide television to announce the Cuban "quarantine," declared that it was unlikely that the Soviets would install nuclear-tipped missiles on the island. The fact remains, however, that the CIA and the other intelligence agencies did discover the Soviet missiles in time for the President to take action, and they presented the facts to Kennedy with no policy recommendations or slanting which could have limited his options. This was how the intelligence process was supposed to work.

The affair started in the late spring of 1962 when CIA analysts noted that the Soviets were sending an increased amount of military assistance to Cuba. These shipments were not viewed with particular alarm in the agency, since there was still much to be done in the Soviet re-equipping of the Cuban army forces, which was then under way. Furthermore, the CIA had ways of keeping track of what arms flowed into Cuba.

Since January 1961, when the Eisenhower administration had broken diplomatic relations with the Castro regime, there had been no agency operators working out of an American embassy in Havana, but the (

DELETED

) Additionally, a steady flow of refugees was arriving in Miami and being debriefed by agency officers permanently assigned there. As was true before the Bay of Pigs, the stories told by many of these refugees were hysterical but oc-

---

lated that Dallas had been a retaliation for this thwarted attempt, although he couldn't prove it."

casionally some valuable nugget of information would be gleaned from their tales.

Based on President Kennedy's request, the USIB had set Cuba as a Priority National Intelligence Objective (PNIO), and the various military intelligence agencies had been assigned extensive collection requirements by the USIB. New requirements were almost continually levied in response to the specific needs of the analysts. The Air Force and the Navy carefully watched the shipping lanes and photographed Soviet ships destined for Cuba. Surveillance was provided by the Sixth Fleet in the Mediterranean, by the Atlantic fleet (which even had a listening post at Guantanamo Bay inside Cuba), and by the Air Force. U.S. intelligence photographed ship movements and listened in electronically on Cuban communications. The National Security Agency tuned its huge antennae in on **Soviet shipping** and Cuban communications. ITT had operated much of the Cuban communications system before Castro's nationalizations, and the company **worked closely with the CIA and NSA to intercept messages.** Much of the old equipment was still in use, and the NSA was collecting large amounts of information. Finally, the CIA was flying two U-2 missions each month over Cuba, and the photographs taken by these spy planes were quickly turned over to the analysts.

So while Soviet military (and economic) assistance to Castro was on the upswing in the late spring of 1962, there seemed little cause for alarm in the CIA or elsewhere in the U.S. government. Moscow had recently eased tensions in Berlin, much to the relief of Washington policy-makers, whose strong stand in that divided city appeared to have paid off. But still there were a few ominous signs. The **CIA learned that Soviet military personnel were being secretly used in combat roles as submarine crews in Indonesia and as bomber crews in Yemen, a** drastic departure from previous Soviet practice. Then, by July the analysts noted further increases in the arms being shipped to Cuba, along with the arrival of a large number of young men from the Soviet Union—who Moscow claimed were technical advisors to assist in economic development programs. The CIA doubted this, for, among other reasons, all the "civilians" were young, seemed to have a military bearing, and

wore only two kinds of sport shirt. It was becoming clear that the Soviets were supplying too much military equipment for the Cuban armed forces to absorb. A small group of CIA analysts, expert in deciphering the ways Moscow and its allies conducted their foreign aid programs, became convinced that an unprecedented military build-up was occurring in Cuba. Their efforts during August to alert top U.S. officials to this threat were hampered, surprisingly, by military intelligence agencies, namely the DIA and the NSA, which viewed the intensified Soviet activity on the island as mostly economic assistance. Perhaps it was because the CIA had performed so poorly with its inaccurate reporting on Cuba as a prelude to the Bay of Pigs that even the hawkish U.S. military establishment was now leery of the agency's ability to assess the Cuban situation. In any event, both the DIA and the NSA saw fit to counter the CIA intelligence reports with rebuttals in late August 1962.

The basic reason that the CIA analysts were able to monitor the Soviet arms build-up more closely than the other intelligence agencies, which had essentially the same information available, was the more refined technique that the CIA had developed, including a special analytical tool known as "crate-ology"—a unique method of determining the contents of the large crates carried on the decks of the Soviet ships delivering arms. With a high degree of accuracy, the specialists could look at photographs of these boxes, factor in information about the ship's embarkation point and Soviet military production schedules, and deduce whether the crates contained transport aircraft or jet fighters. While the system was viewed with caution by many in the intelligence community, CIA Director John McCone accepted its findings, and his confidence in the technique proved to be justified.

Nevertheless, the CIA's analysts did not spot the first shipments of Soviet offensive missiles, which arrived in Cuba during the early part of September. The Soviets escaped the scrutiny of the "crate-ologists" by sending the weapons in the holds of huge freighters, not in crates carried on deck as had been their usual practice when delivering bulky military equipment. On September 19, the USIB approved the National Intelligence Estimates which, while noting the disturbing Soviet arms build-up, declared it unlikely that the

Russians would bring in nuclear-tipped missiles. During this period McCone personally suspected the worst of the Soviets, but, to his credit, he did not put his private views forward as the CIA position since, as he would later say, it was based on "intuition," not "hard intelligence." Nevertheless, he did urge the White House to approve an increased schedule of U-2 flights. The President agreed in early October, but, at Defense Secretary McNamara's urging, responsibility for the reconnaissance missions was turned over from the CIA to the Air Force because of the danger that Soviet SAMs (surface-to-air missiles) posed to more frequent flights.*

On October 14 an Air Force U-2 brought back photographs of six medium-range ballistic-missile sites which were nearing operational readiness and four intermediate-range sites in the early stage of construction. CIA analysts were able to verify these pictures indisputably with the help of information previously provided by satellite surveillance of similar installations in the U.S.S.R. and from documents supplied by Penkovsky, and also by comparing the (

DELETED

) And thus the Cuban missile crisis began.

By the end of October, Nikita Khrushchev had been outmaneuvered by Kennedy and he promised to withdraw his country's offensive weapons from Cuba, in return for an American pledge not to invade the island. (This was a pledge that the CIA, with White House approval, seems to have violated systematically by continuing its guerrilla raids on Cuba until the late 1960s.) The CIA and several military intelligence agencies maintained their surveillance of Cuba to make sure the withdrawal was complete. It was, despite persistent rumors in the press that the Soviets had hidden some of the missiles in caves. The CIA even noted that a group of

* Just as the new wave of U-2s was starting surveillance of Cuba, on October 9, 1962, the mainland Chinese used a SAM to bring down a CIA U-2 flown by a Nationalist Chinese pilot. A SAM of the same model had knocked Francis Gary Powers out of the air over the Soviet Union two years earlier and would down an Air Force plane over Cuba late in October at the height of the missile crisis.

IL-28 jet bombers had been removed from a hiding place which the agency had (unknown to the Soviets) previously discovered.

President Kennedy chose later to view the missile crisis as a nearly disastrous intelligence failure, since the CIA had been unable to give early warning of the Soviet offensive build-up and had predicted in its last estimate the unlikelihood of Soviet missiles being placed on the island. He was not willing to concede that the agency's warning of heavily increased Soviet military activity on the island during the summer months (when military intelligence was claiming otherwise) compensated for the CIA's inability to predict that nuclear-missile sites would be constructed—even though it was as a direct result of the agency's warning that surveillance of the island was intensified and ultimately led to the discovery of the missiles. To what extent the President still mistrusted the CIA for its Bay of Pigs blunder is unclear, but Kennedy obviously expected better information.

The Cuban missile crisis illustrated the inherent limitations of intelligence, among the most important of which is that certain events simply cannot be predicted with accuracy or confidence. Khrushchev's decision to install nuclear missiles in Cuba was not knowable until the Soviets had actually embarked on that course of action. Careful psychological studies of Khrushchev's character could provide suppositions that he might act in an unpredictable way, but to have known exactly what he would do would have required divine analytical wisdom or spies in the inner reaches of the Kremlin—neither of which the CIA possessed. As for those people in the intelligence community whose visceral feelings led them to expect the worst of Khrushchev and Castro before either had contemplated the missile gamble—to have accepted their speculations as intelligence would have been the height of irresponsibility. Allen Dulles and his Clandestine Services lieutenants had had their own gut reactions to events in Cuba nearly two years earlier, and when their "feelings" were presented to the nation's leaders as intelligence, the outcome was the Bay of Pigs. John McCone proved himself a much more responsible intelligence officer than his predecessor when, unlike Dulles, he refused to impose his own suspicions upon the President. Hindsight may in-

dicate that the Dulles technique, employed by McCone, would have had more favorable results—but hindsight is too easy.

The CIA and the rest of the intelligence community conducted extensive post-mortems of the missile crisis. They found that enough bits and pieces of information and other tenuous evidence had been available to have warranted an earlier judgment that the Soviets were installing their missiles. Bureaucratic entanglements and frictions, coupled with some degree of human imperfection, however, prevented even the most astute intelligence officers from determining the true purpose of Khrushchev's actions. Yet intelligence seems to have done the best it could in the existing circumstances; the one or two accurate agent reports picked up during September were buried among thousands of useless, inaccurate, or misleading ones. The collection of huge amounts of secret information from a multitude of sources and the availability of analytical staffs even larger than those available at the time are by themselves no guarantee that the CIA and the intelligence community will produce correct predictions. Intelligence is in essence a guessing game, albeit one that is grounded in fact, logic, and experience. It can be a useful tool to the policy-makers, but it is not, even in its purest form, a magic art.

Abusing the Product

Unfortunately, intelligence reports are often sent to the nation's leaders in a far from pure form, especially when the subject is Soviet military capabilities. Yet, estimating the quantity and quality of Soviet weapons is probably the intelligence community's most important task, since the Soviet Union, on a strategic basis, is the only country in the world that offers a real threat to the security of the United States. (The Chinese strategic threat is more potential than real.) Every President since World War II has wanted to know about any dangerous imbalances between American and Soviet forces, and presidential decisions on whether or not to go ahead with the development of new and expensive weapons systems

have been based, to a great extent, on intelligence estimates of how strong the Russians are (although domestic political considerations and the views of America's allies also play a large role).

The Pentagon knows all too well that to justify its constant demands for new weapons and larger forces, intelligence must show that the Soviets are moving into a position of strength.* To support a request for additional ships, the Navy will often magnify an increased threat from the Soviet fleet. The Air Force can much more easily obtain funds for a new bomber if it can show that the Soviets are developing one. Similar justifications can be—and have been—made for missiles, tanks, and even the continuance of American programs for chemical and biological warfare. Military analysts have tended to take a "worst case" view of the Soviets, from which they predict the most dire possible consequences from Soviet actions. Major General Daniel Graham, formerly chief of estimates at the DIA, described the process in an April 1973 article in *Army Magazine*: "To put it bluntly, there is a considerable body of opinion among decision-makers, in and out of DOD [Department of Defense], which regards threat estimates prepared by the military as being self-serving, budget oriented, and generally inflated." While Graham conceded that the lack of confidence in military estimates is "fully understandable," stemming "from a series of bad overestimates, later dubbed 'bomber gap,' 'missile gap,' and 'megaton gap,' " he asserted that military intelligence has now vastly improved and is capable of making objective estimates. While most observers of the intelligence community would agree with his assessment of the military's bad record in estimates, few outside the Pentagon would accept his assertion that objectivity has returned to the Pentagon's appraisals of the Soviets, although these appraisals are unquestionably closer to reality than they were ten years ago.

Graham illustrated another basic point that "is beginning to be understood in military planner circles." He stated:

* Senator Stuart Symington has pointed out that scare stories about Soviet military strength appear at congressional budget time in springtime Washington as regularly as the cherry blossoms.

Estimates of future enemy forces and hardware are by nature of *intent*—not just *capability*. The old arguments about "capability versus intent" are heard less now in DOD. It remains true that intelligence should emphasize capability in descriptions of current and near-future enemy forces. But the minute you tackle the usual problem of estimating enemy forces (or hardware) a year or so into the future, you have entered the realm of intent. For example, since World War II the Soviets have never to our knowledge deployed forces of fielded hardware as fast as their total capability permitted. To estimate that they would do so with regard to some weapon system or type of force in the future would make little sense. . . . It is remarkable how long it has taken some of our military users to wise up to it.

As a result of the military's propensity to overestimate, the CIA (usually supported by the State Department) is almost always suspicious of Pentagon positions. Thus, the agency tends to resist and counter military judgments, which in turn has led to CIA underestimation. In the national-security bureaucracy, the agency's tendency to be wrong on the low side, while occurring far less frequently than the Pentagon's errors, is considered more serious, since if estimates of Soviet capabilities run too high, that provides a margin for safety to the military planners, who may well spend billions of dollars reacting to a non-existent threat but who at least do not endanger the country by developing too few weapons.

This continuing conflict between the military agencies and the civilians in the intelligence community was most evident in the preparation of the National Intelligence Estimates (NIEs), which until 1973 were considered the highest form of national intelligence.

In the internal CIA reshuffling begun by James Schlesinger during his short stay at the agency and continued by present Director Colby, the twelve-to-fourteen-man Board of National Estimates and its staff of forty to fifty specialists have been largely phased out—along with the production of thoroughly researched and well-thought-out community-wide NIEs. These documents, long the

epitome of finished intelligence production, were found to be inadequate for the more immediate foreign-policy purposes of Henry Kissinger and the Nixon administration. Thus, the BNE has been replaced by a group of eight senior officers known as National Intelligence Officers who on short notice produce brief (no more than ten- or twelve-page) assessments of whatever international situation is of immediate concern to Kissinger's NSC staff.

The net result of this change has been that long-term estimates on broad subjects (e.g., the Outlook on Latin America Over the Next Decade, Soviet Strategic Strike Capabilities for the Next Five Years, etc.) have given way to short-term predictions which are little more than extensions of current intelligence analysis. But the intelligence system is the servant of the policy-maker and must meet his needs and demands. Even so, the CIA's new estimating system has failed to satisfy the NSC staff and the White House. The tactical approach to world problems has proved to be of no more value—and probably less—than the traditional strategic view.

In the past, while the majority of the fifty or more NIEs written each year dealt with political matters, both the CIA and the Pentagon devoted the most work and attention to estimates that dealt with foreign military capabilities—especially the Soviet Union's. These NIEs, on such subjects as Soviet strategic strike forces, air defense forces, and general-purpose forces, influenced large decisions about the American military budget, and each branch of the service as well as the DIA (representing the Defense Department) as a whole would fight fiercely to have its point of view included.

For example, in the 1963-to-1965 period when the Pentagon was seeking funds to build an anti-ballistic-missile (ABM) system, the military services joined together to promote the idea that Moscow was in the process of deploying its own ABM which would nullify the offensive nuclear threat of American strategic forces. Thus, the Pentagon reasoned, the United States would no longer have the power to stop the Soviets from taking bold initiatives in Western Europe and the Third World, and the security of the United States itself would be threatened. Although the military may have believed sincerely that the Soviets were

outdistancing the United States and that Moscow would go on the offensive once it had an advantage, the benefits to be received by the armed services through an ABM system were still tremendously large. The Army stood to receive billions of dollars to build the system (and, not incidentally, get itself into the strategic-missile field, which the Air Force and Navy had managed to pre-empt). The Air Force could justify its requests for more long-range missiles in order to overcome the Soviet ABM defenses, and the Navy, on similar grounds, could ask for additional funds for its missile-equipped submarines.

The CIA and the State Department, on the other hand, did not see the Soviet ABM construction to be such a large threat to the United States. Neither ascribed such hostile intentions to the Soviets as the Pentagon did, and many analysts were not even convinced that any sort of ABM could ever be developed which could effectively stop the other side's intercontinental missiles. (In fact, quite a few cynical observers of the 1972 S.A.L.T. agreements believe that the reason the American and Soviet governments agreed to a limitation of two ABM sites each was that neither country had real confidence that its own ABM would work properly and thus was just as happy to be able to divert the money into other sorts of weaponry.)

While the ABM debate was raging within the intelligence community, both the civilian and the military analysts had access to the same fragmentary information about what the Soviets were doing in the field. There was tremendous pressure for additional intelligence and the USIB was frequently setting new collection requirements. Overt sources such as U.S. diplomats and Soviet periodicals produced some data, and Air Force spy planes flying along the fringes of the Soviet Union picked up more. Huge radars and other electronic sensors located in (**DELETED**) also made a contribution. And the most valuable information was supplied by the photographic satellites.

Yet, the overall picture on the Soviet ABM was incomplete, and the analysts were forced to make conclusions without having all the pieces of the jigsaw puzzle before them. Often they turned

to experts at the private "think tanks" for advice. They also consulted with American corporations—especially Bell Laboratories—that were performing research and development for the U.S. ABM in the hope that some of the fragmentary data amassed would make sense to the people working on similar systems at home.

Both the civilian and the military analysts agreed that the Soviets were constructing some sort of new defense system at Leningrad, and something else at Moscow. Most of the civilians believed that the Leningrad system was aimed against American bombers, and that the Moscow system was probably an ABM defense still undergoing research and development. The military claimed that the Leningrad site was actually an ABM, and that research had been completed for a more advanced ABM system which would be constructed around Moscow.

In those years from 1963 to 1965 the military entered footnote after footnote in the NIEs, and the views of a divided community went forward to the White House. The Johnson administration made hundreds of millions of dollars of development funds available to the Army for the American ABM, although the Pentagon would have liked even more money to speed up development. Several years later, intelligence learned that the Leningrad system was indeed aimed against planes, not missiles (although the military quickly maintained—and still do today—that the Leningrad site could be quickly "upgraded" to have ABM capability), but that at Moscow the Soviets were building a true but limited ABM. The civilian estimate had been much closer to the truth than the military's, but the Pentagon got the funding it wanted from the Johnson and the Nixon administrations to proceed with the deployment of an ABM system.

These intelligence wars are not just fought out in the privacy of the intelligence community. All the members have on occasion selectively disclosed secret data to the press and to members of Congress in support of their budgetary requests. But as columnist Joseph Kraft has written, ". . . far, far more than the civilians in the government, the uniformed military are in the habit of leaking

information to serve their own interests." The sanctity of classified information seems to fall apart when fights for additional funds are under way in Congress. Former Assistant CIA Director for Research Herbert Scoville, Jr., was absolutely correct when he told the Senate Foreign Relations Committee on March 28, 1972, that "the history of the past twenty years is dotted with example after example of intelligence being misused to promote within the Congress the programs of individual organizations or even of the administration as a whole."

Newsmen friendly to the Pentagon, such as Joseph Alsop (who helped promote the Pentagon's mythical bomber, missile, megaton, and ABM gaps, and is currently pushing the military's latest fright gimmick, the "technological" gap), and William Beecher,* have long received leaks of material marked HIGHER THAN TOP SECRET to buttress the military's case in a particular dispute. Included have been numerous reports based on satellite photography and communications intercepts—collection methods so sensitive that the overwhelming majority of government employees *with* security clearances are not authorized access to the information received.

Then Secretary of Defense Melvin Laird and other Defense officials publicly quoted and leaked such one-sided intelligence during the 1969 congressional debate over the ABM that someone—probably in the CIA or the State Department—countered by providing the *New York Times* with the draft of a USIB estimate that refuted most of the Pentagon arguments about the danger posed by the Soviet ABM. In 1971 the Defense Department passed satellite-photo-based material concerning alleged Soviet construction of a new and larger type of missile to military-spending

---

* Beecher, for many years the *New York Times'* Pentagon correspondent, left the paper in early 1973 to become a Deputy Assistant Secretary of Defense for Public Affairs. Ironically, his 1969 story about the secret American bombing of Cambodia and his 1971 piece on the classified American bargaining position at the S.A.L.T. talks have been credited by the Nixon administration as being among the principal reasons, along with the more important leak of the Pentagon Papers, for the formation in June 1971 of the so-called White House plumbers to stop unauthorized disclosures in the press.

champion Senator Henry Jackson. Calling the development "ominous indeed," Jackson warned the country on March 7 about what the Soviets were supposedly doing, at the same time that Congress was considering the military budget. Melvin Laird corroborated Jackson's disclosure three days later in a television interview, and on April 22 cited fresh intelligence "confirming the sobering fact that the Soviet Union is involved in a new—and apparently extensive—ICBM construction program." Additionally, the threat described by Jackson and Laird was made even more vivid by a spate of unattributed supporting leaks.

Finally, an anonymous CIA employee struck back at the Pentagon. He knew that the agency had concluded that the Soviets were only "hardening" their missile sites rather than deploying a huge new missile system, and that over two thirds of the excavations mentioned by Jackson and Laird were intended for an older and relatively small ICBM. So this CIA man publicly disclosed the agency's secret finding, according to the *New York Times* of May 26, 1971, through "non-government arms control experts" and "Senate Republican sources." Even though the CIA appraisal turned out to be much closer to the truth than the Pentagon's gloomy version, at least for another year, no one in the U.S. intelligence community knew for sure what the Soviet missile builders were really doing. In the meantime, the military scare stories—offset to some extent by the CIA's counter-leak—undoubtedly had a psychological effect on the Congress, which in 1971, as usual approved almost the whole Pentagon budget request.

The tragedy of all this maneuvering is that, despite the $6 billion paid out each year for intelligence, neither the Congress nor the public receives a true or worthwhile picture of Soviet military capabilities. Intelligence professionals explain that the sensitivity of the sources and methods involved in collecting this information makes the high degree of secrecy necessary, and they have resisted congressional attempts to create a regular procedure for sharing data with the legislative branch. Yet the professionals do not hesitate to leak the most highly classified intelligence when it serves their departmental interests. Moreover, the intelligence

community regularly provides friendly foreign countries with detailed estimates of Soviet military strength, and during the S.A.L.T. talks the nation's negotiators even told their Soviet counterparts how much the United States really knew about Soviet missiles.* Yet, the American Congress, which has the constitutional responsibility to approve funds for the military budget, cannot get the same information.

Congress, however, has always had the legislative power to insist that the CIA and the rest of the community share with it information on Soviet military capabilities—or any other subject, for that matter. Yet, to date, Congress as a whole has refused to take such action, despite the loud protests of a vocal minority. And Congress' unwillingness to take even so small a step to make itself better informed about the data used to justify military spending is symptomatic of the legislative branch's much larger failing: its refusal to exercise any degree of meaningful control over American intelligence activities.

* In fact, the American S.A.L.T. negotiators were so explicit in their descriptions of Soviet capabilities that at one point, according to John Newhouse's account in his book *Cold Dawn*, the ranking Soviet general took an American military man aside and asked that the U.S. not give the Soviet civilian negotiators such detailed information on *Soviet* missiles.

TEN

Controlling
the CIA

I submit that there is no federal
agency of our government whose
activities receive closer scrutiny
and "control" than the CIA.

—LYMAN KIRKPATRICK
former Executive Director, CIA
October 11, 1971

The reverse of that statement
[Kirkpatrick's] is true in my
opinion, and it is shameful for
the American people to be so
misled. There is no federal
agency of our government
whose activities receive less
scrutiny and control than the CIA.

—SENATOR STUART SYMINGTON
Member, Joint Senate
Committee for CIA Oversight
November 23, 1971

ALTHOUGH Harry Truman wrote in 1963 that "I never had any thought when I set up the CIA that it would be injected into peacetime cloak-and-dagger operations," he—and each President after him—willingly employed the agency to carry out clandestine espionage and covert intervention in the internal affairs of other countries—those activities, in short, subsumed under the "such other functions and duties" language in the enabling legislation. In that phrase lies the authority, according to Richard Helms, for overthrowing foreign governments, subverting elections, bribing officials, and waging "secret" wars. As Helms told the American Society of Newspaper Editors in 1971, this "language was designed to enable us to conduct such foreign activities as the national government may find it convenient to assign to what can best be described as a 'secret service.'"

From its beginning, the CIA's actual functions were couched in deception and secrecy. Richard Bissell's notorious Council on Foreign Relations speech in 1968 (see p. 381) stressed that the original legislation was "necessarily vague." He continued:

> CIA's full "charter" has been frequently revised, but it has been, and must remain, secret. The absence of a public charter leads people to search for the charter and to question the Agency's authority to undertake various activities. The problem of a secret "charter" remains as a curse, but the need for secrecy would appear to preclude a solution.

There was never any doubt in the minds of men like Bissell that the CIA's functions should not be a matter of public record. In fact, the National Security Act of 1947 and the supporting Central Intelligence Act of 1949 are little more than legal covers which

provide for the existence of the CIA and authorize it to operate outside the rules affecting other government agencies. The CIA's actual role is spelled out in Bissell's "secret charter"—that series of classified executive orders called National Security Intelligence Directives (NSCIDs or "en-skids"). These directives were "codified" in 1959, but remain unavailable to all but a few key government officials. Not until July 1973 did the CIA offer the congressional subcommittees which supposedly oversee its activities a glimpse at the "secret charter." And the public still has no way of knowing if the agency is exceeding its mandate, because it has no way of knowing what that mandate is.

During the 1947 congressional debate concerning the agency's formation, Representative Fred Busby asked, "I wonder if there is any foundation for the rumors that have come to me to the effect that through this CIA they are contemplating operational activities." The rumors were indeed accurate, and the following year President Truman approved NSC directive 10/2 which authorized first the semi-independent Office of Policy Coordination, and then in 1951 the CIA itself, to carry out "dirty tricks" overseas, with the two stipulations that the operations be secret and "plausibly deniable." A whole series of NSCIDs expanding the CIA's activities were issued in the years that followed. **One, NSCID 7, gave the CIA powers inside the United States to question Americans about their foreign travels, and to enter into contractual arrangements with American universities,** even though the National Security Act of 1947 forbade the agency to exercise any "police, subpoena, law enforcement powers, or internal security functions." Another NSCID was apparently shown to the judge in the 1966 court case in which one Estonian-American slandered a fellow refugee and then claimed "absolute privilege" to have done so because he was acting under the CIA's orders. Having seen the secret directive, the judge ruled that the agency had the power to operate among émigré groups in the United States, and he dismissed the suit. **Yet another, NSCID 6, apparently spells out the functions of the National Security Agency** (which itself was created by executive order), since in the Nixon administration's 1970 secret plan for domestic espionage there is a recommendation that

this directive be revised to allow NSA "coverage of the communications of U.S. citizens using international facilities."

The essential point is that successive Presidents have regularly enlarged the functions of the CIA by executive fiat. No new laws have been passed, and only a handful of Congressmen have been informed of what was happening. And sometimes Presidents have acted without informing even these normally indulgent congressional "watchdogs," as was the case when President Nixon approved the domestic spying program, and received the CIA's cooperation. The CIA, if nothing else, has always considered that anything a President told it to do was permissible—indeed, necessary—for the defense of the country.

"Out of the crisis of World War II and ensuing cold war," Senator Jacob Javits said on July 18, 1973, "lawyers for the President had spun a spurious doctrine of 'inherent' commander-in-chief powers broad enough to cover virtually every 'national security' contingency." Top CIA officials heartily endorse this broad interpretation of presidential powers, even though they understand that the agency's activities often are of doubtful legality. Senator Symington asked Director-designate William Colby on July 2, 1973, "Do not large-scale operations, such as the war in Laos, go considerably beyond what Congress intended when it provided [in the 1947 act] for other functions and duties related to intelligence?" Colby replied, "I think it undoubtedly did." But Colby justified the Laotian operation on the grounds it was carried out with "proper review, instructions, and direction of the National Security Council" and—most important—the President. The legality of the matter, in Colby's apparent view, stemmed from the chief executive's authorization, not the law. Senator Harold Hughes later asked Colby, "Do you believe it is proper under our Constitution for such military operations to be conducted without the knowledge or approval of the Congress?" Colby's written response is an interesting commentary on the modern meaning of congressional approval:

> The appropriate committees of the Congress and a number of individual senators and congressmen were briefed on CIA's

activities in Laos during the period covered. In addition, CIA's programs were described to the Appropriations Committees in our annual budget hearings.*

Colby's explanation reflects the general belief in the CIA that legislative and judicial restraints simply do not apply to the agency—as long as it is acting under presidential order. The CIA sees itself, in Senator Symington's words, as "the King's men or the President's army." Nevertheless, Congress must take some responsibility for contributing to the agency view of being "above the law," since it specifically exempted the CIA from all budgetary limitations which apply to other government departments. The 1949 statute reads: "Notwithstanding any other provision of law, sums made available to the Agency by appropriation otherwise may be expended for purposes necessary to carry out its functions. . . ." This law, which also gives the DCI the right to spend unvouchered funds,† does not say, however, that the CIA should not be accountable to Congress; but that, essentially, has been the experience of the past twenty-five years.

The 40 Committee

The executive branch has its own mechanisms to control the CIA. While these procedures are slanted greatly to favor the agency's position, they do require high-level—usually presidential—ap-

---

* Colby's claim that these committees were informed conflicts directly with the 1971 statements of the late Senate Appropriations Committee Chairman, Allen Ellender (quoted later in this chapter), that he knew nothing about the CIA's 36,000-man "secret" army in Laos.

† These provisions, along with Congress' practice of hiding the CIA's budget in appropriations to other government departments, may well violate the constitutional requirement that "No money shall be drawn from the Treasury, but in Consequence of Appropriations made by law; and a regular Statement and Account of the Receipts and Expenditures of all public Money shall be published from time to time." A legal challenge (Higgs et al. v. Helms et al.) to the CIA's secrecy in budgetary matters, based on these constitutional grounds, is currently pending in the federal court system.

proval of all major covert operations except the CIA's classical espionage activities.

By the 1947 law, the CIA falls under the National Security Council, reports to the President through it, and takes its orders from it. But the NSC has, in fact, become a moribund body during the Nixon administration, and the agency reports sometimes to the President but more often to the NSC staff headed by Henry Kissinger. By levying intelligence-collection priority requirements and requesting analytical contributions to policy studies, the Kissinger staff plays a large part in directing the CIA's information-gathering effort. As far as the agency is concerned, however, the NSC itself is little more than a conduit from the President and Kissinger to the CIA, a legal fiction which is preserved because the 1947 law gives it authority over the agency.

Every major CIA proposal for covert action—including subsidies for foreign political leaders, political parties, or publications, interference in elections, major propaganda activities, and paramilitary operations—still must be approved by the President or the 40 Committee.* The nearly ubiquitous Kissinger chairs this committee, just as he heads the three other principal White House panels which supervise the intelligence community.

Allen Dulles described the 40 Committee's role in *The Craft of Intelligence*: "The facts are that the CIA has never carried out any action of a political nature, given any support of any nature to any persons, potentates or movements, political or otherwise, without appropriate approval at a high political level in our government *outside the CIA*" (Dulles' italics). Dulles' statement was and is correct, but he carefully omitted any mention of the CIA's espionage activities. He also did not mention that the 40 Committee functions in such a way that it rarely turns down CIA requests for covert action.

The committee is supposed to meet once a week, but the busy

---

* Over the last twenty-five years this body has also been called the Special Group, the 54–12 Group, and the 303 Committee. Its name has changed with new administrations or whenever its existence has become publicly known.

schedule of its members* causes relatively frequent cancellations. When it does meet—roughly once or twice a month in the Nixon administration—intentionally incomplete minutes are kept by its one permanent staff member, who is always a CIA officer. All the proposals for American intervention overseas that come before the committee are drafted by the CIA's Clandestine Services, and thus are likely to maximize the benefits to be gained by agency action and to minimize the disadvantages and risks. More often than not, these proposals are put into final form only a few days before the 40 Committee meets. Thus, the non-CIA members often have little time to investigate the issues adequately. And even when sufficient prior notice is given, the staff work that can be done is extremely limited by the supersecrecy surrounding the 40 Committee's deliberations and the fact that only a handful of people outside the agency are cleared to know about its activities. Even within the CIA the short deadlines and the excessive secrecy allow for little independent review of the projects by the Director's own staff.

The 40 Committee's members have so many responsibilities in their own departments that they usually have only a general knowledge about most countries of the world. On specific problems, they generally rely on advice from their agency's regional experts, but these officials are often denied access to 40 Committee proposals and never are allowed to accompany their bosses to committee sessions. Only the DCI is permitted to bring with him an area specialist, and the other high officials, deprived of their own spear carriers, are at a marked disadvantage. Moreover, the 40 Committee members are men who have been admitted into the very private and exclusive world of covert operations, and they have an overwhelming tendency to agree with whatever is proposed, once they are let in on the secret. The non-CIA members of the committee have had little or no experience in covert operations, and they tend to defer to the views of the "experts." Columnist Stewart

* In addition to Kissinger, they are currently the Under Secretary of State for Political Affairs, the Deputy Secretary of Defense, the Director of Central Intelligence, and the Chairman of the Joint Chiefs of Staff.

Alsop, himself an OSS veteran, described in the May 25, 1973, *Washington Post* how the brightest men in the Kennedy administration could have approved an adventure with so small a chance of success as the Bay of Pigs invasion, and his explanation applies just as well to other CIA activities. Alsop stated, "The answer lies somewhere in the mystique of the secret-service professional *vis-à-vis* the amateur. Somehow in such a confrontation, the amateur tends to put a childish faith in the confident assertions of the professional." Similarly, Marilyn Berger in the May 26, 1973, *Washington Post* quoted a veteran intelligence official about his experiences in dealing with the 40 Committee: "They were like a bunch of schoolboys. They would listen and their eyes would bug out. I always used to say that I could get $5 million out of the Forty Committee for a covert operation faster than I could get money for a typewriter out of the ordinary bureaucracy."

The 40 Committee process is further loaded in favor of the CIA because the agency prepares the proposals, and discussion is thereby within the CIA's terms of reference. The non-CIA members have no way of verifying that many of the agency's assertions and assumptions are correct, for example, (

DELETED

) The non-CIA members had to accept the agency's word that this program would have a chance of success. For security reasons, the specific people and methods that the CIA intends to use in a secret operation of this type are never included in the proposal. 40 Committee members can ask about the details at the actual meetings, but they have no way of knowing, without their own regional experts present, whether or not the CIA is providing them with self-serving answers.

In fact, much of the intelligence upon which the recommended intervention is based comes from the Clandestine Services' own sources, and this mixing of the CIA's informational and operational functions can cause disastrous results, as occurred when the

agency led the Kennedy administration to believe in 1961 that a landing of an exile military force would lead to a general uprising of the Cuban people. A more recent if less cataclysmic case occurred in 1970 when intervention in the Chilean elections was under government consideration. At (

DELETED

) the content of the report provided a strong argument for U.S. intervention to forestall Soviet gains. This report may or may not have been genuine. In either case, it was disseminated by the people in the Clandestine Services who favored intervention, and they were well aware of the effect it would have on the 40 Committee members. If, in this instance, the covert operators were not actually misleading the committee, they certainly could have been, and there was no way that any independent check could be made on them.

Until the 1967 disclosure of secret CIA funding of the National Student Association and scores of other ostensibly private organizations, the 40 Committee was called on only to give initial approval to covert-action programs.* Thus, most CIA-penetrated and subsidized organizations went on receiving agency funds and other support year after year without any outside review whatever of

---

* Final approval for a covert-action program is normally given by the 40 Committee chairman—still Henry Kissinger, even since he has become Secretary of State. He, in turn, notifies the President of what has been decided, and if there is a matter on which the committee was in disagreement, the chief executive makes the final decision. Although the President either reviews or personally authorizes all these secret interventions in other countries' internal affairs, he never signs any documents to that effect. Instead, the onus is placed on the 40 Committee, and if he chooses, the President can "plausibly deny" he has been involved in any illegal activities overseas.

the continuing worthiness of the project. But the 1967 scandal caused the 40 Committee to revise its procedures so that all ongoing non-espionage operations were regularly reviewed. In these reviews, however, the committee is perhaps even more dependent on the CIA for information and guidance than with new programs. For unless there has been a public controversy, only the Clandestine Services usually know whether their efforts to subsidize a particular organization or undermine a certain government have been successful. And the Clandestine Services would be unlikely to admit that their own operation was going badly, even if that were the case. (

DELETED

) American officials hoped that through this "democratic front" Thieu could widen his political base by rallying various non-communist opposition elements to his camp. The effort was a resounding failure from the American point of view, since Thieu showed no interest in broadening his support—as long as the Vietnamese army and the U.S. government still supported him. Even though this was one of the few instances where the State Department, through its diplomatic reporting from Saigon, (

DELETED

)

Even Richard Bissell in his 1968 Council on Foreign Relations talk admitted that the 40 Committee "is of limited effectiveness." Bissell stated that if the committee were the only control instrument, he would "view it as inadequate," but he believed that prior discussions on covert projects at working levels in the bureaucracy compensated for the failings of the "interdepartmental committee composed of busy officials who meet only once a week." To some extent what Bissell says is true, but he omits the fact that the most important projects, such as the Bay of Pigs, are considered so sensitive that the working levels outside the CIA are forbidden all knowledge of them. And he does not state that even

when a few outside officials at the Assistant Secretary level or just below are briefed on covert operations, they are told the programs are so secret that they cannot talk to any of their colleagues about them, which prevents them from calling into play the bureaucratic forces usually needed to block another agency's projects. Furthermore, these officials, having been let in on the U.S. government's dirtiest and darkest activities, are often reluctant to do anything in opposition that will jeopardize their right to be told more secrets at a later time. Nevertheless, the bureaucracy in State and, to a much lesser extent, in Defense does have some effect in limiting the CIA's covert operations, although not nearly so much as Bissell claimed.

As previously mentioned, there is one CIA activity, classical espionage, over which there is no outside control—not from the 40 Committee, from the bureaucratic working level, nor from Congress. The Director of Central Intelligence has a statutory responsibility to protect intelligence sources and methods from unauthorized disclosure, and every DCI since Allen Dulles has taken this to mean that the CIA cannot inform any other government agencies of the identity of its foreign agents—the agency's most closely guarded secrets. While this secrecy in order not to jeopardize the lives of foreigners (or Americans) who spy for the CIA is understandable, the use of a particular agent can sometimes have a political effect as large as, or larger than, a covert-action program. For example, if the CIA recruits a foreign official who is or becomes his country's Minister of Interior (e.g., Antonio Arguedas in Bolivia), then discovery of his connection to the agency can cause an international incident (as occurred in 1968 when Arguedas publicly admitted that he had worked for the CIA). In other instances, there have been Foreign Ministers and even Prime Ministers who were CIA agents, but the 40 Committee never was permitted to rule on whether or not the agency should continue its contact with them. Sometimes the CIA station chief in a particular country will advise the American ambassador that one of his agents is in a very high place in the local government or that he intends to recruit such a man, but the station chief does so at his own discretion.

The recruitment of lower-level foreigners can also have an important effect, especially if something goes wrong. This was the case in Singapore in 1960 (described in Chapter 9) when a CIA lie-detector expert blew a fuse, wound up in jail, caused the U.S. government to be subjected to blackmail, and damaged America's reputation overseas. The point to be noted is that since the CIA lie-detector man was putting a potential spy through the "black box," his mission was part of an espionage operation and hence not subject to control outside the agency. Similarly, during the mid-1960s (

DELETED

)

Prepared by the Pentagon's National Reconnaissance Office, the Joint Reconnaissance Schedule is always several inches thick and filled with hundreds of pages of highly technical data and maps. To a non-scientist, it is a truly incomprehensible collection of papers, and the staffs of the various 40 Committee members usually have only a day or two to look it over before the meetings. Under these conditions, the 40 Committee usually passes the schedule with little or no discussion. From time to time, the State Department will object to a particularly dangerous flight, such as sending an Air Force drone over South China subsequent to the American invasion of Cambodia, but nearly always missions—including the cruise of the *Liberty* (attacked by the Israelis during the 1967 Six Day War), the voyage of the spy ship *Pueblo* (captured by the North Koreans in 1968), and the flight of the EC-121 (shot down by the North Koreans in 1969)—are routinely approved.

(

DELETED

DELETED

)

Even as the 40 Committee fails to keep a close watch on secret reconnaissance activities, is relatively ineffective in monitoring the CIA's covert operations, and is totally in the dark on espionage operations, President Nixon and especially Henry Kissinger are unquestionably aware of its shortcomings and have done little to change things. Institutionally, the committee could easily provide better control over American intelligence if its internal procedures were altered, if it were provided with an adequate staff, and if it could develop its own sources for information and evaluation independent of the agency's Clandestine Services. But it is the President and Kissinger who ultimately determine how the CIA operates, and if they do not *want* to impose closer control, then the *form* of the control mechanism is meaningless. The fact remains that both men believe in the need for the United States to use clandestine methods and "dirty tricks" in dealing with other countries, and the current level and types of such operations obviously coincide with their views of how America's secret foreign policy should be carried out.

Therefore, as long as the CIA remains the President's loyal and personal tool to be used around the world at his and his top advisor's discretion, no President is likely, barring strong, unforeseen pressure, to insist that the agency's operations be brought under closer outside scrutiny.

The PFIAB and the OMB

In addition to the 40 Committee, the President has two other bodies in the executive branch which could conceivably assist him in controlling the CIA. One of these is the President's Foreign Intelligence Advisory Board (PFIAB), a group of eleven presidentially appointed private citizens who meet several times a year to evaluate the activities of the intelligence community and to make recommendations for needed change. President Eisenhower originally set up the PFIAB in 1956 under the chairmanship of Dr. James Killian of MIT, and its other heads have been General John Hull, Clark Clifford, General Maxwell Taylor, and, currently, retired Admiral George Anderson. The majority of its members have always been people with close ties to the Pentagon and defense contractors,* and it has consistently pushed for bigger (and more expensive) intelligence-collection systems.

The PFIAB meets approximately once a month in Washington, and is thus of limited value as a permanent watchdog committee. It is further handicapped by its status as an advisory group, with the resulting lack of bureaucratic authority. In general, the various members of the intelligence community look on the board as more of a nuisance than a true control mechanism. Periodically, when PFIAB is in session, CIA officials brief the members on current intelligence collection and the latest national estimates. The Clandestine Services' activities—particularly covert-action opera-

---

* In February 1974, the PFIAB's members in addition to Admiral Anderson were Dr. William Baker, Bell Telephone Laboratories' Vice President for Research; John Connally, former Governor of Texas and Secretary of the Navy and the Treasury; Leo Cherne, Executive Director of the Research Institute of America; Dr. John Foster, former Director of Defense Department Research and Engineering; Robert Galvin, President of Motorola; Gordon Gray, former Assistant to the President for National Security Affairs; Dr. Edwin Land, President of Polaroid; Clare Boothe Luce, former Congresswoman and ambassador; Nelson Rockefeller, former Governor of New York; and Dr. Edward Teller, nuclear physicist and "father" of the hydrogen bomb.

tions—are almost never considered unless an operation has already been publicly disclosed.

Over the years, Presidents have tended to use the PFIAB as a prestigious but relatively safe "in-house" investigative unit, usually at times when the chief executive was displeased with the quality of intelligence he was receiving. Whenever an intelligence failure is suspected in connection with a foreign-policy setback, the board is usually convened to look into the matter. President Kennedy called on it to recommend ways to reorganize the intelligence community after the 1961 Bay of Pigs debacle, but virtually no changes resulted from the PFIAB's efforts. The following year Kennedy asked the PFIAB to find out why the CIA had not discovered sooner that there were Soviet offensive missiles in Cuba, and the PFIAB found the two accurate agent accounts of the Soviet build-up buried among the thousands of misleading or irrelevant reports which had piled up at the agency in the month before the crisis. With perfect hindsight the PFIAB declared that the CIA should have recognized the truth of these reports and rejected all the others. Similarly, in 1968 President Johnson had the board investigate why the CIA had not determined the precise timing of the Soviet invasion of Czechoslovakia in advance.

These PFIAB post-mortems can be of great value to the intelligence community in pinpointing specific weaknesses and recommending solutions; they could be even more useful in making clear that certain events simply cannot be predicted in advance, even by the most efficient intelligence system. However, the PFIAB has tended to operate with the assumption that all information is "knowable" and that the intelligence community's problems would be solved if only more data were collected by more-advanced systems. This emphasis on quantity over quality has served to accentuate the management problems that plague American intelligence and, in recent years at least, has often been counterproductive.

Probably the PFIAB's most notable contribution to the nation's intelligence effort occurred in the 1950s and early 1960s when one of its subcommittees, headed by Polaroid's Dr. Edwin Land, conceived several new technical collection programs. Land's sub-

committee was instrumental in advancing the development of the U-2 spy plane, which, with the exception of the ill-fated Powers flight over the Soviet Union, may be considered one of the CIA's greatest successes. (

DELETED

) **The new systems are technologically feasible, but they are fantastically expensive, costing billions of dollars, and the intelligence benefits to be gained are marginal.**

The President's last potential regulatory body for intelligence affairs is the Office of Management and Budget (OMB). Known as the Bureau of the Budget until 1969, the OMB is the White House agency which closely scrutinizes the spending of all government departments and determines fiscal priorities for the administration. It has the power to cut the spending of federal agencies and even eliminate entire programs. Cabinet secretaries can sometimes appeal the OMB's decisions to the President, but he is understandably reluctant to overrule his own budgetary watchdog. For the CIA, however, the OMB (and the BOB before it) has never been more than a minor irritant. Its International Affairs Division's intelligence branch, which in theory monitors the finances of the intelligence community, has a staff of only five men: a branch chief and one examiner each for the CIA, the NSA, the **National Reconnaissance Office,** and the DIA (including the rest of military intelligence). These five men could not possibly do a complete job in keeping track of the $6 billion spent annually for government spying, even if they received full cooperation from the agencies involved—which they do not.

The theology of national security, with its emphasis on secrecy and deception, greatly limits the effectiveness of the President's budget examiners, who are generally treated as enemies by the intelligence agencies. In this regard, the CIA has been particularly guilty. When the OMB started monitoring the agency in the 1950s,

the budget man was refused a permanent pass to visit headquarters. He was regularly forced to wait at the building's entrance while a CIA official upstairs was telephoned and asked to verify the auditor's credentials. The situation improved somewhat in 1962 after Robert Amory, former CIA Deputy Director for Intelligence, became head of the OMB's International Division, and the examiner received his own badge. (The former examiner was meanwhile recruited by the CIA and assigned to deal with the OMB, and the new examiner turned out to be himself a former agency employee, who eventually returned also to handle relations with the OMB.)

In the mid-1960s President Johnson gave the OMB expanded power to scrutinize agency spending, but even this presidential mandate did not appreciably improve the bureau's access. For example, after the (

DELETED

) the OMB examiner wanted to look into how the money was being spent. At one point, he came to the agency with the intention of speaking to the knowledgeable personnel in the Clandestine Services, after first stopping off to see one of the CIA's Planning, Programming, and Budgeting (PPB) officers. The PPB man was told not to let the OMB representative leave his office while Director Helms was being informed of what the OMB was trying to investigate. Helms promptly called a high White House official to complain that the OMB was interfering with a program already approved by the 40 Committee. The White House, in turn, ordered the OMB to drop its inquiry. (

DELETED

)

The significance of this incident is not so much that the CIA makes life difficult for the OMB and gets away with it. Rather, what happened reflects the agency's attitude that its operations are above normal bureaucratic restraints and that when the President

has given his approval, not even the technicalities can be questioned.

The CIA has also resorted to the use of outright lies and deceit to prevent the OMB from being informed about its activities. In 1968 an examiner made a fact-finding tour of CIA installations in Europe and the Middle East. He was accompanied by an agency officer from headquarters, and his escort was specifically told by the Clandestine Services' European Division chief that the budget man should not be allowed to see anything "which might later cause us difficulty or embarrassment." The examiner was to be entertained, given cursory briefings, but not educated. (

DELETED

)*

CIA headquarters knew that the OMB man was extremely interested in guns and police work, and the field stations were so informed. (

DELETED

) he was asked if he would first like to visit Scotland Yard. With his interest in police work, he was unable to resist such an offer and, by prearrangement, the British police snowed him under with extensive briefings and tours of the

* (

DELETED

)

facilities. This diversion, which had nothing to do with the purpose of his trip, cost him a whole day out of his tight schedule. The next day he was slated to drive to another CIA installation about a hundred miles from London. But the agency did not want him to have much time to ask questions or to look around. Thus, his route was planed to pass through Banbury, the picturesque old English town whose cross is of nursery-rhyme fame. As the agency's operators had suspected, he could not forgo the pleasure of stopping in a typical English pub for lunch and then doing some sightseeing. The better part of another day was killed in this fashion, and he never had time to dig deeply into matters the agency did not want him to know about. Soon after, he left England without ever closely inspecting the agency's extensive activities there (aimed principally at Third World countries). To be sure, he had hardly been assiduous in his effort to penetrate the CIA smoke screen.

In the Near East, things worked out better for the man from OMB. The head of that division, unlike the European Division clandestine chief, saw the tour as an opportunity to impress the OMB examiner with the agency's activities. Thus, the escort officer was instructed to give the visitor "the full treatment," and the clandestine operators in the field were told to confide in him in order to win him over to the CIA side.

This examiner's experience was not exceptional. Many similar instances point up the OMB's—and, earlier, the BOB's—failure to exercise any degree of meaningful control over the CIA. As Director, Richard Helms was fully aware and indeed encouraging of the agency's efforts to escape OMB scrutiny. Still, he could apparently in good conscience tell the American Society of Newspaper Editors in 1971, "Our budget is gone over line for line by the Office of Management and Budget."

The Ambassador

The American ambassador in each country where the United States maintains diplomatic relations is, in theory, the head of the "country team," which is made up of the chiefs of all the U.S. govern-

ment agencies operating in that country, including the CIA. The Eisenhower administration originated this expanded role for the ambassador, but also issued a secret directive exempting the CIA from his supervision. President Kennedy, shortly after taking office, reiterated that the ambassador should supervise all the agencies and then sent out a secret letter which said the CIA was *not* to be excluded. The Kennedy letter remains in effect today, but its application varies from country to country.

In nearly every case, the personalities of the ambassador and the CIA station chief determine the degree to which the ambassador exercises control over the CIA. Strong-willed diplomats like G. McMurtrie Godley, first in the Congo and then in Laos (where he became known as the "field marshal"), and Ellsworth Bunker in Vietnam have kept the agency under close supervision, but they are also stanch advocates of extensive clandestine operations. Some ambassadors insist, as did Chester Bowles in India, that they be informed of all CIA activities, but usually do not try to exert any control over the operations. Still others, because of a lack of forcefulness or a lack of interest, give the CIA a free hand and do not even want to be informed of what the agency is up to.

Again, quoting the Bissell doctrine:

Generally the Ambassador had a right to know of any covert operations in his jurisdiction, although in special cases (as a result of requests from the local Chief of State or the Secretary of State) the [CIA] chief of station was instructed to withhold information from the Ambassador. Indeed, in one case the restriction was imposed upon the specific exhortation of the Ambassador in question, who preferred to remain ignorant of certain activities.

One ambassador, John C. Pritzlaff, Jr., refused to play such a passive role and, in a fashion highly uncharacteristic of American envoys, stood up to the CIA. In the process, Pritzlaff, a political appointee, became something of a hero to the few State Department officers familiar with the way he virtually banned CIA covert activities from his country of assignment, Malta. The problem

started early in 1970 when retired Admiral George Anderson took a trip through the Mediterranean countries and became alarmed that leftist Dom Mintoff might win the Maltese elections scheduled for the end of the year. As a Navy man, Anderson was a strong sea-power advocate, and he feared Malta might be lost to N.A.T.O. forces and become a base for the Soviet fleet. Although he was not yet head of PFIAB, he used his White House connections to urge the Clandestine Services to intervene in the Maltese elections. The agency was not enthusiastic about the project, partly because of its lack of "assets" on the island, but it agreed to send a clandestine operative to make a study of how the election could be fixed. Ambassador Pritzlaff, in telegram after telegram, resisted even this temporary assignment of an agency operative to his country. In the end, the Clandestine Services did not intervene and Mintoff was elected. N.A.T.O. retained access to the island through British bases.*

Congress

Congressional control of the CIA can be broken down into two distinct periods: before and after Watergate. In the agency's first twenty-six years, the legislative branch was generally content to vote the CIA more than enough money for its needs, without seriously questioning how the funds would be spent. In fact, only a handful of Congressmen even knew the amount appropriated, since all the money was hidden in the budgets of other government agencies, mainly the Defense Department. To be sure, four separate subcommittees of the House and Senate Armed Services committees were responsible for monitoring the CIA, but their supervision was minimal or nonexistent. In the House, the names of the members were long kept secret, but they were generally the most senior

* Anderson's fears seemed partially justified, however, in 1971, when Mintoff precipitated a mini-crisis by expelling the N.A.T.O. commander from the island and by greatly increasing the cost to Britain of keeping its facilities there. In an incident reminiscent of Cyprus President Makarios' blackmail of U.S. intelligence several years before, the U.S. government was forced to contribute several million dollars to help the British pay the higher rent for the Maltese bases.

(and thus often the most conservative) men on their respective committees. (Allen Dulles was reported by the *New York Times* in April 1966 to have had "personal control" over which Congressmen would be selected.) In August 1971, House Armed Services chairman F. Edward Hébert of Louisiana broke with past practice and dipped down his committee's seniority ladder to appoint Lucien Nedzi, a hard-working liberal from Michigan, head of the oversight subcommittee. Hébert, however, kept complete control of the subcommittee's staff, and Nedzi is the only non-conservative among the panel's five permanent and two *ex officio* members. When Hébert made his unusual choice, it was widely speculated that he was trying to defuse outside criticism of the subcommittee's performance by naming a liberal as chairman, and that he felt he could keep Nedzi isolated. Nedzi had little time for overseeing the CIA during 1972, his first full year as chairman, because he faced tough primary and re-election challenges. In 1973 he launched a comprehensive inquiry into the agency's role in the Watergate affair, but it remains to be seen whether his subcommittee will delve any deeper into CIA covert operations than the House panels have done in the past. In the Senate the Armed Services and Appropriations subcommittees have traditionally met together to maintain joint oversight of the CIA. As is true in the House, the members have almost all been conservative, aging, military-oriented legislators.

Many Congressmen and Senators—but by no means a majority—believe that these oversight arrangements are inadequate, and since 1947 nearly 150 separate pieces of legislation have been introduced to increase congressional surveillance of the CIA. None has passed either chamber, and the House has never even had a recorded vote on the subject. The Senate, by a 59–27 margin in 1956, and by 61–28 in 1966, has turned down proposals for expanded and more active watchdog committees for the agency and the rest of the intelligence community. To strengthen his case for maintaining the *status quo* at the time of the 1966 vote, Senator Richard Russell, then chairman of the Armed Services Committee, agreed that starting in 1967 the three senior members of the Foreign Relations Committee would be allowed unofficially to sit

in on the joint oversight subcommittee's meetings. But after this arrangement was in effect for several years, Senator John Stennis, Russell's successor as chairman, simply stopped holding sessions. There was not a single one in either 1971 or 1972. Stennis is generally believed to have ended the subcommittee's functions because foreign-policy liberals J. William Fulbright and Stuart Symington would have been present for the secret deliberations. Neither man was trusted at the time by either the CIA or by the conservative Senators who have kept oversight of the CIA as their own private preserve. In the absence of any joint subcommittee meetings, the five senior members of the Appropriations Committee, all of whom were stanch hawks and administration supporters, met privately to go over the agency's budget.

Senator Symington challenged this arrangement on November 23, 1971, when, without prior warning, he introduced a floor amendment which would have put a $4 billion limit on government-wide intelligence spending—roughly $2 billion less than what the administration was requesting. Although Symington's amendment was defeated 51–36, it produced perhaps the most illuminating debate on intelligence ever heard in the Senate.

Symington berated the fact that the Senate was being asked to vote billions of dollars for intelligence with only five Senators knowing the amount; and in a colloquy with the Appropriations chairman, the late Allen Ellender, Symington established that even those five Senators had limited knowledge of the CIA's operations. Ellender replied to Symington's question on whether or not the appropriations subcommittee had approved the financing of a 36,000-man "secret" army in Laos:

> I did not know anything about it. . . . I never asked, to begin with, whether or not there were any funds to carry on the war in this sum the CIA asked for. It never dawned on me to ask about it. I did see it published in the newspapers some time ago.

Laos was, of course, the CIA's largest operation at the time that supposed overseer Ellender admitted ignorance about it.

Richard Russell, too, had had a similar lack of interest in what the CIA was doing. He had once even told CIA Director Helms— privately—that there were certain operations he simply did not want to know about. Senator Leverett Saltonstall, who served for many years as ranking Republican on the oversight subcommittee, expressed the same view publicly in 1966: "It is not a question of reluctance on the part of CIA officials to speak to us. Instead it is a question of our reluctance, if you will, to seek information and knowledge on subjects which I personally, as a Member of Congress and as a citizen, would rather not have."

Faced with this rejection of responsibility on the part of the congressional monitors, the CIA has chosen to keep the subcommittee largely in the dark about its covert operations—unless a particular activity, such as the 1967 black-propaganda effort against mainland China, has been successful in the agency's eyes and could be bragged about to the legislators. Helms did make frequent visits to Capitol Hill to give secret briefings, but these usually concerned current intelligence matters and estimates of the communist countries' military capabilities—not the doings of the Clandestine Services. Yet Helms won a reputation among lawmakers as a man who provided straight information.* Senator J. William Fulbright, who sat in on Helms' briefings to the joint oversight committee until they were discontinued in 1971, described the proceedings to author Patrick McGarvey for the latter's *CIA: The Myth and the Madness:*

> The ten minute rule is in effect, so the members have little if any chance to dig deep into a subject. The director of CIA spends most of the time talking about the Soviet missile threat

---

* Although Helms had been for many years providing current intelligence and estimates to congressional committees in secret oral briefings, the CIA officially opposed legislation introduced in 1972 by Senator John Sherman Cooper of Kentucky which would have provided the appropriate committees with the same sort of data in the form of regular CIA reports. The bill was favorably approved by the Foreign Relations Committee, but subsequently died in Armed Services. Director-designate William Colby told the latter committee in July 1973 that he thought this information could be supplied on an informal basis "without legislation."

and so on. The kind of information he provides is interesting, but it really is of little help in trying to find out what is going on in intelligence. He actually tells them only what he wants them to know. It seems to me that the men on the committee are more interested in shielding CIA from its critics than in anything else.

Once a year the CIA does come before the appropriations subcommittees in both houses to make its annual budget request. These sessions, however, are completely on the agency's terms. Prior to the meeting, CIA electronics experts make an elaborate show of sweeping the committee rooms for bugging devices, and blankets are thrown over the windows to prevent outside surveillance. The transcripts of the sessions are considered so secret that copies are locked up at CIA headquarters. Not one is left with the subcommittees for future study. Committee staff members, who normally do most of the substantive preparation for hearings, are banned at the CIA's request.*

Allen Dulles set the tone for these CIA budget presentations in the 1950s when he commented to a few assistants preparing him for his annual appearance, "I'll just tell them a few war stories." A more current example of the CIA's evasive tactics occurred in 1966 when the Senate appropriations subcommittee was thought to have some hard questions to ask about the growing costs of technical espionage programs. DCI Helms responded to the senatorial interest by bringing with him the CIA's Deputy Director for Science & Technology, Dr. Albert D. "Bud" Wheelon, who loaded himself up with a bag full of spy gadgets—a camera hidden in a tobacco pouch, a radio transmitter hidden in false teeth, a tape recorder in a cigarette case, and so on. This equipment did not

---

* A relatively similar procedure is followed when an individual Senator or Congressman writes to the CIA about a covert operation. Instead of sending a letter in return, an agency representative offers to brief the legislator *personally* on the matter, on the condition that no staff members are present. This procedure puts the busy lawmaker at a marked disadvantage, since his staff is usually more familiar with the subject than he is— and probably wrote the original letter.

even come from Wheelon's part of the agency but was manufactured by the Clandestine Services; if, however, the Senators wanted to talk about "technical" matters, Helms and his assistant were perfectly willing to distract them with James Bond–type equipment.

Wheelon started to discuss the technical collection programs, but as he talked he let the Senators inspect the gadgets. Predictably, the discussion soon turned to the spy paraphernalia. One persistent Senator asked two questions about the new and expensive technical collection systems the CIA was then putting into operation, but Wheelon deftly turned the subject back to the gadgets. When the Senator asked his question a third time, Chairman Russell told him to hold his inquiry until the CIA men were finished. But the Senators became so enthralled with the equipment before them that no more questions were asked.*

In 1967 the CIA, as usual, prepared its budget request with a dazzling collection of slides and pictures, emphasizing the agency's role in fighting communism around the world and producing intelligence on the military threat posed by the Soviet Union and China. Also included in the "canned" briefing was a description of the CIA's technical collection expertise, its work with computers and other information-processing systems, and even its advanced techniques in printing—but, again, no "dirty tricks." The presentation was rehearsed several times at CIA headquarters while calls were awaited from Capitol Hill to set specific dates. A Congressman serving on the House appropriations oversight group was even invited to come out to the agency to see one of the dry runs. A few days later a staff man on the House panel telephoned the CIA to say that the Congressman who had seen the rehearsal said that everything seemed in order and that the chairman simply did not have the time to hear the presentation, but that the committee would approve the full budget request of nearly $700 million anyway. Shortly thereafter a similar call came from the Senate committee. The chairman had apparently been told by his opposite

* Seven years later, the same panel would investigate the 1971 assistance furnished by the Clandestine Services to E. Howard Hunt and Gordon Liddy for their "plumbers" operations—assistance comprised of many of the same gadgets that amused the Senators in 1966.

number in the House that the CIA request seemed reasonable, and on the strength of the House recommendation the Senate would also approve the full amount without a hearing.

Thus, in 1967 the CIA did not even *appear* in front of its budgetary oversight committees. The experience that year was extreme, but it does illustrate how little congressional supervision the agency has been subject to over the years.

Many congressional critics of the CIA have advocated broadening the membership of the CIA oversight subcommittees to include legislators who will hold the agency up to the same sort of scrutiny that other government departments receive. They argue that in the equally sensitive field of atomic energy a joint congressional committee has kept close track of the Atomic Energy Commission without any breach in security. However, some liberals who advocate greater control of the CIA fear that a joint CIA committee analogous to the Joint Atomic Energy Committee might easily be "captured" by the agency, just as the atomic energy committee has, to a large extent, been co-opted by the AEC.

Those who oppose increased congressional control of the agency claim that if the CIA is to operate effectively, total secrecy must be maintained, and that expanding the functions and the membership of the oversight subcommittees would mean much greater likelihood of breaches in security. They fear that larger subcommittees would necessarily lead to the presence of administration opponents who might exploit agency secrets for political gains. Moreover, it is said that friendly foreign intelligence services would be reluctant to cooperate or share secrets with the agency if they knew that their activities would be revealed to the American Congress.

No matter what the merits of the arguments for closer congressional control, there was no chance that a majority of either house would vote for any appreciable change until the Watergate affair broke wide open in early 1973. Suddenly the long-dormant oversight subcommittees began to meet frequently to investigate the degree of CIA involvement in the illegal activities sponsored by the White House and the Committee to Re-Elect the President. The obvious abuses of power by the administration and its supporters stirred even conservative legislators into demands for cor-

rective action. And the administration, in trying to justify its excesses on the grounds of protecting the "national security"—a justification largely unacceptable to Congress—seriously weakened the position of those who claimed that the CIA's actions should escape scrutiny on those same "national security" grounds. Furthermore, there was a widespread public and media outcry against concentration of power in the White House, and against President Nixon's penchant for taking unilateral actions without the approval or even the advice of Congress. The CIA, as the President's loyal tool—tainted to some extent by involvement in Watergate-related activities—also became vulnerable.

The four oversight subcommittees which met so frequently in the first six months of 1973 are still made up of the same overwhelmingly conservative members. But, pushed by either their own revulsion over Watergate or by public reaction to it, they seem likely to take some action to increase congressional surveillance of the CIA.

For example, John Stennis, the Senate Armed Services chairman, declared on July 20, 1973: "The experience of the CIA in Laos, as well as the more recent disclosures here at home have caused me to definitely conclude that the entire CIA act should be entirely reviewed." This is the same Stennis who nineteen months earlier, when the CIA's "secret" war in Laos was at its peak, stated:

> This agency is conducted in a splendid way. . . . As has been said, spying is spying. But if we are going to have an intelligence agency, . . . it cannot be run as if you were running a tax collector's office or the HEW or some other such department. You have to make up your mind that you are going to have an intelligence agency and protect it as such, and shut your eyes some and take what is coming.

Yet, from all indications, Stennis has become sincerely convinced that the chief executive, on his own, should never again be able to take the country into a Vietnam-type conflict. On October 18, 1973, he introduced legislation—while reserving his right to change it after study and hearings extending into 1974—which

would modify the CIA's legal base. First, it would limit the agency's domestic activities to "those which are necessary and appropriate to its foreign intelligence mission," apparently defining this in a way to abolish covert activities in the United States. Second, it would set up tighter procedures for congressional oversight, while "recognizing essential security requirements."

A simple majority in either chamber would be sufficient to change the present system of CIA oversight. As much as the agency wants to keep its activities secret, it would have little choice but to comply with serious congressional demands for more information and more supervision. The power of the purse gives the legislative branch the means to enforce its will on a reluctant CIA, and even one house standing alone could use this power as a control mechanism. That is, assuming that Congress is willing to accept the responsibility.

CIA and the Press

In a recent interview, a nationally syndicated columnist with close ties to the CIA was asked how he would have reacted in 1961 if he had uncovered advance information that the agency was going to launch the Bay of Pigs invasion of Cuba. He replied somewhat wistfully, "The trouble with the establishment is that I would have gone to one of my friends in the government, and he would have told me why I shouldn't write the story. And I probably wouldn't have written the story."

It was rather fitting that this columnist, when queried about exposing a CIA operation, should have put his answer in terms of the "establishment" (of which he is a recognized member), since much of what the American people have learned—or have not learned—about the agency has been filtered through an "old-boy network" of journalists friendly to the CIA. There have been exceptions, but, by and large, the CIA has attempted to discourage, alter, and even suppress independent investigative inquiries into agency activities.

The CIA's principal technique for fending off the press has been to wrap itself in the mantle of "national security." Reporters have

been extremely reluctant to write anything that might endanger an ongoing operation or, in Tom Wicker's words, "get an agent killed in Timbuktu." The CIA has, for its part, played upon these completely understandable fears and used them as a club to convince newsmen that certain stories should never be written. And many reporters do not even have to be convinced, either because they already believe that the CIA's activities are not the kind of news that the public has a right to know or because in a particular case they approve of the agency's aims and methods.

For example, on September 23, 1970, syndicated columnist Charles Bartlett was handed, by a Washington-based official of ITT, an internal ITT report sent in by the company's two representatives in Chile, Hal Hendrix and Robert Berrellez. This eight-page document—marked PERSONAL AND CONFIDENTIAL—said that the American ambassador to Chile had received the "green light to move in the name of President Nixon . . . [with] maximum authority to do all possible—short of a Dominican Republic-type action—to keep Allende from taking power." It stated that the Chilean army "has been assured full material and financial assistance by the U.S. military establishment" and that ITT had "pledged [its financial] support if needed" to the anti-Allende forces. The document also included a lengthy rundown of the political situation in Chile.

With the material for an exposé in his hands, Bartlett did not launch an immediate investigation. Instead, he did exactly what ITT hoped he would do: he wrote a column about the dangers of a "classic Communist-style assumption of power" in Chile. He did see some hope that "Chile will find a way to avert the inauguration of Salvador Allende," but thought there was little the United States could "profitably do" and that "Chilean politics should be left to the Chileans." He did not inform his readers that he had documentary evidence indicating that Chilean politics were being left to the CIA and ITT.

Asked why he did not write more, Bartlett replied in a 1973 telephone interview, "I was only interested in the political analysis. I didn't take seriously the Washington stuff—the description of

machinations within the U.S. government. [The ITT men who wrote the report] had not been in Washington; they had been in Chile." Yet, by Bartlett's own admission, his September 28 column was based on the ITT report—in places, to the point of paraphrase. He wrote about several incidents occurring in Chile that he could not possibly have verified in Washington. Most reporters will not use material of this sort unless they can check it out with an independent source, so Bartlett was showing extraordinary faith in the reliability of his informants. But he used their material selectively —to write an anti-Allende scare piece, not to blow the whistle on the CIA and ITT.

An ITT official gave the same report to *Time*'s Pentagon correspondent, John Mulliken. Mulliken covered neither the CIA nor Chile as part of his regular beat, and he sent the ITT document to *Time*'s headquarters in New York for possible action. As far as he knows, *Time* never followed up on the story. He attributes this to "bureaucratic stupidity—the system, not the people." He explains that *Time* had shortly before done a long article on Chile, and New York "didn't want to do any more."

Thus, the public did not learn what the U.S. government and ITT were up to in Chile until the spring of 1972, when columnist Jack Anderson published scores of ITT internal documents concerning Chile. Included in the Anderson papers, as one of the most important exhibits, was the very same document that had been given eighteen months earlier to Bartlett and *Time* magazine.

Jack Anderson is very much a maverick among Washington journalists, and he will write about nearly anything he learns—and can confirm—about the U.S. government and the CIA. With a few other notable exceptions, however, the great majority of the American press corps has tended to stay away from topics concerning the agency's operations. One of the reasons for this is that the CIA, being an extremely secretive organization, is a very hard beat to cover. Newsmen are denied access to its heavily guarded buildings, except in tightly controlled circumstances. No media outlet in the country has ever assigned a full-time correspondent to the agency, and very few report on its activities even on a part-time basis.

Except in cases where the CIA wants to leak some information, almost all CIA personnel avoid any contact whatsoever with journalists. In fact, agency policy decrees that employees must inform their superiors immediately of any and all conversations with reporters, and the ordinary operator who has too many of these conversations tends to become suspect in the eyes of his co-workers.

For the general view in the CIA (as in some other parts of the federal government) is that the press is potentially an enemy force —albeit one that can be used with great success to serve the agency's purposes. Former Deputy Director for Intelligence Robert Amory was speaking for most of his colleagues when in a February 26, 1967, television interview he said that press disclosures of agency funding of the National Student Association and other private groups were "a commentary on the immaturity of our society." With the pronounced Anglophile bias and envy of Britain's Official Secrets Act so common among high CIA officials, he compared the situation to our "free motherland in England," where if a similar situation comes up, "everybody shushes up in the interest of their national security and . . . what they think is the interest of the free world civilization."

Former CIA official William J. Barnds* was even more critical of journalistic probes of the agency in a January 1969 article in the influential quarterly *Foreign Affairs:*

The disclosure of intelligence activities in the press in recent years is a clear national liability. These disclosures have created a public awareness that the U.S. government has, at least at times, resorted to covert operations in inappropriate situations, failed to maintain secrecy and failed to review ongoing operations adequately. The public revelations of those weaknesses, even though they are now partially corrected, hampers

---

* Barnds had been with the agency's Office of National Estimates until he joined the staff of the Council on Foreign Relations in the mid-1960s. In 1968 he was the secretary at the CFR session where Richard Bissell laid out his views on covert operations.

CIA (and the U.S. government) by limiting those willing to cooperate with it and its activities. As long as such disclosures remain in the public mind, any official effort to improve CIA's image is as likely to backfire as to succeed.

Barnd's admission that the CIA has certain weaknesses is unusual coming from a former (or present) agency official, but very few in the CIA would disagree with his statement that press stories about intelligence operations are a "national liability."

The CIA's concern about how to deal with reporters and how to use the press to best advantage dates back to the agency's beginnings. During the 1950s the agency was extremely wary of any formal relations with the media, and the standard answer to press inquiries was that the CIA "does not confirm or deny published reports."

To be sure, there was a CIA press office, but it was not a very important part of the agency's organization. To CIA insiders, its principal function seemed to be to clip newspaper articles about the CIA and to forward them to the interested component of the agency. The press office was largely bypassed by Director Allen Dulles and a few of his chief aides who maintained contact with certain influential reporters.

Dulles often met his "friends" of the press on a background basis, and he and his Clandestine Services chief, Frank Wisner, were extremely interested in getting across to the American people the danger posed to the country by international communism. They stressed the CIA's role in combating the communist threat, and Dulles liked to brag, after the fact, about successful agency operations. The reporters who saw him were generally fascinated by his war stories of the intelligence trade. Wisner was particularly concerned with publicizing anti-communist émigré groups (many of which were subsidized or organized by the CIA), and he often encouraged reporters to write about their activities.

According to an ex-CIA official who worked closely with Wisner, the refugees from the "captive nations" were used by the CIA to give credence to the idea that the United States was truly

interested in "rolling back the Iron Curtain." This same former CIA man recalls Dulles and Wisner frequently telling subordinates, in effect: "Try to do a better job in influencing the press through friendly intermediaries."

Nevertheless, the agency's press relations during the Dulles era were generally low-keyed. Reporters were not inclined to write unfavorable or revealing stories about the CIA, and the agency, for its part, received a good deal of useful information from friendly newsmen. Reporters like Joseph Alsop, Drew Pearson, Harrison Salisbury, and scores of others regularly sat down with CIA experts to be debriefed after they returned from foreign travels. These newsmen in no way worked for the agency, but they were glad to provide the incidental information that a traveler might have observed, such as the number of smokestacks on a factory or the intensity of traffic on a railroad line. The Washington bureau chief of a large newspaper remembers being asked, after he returned from Eastern Europe, "to fill in the little pieces which might fit into the jigsaw puzzle." This type of data was quite important to the intelligence analyst in the days before the technical espionage programs could supply the same information. The agency's Intelligence Directorate routinely conducted these debriefings of reporters, as it does today. Selected newsmen, however, participated in a second kind of debriefing conducted by the Clandestine Services. In these the emphasis was on the personalities of the foreign officials encountered by the newsmen (as part of the unending probe for vulnerabilities) and the operation of the internal-security systems in the countries visited.

At the same time the CIA was debriefing newsmen, it was looking for possible recruits in the press corps or hoping to place a CIA operator under "deep cover" with a reputable media outlet. The identities of these bogus "reporters" were (and are) closely guarded secrets. As late as November 1973, according to Oswald Johnston's *Washington Star-News* report (confirmed by other papers), there were still about forty full-time reporters and free-lancers on the CIA payroll. Johnston reported that CIA Director Colby had decided to cut the "five full-time staff cor-

respondents with general-circulation news organizations," but that the other thirty-five or so "stringers" and workers for trade publications would be retained. American correspondents often have much broader entrée to foreign societies than do officials of the local American embassy, which provides most CIA operators with their cover, and the agency simply has been unable to resist the temptation to penetrate the press corps, although the major media outlets have almost all refused to cooperate with the CIA.

William Attwood, now publisher of *Newsday*, remembers vividly that when he was foreign editor of *Look* during the 1950s a CIA representative approached him and asked if *Look* needed a correspondent in New Delhi. The agency offered to supply the man for the job and pay his salary. Attwood turned the agency down.

Clifton Daniel, former managing editor of the *New York Times* and now that paper's Washington bureau chief, states that in the late 1950s "I was very surprised to learn that a correspondent of an obscure newspaper in an obscure part of the world was a CIA man. That bothered me." Daniel promptly checked the ranks of *Times* reporters for similar agency connections, but found "there did not seem to be any." He believes that one reason why the *Times* was clean was that "our people knew they would be fired" if they worked for the agency.

In 1955 Sam Jaffe applied for a job with CBS News. While he was waiting for his application to be processed, a CIA official whom Jaffe identifies as **Jerry Rubins** visited his house in California and told him, "If you are willing to work for us, you are going to Moscow" with CBS. Jaffe was flabbergasted, since he did not even know at that point if CBS would hire him, and he assumes that someone at CBS must have been in on the arrangement or otherwise the agency would never have known he had applied for work. Moreover, it would have been highly unusual to send a new young reporter to such an important overseas post. **Rubins** told Jaffe that the agency was "willing to release certain top-secret information to you in order that you try and obtain certain information for us." Jaffe refused and was later hired by CBS for a domestic assignment.

Before the CIA's successful armed invasion of Guatemala in 1954, a *Time* reporter dropped off the staff to participate, by his own admission, in the agency's paramilitary operations in that country. After the Guatemalan government had been overthrown, he returned to the *Time* offices in New York and asked for his old job back. According to another *Time* staffer, the managing editor asked the returned CIA man if he were still with the agency. The man said no. The managing editor asked, "If you were still really with the CIA and I asked you about it, what would you say?" The returned CIA man replied, "I'd have to say no." *Time* rehired him anyway.*

The Dulles years ended with two disasters for the CIA that newspapers learned of in advance but refused to share fully with their readers. First came the shooting down of the U-2 spy plane over the Soviet Union in 1960. Chalmers Roberts, long the *Washington Post*'s diplomatic correspondent, confirms in his book *First Rough Draft* that he and "some other newsmen" knew about the U-2 flights in the late 1950s and "remained silent." Roberts explains, "Retrospectively, it seems a close question as to whether this was the right decision, but I think it probably was. We took the position that the national interest came before the story because we knew the United States very much needed to discover the secrets of Soviet missilery."

Most reporters at the time would have agreed with Richard Bissell that premature disclosure would have forced the Soviets "to take action." Yet Bissell admitted that "after five days" the Soviets were fully aware that the spy planes were overflying their country, and that the secrecy maintained by the Soviet and American governments was an example "of two hostile governments col-

* More recently CIA men have turned up as "reporters" in foreign countries for little-known publications which could not possibly afford to pay their salaries without agency assistance. Stanley Karnow, formerly the *Washington Post*'s Asian correspondent, recalls, "I remember a guy who came to Korea with no visible means of support. He was supposed to be a correspondent for a small paper in New York. In a country where it takes years to build up acquaintances, he immediately had good contacts, and he dined with the CIA station chief. It was common knowledge he worked for the agency."

laborating to keep operations secret from the general public on both sides."

The whole U-2 incident may well have been a watershed event. For much of the American press and public it was the first indication that their government lied, and it was the opening wedge in what would grow during the Vietnam years into the "credibility gap." But as the Eisenhower administration came to an end, there was still a national consensus that the fight against communism justified virtually any means. The press was very much a part of the consensus, and this did not start to crack until it became known that the CIA was organizing an armed invasion of Cuba.

Five months before the landing took place at the Bay of Pigs, the *Nation* published a secondhand account of the agency's efforts to train Cuban exiles for attacks against Cuba and called upon "all U.S. news media with correspondents in Guatemala," where the invaders were being trained, to check out the story. The *New York Times* responded on January 10, 1961, with an article describing the training, with U.S. assistance, of an anti-Castro force in Guatemala. At the end of the story, which mentioned neither the CIA nor a possible invasion, was a charge by the Cuban Foreign Minister that the U.S. government was preparing "mercenaries" in Guatemala and Florida for military action against Cuba. Turner Catledge, then the managing editor of the *Times,* declared in his book *My Life and The Times*: "I don't think that anyone who read the story would have doubted that something was in the wind, that the United States was deeply involved, or that the *New York Times* was onto the story."

As the date for the invasion approached, the *New Republic* obtained a comprehensive account of the preparations for the operation, but the liberal magazine's editor-in-chief, Gilbert Harrison, became wary of the security implications and submitted the article to President Kennedy for his advice. Kennedy asked that it not be printed, and Harrison, a friend of the President, complied. At about the same time, *New York Times* reporter Tad Szulc uncovered nearly the complete story, and the *Times* made preparations to carry it on April 7, 1961, under a four-column headline. But *Times* publisher Orvil Dryfoos and Washington bureau chief

James Reston both objected to the article on national-security grounds, and it was edited to eliminate all mention of CIA involvement or an "imminent" invasion. The truncated story, which mentioned only that 5,000 to 6,000 Cubans were being trained in the United States and Central America "for the liberation of Cuba," no longer merited a banner headline and was reduced to a single column on the front page. *Times* editor Clifton Daniel later explained that Dryfoos had ordered the story toned down "above all, [out of] concern for the safety of the men who were preparing to offer their lives on the beaches of Cuba."

Times reporter Szulc states that he was not consulted about the heavy editing of his article, and he mentions that President Kennedy made a personal appeal to publisher Dryfoos not to run the story. Yet, less than a month after the invasion, at a meeting where he was urging newspaper editors not to print security information, Kennedy was able to say to the *Times'* Catledge, "If you had printed more about the operation, you would have saved us from a colossal mistake."

The failure of the Bay of Pigs cost CIA Director Dulles his job, and he was succeeded in November 1961 by John McCone. McCone did little to revamp the agency's policies in dealing with the press, although the matter obviously concerned him, as became evident when he reprimanded and then transferred his press officer, who he felt had been too forthcoming with a particular reporter. In McCone's first weeks at the agency, the *New York Times* got wind of the fact that the CIA was training Tibetans in paramilitary techniques at an agency base in Colorado, but, according to David Wise's account in *The Politics of Lying*, the Office of the Secretary of Defense "pleaded" with the *Times* to kill the story, which it did. In the Cuban missile crisis of 1962, President Kennedy again prevailed upon the *Times* not to print a story—this time, the news that Soviet missiles had been installed in Cuba, which the *Times* had learned of at least a day before the President made his announcement to the country.*

* According to the *Times'* Max Frankel, writing in the Winter 1973 *Columbia Forum,* there was still a feeling that the paper had been "remiss"

Then, in 1964, McCone was faced with the problem of how to deal with an upcoming book about the CIA, and his response was an attempt to do violence to the First Amendment.

The book was *The Invisible Government*, by reporters David Wise of the *New York Herald Tribune* and Thomas Ross of the *Chicago Sun-Times*. Their work provided an example of the kind of reporting on the agency that other journalists might have done but had failed to do. In short, it was an example of investigative reporting at its best and, perhaps as a result, it infuriated the CIA.

McCone and his deputy, Lieutenant General Marshall Carter, both personally telephoned Wise and Ross's publisher, Random House, to raise their strong objections to publication of the book. Then a CIA official offered to buy up the entire first printing of over 15,000 books. Calling this action "laughable," Random House's president, Bennett Cerf, agreed to sell the agency as many books as it wanted, but stated that additional printings would be made for the public. The agency also approached *Look* magazine, which had planned to run excerpts from the book, and, according to a spokesman, "asked that some changes be made—things they considered to be inaccuracies. We made a number of changes but do not consider that they were significant."

The final chapter in the agency attack against *The Invisible Government* came in 1965 when the CIA circulated an unattributed document on "The Soviet and Communist Bloc Defamation Campaign" to various members of Congress and the press. This long study detailed the many ways used by the KGB to discredit the CIA, including the "development and milking of Western journalists. Americans figure prominently among these." The study singled out as an example of KGB disinformation a Soviet radio broadcast that quoted directly from *The Invisible Government*.

---

in withholding information on the Bay of Pigs, so the *Times* extracted a promise from the President that while the paper remained silent he would "shed no blood and start no war." Frankel notes that "no such bargain was ever struck again, though many officials made overtures. The essential ingredient was trust, and that was lost somewhere between Dallas and Tonkin."

The agency's message was not too subtle, but then the CIA never put its name on the document.

When Richard Helms took over the agency in 1966, press relations changed noticeably. Helms himself had been a reporter with United Press in Germany before World War II, and he thought of himself as an accomplished journalist. He would tell his subordinates, when the subject of the press came up in the agency's inner councils, that he understood reporters' problems, how their minds worked, what the CIA could and could not do with them. He had certain writing habits (which may have originated either with a strict bureau chief or a strict high-school English teacher) which set him apart from others in the clandestine part of the agency, where writing is considered a functional, as opposed to a literary, skill. For instance, he would not sign his name to any document prepared for him that included a sentence beginning with the words "however" or "therefore."

It soon became clear within the agency that Helms was intent on taking care of most of the CIA's relations with the press himself. Acutely aware that the agency's image had been badly tarnished by the Bay of Pigs and other blown operations during the early 1960s, he was determined to improve the situation. He later told a congressional committee, "In our society even a clandestine outfit cannot stray far from the norms. If we get . . . the public, the press or the Congress against us, we can't hack it."

So Helms began to cultivate the press. He started a series of breakfasts, lunches, and occasional cocktail and dinner parties for individual reporters and groups of them. On days when he was entertaining a gathering of journalists, he would often devote part of his morning staff meeting to a discussion of the seating arrangements and make suggestions as to which CIA official would be the most compatible eating partner for which reporter. While a few senior clandestine personnel were invited to these affairs, Helms made sure that the majority came from the CIA's analytical and technical branches. As always, he was trying to portray the agency as a predominantly non-clandestine organization.

Helms' invitations were not for every reporter. He concentrated on what the *New York Times'* John Finney calls the "double-domes —the bureau chiefs, columnists, and other opinion makers." David Wise, who headed the *New York Herald Tribune*'s Washington staff, has a similar impression: "In almost every Washington bureau, there's one guy who has access to the agency on a much higher level than the press officer. Other reporters who call up get the runaround." Finney states that Helms and his assistants would "work with flattery on the prestige of" these key journalists. CBS News' Marvin Kalb, who attended several of Helms' sessions with the press (and who was recently bugged by the Nixon administration), recalls that Helms "had the capacity for astonishing candor but told you no more than he wanted to give you. He had this marvelous way of talking, of suggesting things with his eyes. Yet, he usually didn't tell you anything."

Helms' frequent contact with reporters was not a sinister thing. He was not trying to recruit them into nefarious schemes for the CIA. Rather, he was making a concerted effort to get his and his agency's point of view across to the press and, through them, to the American public—a common activity among top government officials. Furthermore, Helms was an excellent news source—for his friends. Columnist Joseph Kraft (another Nixon-administration bugging victim) generally sums up the view of Helms by reporters who saw him frequently: "I wanted to see Helms a lot because he was talking with the top men in government. He was a good analyst —rapid, brief, and knowledgeable about what was going on." Kraft recalls that Helms was the only government official who forecast that South Vietnamese President Thieu would successfully block implementation of the Vietnamese peace accords until after the 1972 American election, and other reporters tell similar stories of Helms being among the most accurate high government sources available on matters like Soviet missiles or Chinese nuclear testing. He did not usually engage in the exaggerated talk about communist threats that so often characterizes "informed sources" in the Pentagon, and he seemed to have less of an operational ax to grind than other Washington officials.

The source of a news leak is not usually revealed in the newspapers. Yet when Helms, or any other government official, gives a "not-for-attribution" briefing to reporters, he always has a reason for doing so—which is not necessarily based on a desire to get the truth out to the American people. He may leak to promote or block a particular policy, to protect a bureaucratic flank, to launch a "trial balloon," to pass a message to a foreign government, or simply to embarrass or damage an individual. Most reporters are aware that government officials play these games; nevertheless, the CIA plays them more assiduously, since it virtually never releases any information overtly. The *New York Times* Washington bureau chief, Clifton Daniel, notes that although the agency issues no press releases, it leaks information "to support its own case and to serve its own purposes. . . . It doesn't surprise me that even secret bureaucrats would do that." Daniel says, however, that he "would accept material not-for-attribution if the past reliability of the source is good. But you have to be awfully careful that you are not being used."

In early 1968, *Time* magazine reporters were doing research on a cover story on the Soviet navy. According to *Time*'s Pentagon correspondent, John Mulliken, neither the White House nor the State Department would provide information on the subject for fear of giving the Soviets the impression that the U.S. government was behind a move to play up the threat posed by the Soviet fleet. Mulliken says that, with Helms' authorization, CIA experts provided *Time* with virtually all the data it needed. Commenting on the incident five years later, Mulliken recalls, "I had the impression that the CIA was saying 'the hell with the others' and was taking pleasure in sticking it in." He never did find out exactly why Helms wanted that information to come out at that particular time when other government agencies did not; nor, of course, did *Time*'s readers, who did not even know that the CIA was the source of much of the article which appeared on February 23, 1968.

From the days of Henry Luce and Allen Dulles, *Time* had always had close relations with the agency. In more recent years, the magazine's chief Washington correspondent, Hugh Sidey, re-

lates, "With McCone and Helms, we had a set-up that when the magazine was doing something on the CIA, we went to them and put it before them. . . . We were never misled."

Similarly, when *Newsweek* decided in the fall of 1971 to do a cover story on Richard Helms and "The New Espionage," the magazine, according to a *Newsweek* staffer, went directly to the agency for much of its information. And the article, published on November 22, 1971, generally reflected the line that Helms was trying so hard to sell: that since "the latter 1960s . . . the focus of attention and prestige within CIA" had switched from the Clandestine Services to the analysis of intelligence, and that "the vast majority of recruits are bound for" the Intelligence Directorate. This was, of course, written at a time when over two thirds of the agency's budget and personnel were devoted to covert operations and their support (roughly the same percentage as had existed for the preceding ten years). *Newsweek* did uncover several previously unpublished anecdotes about *past* covert operations (which made the CIA look good) and published at least one completely untrue statement concerning a multibillion-dollar technical espionage program. Assuming that the facts for this statement were provided by "reliable intelligence sources," it probably represented a CIA disinformation attempt designed to make the Russians believe something untrue about U.S. technical collection capabilities.

Under Helms, the CIA also continued its practice of intervening with editors and publishers to try to stop publication of books either too descriptive or too critical of the agency. In April 1972 this book —as yet unwritten—was enjoined; two months later, the number-two man in the Clandestine Services, Cord Meyer, Jr., visited the New York offices of Harper & Row, Inc., on another anti-book mission. The publisher had announced the forthcoming publication of a book by Alfred McCoy called *The Politics of Heroin in Southeast Asia,* charging the agency with a certain degree of complicity in the Southeast Asian drug traffic. Meyer asked old acquaintances among Harper & Row's top management to provide him with a copy of the book's galley proofs. While the CIA obviously hoped to handle the matter informally among friends, Harper & Row asked the agency for official confirmation of its request. The CIA's General Counsel,

Lawrence Houston, responded with a letter of July 5, 1972, that while the agency's intervention "in no way affects the right of a publisher to decide what to publish . . . I find it difficult to believe . . . that a responsible publisher would wish to be associated with an attack on our Government involving the vicious international drug traffic without at least trying to ascertain the facts." McCoy maintained that the CIA had "no legal right to review the book" and that "submitting the manuscript to the CIA for prior review is to agree to take the first step toward abandoning the First Amendment protection against prior censorship." Harper & Row apparently disagreed and made it clear to McCoy that the book would not be published unless first submitted. Rather than find a new publisher at that late date, McCoy went along. He also gave the entire story to the press, which was generally critical of the CIA.

The agency listed its objections to Harper & Row on July 28, and, in the words of the publisher's vice president and general counsel, B. Brooks Thomas, the agency's criticisms "were pretty general and we found ourselves rather underwhelmed by them." Harper & Row proceeded to publish the book—unchanged—in the middle of August.

The CIA has also used the American press more directly in its efforts against the KGB. On October 2, 1971, the week after the British government expelled 105 Soviet officials from England because of their alleged intelligence activities, the *New York Times* ran a front-page article by Benjamin Welles about Soviet spying around the world. Much of the information in the article came from the CIA, and it mentioned, among other things, that many of the Russians working at the United Nations were KGB operators. According to Welles, the agency specifically "fingered as a KGB man" a Russian in the U.N. press office, Vladimir P. Pavlichenko, and asked that he be mentioned in the article. Welles complied and included a paragraph of biographical information on the Russian, supplied by the CIA. Ten days later the Soviet Union made an official protest to the U.S. government about the "slanderous" reports in the American press concerning Soviet officials employed at the U.N.

The *Times'* charges about espionage activities of the Soviets at

the U.N. were almost certainly accurate. But, as a Washington-based media executive familiar with the case states, "The truth of the charges has nothing to do with the question of whether an American newspaper should allow itself to become involved in the warfare between opposing intelligence services without giving its readers an idea of what is happening. If the CIA wants to make a public statement about a Soviet agent at the U.N. or the U.S. government wants to expel the spy for improper activities, such actions would be legitimate subjects for press coverage—but to cooperate with the agency in 'fingering' the spy, without informing the reader, is at best not straightforward reporting."

The CIA has often made communist defectors available to selected reporters so news stories can be written (and propaganda victories gained). As was mentioned earlier, most of these defectors are almost completely dependent on the CIA, and are carefully coached on what they can and cannot say. Defectors unquestionably are legitimate subjects of the press's attention, but it is unfortunate that their stories are filtered out to the American people in such controlled circumstances.

David Wise remembers an incident at the *New York Herald Tribune* in the mid-1960s when the CIA called the paper's top officials and arranged to have a Chinese defector made available to reporters. According to Wise, CIA officials "brought him down from Langley [for the interview] and then put him back on ice." Similarly, in 1967 the agency asked the *Times'* Welles to come out to CIA headquarters to talk to the Soviet defector Lieutenant Colonel Yevgeny Runge. On November 10 Welles wrote two articles based on the interview with Runge and additional material on the KBG supplied by CIA officers. But Welles also included in his piece several paragraphs discussing the CIA's motivation in making Runge available to the press. The article mentioned that at least some U.S. intelligence officials desired "to counter the international attention, much of it favorable, surrounding the Soviet Union's 50th anniversary," which was then taking place. Publicizing the defection, Welles continued, "also gave United States intelligence men a chance to focus public attention on what they consider a growing emphasis on the use of 'illegal' Soviet agents around the world."

According to Welles, these paragraphs stating, in effect, that the CIA was exploiting Runge's defection for its own purposes infuriated the agency, and he was "cut off" by his CIA sources. He experienced "long periods of coolness" and was told by friends in the agency that Helms had personally ordered that he was to be given no stories for several months.

The CIA is perfectly ready to reward its friends. Besides provision of big news breaks such as defector stories, selected reporters may receive "exclusives" on everything from U.S. government foreign policy to Soviet intentions. Hal Hendrix, described by three different Washington reporters as a known "friend" of the agency, won a Pulitzer Prize for his 1962 *Miami Daily News* reporting of the Cuban missile crisis.* Much of his "inside story" was truly inside: it was based on CIA leaks.

Because of the CIA's clever handling of reporters and because of the personal views held by many of those reporters and their editors, most of the American press has at least tacitly gone along, until the last few years, with the agency view that covert operations are not a proper subject for journalistic scrutiny. The credibility gap arising out of the Vietnam war, however, may well have changed the attitude of many reporters. The *New York Times'* Tom Wicker credits the Vietnam experience with making the press "more concerned with its fundamental duty." Now that most reporters have seen repeated examples of government lying, he believes, they are much less likely to accept CIA denials of involvement in covert operations at home and abroad. As Wicker points out, "Lots of people today would believe that the CIA overthrows governments," and most journalists no longer "believe in the sanctity of classified material." In the case of his own paper, the *New York Times*, Wicker feels that "the Pentagon Papers made the big difference."

The unfolding of the Watergate scandal has also opened up the agency to increased scrutiny. Reporters have dug deeply into the

* This is the same Hal Hendrix who later joined ITT and sent the memo saying President Nixon had given the "green light" for covert U.S. intervention in Chile. See p. 350 above.

CIA's assistance to the White House "plumbers" and the attempts to involve the agency in the Watergate cover-up. Perhaps most important, the press has largely rejected the "national security" defense used by the White House to justify its actions. With any luck at all, the American people can look forward to learning from the news media what their government—even its secret part—is doing. As Congress abdicates its responsibility, and as the President abuses his responsibility, we have nowhere else to turn.

ELEVEN

Conclusions

In the eyes of posterity it will
inevitably seem that, in
safeguarding our freedom, we
destroyed it; that the vast
clandestine apparatus we built up
to probe our enemies' resources
and intentions only served in the
end to confuse our own purposes;
that the practice of deceiving
others for the good of the state
led infallibly to our deceiving
ourselves; and that the vast army
of intelligence personnel built up
to execute these purposes were
soon caught up in the web of their
own sick fantasies, with
disastrous consequences
to them and us.

—MALCOLM MUGGERIDGE
May 1966

I<small>T</small> is a multi-purpose, clandestine arm of power . . . more than an intelligence or counterintelligence organization. It is an instrument for subversion, manipulation, and violence, for the secret intervention in the affairs of other countries." Allen Dulles wrote those words about the KGB in 1963 so that Americans would better understand the nature of the Soviet security service. His description was a correct one, but he could—just as accurately—have used the same terms to describe his own CIA. He did not, of course, because the U.S. leaders of Dulles' generation generally tried to impute the worst possible methods and motives to the forces of international communism, while casting the "defensive actions of the free world" as honest and democratic. Both sides, however, resorted to ruthless tactics. Neither was reluctant to employ trickery, deceit, or, in Dulles' phrase, "subversion, manipulation, and violence." They both operated clandestinely, concealing their activities not so much from the "opposition" (they couldn't) as from their own peoples. Secrecy itself became a way of life, and it could not be challenged without fear of a charge that one was unpatriotic or unmindful of the "national security."

In the dark days of the Cold War the communist threat was real to most Americans. Sincere men believed that the enemy's dirtiest tricks must be countered. Fire was to be fought with fire, and America's small élite corps of intelligence professionals claimed they knew how to do this. The public and the country's leaders were willing to go along, if not always enthusiastically, at least without serious opposition. Consequently, clandestine operatives from the United States as well as the Soviet Union were turned loose in virtually every nation in the world. Each side won secret victories, but the overall results were decidedly mixed. For its part, the CIA played some role in forestalling a communist takeover of Western

Europe, but the agency's record in the Middle East, Asia, and elsewhere in the world left much to be desired.

When the CIA's invaders were defeated in 1961 on the beaches of the Bay of Pigs, it should have been a signal to the country that something was wrong—both with the CIA and the government that directed the secret agency's activities. It should have been clear that events in the Third World could (and should) no longer be easily and blatantly manipulated by Washington. It should have been obvious that the times were rapidly changing; that the fears, following on the heels of World War II, that the "communist monolith" was on the verge of dominating the "free world" were invalid. It should have been apparent to the American public that the CIA was living in the past.

Columnist Tom Braden, a former high-ranking CIA covert expert, reflecting on the latter-day life of the CIA, wrote in January 1973: "Josef Stalin's decision to attempt conquest of Western Europe by manipulation, the use of fronts and the purchasing of loyalty turned the Agency into a house of dirty tricks. It was necessary. Absolutely necessary, in my view. But it lasted long after the necessity was gone."

Yet after the initial public outcry over the Cuban fiasco, the personnel shake-up at the agency and the high-level reviews of its performance ordered by President Kennedy had little effect. The CIA went back to operating essentially the same way it had for the previous decade, again with at least the tacit acceptance of the American public. Not until the Indochinese war shocked and outraged a significant part of the population were CIA's tactics, such as secret subsidies, clandestine armies, and covert coups, seriously called into question. Now Watergate has brought the issue of an inadequately controlled secret intelligence agency home to us. The clandestine techniques developed over a quarter-century of Cold War have, at last, been dramatically displayed for the people of this country, and the potential danger of a CIA which functions solely at the command of the President has been demonstrated to the public.

The CIA has a momentum of its own, and its operatives continue to ply their trade behind their curtain of secrecy. They do not want to give up their covert activities, their dirty tricks. They believe in these methods and they rather enjoy the game. Of course, without a presidential mandate they would have to stop, but the country has not had a chief executive since the agency's inception who has not believed in the fundamental need and rightness of CIA intervention in the internal affairs of other nations. When a President has perceived American interests to be threatened in some faraway land, he has usually been willing to try to change the course of events by sending in the CIA. That these covert interventions often are ineffective, counterproductive, or damaging to the national interest has not prevented Presidents from attempting them.

(

DELETED

) Kissinger and Nixon were concerned with what they believe to be a legitimate end—preventing a Marxist from being elected President of Chile—and the means employed mattered little to them, as long as secrecy could be maintained.

The new CIA Director, William Colby, has indicated on the public record that he intends to keep the agency functioning largely as it has in the past (while pledging to shun future "Watergates"). When Senator Harold Hughes asked him where the line should be drawn between the use of CIA paramilitary warriors and the regular U.S. armed forces, Colby replied that the dividing line should be "at the point in which the United States acknowledges involvement in such activities." Senator Hughes specifically put this answer into perspective when he said on August 1, 1973, "Mr. Colby believes that CIA-run military operations are perfectly acceptable as long as they can be concealed."

Colby's—and the CIA's and the Nixon administration's—view that "deniability" somehow allows the United States a free hand

for covert intervention abroad (and at home) is an anachronistic hangover from the Cold War. Perhaps such actions could once have been justified when the future of the country was seemingly at stake, but no such threat now looms on the horizon. The only two foreign powers with the potential to threaten the United States —the Soviet Union and China—have long ceased to be meaningful targets of CIA secret operations. Instead, the agency works mainly in the Third World, in nations that pose no possible threat to American security (

DELETED

) The CIA is not defending our national security. It seeks rather to maintain the *status quo*, to hold back the cultural clock, in areas that are of little or no significance to the American people. These efforts are often doomed to failure. In fact, at least since 1961, the CIA has lost many more battles than it has won, even by its own standards. Furthermore, the very fact that the United States operates an active CIA around the world has done incalculable harm to the nation's international position. Not only have millions of people abroad been alienated by the CIA's activities, but so have been a large number of Americans, especially young people.

The time has come for the United States to stand openly behind its actions overseas, to lead by example rather than manipulation. The changeover might disturb those government officials who believe in the inherent right of the United States to exercise its power everywhere, clandestinely when that seems necessary; but in the long run non-interference and forthrightness would enhance America's international prestige and position.

Even in an era when the public is conditioned to ever expanding and ever more expensive government activities, the $6 billion yearly cost of American intelligence represents a significant slice of the national treasure. The government spends more money on the various forms of spying than it does on the war against crime and drugs, community development and housing, mass transportation systems, and even the country's overt international programs carried out by the State Department, the USIA, and the AID combined. Yet, unlike other federal activities, information on the intelligence

community—how much money is being spent and where the money goes—is systematically withheld from the American people and all but a handful of Congressmen. Behind this wall of secrecy (which exists as much to conceal waste and inefficiency as to protect "national security") intelligence has grown far beyond the needs of the nation.

The time has come to demysticize the intelligence profession, to disabuse Americans of the ideas that clandestine agents somehow make the world a safer place to live in, that excessive secrecy is necessary to protect the national security. These notions simply are not true; the CIA and the other intelligence agencies have merely used them to build their own covert empire. The U.S. intelligence community performs a vital service in keeping track of and analyzing the military capability and strengths of the Soviet Union and China, but its other functions—the CIA's dirty tricks and classical espionage—are, on the whole, a liability for the country, on both practical and moral grounds.

But because of bureaucratic tribalism, vested interests, and the enormous size of the intelligence community, internal reform never makes more than a marginal dent in the community's operations. The people in charge like things essentially as they are, and they have never been subjected to the kind of intense outside pressure which leads to change in our society. Presidents, furthermore, have not wanted to greatly disturb the existing system because they have always wanted more, if not better, intelligence; because they were afraid of opening up the secret world of intelligence to public scrutiny; because they did not want to risk losing their personal action arm for intervention abroad.

The Congress, which has the constitutional power and, indeed, the responsibility to monitor the CIA and U.S. intelligence, has almost totally failed to exercise meaningful control. Intelligence has always been the sacred shibboleth which could not be disturbed without damaging the "national security," and, despite loud protests from a few outspoken critics, neither legislative house has been willing to question seriously the scope or the size of intelligence activities. Yet, if there is to be any real, meaningful change in the intelligence community, it must come from Congress, and,

judging from past experience, Congress will act only if prodded by public opinion. The Watergate affair has, to some extent, played such a role, and the full review of the CIA's secret charter promised by Senate Armed Services chairman John Stennis should be the first step in limiting the CIA's covert operations and cutting down the duplication and inefficiency of the rest of the community.

Congress should require the various intelligence agencies to keep it informed of the information collected. This kind of data should be routinely supplied to the legislative branch so it can properly carry out its foreign-policy functions and vote funds for the national defense. If the same information can be given to foreign governments and selectively leaked to the press by administrations in search of votes on military-spending issues, then there is no "security" reason why it must be denied to the Congress. The Soviets know that U.S. spy satellites observe their country and that other electronic devices monitor their activities; it makes little sense to classify the intelligence gathered "higher than top secret." No one is asking that technical details such as how the cameras work be given to the Congress or made public—but the excessive secrecy which surrounds the finished intelligence product could certainly be eased without in any way limiting the nation's ability to collect raw intelligence data by technical means.

As for the CIA proper, Congress should take action to limit the agency to the role originally set out for it in the National Security Act of 1947—namely, the CIA should concern itself exclusively with coordinating and evaluating intelligence. At the minimum, if clandestine activities must be continued by the U.S. government, the operational part of the CIA should be separated from the non-covert components. In the analytical and technical field the agency can make its most important contribution to the national security, but these functions have been neglected and at times distorted by the clandestine operatives who have almost always been in control of the CIA. Intelligence should not be presented to the nation's policy-makers by the same men who are trying to justify clandestine operations. The temptation to use field information selectively and to evaluate information to serve operational interests can be irresistible to the most honest men—let alone to the clandestine operatives.

However, the best solution would be not simply to separate the Clandestine Services from the rest of the CIA, but to abolish them completely. The few clandestine functions which still serve a useful purpose could be transferred to other government departments, but, for the most part, such activities should be eliminated. This would deprive the government of its arsenal of dirty tricks, but the republic could easily sustain the loss—and be the better for it.

The Clandestine Services' espionage operations using human agents have already been made obsolete by the technical collection systems which, along with open sources, supply the United States government with almost all the information it needs on the military strength and deployments of the Soviet Union and China. The truly valuable technical systems—the satellites and electronic listening devices—should be maintained, although without the present duplication and bureaucratic inefficiency. Since Oleg Penkovsky's arrest by Soviet authorities in 1962, there has been no CIA spy who has supplied the United States with important information about any communist power, and it is difficult to justify the expenditure of over $1 billion in the last decade for classical espionage simply on the hope that another Penkovsky will someday offer himself up as a CIA agent. Assuming that the CIA's most valuable agents will continue to be volunteers—"walk-ins" and defectors— a small office attached to the State Department and embassy contacts could be established to receive the information supplied by these sources.

While the CIA has been much more successful in penetrating the governments of the Third World and some of America's allies, the information received is simply not that important and can be duplicated to some extent through diplomatic and open sources. While it might be interesting to know about the inner workings of a particular Latin American, Asian, or African country, this intelligence has little practical use if the CIA has no intention of manipulating the local power structure.

The Clandestine Services' counterespionage functions should be taken over by the FBI. Protecting the United States against foreign spies is supposed to be the bureau's function anyway, and the incessant game-playing with foreign intelligence services—the prov-

ocations, deceptions, and double agents—would quickly become a relic of the past if the CIA were not involved in its own covert operations. Playing chess with the taxpayers' money against the KGB is unquestionably a fascinating exercise for clandestine operatives, but one that can properly be handled by the internal-security agency of the United States, the FBI.

As for the CIA's paramilitary tasks, they have no place in an intelligence agency, no place in a democratic society. Under the Constitution, only Congress has the power to declare war, and the United States should never again become involved in armed conflict without full congressional approval and public knowledge. If "American advisors" are needed to assist another country legitimately, they can be supplied by the Pentagon. The other forms of covert action—propaganda, subversion, manipulation of governments—should simply be discontinued. These are more often than not counterproductive and, even when successful, contrary to the most basic American ideals. The CIA's proprietary companies should be shut down or sold off. The agency would have little use for one of the largest aircraft networks in the world if it were not constantly intervening in foreign countries. The proprietaries, with their unregulated profits, potential conflicts of interest, and doubtful business practices, should in no case be allowed to continue operations.

The other countries of the world have a fundamental right not to have any outside power interfere in their internal affairs. The United States, which solemnly pledged to uphold this right when it ratified the United Nations charter, should now honor it. The mechanisms used to intervene overseas ignore and undermine American constitutional processes and pose a threat to the democratic system at home. The United States is surely strong enough as a nation to be able to climb out of the gutter and conduct its foreign policy in accordance with the ideals that the country was founded upon.

APPENDIX

The Bissell Philosophy

**Minutes of the 1968
"Bissell Meeting" at the
Council on Foreign Relations
as reprinted by the Africa
Research Group**

The third meeting of the Discussion Group on Intelligence and Foreign Policy *was held at the Harold Pratt House on January 8, 1968, at 5:00 p.m. Present were: Richard M. Bissell, Jr., Discussion Leader; Douglas Dillon, Chairman; William J. Barnds, Secretary; William R. Harris, Rapporteur; George Agree, Frank Altschul, Robert Amory, Jr., Meyer Bernstein, Col. Sidney B. Berry, Jr., Allen W. Dulles, George S. Franklin, Jr., Eugene Fubini, Julius C. Holmes, Thomas L. Hughes, Joseph Kraft, David W. MacEachron, Philip W. Quigg, Harry Howe Ransom, Theodore C. Sorensen, David B. Truman.*

The Chairman, Mr. Dillon, opened the meeting, noting that although this entire series of discussion was "off-the-record," the subject of discussion for this particular meeting was especially sensitive and subject to the previously announced restrictions.

Mr. Dillon noted that problems involving CIA's relationships with private institutions would be examined at a later meeting, though neither Mr. Bissell nor others should feel restricted in discussion of such problems this evening.

As the session's discussion leader, Mr. Bissell offered a review and appraisal of covert operations in U.S. foreign policy.

Touching briefly upon the question of responsibility, of whether these agencies are instruments of national policy, Mr. Bissell remarked that, in such a group, he needn't elaborate on CIA's responsiveness to national policy; that we could assume that, although CIA participates in policy making (as do other "action agencies," such as AID, the military services and Departments, in addition to the Department of State), CIA was a responsible agency of national policy.

Indeed, in Mr. Bissell's personal experience, CIA's role was more carefully circumscribed and the established limits observed more attentively than in ECA, where Mr. Bissell had previously worked.

The essential control of CIA resided in a Cabinet-level committee, comprising a representative of the White House staff, the Under Sec-

retary of State, Deputy Secretary of Defense, and in recent years the personal participation of the Director of Central Intelligence. Over the years this committee has become a more powerful and effective device for enforcing control. It reviews all new projects, and periodically scrutinizes ongoing projects.

As an interdepartmental committee composed of busy officials who meet only once per week, this control group is of limited effectiveness. Were it the only control instrument, Mr. Bissell would view it as inadequate, but in fact this committee is merely the summit of control, with a series of intermediate review procedures as lower levels. Projects are usually discussed in the relevant office of the Assistant Secretary of State, and, if at all related to Defense Department interests, at a similar level in DoD, frequently after consideration at lower levels in these departments. It was rare to take an issue before the Special Group prior to discussion at lower levels, and if there was objection at lower levels, most issues were not proposed to the Special Group—excepting large projects or key issues, which would be appealed at every level, including the Special Group.

Similar procedures applied in the field. Generally the Ambassador had a right to know of any covert operations in his jurisdiction, although in special cases (as a result of requests from the local Chief of State or the Secretary of State) the chief of station was instructed to withhold information from the Ambassador. Indeed, in one case the restriction was imposed upon the specific exhortation of the Ambassador in question, who preferred to remain ignorant of certain activities.

Of the "blown" operations, frequently among the larger ones, most are known to have been approved by the President himself. The U-2 project, for example, was an off-shoot of the Land (intelligence) Committee of the Killian panel on surprise attack; it was proposed as a Killian panel recommendation to the President, supported by USIB; its procurement, in utmost secrecy, was authorized by the President, and, with the exception of the first few flights (the initial authorization being to operate for a period of ten days, "weather permitting"), each individual flight was authorized by the President, with participation by the Secretary of State and Secretary of Defense.

Covert operations should, for some purposes, be divided into two classifications: (1) *Intelligence collection*, primarily espionage, or the obtaining of intelligence by covert means; and (2) *Covert action*, attempting to influence the internal affairs of other nations—sometimes called "intervention"—by covert means.

Although these two categories of activity can be separated in theory, intelligence collection and covert action interact and overlap. Efforts have been made historically to separate the two functions but the result has usually been regarded as "a total disaster organizationally." One such attempt was the establishment in the early days of CIA (1948) of the OPC under Frank G. Wisner as a separate organ for covert action. Although supported and given cover by the CIA, this organization was independent and Wisner reported directly to the Secretaries of State and Defense. "Beedle" Smith decided when he became Director of Central Intelligence that, if he were responsible for OPC, he was going to run it and it was merged with the clandestine intelligence organization in such a way that within the combined Clandestine Service there was a complete integration of intelligence collection and covert action functions in each area division.

In addition to our experience with OPC, the Germans and the British for a time during the war had organizations for covert special operations separate from, and inevitably in competition with, their espionage services. In every case the experience has been unfortunate. Although there are many disagreements within CIA on matters of doctrine, the view is unanimous that the splitting of intelligence and covert action services would be disastrous, with resulting competition for recruitment of agents, multiple recruitment of the same agents, additional security risks, and dissipation of effort.

Concerning the first category, *intelligence collection*, we should ask: (a) What is the scope of "covert intelligence collection"? (b) What intelligence collection functions can best be performed covertly?

The scope of covert intelligence collection includes: (1) reconnaissance; (2) communications and electronic intelligence, primarily undertaken by NSA; and (3) classical espionage, by agents. In gauging their utility, Mr. Bissell ranked (1) the most important, (2) slightly below, and (3) considerably below both (1) and (2).

Although it is less effective, classical espionage is "much the least costly," with the hardware components of recon and NSA activities raising their costs considerably.

(In the after-dinner discussion, an authority on communications-electronics expressed his concurrence in Mr. Bissell's relative rankings. Notwithstanding technological advances in cryptology, the increased sophistication in most cryptosystems assured that (1) (reconnaissance) outranked (2). Another observer noted that the budgets correlated in similar manner, the former speaker concurring and noting that, how-

ever surprising, the budgets approximated maximum utility according to cost-effectiveness criteria.)

Postwar U.S. reconnaissance operations began, historically, as "covert" operations, primarily a series of clandestine overflights of Communist territory in Eastern Europe, inaugurated in the early 1950s. These early efforts were followed by the U-2 project, which provided limited coverage but dramatic results.

Now we have reconnaissance satellites. Overhead reconnaissance is one of the most open of "secrets" in international affairs; it is no longer really a "covert activity," and bureaucratic responsibility for it now resides in the Pentagon.

Classical espionage, in the early postwar years, was conducted with special intensity in West Germany, and before the Berlin wall, in that city, which was ideal for the moving of agents in both directions, providing a sizable flow of political and economic intelligence (especially from East Germany).

Throughout the period since the early fifties, of course, the Communist bloc, and more especially the U.S.S.R. itself, has been recognized as the primary target for espionage activities. Circumstances have greatly limited the scale of operations that could be undertaken within the bloc so much of the effort has been directed at bloc nationals stationed in neutral or friendly areas, and at "third country" operations that seek to use the nationals of other non-Communist countries as sources of information on the Soviet bloc.

More recently there has been a shift in priorities for classical espionage toward targets in the underdeveloped world. Partly as a result of this change in priorities and partly because of other developments, the scale of the classical espionage effort mounted in Europe has considerably diminished. The U.S.S.R. remains a prime target but Communist China would today be given the same priority.

As to the kinds of information that could be obtained, espionage has been of declining relative importance as a means of learning about observable developments, such as new construction, the characteristics of transportation systems, the strength and deployment of military forces and the like because reconnaissance has become a far more effective collection technique and (except in China) travel is freer and far more extensive than some years ago. It had been hoped that espionage would contribute to the collection of intelligence on Soviet and East European technology, since this is a body of information not readily observable (until embodied in operational systems). Another

type of intelligence for which espionage would seem to be the only available technique is that concerning enemy intentions. In practice however espionage has been disappointing with respect to both these types of intelligence. They are for obvious reasons closely guarded and the task is just too difficult to permit results to be obtained with any dependability or regularity. With respect to the former category—technology—the published literature and direct professional contacts with the scientific community have been far richer sources.

(A communications-electronics expert interjected the observation that the same reasoning applied to inadequacies in S&T intelligence collection; technology is just too difficult for agents, who are insufficiently trained to comprehend what they observe as the technologies become increasingly complicated.)

As to friendly neutrals and allies, it is usually easier to learn what one wishes by overt contacts, human contacts of overt members of the U.S. mission or private citizens. We don't need espionage to learn British, or even French intentions.

(The speaker was questioned as to whether the other side's espionage was of similarly limited utility, or whether—with their Philbys—they were more successful?)

Mr. Bissell remarked that Soviet Union successes were primarily in counterintelligence, though going back aways, the Soviet Union had been more successful in recruiting U.S. scientists.

(The question was raised as to whether Burgess and MacLean constituted merely C.I. successes.)

Mr. Bissell thought so.

(In another's recollection, Soviet atomic intelligence efforts had been of substantial assistance in facilitating the Soviet nuclear weapons program. Although it is not possible to estimate with precision the effects of this intelligence, it was Lewis Strauss's guess that atomic intelligence successes allowed the Soviets to detonate their first device at least one and one-half and perhaps as much as two and one-half years before such a test would have been possible with purely indigenous efforts.)

The general conclusion is that against the Soviet bloc or other sophisticated societies, espionage is not a primary source of intelligence, although it has had occasional brilliant successes (like the Berlin Tunnel and several of the high level defectors). A basic reason is that espionage operates mainly through the recruitment of agents and it is enormously difficult to recruit high level agents. A low level agent,

even assuming that he remained loyal and that there is some means of communicating with him[,] simply cannot tell you much of what you want to know. The secrets we cannot find out by reconnaissance or from open sources are in the minds of scientists and senior policy makers and are not accessible to an ordinary citizen even of middle rank.

In contrast, the underdeveloped world presents greater opportunities for covert intelligence collection, simply because governments are much less highly oriented; there is less security consciousness; and there is apt to be more actual or potential diffusion of power among parties, localities, organizations, and individuals outside of the central governments. The primary purpose of espionage in these areas is to provide Washington with timely knowledge of the internal power balance, a form of intelligence that is primarily of tactical significance.

Why is this relevant?

Changes in the balance of power are extremely difficult to discern except through frequent contact with power elements. Again and again we have been surprised at *coups* within the military; often, we have failed to talk to the junior officers or non-coms who are involved in the *coups*. The same problem applies to labor leaders, and others. Frequently we don't know of power relationships, because power balances are murky and sometimes not well known even to the principal actors. Only by knowing the principal players well do you have a chance of careful prediction. There is real scope for action in this area; the technique is essentially that of "penetration," including "penetrations" of the sort which horrify classicists of covert operations, with a disregard for the "standards" and "agent recruitment rules." Many of the "penetrations" don't take the form of "hiring" but of establishing a close or friendly relationship (which may or may not be furthered by the provision of money from time to time).

In some countries the CIA representative has served as a close counselor (and in at least one case a drinking companion) of the chief of state. These are situations, of course, in which the tasks of intelligence collection and political action overlap to the point of being almost indistinguishable.

(The question was raised as to why ordinary diplomats couldn't maintain these relationships.)

Mr. Bissell observed that often they could. There were special cases, however, such as in one Republic where the chief of state had a "special relationship" with the senior CIA officers without the knowledge of the U.S. Ambassador because the President of the Republic

had so requested it. The CIA man sent reports by CIA channels back to the Secretary of State, but the Ambassador in the field, as agreed by the Secretary of State, wasn't to be informed. In this case, a problem arose when the relevant Assistant Secretary of State (who had received cables from the CIA man) became the new Ambassador, but the President of the Republic liked the new Ambassador and asked that a "special relationship" be established with him too.

Aside from this unique case, it seems to have been true generally that the Ambassador has to be a formal representative of the United States most of whose relations with the government to which he is accredited are through or with the knowledge of its foreign office. On the other hand, the CIA representative can maintain a more intimate and informal relationship the privacy of which can be better preserved both within the government of the country in question and within the United States government. Moreover, if a chief of state leaves the scene or changes his mind, you can quietly move a station chief, but it could be embarrassing if it were necessary suddenly to recall the U.S. Ambassador.

(Was the previously described relationship really a "covert operation"?)

The "cover" may be to shield visibility from some junior officials or, in the case of a "private adviser" to a chief of state, to shield this fact from politicians of the local government.

(Another observation was that the method of reporting, through CIA channels, constituted one difference and had some influence. A chief of state who knew that CIA's reports would be handled in a smaller circle, with less attendant publicity, might prefer these channels for some communications.)

Concerning the second category, *covert action*:

The scope of covert action could include: (1) political advice and counsel; (2) subsidies to an individual; (3) financial support and "technical assistance" to political parties; (4) support of private organizations, including labor unions, business firms, cooperatives, etc.; (5) covert propaganda; (6) "private" training of individuals and exchange of persons; (7) economic operations; and (8) paramilitary [or] political action operations designed to overthrow or to support a regime (like the Bay of Pigs and the programs in Laos). These operations can be classified in various ways: by the degree and type of secrecy required [,] by their legality, and, perhaps, by their benign or hostile character.

From whom is the activity to be kept secret? After five days, for example, the U-2 flights were not secret from the Russians but these operations remained highly secret in the United States, and with good reason. If these overflights had "leaked" to the American press, the U.S.S.R. would have had been forced to take action. On a less severe level the same problem applies to satellite reconnaissance. These are examples of two hostile governments collaborating to keep operations secret from the general public of both sides. "Unfortunately, there aren't enough of these situations."

(The remark was interjected that there was another reason for secrecy; if one had to admit to the activity, one would have to show the results, and exactly how good or bad they were.)

Covert operations could be classified by their legality or illegality. Many of them are legal.

They can also be classified as "benign" or "hostile." Most operations in Western Europe have been "benign," though involving the gravest improprieties, and in some cases clearly illegal action. (E.g., covert support of political parties.)

In the case of a large underdeveloped country, for example, money was put into a party's funds without the knowledge of that party. The relatively few economic operations that have been undertaken have been both benign and legal. One of these involved the provision by CIA of interim ostensibly private financing of an overt project pending an overt and official loan by AID. Its purpose was to give AID time for some hard bargaining without causing a complete failure of the transaction. The stereotype, of course, is that all covert operations are illegal and hostile, but this is not really the case.

The role of covert intervention can best be understood by contrast with the overt activities of the United States government. Diplomacy seeks results by bargaining on a government-to-government basis, sometimes openly—sometimes privately. Foreign economic policy and cultural programs seek to modify benignly the economies of other countries and the climate of opinion within them. Covert intervention is usually designed to operate on the internal power balance, often with fairly short-term objectives in view. An effort to build up the economy of an underdeveloped country must be subtle, long continued, probably quite costly, and must openly enlist the cooperation of major groups within the country if it is to have much influence. On the other hand an effort to weaken the local Communist party or to win an election,

and to achieve results within at most two or three years, must obviously be covert, it must pragmatically use the people and the instrumentalities that are available and the methods that seem likely to work. It is not surprising that the practitioners within the United States government of these two types of intervention differ temperamentally and in their preferences for methods, friends, and ideologies.

The essence of such intervention in the internal power balance is the identification of allies who can be rendered more effective, more powerful, and perhaps wiser through covert assistance. Typically these local allies know the source of the assistance but neither they nor the United States could afford to admit to its existence. Agents for fairly minor and low sensitivity interventions, for instance some covert propaganda and certain economic activities, can be recruited simply with money. But for the larger and more sensitive interventions, the allies must have their own motivation. On the whole the Agency has been remarkably successful in finding individuals and instrumentalities with which and through which it could work in this fashion. Implied in the requirement for a pre-existing motivation is the corollary that an attempt to induce the local ally to follow a course he does not believe in will at least reduce his effectiveness and may destroy the whole operation. It is notably true of the subsidies to student, labor, and cultural groups that have recently been publicized that the Agency's objective was never to control their activities, only occasionally to point them in a particular direction, but primarily to enlarge them and render them more effective.

Turning to relations with other agencies, Mr. Bissell was impressed by the degree of improvement in relations with the State Department. Seen from the Washington end, there has been an increase in consultation at the country-desk level, more often at the Bureau level or the Assistant Secretary of State level as the operation shapes up. The main problem some five to six years ago was not one of responsibility or authority but of cover arrangements.

Mr. Bissell provided a brief critique of covert operations, along the following lines:

That aspect of the Agency's operations most in need of change is the Agency's use and abuse of "cover." In this regard, the "background paper" for this session raised many cover-oriented questions.

On disclosure of private institutional support of late, it is very clear that we should have had greater compartmenting of operations.

If the Agency is to be effective, it will have to make use of private institutions on an expanding scale, though those relations which have "blown" cannot be resurrected.

We need to operate under deeper cover, with increased attention to the use of "cut-outs." CIA's interface with the rest of the world needs to be better protected.

If various groups hadn't been aware of the source of their funding, the damage subsequent to disclosure might have been far less than occurred.

The CIA interface with various private groups, including business and student groups, must be remedied.

The problem of Agency operations overseas is frequently a problem for the State Department. It tends to be true that local allies find themselves dealing always with an American and an official American—since the cover is almost invariably as a U.S. government employee. There are powerful reasons for this practice, and it will always be desirable to have some CIA personnel housed in the Embassy compound, if only for local "command post" and communications requirements.

Nonetheless, it is possible and desirable, although difficult and time-consuming, to build overseas an apparatus of unofficial cover. This would require the use or creation of private organizations, many of the personnel of which would be non-U.S. nationals, with freer entry into the local society and less implication for the official U.S. posture.

The United States should make increasing use of non-nationals, who, with effort at indoctrination and training, should be encouraged to develop a second loyalty, more or less comparable to that of the American staff. As we shift our attention to Latin America, Asia, and Africa, the conduct of U.S. nationals is likely to be increasingly circumscribed. The primary change recommended would be to build up a system of unofficial cover; to see how far we can go with non-U.S. nationals, especially in the field. The CIA might be able to make increasing use of non-nationals as "career agents" that is with a status midway between that of the classical agent used in a single compartmented operation perhaps for a limited period of time and that of a staff member involved through his career in many operations and well informed of the Agency's capabilities. Such career agents should be encouraged with an effort at indoctrination and training and with a prospect of long-term employment to develop a second loyalty and they could of course never be employed in ways that would conflict with

their primary loyalties toward their own countries. This still leaves open, however, a wide range of potential uses. The desirability of more effective use of foreign nationals increases as we shift our attention to Latin America, Asia, and Africa where the conduct of United States nationals is easily subject to scrutiny and is likely to be increasingly circumscribed.

These suggestions about unofficial cover and career agents illustrate and emphasize the need for continuing efforts to develop covert action capabilities even where there is no immediate need to employ them. The central task is that of identifying potential indigenous allies—both individuals and organizations—making contact with them, and establishing the fact of a community of interest.

There is some room for improvement, Mr. Bissell thought, in the planning of covert action country by country. Covert intervention is probably most effective in situations where a comprehensive effort is undertaken with a number of separate operations designed to support and complement one another and to have a cumulatively significant effect. The Agency probably finds itself involved in too many small covert action operations having no particular relationship with one another and having little cumulative impact.

There is no doubt that some covertly funded programs could be undertaken overtly, Mr. Bissell thought. Often activities have been initiated through CIA channels because they could be started more quickly and informally but do not inherently need to be secret. An example might be certain exchange of persons programs designed to identify potential political leaders and give them some exposure to the United States. It should be noted, however, that many such innocent programs are more effective if carried out by private auspices than if supported officially by the United States government. They do not need to be covert but if legitimate private entities such as the foundations do not initiate them, there may be no way to get them done except by covert support to "front" organizations.

Many propaganda operations are of declining effectiveness. Some can be continued at slight cost, but some of the larger ones (radio, etc.) are pretty well "blown" and not inexpensive. USIA doesn't like them, and although they did have a real justification some ten to fifteen years ago as the voice of refugees and emigrés, groups which also have declined in value, and in the view of some professionals are likely to continue declining in value.

In his last two years in the Agency, Mr. Bissell felt that the Clandestine Services could have been smaller.

Indeed, steps were taken to reduce their size. It is impossible to separate the issue of size from personnel and cover problems. It was Mr. Bissell's impression that the Clandestine Services were becoming increasingly a career service, too much like the Foreign Service (personnel looking to a succession of overt posts in a safe career). One result was the circumscription of local contacts. There was a subtle change taking place, which threatened to degrade some of CIA's former capabilities. Formally, the CIA had a staff with a wide variety of backgrounds, experiences, and capabilities. Its members were recruited from every sort of public and private occupation. If this diversity and variety is lost through the process of recruiting staff members from college, training them in a fairly standard pattern, and carrying them through orderly planned careers in the Agency, one of the organization's most valuable attributes will disappear.

Finally, Mr. Bissell remarked on large operations. It is self-evident that if an operation is too large, it can't remain a deeply kept secret. At best, one can then hope for a successful formal disclaimer. The worst of many faults of the Bay of Pigs operation was excessive reliance on the operation's disclaimability.

It has been a wise decision that operations of that scale not be undertaken by the Agency, except in theaters such as Vietnam, where the stakes and standards are different.

Covert action operations are generally aimed at short-term goals and the justification for the control machinery is that bias of operators to the short run can be compensated for in the review process. Mr. Bissell can conceive of no other way to force greater attention to long-range costs and values. One alternative is that caution will lead to ineffectuality. "Operational types" will be risk-takers; the counterweight is, and should be, applied by the other agencies in government.

In the discussion following Mr. Bissell's talk, the issue of CIA cover was cited as among the more interesting from the perspective of a former State Department appointee. The size of covert operations known to other governments was a continuing embarrassment, and the overseas staff maintained for these purposes and known to host governments was a similar source of embarrassment. From time to time, efforts were made to reduce overseas staff; although agreement in

principle was readily forthcoming, the particulars of staff reduction were difficult to obtain.

A former member of the Special Group (who served eighteen months on that committee) agreed with Mr. Bissell's earlier remarks on control mechanisms, insofar as they applied to review of new projects. These received most careful scrutiny. Insofar as the Special Group considered ongoing projects during this eighteen-month period, it was recalled that there was not any systematic, thorough procedure for such review, the committee finding itself busy with all the new proposals. If it were true that most operations were most useful for short-term goals, then perhaps there should be greater attention to review of ongoing projects, and termination of more projects earlier than in past practice.

A continuing problem which worries one former official was that concerning the "charter" of CIA, the public expression of which, in the National Security Act of 1947, was necessarily vague. CIA's full "charter" has been frequently revised, but it has been, and must remain[,] secret. The absence of a public charter leads people to search for the charter and to question the Agency's authority to undertake various activities. The problem of a secret "charter" remains as a curse, but the need for secrecy would appear to preclude a solution.

Another former official remarked on the inadequacy of clandestine intelligence as a means of obtaining enemy intentions. Sherman Kent (former Chairman, Board of National Estimates) distinguishes "the knowable" from "the unknowable," and we should recognize that much remains impossible to know, including, frequently, enemy intentions.

Respecting the reduction of overseas personnel and programs of declining utility, it was noted that the curtailment of over-age and unproductive personnel was a thorny issue. Recognizing the likelihood of appeal to the President and the absence of widespread participation in a manpower review, a former budget official arranged the participation of the Bureau of the Budget, CIA, FIAB, and relevant Under Secretaries in considerations of budgetary modifications. What emerged was an inertia, partly the inertia of the cold war. Parenthetically, a couple of much-criticized public media projects (cited by name) had proven of value, as the fall of Novotny in Czechoslovakia suggested, but a number of ineffective programs were retained. The problem was to free the budget, to do something new, in the place of old programs, not to

reduce the budget, but unfortunately, the chiefs in CIA wanted to control their working capital. If it were only possible to tell these officials not to worry, that we were setting aside $xxx million for CIA, and merely seeking to encourage better use of the same dollar amounts, then it would have been possible to move around some money. The big "iffy" question was a particular (named) foundation, which received a sizable allocation. Finally, everything was cleared up, and the next big review was scheduled, but never really effected as a consequence of the Cuban missile crisis. The review was geared up in 1963 once again.

Another observer, drawing upon work with the "combined cryptologic budget" and private industry, concluded that it was usually impossible to cut a budget; usually it was only possible to substitute a new project for an old one.

The Chairman suggested a number of questions: What are the effects of covert operations being blown? What can be done to improve the image of the Agency? What can be done to improve relations between the Agency and the press?

It was thought that a journalist's perspective might aid in discussing these questions, but a number of prior issues were thought to require attention:

(1) The matter of size required attention. In any government agency size can become a problem; increasingly there is a realization that the government is too big and "an ever-swelling tumor." At some point there will have to be a fairly sharp cutback in the U.S. foreign policy establishment.

(2) One was not overly impressed by the use of CIA in the developing world; in any case, we could have increased confidence in the range of choice in most developing areas. Conversely, it might not be as easy as Mr. Bissell suggested to know the power structure in more developed areas, in Western Europe and Japan.

(A query was interjected: Why should we have increasing confidence in the range of choice in developing areas?

Perhaps there are less variations than we earlier thought. "Things are evening out and we can live more comfortably.")

(3) Where do you bury the body? One is not completely convinced by citation of the experience with Frank Wisner's OPC. We could get around the responsibility issue raised by "Beedle" Smith; we could get around conflicting chains of command.

(4) Related to (3). Maybe there is a cost to be paid for having covert operations under CIA. Perhaps we could have intelligence col-

lection under State and covert operations under the Special Assistant to the President for National Security Affairs.

In response to items (3) and (4) some earlier remarks were clarified: one would not claim that the operational side of CIA need be where it is. Rather, one would inveigh against the splitting of covert intelligence collection and covert operations. One could, however, split the operational side from the analytic side. This is a plausible case, a solution for which could be worked out (though, on balance, the speaker was against it). But to split the operational side—as the German case, the British case for a time, and our own for a time suggested—would be disastrous.

Remarking on labor activities, one participant stated that before May 1967 it was common knowledge that there had been some CIA support for labor programs, but first *Ramparts* and then Tom Braden spelled out this support in public. Those in international labor affairs were dismayed, and certain newspapermen compounded their difficulties by confusing AID with CIA, and claiming that the AFL-CIO's Free Labor Development program was tainted.

Since these disclosures, the turn of events has been unexpected. First, there hasn't been any real trouble with international labor programs. Indeed, there has been an increase in demand for U.S. labor programs and the strain on our capacity has been embarrassing. Formerly, these foreign labor unions knew we were short of funds, but now they all assume we have secret CIA money, and they ask for more help.

Worse yet, Vic Reuther, who had been alleging that others were receiving CIA money, and whose brother's receipt of $50,000 from CIA in old bills was subsequently disclosed by Tom Braden, still goes on with his charges that the AFL-CIO has taken CIA money. Here again, no one seems to listen. "The net result has been as close to zero as possible. We've come to accept CIA, like sin." So, for example, British Guiana's labor unions were supported through CIA conduits, but now they ask for more assistance than before. So, our expectations to the contrary, there has been almost no damage.

A former State Department official offered some remarks on intelligence operations as seen from the field. He concurred in Mr. Bissell's remarks on "cover." The initial agreement between the Agency and State was intended to be "temporary," but "nothing endures like the ephemeral."

How are Agency officials under "official cover" specially equipped to handle covert operations? If the Agency station chief has a "special

relationship" with the chief of state, one would submit that it was because the Ambassador wasn't worth a damn. Moreover, such a "special relationship" created the risk that the chief of state, seeing two channels to Washington, could play one off against another. Some foreign statesmen are convinced that an "invisible government" really exists, and this impression shouldn't be allowed.

Also, prejudice in favor of covertly obtained intelligence is a troublesome thing.

One way to overcome the misconceptions is to make CIA a *truly* secret service, and not merely an agency duplicating the Foreign Service. With money shortages CIA has often filled a vacuum, but this does not make it right.

Another questioned the discussion leader's proposal for greater utilization of non-U.S. nationals. How could you get non-nationals to do the job and to develop loyalty to the United States?

One was not sure that it was doable, but it was worth trying. It would be more prone to work if you used a national of Country B to work in Country C, if what you are asking is neither (1) against the interest of Country B, nor (2) nefarious. You do need some cover, and the natural vehicle is an organization with non-American nationals.

Another observer was struck by the lack of interest in the "blowing" of covertly sponsored radio activities. Why has there been so little interest in these activities, in contrast to the immense concern over the CIA-NSA relationship? One might conclude that the public is not likely to be concerned by the penetration of overseas institutions, at least not nearly so much as by penetration of U.S. institutions. "The public doesn't think it's right; they don't know where it ends; they take a look at their neighbors." Does this suggested expansion in use of private institutions include those in the United States, or U.S. institutions operating overseas?

In response, attention was drawn to the clear jurisdictional boundaries between CIA and the FBI, CIA being proscribed from "internal security functions." CIA was averse to surveillance of U.S. citizens overseas (even when specifically requested), and averse to operating in the United States, excepting against foreigners here as transients. One might want CIA to expand its use of U.S. private corporations, but for objectives outside the United States. It was recalled that the Agency funding of the National Student Association was, in every case, for activities outside the United States or for activities with overseas objectives.

Why, we might ask, should the U.S. government use nongovernmental institutions more, and why should it deal with them in the United States? If dealings are overseas, then it is necessary to maintain an overseas bureaucracy to deal with the locals. It is also necessary to engage in communications in a possibly hostile environment. If one deals through U.S. corporations with overseas activities, one can keep most of the bureaucratic staff at home and can deal through the corporate headquarters, perhaps using corporate channels for overseas communications (including classified communications). In this opinion, the policy distinction should involve the use to which the private institution is put, not whether or not to use private institutions.

In another view it was desirable for this discussion group to examine different types of institutions. For example, should CIA use educational institutions? Should CIA have influenced the selection of NSA officers?

One was not aware that CIA had influenced the election of NSA officers; if it had, it shouldn't have done so, in one's opinion.

Mightn't it be possible to deal with individuals rather than organizations?

Yes, in many cases this would be preferable. It depended upon skill in the use of our operating capabilities.

As an example of the political use of secretly acquired intelligence, a former official noted the clandestine acquisition of Khrushchev's "secret speech" in February 1956. The speech was too long for even Khrushchev to memorize, and over one hundred people had heard it. We targeted it, and by secret means acquired a copy. The State Department released the text and *The New York Times* printed it in full. The repercussions were felt around the world, and particularly within the Communist bloc. The Soviets felt unable to deny the authenticity of the text we released, and the effect upon many of the satellite states was profound. It was the beginning of the split in the Communist movement. If you get a precise target, and go after it, you can change history.

Another observer was troubled by the earlier-expressed point about increased use of private institutions. Most demoralizing in the academic community was the sense of uncertainty about institutions with which individuals were associated. There is a profound problem in penetrating institutions within the country when there is a generalized loss of faith, a fear that nothing is what it seems.

It was noted that the next session, on February 15, 1968, would concentrate upon relations with private institutions.

To one observer, part of this solution would be found in the political process, involving extragovernmental contacts in the sphere of political action.

In response to a query, the relative utilities of types of intelligence data were reviewed. Most valuable was reconnaissance, then communications-electronic intelligence, then classical espionage.

We have forgotten, it was noted, the number one over-all source, namely, overt data.

The meeting was adjourned at 9:15 p.m., and participants were reminded of the next meeting on February 15.

WILLIAM R. HARRIS
RAPPORTEUR

Index

A Note on the Type

The text of this book was set on the Linotype in a face called Times Roman, designed by Stanley Morison for *The Times* (London) and first introduced by that newspaper in 1932.

Among typographers and designers of the twentieth century, Stanley Morison has been a strong forming influence, as typographical adviser to the English Monotype Corporation, as a director of two distinguished English publishing houses, and as a writer of sensibility, erudition, and keen practical sense.

Composed, printed, and bound by The Haddon Craftsmen, Inc., Scranton, Pennsylvania.